Language Arts for
Today's Children

Prepared by

THE COMMISSION ON THE ENGLISH CURRICULUM

Vol. I   The English Language Arts

Vol. II   Language Arts for Today's Children

Vol. III   The English Language Arts in the Secondary School
in preparation

Vol. IV   The College Teaching of English
in preparation

Vol. V   The Preparation of Teachers of the English Language Arts
in preparation

Language Arts for Today's Children

Prepared by

THE COMMISSION ON THE ENGLISH CURRICULUM

of the

NATIONAL COUNCIL OF TEACHERS OF ENGLISH

New York

APPLETON-CENTURY-CROFTS, INC.

Preface

How such a volume as *Language Arts for Today's Children* will be used depends upon who the reader is and what his purposes may be.

The volume is divided into four distinct but related parts. Part I sets forth the sources from which any effective program in the language arts must stem—the needs for language among children living in the world today, a knowledge of what children are like and how they develop, and the nature of a language program that is planned to fit their growing powers.

Part II treats separately each of the four strands of the language arts program—listening, speaking, reading, and writing—showing the sequential development and conditions which foster wholesome growth in each area.

Part III brings the four phases of language which were temporarily separated for analysis in Part II back into functional relationships both among themselves and with the ongoing experiences of classroom living. Programs in action at each level of the elementary school are described in relation to the opportunities for children to grow in effective oral and written communication as well as in the skills of spelling, handwriting, and reading.

Part IV deals with basic considerations involved in setting up and appraising a sound language arts program whether undertaken by an individual school, a county or city system, or a state curriculum committee. In this part also ways for parents and teachers to work together in promoting language growth are explored along with helpful procedures for evaluating the language arts program.

v

Readers who are interested in the goals of such a program may wish to turn first to that portion of Chapter II in which these are summarized. Classroom teachers may prefer to begin with the descriptions of practice in Part III. Whatever the order in which the material is read, it is important that each section be seen in relation to the rest of the volume.

The committee which produced *Language Arts for Today's Children* found stimulation and gained added insight through coöperative endeavor and face-to-face discussions out of which grew a common point of view. It commends the method to all those concerned with building, improving, or appraising language arts programs in the elementary school. Teachers, principals, supervisors, parents, and if possible, children themselves, all should have a significant part in planning if the program is to be a dynamic one. The importance today of effective listening, speaking, reading, and writing justifies this total involvement of all concerned.

H. K. M.

E. G.

MEMBERS OF THE COMMISSION ON THE ENGLISH CURRICULUM

NATIONAL COUNCIL OF TEACHERS OF ENGLISH
Urbana, Illinois

DIRECTOR

Dora V. Smith, Professor of Education
University of Minnesota, Minneapolis
Minnesota

ASSOCIATE DIRECTORS

Angela M. Broening, Director of Publications
Baltimore Public Schools, Baltimore
Maryland

Helen K. Mackintosh, Associate Chief
Elementary Section, Division of State
and Local School Systems, U.S. Office
of Education, Department of Health,
Education, and Welfare
Washington, D.C.

Porter G. Perrin, Professor of English
University of Washington, Seattle
Washington

MEMBERS OF THE COMMISSION

Harlen M. Adams, Executive Dean
Chico State College
Chico, California

Harold A. Anderson
Department of Education
University of Chicago
Chicago, Illinois

Roy P. Basler, Associate Director
Reference Department
Library of Congress
Washington, D.C.

Simon Certner, Department of English
Morris High School
New York City, New York

Herbert L. Creek, Professor Emeritus
Department of English
Purdue University
Lafayette, Indiana

Muriel Crosby, Director of Elementary Education, Wilmington Public Schools
Wilmington, Delaware

Carter Davidson, President and Professor of English, Union College and University
Schenectady-Albany, New York

John J. DeBoer, Professor of Education
University of Illinois
Urbana, Illinois

John C. Gerber, Professor of English and Coördinator of Communication Skills
University of Iowa
Iowa City, Iowa

Margaret R. Greer, formerly Librarian, Board of Education Library
Minneapolis, Minnesota

vii

PRODUCTION COMMITTEE FOR VOLUME II

Co-Chairmen

Elizabeth Guilfoile
Principal, Hoffman School
Cincinnati, Ohio

Helen K. Mackintosh
Associate Chief, Elementary
Schools Section
United States Office of Education
Washington, D.C.

Althea Beery
Supervisor of Elementary Education
Cincinnati Public Schools
Cincinnati, Ohio
Muriel Crosby
Director of Elementary Education
Wilmington, Delaware
Mildred A. Dawson
Professor of Education
Appalachian State Teachers College
Boone, North Carolina
Dorothea McCarthy
Professor of Psychology
Fordham University Graduate School
New York City, New York

Grace Rawlings, Principal
Liberty School
Baltimore, Maryland
Nila B. Smith
Professor of Educational Psychology
New York University
New York City, New York
Ruth Strickland
Department of Education
Indiana University
Bloomington, Indiana
Charlotte G. Wells
Professor of Speech
University of Missouri
Columbia, Missouri

ix

Contents

PAGE

Preface V

PART I

BASES FOR THE LANGUAGE ARTS PROGRAM

CHAPTER

1. The Language Needs of Today's Children 3

2. Child Development and Its Relationship to the Language Arts Program 18

3. Continuity in Language Development 42

PART II

FACETS OF THE LANGUAGE ARTS

4. Listening 71

5. Speaking 106

6. Reading 144

7. Writing 206

PART III

THE PROGRAM IN ACTION

8. Early Childhood 261

9. The Middle Grades 283

10. The Upper Years 302

PART IV

BUILDING AND APPRAISING A LANGUAGE ARTS PROGRAM

CHAPTER   PAGE

11. Factors Which Facilitate a Good Language Arts Program 319

12. Coöperation of Home and School in Promoting Language Growth 358

13. Evaluation of the Language Arts Program . . . 386

Appendix 415

Index 425

Illustrations

Between pp. 16–17

Your Own Voice Surprises You
  Florida State University, Tallahassee, Florida
Storytelling Time Is Really Fun
  Cleveland Public Schools, Cleveland, Ohio
Making Good Tortillas Calls for Careful Reading
  California State Department of Education, Bureau of Audio-
  Visual Education, Sacramento, California
How Well Can You Use the Telephone?
  Kingston Public Schools, Kingston, New York (Freeman
  Photo)
It's as Real as Though You Were There!
  University of Minnesota, St. Paul, Minnesota
The Telephone Makes the World Seem Smaller
  Milwaukee Public Schools (Milwaukee Journal Photo)
We Help Each Other
  Grand Rapids Public Schools, Grand Rapids, Michigan
  (J. Warren Southwick)

Between pp. 48–49

They Learn to Do by Doing
  Baltimore Public Schools, Baltimore, Maryland
We'll All Watch. Some of Us Will Talk
  Denver Public Schools, Denver, Colorado
You Can Believe It When You See It
  Public Schools, Washington, D.C. (Photograph by The
  Washington Post, 1952)
Informal Play Tests Out Ideas
  California State Department of Education, Sacramento, Cali-
  fornia

xiii

Which Story Do You Like Best?
  Minneapolis Public Schools, Minneapolis, Minnesota
That's My Favorite Program
  Department of Instructional Materials, Portland, Oregon, Public Schools
It Pays to Listen to the Forest Ranger
  Newton Public Schools, Newton, Massachusetts
A Sound Recorder Helps to Improve His Talk
  Department of Education, Nutley, New Jersey
Spontaneous Combustion
  Petworth School, Washington, D.C.
He Makes It So Clear
  Newton Public Schools, Newton, Massachusetts
His Puppet Thinks and Speaks
  Western Washington College of Education, Bellingham, Washington
The Goblin Scares the Audience
  University of Minnesota, Minneapolis, Minnesota
Have You Tried Yourself Out with a Tape Recorder?
  Newton Public Schools, Newton, Massachusetts
Almost Right—Try Again
  Board of Education of Baltimore County, Towson, Maryland

Between pp. 144–145

Elmer Helps Children Learn to Read
  Minneapolis Public Schools, Minneapolis, Minnesota
That's My Story—What's Yours?
  Petworth School, Washington, D.C.
You Write—You Read—You Look
  Petworth School, Washington, D.C.
In a Group or by Yourself, You Read
  Office of County Superintendent of Schools, Los Angeles, California
Research Skills Help Find the Answers
  Office of County Superintendent of Schools, Los Angeles, California
I Found It Right on This Page
  Department of Instructional Materials, Portland, Oregon Public Schools

Between pp. 208–209

Your Name Says It's Yours
   Seattle Public Schools, Seattle, Washington (Photograph by The Seattle Times)
A Third Grade's Idea of a Dictionary Box
   Office of County Superintendent of Schools, Los Angeles, California
Here's How You Use the Dictionary Box
   Office of County Superintendent of Schools, Los Angeles, California
This Is *My* Autobiography
   University of Wyoming, Laramie, Wyoming
All Kinds of Dictionaries Help with Writing
   Baltimore Public Schools, Baltimore, Maryland
Words—Words—Words—Make a Vocabulary
   Newton Public Schools, Newton, Massachusetts
A Newspaper Calls for Teamwork in Writing
   Office of County Superintendent of Schools, Los Angeles, California

Between pp. 272–273

When You Varnish a Doll Bed, You Can Tell About It
   Ohio State University, Columbus, Ohio
You Be the Mother, I'll Be the Neighbor
   Minneapolis Public Schools, Minneapolis, Minnesota
Be Careful, He's Our Only Hamster
   Ohio State University, Columbus, Ohio
Cocky's School Visit Brings Questions and Answers
   Ohio State University, Columbus, Ohio
This Is the Best Story Yet
   Board of Education, New York, New York
Your Own Painting Gives You Something to Talk About
   Public Schools, Norfolk, Virginia (Will Photo Service)
Let's Show and Tell
   Western Washington College of Education, Bellingham, Washington

Between pp. 320–321

We Use Our Language Arts Skills to Persuade the Principal
  Whittier School, Phoenix, Arizona
A Daily Diary Keeps Track of the Highlights
  Whittier School, Phoenix, Arizona
Sixth Graders Interview a Teacher
  Whittier School, Phoenix, Arizona
Selecting, Cutting, and Pasting Are Part of the Job
  Whittier School, Phoenix, Arizona
Mimeographing the Newspaper Calls for Planning
  Public Schools, Grand Rapids, Michigan (J. Warren Southwick)
Summing Up What We Know about Aviation
  Board of Education, Chattanooga, Tennessee
Listening, Speaking, Reading, and Writing Are Part of Playing
  Bountiful Elementary School, Davis County, Utah
It Takes Many Skills to Prepare a Report
  Office of County Superintendent of Schools, Los Angeles, California

Between pp. 384–385

A Time—A Place—The Right Books
  Western Washington College of Education, Bellingham, Washington
Fifth Graders Flash the World News
  Newton Public Schools, Newton, Massachusetts
Parents Help Children Grow in Reading
  Lincoln School, Oak Park, Illinois
Child, Mother, Teacher Evaluate
  Baltimore Public Schools, Baltimore, Maryland
You Get the Facts When You See What's Happening
  Newton Public Schools, Newton, Massachusetts
Fifth Graders Interview the Mayor
  Department of Education, Elizabeth, New Jersey
A Library with Everything to Offer
  Spokane Public Schools, Spokane, Washington

PART I

Bases for the Language Arts Program

CHAPTER 1

The Language Needs of Today's Children

ANNETTE, at sixteen months, capers before the television set in response to the dancing of the figures on the screen. She claps her hands and cries, "Baby." Michael, her brother, was five before he saw a television program. Their father, aged thirty-one, had never heard a radio broadcast until he was twelve, but at twenty he talked to other pilots of his squadron in flight over Japan. The grandfather, now aged fifty-six, grew up in his village home without a telephone. A great aunt who is seventy-seven did not see a movie until her children were in high school, and she had read a newspaper only once weekly until after she was a grandmother.

RECOGNIZING THE CHANGES IN LANGUAGE NEEDS

This experience of a single family points to the startling changes in mass communication which have swept the country and how they have affected the homes of America in the span of one generation. A similar illustration could show the rapid changes which have taken place recently in transportation facilities—from horse-and-buggy to automobile to airplane, all within the first half of our present century. The consequent shortening of distance brings with it closer communication in social life, domestic politics, and international relations.

Mass communication and rapid transportation are of course but two results of the tremendous technological de-

velopment which has occurred in recent years. This development has led to fundamental changes in our society such as
mass production, with even larger numbers of people working for others instead of for themselves, with shorter hours of
labor and increased time for recreation. American children
like Annette and Michael are growing up in a world that is
different because of changes in the very nature of living and
of communication.

On the other hand, as the Commission on the English Curriculum has already pointed out in Volume I of this series,
"the goals of teaching the language arts are as old as the
ideals of Western civilization." To think clearly and honestly,
to read thoughtfully, to communicate effectively, and to listen intelligently are as important today as they ever were.
"Yet each generation faces the task of interpreting these goals
anew in the light of the conditions of its own age." [1]

Existing changes in environmental conditions affect the
language needs of individuals; so also do the current aspects
of world society. Confusions and misunderstandings are ram-
pant; feelings of uncertainty and insecurity are the common
experience. Whatever the provisions are that education
should make for helping children and adults meet the per-
plexities and anxieties of their times, certainly language has a
fundamental role to play. The program set forth in this
volume has been developed upon this basic assumption.

MEETING THE PERSONAL NEEDS OF BOYS
AND GIRLS

The child's growth in language is closely bound up with
the development of his own personality. In an age of increasing pressures and tensions, he needs especially warm interpersonal relationships with other children and with adults.

[1] National Council of Teachers of English, Commission on the English
Curriculum, *The English Language Arts*, N.C.T.E. Curriculum Series, Vol. I
(New York, Appleton-Century-Crofts, Inc., 1952), p. 1.

The emotional tone of his life is expressed through the communication essential to ordinary everyday living. Conversation and, in much smaller degree, letter-writing are the basic language activities through which these interpersonal relationships are achieved.

The Contribution of Reading and Literature to Personal Development

For his total growth the individual needs all the language arts. Reading serves not only for the practical purposes of daily life, but also for the extension of experience, for the development of social understanding and a personal sense of values, for release of tensions, and for appreciation of beauty and sheer enjoyment. Literature is first of all for delight, but by reason of its power over the emotions it helps to develop in boys and girls an unconscious sensitivity to the ideas and ideals of their own heritage. The spiritual insight so gained tends to give stability in time of change and perspective at a moment when all values seem fleeting.

The daily newspaper and the weekly periodical keep the reader informed concerning current events, but there are vast quantities of books—science, biography, travel, folklore, poetry, and fiction—which help him to know life, to interpret it, or to escape from it as the case may be. *Willie's Walk to Grandmama*, for example, gives little children a glowing sense of both security and good fellowship in family relations, whereas they see themselves and their daily doings in Marchette Chute's "On Going to Bed" or Robert Louis Stevenson's "My Shadow." In *Blueberries for Sal* they not only find a good laugh, but they share a universal sense of safety with mother near at hand. Older children find a similar family feeling in *The Fair Adventure*, in *Caddie Woodlawn*, or in *The Bounces of Cynthiann'*.

An equal sense of pride in their American heritage comes from the many good stories of other children in the American family, like Hetty and Hank in *Down, Down the Mountain* or E-Ye-Shure in *I Am a Pueblo Indian Girl*. The Wilder saga of pioneer days in such books as *The Little House in the Big Woods* takes them back to the days celebrated in Arthur Guiterman's "The Pioneer." Joaquin Miller's "Columbus" and the Benéts' "Miles Standish" give them an imaginative interpretation of forces that have made America great. Other nations, too, have their heroes and their aspirations—many of them shared with American children whose parents brought them from a far-off land—but to boys and girls, Hansi spending his Christmas in Switzerland, Miki enjoying Easter in Hungary, and the Irish children hiking the hills to the cottage at Bantry Bay seem, fortunately, very much like themselves. What greater need has the world today than for just that kind of assurance?

Or it may be, the children ask simply good fun from books or a chance to escape from what must seem to them at times a weary and incomprehensible world. *The Five Hundred Hats of Bartholomew Cubbins* may well be on the nearest shelf, or *My Father's Dragon* or *Pecos Bill*. Truly, children today are demonstrating the truth of Emily Dickinson's lines, "There is no frigate like a book, To take us worlds away"— whether those worlds are distant in time or place or whether they exist only in the realm of imagination.

The Importance of Creative Writing and Dramatic Presentation

Language as an expression of individual feeling or aspiration has great significance in these times. The schools, therefore, give ample opportunity for creative writing, which becomes for many an outlet for feelings, an organization of personal experience, an instrument of self-discovery and self-development.

The boy from a minority race who wrote the following and shared it through the school paper was still somewhat vague in his sentence organization, but the impact of his poem is real and indicates that for him this writing was emotional release.

To Bravely Smile

A quick delight that catches the throat
And tunes the key of laughter—
To know beyond a shadowy doubt
That nothing is real—yet smile
To vision within and feel without
An everlasting thrill,
And yet the hurt is always there—
To know the world is not quite fair—
And yet to smile.

Choric speaking and dramatization offer to children in some schools the opportunity for group expression of shared emotions. A class of older boys, academically retarded, were helped to work off some of their aggressiveness toward each other by vigorous chanting in unison of such ballads as the "Grand Old Duke of York." A superior group likewise felt the emotional power of verse in the choral speaking of Tennyson's "Bugle Song." A feeling of the real meaning of Christmas came to the entire class as they chanted together Longfellow's "I Heard the Bells on Christmas Day," concluding with the familiar refrain of "Peace on earth, good will to men."

Younger children, too, have the same sense of sharing emotions when they skip and dance and sway to such familiar poems as "Rock-a-Bye-Baby," "Dance to Your Lady," and "I Saw Three Ships A-Sailing." One has only to watch children acting out favorite scenes from *Picnic in the Woods*, or *Little Women*, or *Robin Hood* to know what delight, what insight into characterization, and what release of their own emotions they gain from dramatic play or dramatization.

The Need for Basic Skills in a Functional Setting

Because of the relationship of language to personal living, the elementary school must concern itself not alone with the child's long-time goals for the language arts, but also with the present-day living of children. Within the life of the school many needs arise for the basic skills of letter-writing, of selecting and organizing ideas for presentation to others, of reading accurately and intelligently for a wide variety of purposes. Many opportunities are provided for extending the child's vocabulary both in speech and in writing and for strengthening his power to express ideas effectively in sentences which grow in clarity and complexity with the increasing maturity of his thinking.

Today's children are growing up in an anxious world. For that reason, not merely the process of learning these skills should be emphasized in school but also the satisfactions which come from success in mastering them. This means elimination of undue pressures toward achievement for which the individual boy or girl is not yet ready. For the child, learning to read should be made an enjoyable task because a wealth of books is waiting to give him new experiences as well as pleasure. As he learns to write, he should discover the fun of keeping in touch with absent friends and loved ones through letters, and the thrill of catching the fleeting images of his own thought in written words. Speaking never need be a matter of sterile formality in school when life offers so much of interest for children to share and when they can gain so much in human understanding by talking things out together. Listening can be a source of interest, fun, and inspiration. The good school of today strives to see to it that learning takes place in an atmosphere of happiness and enthusiasm.

The Influence of Radio and Television

Radio and television are influencing our way of life profoundly. Information of great or small importance is shared by all people at once. Opinion and entertainment are furnished to children and adults for hours every day. The child lives even more than the adult with this volume of sight and sound, some of it good, much of it cheap and overtaxing to the emotions. He must learn to turn his back upon the screen at times and to shut the sound out of his consciousness if he is to do any consecutive thinking or reading at all. He must learn to apportion his leisure time wisely, devoting it to a variety of wholesome activities—now to sports and the out-of-doors, now to reading or writing, and now to constructive pursuits in crafts, in music, or in puppetry, according to his personal interests.

But he also must learn to make the best possible use of sound and screen, to hear accurately, to interpret adequately, and to evaluate carefully, if the floods of information coming over radio and television are to be of use to him. He must learn to check opinions voiced by commentators with what he knows or can learn through observation, through conversation, and through reading. He must learn how to choose the genuine instead of the superficial in drama, the lasting instead of the melodramatic in stories for children. He must copy the clean-cut diction of the best announcers and not the jumbled or slangy speech of those comedians who purposely misuse the language.

The Interplay of Activities of Home and School

The mother of Annette and Michael feels that radio and television are over-stimulating to her children, not only through the programs themselves, but also through a tense-ness of conversational tone that the listening adults develop in response to hourly news broadcasts of war, strikes, political bickering, and daily tragedy. She helps them to find the better programs for children—the puppet presentation of *Cinderella* or *Pinocchio*, the musical version of *Hansel and Gretel*—using these as leads for reading aloud later. She believes, too, that life as it is lived is important along with life as it is represented. She spends much time with the children in the open air, so that the baby and her brother encounter the natural world, the neighbors, the dogs and cats, the milk truck, the mail carrier, and other children.

She preserves for them the story time that was the most precious feature of her own childhood—sometimes the imaginative charm of "The Elves and the Shoemaker," or "Snow

White and the Seven Dwarfs," sometimes the good fun of Paul Bunyan, sometimes the hero stories from the Bible, and sometimes the everyday tales of William who rode in the circus parade, of *White Snow, Bright Snow,* or of the ducklings whose mother led them safely across Charles Street into Boston Gardens. She plans also for times of relaxation with nursery rhymes, picture books, or quiet conversation at bedtime.

The father shares with his children experiences appropriate to their development, but he also provides books for interpretation. When Michael was four, his father picked up *The Little Train* at the bookstore. He and Michael compared texts and pictures with real trains on their weekly walks to the railroad station. Mike learned to identify and name *engine, caboose, freight car, flat car,* and *block signal.* He could review from the pictures what he had learned by observation of the work of the engineer, brakeman, and switchman, enlarging his vocabulary and broadening his concepts daily.

At five, Michael took his book and his ceaseless questions to kindergarten, where *The Little Train* shared table space for a while with *Mother Goose, Millions of Cats, What Animal Is It?* and other picture books of great variety. Then one day when Mike was in the first grade, he and his class took a trip on a train. They bought their own tickets in the downtown station at the ticket window. They explored the diner and saw the cook at work in his tiny kitchen. They watched the porter make up a bed. They got acquainted with the conductor. When the train departed on schedule, they rode in a coach to the nearest suburban station, where they got off and took the trolley bus back to school. From this experience Michael's concept of trains was broadened; his experience in riding on a train gave him something to talk about, and something that he shared with the group. Next day he went to the library with the rest of the children and discovered more books about trains which he could borrow to read with his mother or to share with the other children in the class. All of them enjoyed especially the teacher's reading of Rowena Bennett's poem, "The Modern Dragon," which pictures the train roaring wildly through the darkness, its one eye lighting the way.

Not all mothers so wisely reconcile these newer influences in the field of communication with the developmental needs of young children. Not all schools draw upon children's real-life experiences for school learning. Many children are exposed to an unbalanced program of television, radio, and movies at home and to formal lessons only with traditional materials at school.

It seems, however, that young children who are normally healthy and active will take from radio and television only what has meaning for them. Annette gives brief attention and surprising response to the dancing figures, but after a few minutes she runs away from the screen to more active pursuits.

Michael now turns off the most exciting of "horse operas" to watch and listen while a local naturalist displays on the TV screen birds or other living creatures. His father interested him in this program by talking about the naturalist and his work and by taking him to the Zoological Gardens. In school, Michael's teacher will draw upon this special interest, just as she draws upon the interests of other children to develop their powers in conversation and discussion and to lead them eventually into reading and into writing. She will help them through the extension of these interests to build further constructive experience in home and community. At the same time she makes note of a forthcoming broadcast of *Spunky*, the story of the circus pony, by the Haders, in which Michael and many of the other children will be interested. The following Saturday, also, the story-telling hour at the public library is to feature *Honk the Moose* by Phil Stong, which Michael and others may hear and retell to the entire class.

The teacher recognizes that school and home must accept joint responsibility for the quality of children's experiences and together must help them learn to use the skills of communication which are essential for well-rounded development. She gains much insight into the children's home experiences through their conversation and through the things they bring to school to share with others. She also plans for time to talk with parents and get from them this essential background.

MEETING THE SOCIAL NEEDS OF THE BOYS AND GIRLS

The children of today's world face a striking need to use language in learning to live with others. Good human relations may be impaired or facilitated through the quality of language arts experiences. Growth in this area of living comes as children practice wholesome relationships in an encouraging atmosphere both at home and at school. Above all, they must learn to accept other children as they are.

The Importance of Language Arts in Improving Human Relations

Hubert, as a member of a ten-year-old group, led the change of attitude toward a boy of another race with a simple, "Come on, Jeff, you be on my side."

At sixteen, he was one of a group of young people who challenged the community in debate, in letters to the newspapers, and in radio speeches, when their classmate, a member of a minority group, was denied a national honor he had earned.

Daily in school life children are helped by the wise teacher to a deeper appreciation of others through the use of poetry, stories, dramatic play, or conversation.

"Little Becky, Little Becky," a group of kindergarten children once taunted on the playground, recognizing that the diminutive twelve-year-old was different from themselves in everything but size. Becky, dwarfed from birth, had just entered the school from another community. In the classroom, after calling the children together, the teacher told a brief version of a favorite story of her own childhood, "Thumbelina." The five-year-olds listened, entranced, to the story and then spent some time exploring for "little things" such as the tiny turtle in the terrarium, the miniature furniture which was perched on a shelf in the playhouse, the smallest beads in the bead box. Brief and fleeting as this interest was, the teacher observed that thereafter they welcomed Becky when she left her own sixth-grade group on the playground and drifted to their swings or sandbox.

Older children find a need for the language processes of guest-host relationships which they learn and practice as they entertain their parents or boys and girls from other rooms at school. They learn something of the emotional connotation of words and of the vicious results of stereotyped name-calling. They need to find ways of disagreeing courteously. At the same time, they discover the importance of the language used in making ideas clear to others, of the kinds of usage acceptable in one situation and not in another. They come to recognize the value of a wealth of words and of clarity in thought and expression as they think and talk together with other children.

The Language Arts as Basic to Democratic Life

Learning to use the communication skills effectively in living with other people is, clearly, one of the basic needs of our times. There are other language needs which are worthy of attention if children are to be aided to the fullest extent in becoming useful members of society today.

Literacy. On the elementary school, primarily, rests the responsibility for simple literacy, which is basic to the success of democracy. All thought and decision rest upon having the facts. Accuracy in getting the facts demands basic skills in reading and listening. Available evidence indicates that the schools are doing this job today better than they ever did. The men of World War II read four years in advance of the men of World War I, and this in spite of the fact that the practice of getting rid of those who could not read was on the wane during the years between. But the level of literacy is not good enough even today for the exercise of the duties of intelligent citizenship. That fact alone is a constant challenge to the schools.

Group discussion and decision. Moreover, mere literacy is not enough. To be a good citizen the individual must be well informed, must speak responsibly both at home and abroad. He must think clearly before he speaks, in order to challenge the ideas of others. He must expect evidence for statements made by his fellows, and he must expect to produce evidence for the generalizations in which he himself indulges. He must be conscious of the emotional intent and of the emotional bias of words and must demand simple statements of fact when statements of fact are appropriate to the topic being considered.

An eighth-grade group, questioning what they read and heard about the stand of local councilmen on housing, visited the council chambers after their teacher and a parent made the arrangements. The mayor, presiding, allowed the young people to put their questions which they had formulated carefully. Two council members gave answers from opposite points of view. This experience stimulated further extensive study in their classroom situation. But it did more—as Leander told his father, "This deciding about things looks like everybody's job to me."

At times, too, the individual must write to make his own thought or that of his group effective in action. He must be able to record facts and ideas for future reference. He must master the difficult conventions of writing and of spelling. The road is an uphill one for many children. Great patience is needed both by parents and by teachers in order to give help and encouragement in the long, slow process.

Planning and carrying out plans. In a democracy, the person who can speak well wields a powerful influence. With regard to speech, children come to kindergarten with four years of practice on which the school can build in a larger setting representing all levels of language and all the elements of a democratic society. Children who learn to share, to coöperate, to lead, to follow, to plan together, to carry out plans, to evaluate results, and to use the arts of communication in so doing are learning the fundamental processes by which the people in a democracy work together.

The Moral Implications of Communication

The school must remember also that the individual without moral responsibility may use his communication skills to mislead, to delude, or to corrupt others and to destroy the pattern of life by which the good of all is fostered. Moral courage and a highly developed social conscience must go hand in hand with skill in communication to insure constructive participation in living. For these reasons, it is essential that the development of language skills should take place in a social setting.

Boys of a third-grade group were playing checkers in the classroom during a rainy noon hour, without adult supervision. One of them, after being noisy and disorderly to the point of bringing the principal to the scene, failed to speak up and acknowledge that he had violated the code of reasonable quiet which the group had accepted. The other children were obviously faced with a moral dilemma to tell or not to tell. While the principal waited they appeared individually to debate their action. "Would you like to talk it over without me?" she asked. They eagerly assented, but upon her return after a few minutes they regretfully reported no success.

"Let me talk to Charlie," proposed Clint. All soberly agreed, apparently not regarding this as an open accusation of Charlie.

"Tell exactly what you did and you'll feel better," counseled Clint. "That's what I did when I broke the window, and I know." With a bit more of this counseling Charlie spoke up. All the boys beamed.

The principal recognized the incident as an outcome of the consistent daily discussion in that classroom of pertinent problems in which the teacher always encouraged the children to go far enough to decide in terms of fundamental values.

SUMMARY

In this chapter an attempt has been made to look at all the communication skills as they are needed for social and community living in these times. Each of the separate strands of the language arts assumes greater significance as new forces and patterns evolve in our society.

To be able to read, write, speak, and listen is an essential achievement in a society which grows continuously more complex and depends increasingly upon the use of the written and spoken word. Literacy is essential to earning a living and to sharing in any effective measure in community life.

Speaking and listening have always been recognized as necessary to any kind of satisfactory social and community living, but parents of a hundred years ago, although they valued reading increasingly, did not consider it indispensable to a good life. Today, the child who does not learn to read cannot participate intelligently in the common life and is therefore a source of concern to his parents, to the school he attends, and to the community as well. Writing, once an accomplishment of a very few people, is now recognized as a needed skill for all children in meeting the common demands of day-by-day living.

Such changes sharply delineate new needs for the language arts. It is the purpose of this volume to aid teachers in meeting these needs.

Your Own Voice Surprises You.

Storytelling Time Is Really Fun.

Making Good Tortillas Calls for Careful Reading.

How Well Can You Use the Telephone?

It's as Real as Though You Were There!

The Telephone Makes the World Seem Smaller.

We Help Each Other.

BIBLIOGRAPHY

APPLEGATE, Mauree, *Everybody's Business—Our Children* (Evanston, Illinois, Row, Peterson & Company, 1952).

BECKER, May L., *First Adventures in Reading; Introducing Children to Books* (Philadelphia, J. B. Lippincott Company, 1947).

Children's Book Council, *The World of Children's Books* (New York, 50 West 53rd Street, 1952).

DALE, Edgar, *How to Read a Newspaper* (Chicago, Scott, Foresman and Company, 1941).

DEBOER, John J., "Cultivating Powers of Discrimination in Reading," *School Review*, LVII (January, 1949), pp. 28–36.

EATON, Anne T., *Reading with Children* (New York, Viking Press, Inc., 1940).

Madison Public Schools, *Magazines for Elementary Grades* (Madison, Wisconsin, Curriculum Division, The Public Schools, 1949).

MARTIN, William E., and STENDLER, Celia B., *Child Development: The Process of Growing Up in Society* (New York, Harcourt, Brace & Company, Inc., 1953).

MONROE, Marion, *Growing into Reading; How Readiness for Reading Develops at Home and at School* (Chicago, Scott, Foresman and Company, 1951).

PLATZ, Helen R., "Trash and Treasure in Children's Reading," *Child Study*, XXX (Spring, 1953).

RANLETT, L. Felix, "Magazines for Tens and Teens," *Horn Book Magazine*, XX (July–August, 1944), pp. 271–77.

ROBBINS, Florence, *Educational Sociology: A Study in Child, Youth, School, and Community* (New York, Henry Holt & Company, Inc., 1953).

SIEPMANN, Charles A., *Radio, Television, and Society* (New York, Oxford University Press, 1950).

WITTY, Paul, and BRICKER, Harry, *Your Child and Radio, TV, Comics, and Movies* (Chicago, Science Research Associates, Inc., 1952).

C H A P T E R 2

Child Development and Its Relationship to the Language Arts Program

As KNOWLEDGE of human development increases through many scientific studies, it becomes increasingly evident that the ability to communicate plays an important role both in intellectual development and in the growth of personality. Children at each age level have their characteristic needs for growth as well as their characteristic methods of reaction and response. As teachers learn to fit the language arts program to these needs and to these ways of responding, as they set realistic goals, and as they work *through* rather than *against* children's normal patterns of development, satisfactory growth in language will result. For the language arts program is both end and means. It develops skill in all forms of communication through language, giving children increasing insight into the structure and effective use of their mother tongue and developing their ability to read and to listen as well as to use reading and listening for worth-while purposes in life. At the same time, language is the means by which children acquire knowledge and understanding in all areas of education and in first-hand experience in life.

LANGUAGE AND THE TOTAL DEVELOPMENT
OF THE CHILD

Dollard and Miller show clearly the importance of language in the total pattern of the child's growth.[1] One cannot guide, motivate, nor reassure the infant with words. In fact, many of the acute emotional disturbances of infancy and early childhood are due to lack of development of the processes of reasoning which depend in large measure upon language. Without such powers of thinking, the very young child cannot foresee the outcome of events nor understand the relationships of cause and effect. What happens to him at the present moment is all-important. He is incapable of sacrificing immediate goals for remote ones which he cannot perceive.

The Social Effects of Language

Furthermore, language is a major instrument of social control. As the little child gains in mastery of language, he becomes capable of responding to verbal explanations and directions, and grows through the possibility of interaction between thought and experience and between his ideas and those of others. Insight, for example, into why he may not touch a certain electric wire comes only with increased experience and with command of language. Up to that time, he must act only in obedience to a command. With the acquisition of language, generalization becomes more effective, and generalization is the means by which he substitutes the processes of thinking for the more wasteful techniques of trial and error in facing problem situations. It is also the means by which each generation builds on the experience of the past.

The young child's desire for social approval and conformity influences significantly his growth in language. He is

[1] John Dollard and Neal E. Miller, *Personality and Psychotherapy* (New York, McGraw-Hill Book Company, Inc., 1950), p. 107.

rewarded or reprimanded for his use of certain words. As his efforts at expression meet with praise or ridicule, he learns which phrases are acceptable and which are not. In the same way, he senses the distinction between real and make-believe, between justice or the lack of it. He discovers in time that he is more readily understood when he relates events in order and includes all necessary details in his explanations. If he does not, he fails to get what he desires.[2]

Motivation of growth in language should come, in school as well as outside of school, from the effective use of it in normal social situations and the recognition of the inevitable relationship between control of words and ideas and the achievement of personal and social goals. The purposes will vary; the setting will become broader and more complex, as Baker discovered in his study of group discussion in Grades II, IV, and VI,[3] and the language used will grow in extensiveness and maturity, but the essential social motive will remain.

Language and the Development of Personality

Growth in ability to communicate is also an essential part of the development of the self.[4] The child who learns to communicate with ease and satisfaction tends to build up an outgoing personality and a friendly relationship to others; whereas the one who is retarded in his language development or finds his efforts to communicate frustrated may become timid or inhibited or may turn aggressive and strike out at the world.

Development of both personality and language seems to follow a plan laid down at the beginning of life. It appears true that in the sequence of his growth as a person just as in

[2] *Ibid.*, pp. 116–24.

[3] Harold V. Baker, *Children's Contributions to Elementary School General Discussion*, Child Development Monograph No. 29 (New York, Columbia University, Teachers College Bureau of Publications, 1942). See also summary of this study on pages 118–19 in the discussion of speech.

[4] Erik H. Erikson, *Childhood and Society* (New York, W. W. Norton & Company, Inc., 1950).

the sequence of the growth of his body, the child follows inner laws of development, and needs from adults chiefly encouragement, guidance, and opportunity to try his powers.

Along with increasing control over language, then, children are developing as individual personalities. The first necessity for the infant is to gain a feeling of trust or of confidence in the people and things about him. At the same time, he must learn faith in himself and his ability to meet the demands made upon him in mind and in body. Gradually he discovers himself as an independent human being and faces the task of achieving a feeling of personal adequacy and self-reliance. He continues with this task throughout life, helped by his parents and his teachers during his formative years to develop self-control without loss of self-esteem. Jersild, after a careful study of the problem among both children and young people, came to the conclusion that the school has a primary responsibility for opening new possibilities for self-discovery and acceptance.[5] The language arts have a particularly important part to play in helping the child to draw upon his emotional resources through self-expression rather than to stifle them through too rigid adherence to convention. Through reading, also, the language arts can furnish opportunity both for emotional release and for the understanding of self through stories paralleling the child's own experience or setting forth values which he may be led to accept.

The school also can furnish abundant opportunity to the child to explore, to test his powers, and to make choices. As his experience broadens, his vocabulary increases. As his language and thought power mature, he becomes capable of extending and analyzing his experience. Through the same power of communication, his horizons widen, his trust in other people deepens, and his relationship to the world about him becomes more secure. In school, also, he is a member of a larger social group than either home or neigh-

[5] Arthur T. Jersild, *In Search of Self; An Exploration of the Role of the School in Promoting Self-Understanding* (New York, Columbia University, Teachers College Bureau of Publications, 1952).

borhood has provided. He must continue to develop personal initiative, but now in relation to the common purposes of the group. In the early years of his life, he has exercised this initiative in "make believe" and in dramatic play. Later he is ready for more vigorous learning and a share in the many kinds of activity which combine opportunity with a sense of personal responsibility for effective participation in the group life. From that point on, the child's own relationship to the group assumes special significance for him. Two things are necessary if he is to have that sense of achievement and pride in a job well done [6] which is fundamental to the building of a wholesome personality: he must work within the limits of his own powers, and at the same time he must develop the assurance which comes from the approval of the group.

THE ORDERLY PATTERN OF HUMAN GROWTH

The pattern of human growth is orderly and consistent; yet there are almost as many variations of the pattern as there are growing children. Men of science interested in human growth have made careful studies of the sequence of steps in the development of physique, personality, and language. Each step involves all that has gone before and is itself involved in all that follows. Yet individual differences within age levels and from age to age are so great that generalizations about children of this stage or that must be made with due recognition of such diversity. It is true, however, that the infant who has learned to trust those who care for him may learn to trust himself more readily because of the security he has established. Furthermore, a child who has learned to understand and to control himself and to use his powers with a degree of initiative approaches the task of establishing broader human relationships with other people without the handicap of timidity or lack of self-confidence.

[6] *Ibid.*

The Importance of the "Teachable Moment"

In recent studies of human development the term *teachable moment* has been used to designate the time when a child is "ready" for what he is to be taught. Such readiness may be physical or mental; it may be social or emotional; or it may be all four.[7] Unless there is "synchronization between maturity and opportunity," as Olson says,[8] the child's efforts at learning will meet with frustration. Quite as important as physical and mental maturity is the child's attitude toward what is being taught. If he resists the learning, his intelligence will be of little use. Teachers should be alert to the child's interest of the moment, to the need which he feels in any given enterprise for increased facility in a certain skill or for additional knowledge on a particular subject. This is not a matter of so-called "toadying" to children's whims; it is rather a matter of the teacher's being intelligent enough to recognize and use the child's immediate interests and needs and to develop real and vital experiences in the classroom which will stimulate essential drives for learning. For example, a child who has been completely disinterested in correct form in the heading of a letter may suddenly wish to know how to write it when a new interest in how to care for a parakeet demands writing for a pamphlet of information. Entertaining members of the community at an exhibit of work completed in the classroom may arouse a real sense of need for knowing what to say in introducing a child to an adult. A visit to a nearby flour mill may furnish the drive which sends a ten-year-old boy to a children's encyclopedia for the first time. No engineer is so foolish as to try to make water run up hill if by making it run down hill, he can have the forces of gravity on his side. Teachers should be alert not

[7] Robert J. Havighurst, *Developmental Tasks and Education*, 2nd ed. (New York, Longmans, Green & Company, 1952).

[8] Willard C. Olson, *Child Development* (Boston, D. C. Heath & Company, 1949).

only to detect the "teachable moments," but to promote them by the richness and reality of the experiences furnished in the classroom. Efforts to teach what a child is not ready to learn are largely wasted; witness the futility of efforts to initiate every school beginner into reading and to demand a uniform quality of handwriting of all children in a class whether they are physically and emotionally ready for the task or not.

Caring for Individual Differences in Development

Some children are consistently slow in growth, but their gains, which are nevertheless solid and substantial, follow a normal sequence. Others are definitely retarded. It must be recognized that some of them will never catch up with the group. Some children are consistently rapid in growth, whereas others progress in irregular spurts. If the child's sequence of growth follows the usual pattern and each step forms a secure foundation for the next, he may be said to be developing normally. The task of parents and teachers is to study the process of his growth and to provide the stimulation and experience he needs at each point along the way.

Many school systems, therefore, have recently attempted to build programs which recognize a natural sequence of growth on the part of children and accept the fact that each must work through various stages at his own rate and to the extent of his individual capacity.[9] It is well, then, to ask early in the process of making a curriculum what children are like at successive periods in their development and how the school may best furnish an environment and a natural motivation suited to each of them.

[9] Grand Rapids Public Schools, *Growing by Doing* (Grand Rapids, Michigan, Board of Education, 1951).

Ohio State University Laboratory Schools, *How Children Develop*, School Series, No. 3 (Columbus, Ohio, The University, 1946).

New York City Public Schools, *Chart for Growth in the Language Arts* (New York City Public Schools, Curriculum Division, Brooklyn, 1946).

THE PRESCHOOL CHILD

The child of two to five years of age may be at home or in the nursery school or kindergarten. He may be an only child among adults, or he may be living with a lively group of brothers and sisters. He develops early many skills necessary for coping with the complex world about him, among them the growing use of voice and speech. If adults take time to talk with him and answer his continuous flow of questions, he acquires vocabulary at a rapid pace and grows in ability to think and to express his thoughts clearly. He seeks companionship in carrying on his activities but often plays alongside others rather than with them. His ability to share and to coöperate extends only to things that interest him and then for short periods of time. As he talks with other children he is likely to be concerned primarily with himself and his own interests. There is little interaction except for occasional disputes over possessions and privileges. If he has no playmates, a child of this age often invents imaginary ones who fill his need for companionship until he goes to school and finds real companions. He adjusts to organized groups slowly and turns to adults for help and approval fully as often as to his playmates.

The dramatic play of this period tends to reproduce adult activities as the child explores his own world by playing house, store, deliveryman, or postman and impersonates one after another the characters he meets on radio or television, in picture books, and in stories which are read or told to him.

His imagination takes care of most properties, though he may demand a gun or lasso or mother's hat or high-heeled shoes for "dress up" purposes. He enters into his dramatizing so thoroughly that he *is* Cowboy Small in Lois Lenski's story and demands to be treated accordingly. One small boy even refused to have his cowboy suit laundered because Cowboy Small did not have his laundered in the story.

Children of four and five are keenly interested in words—especially new and unusual sounding ones—and will play with them, toss them about gleefully, and invent all sorts of distortions of them. They like to imitate adult talk and will copy adult behavior and conversation in their play of housekeeping, calling on the neighbors, and serving as teacher or storekeeper.

Poetry and stories suited to their maturity and interests fascinate them at this age. They delight especially in books of their own and will carry them around, talk about them, and even pretend to read them if an adult will listen.

As the child builds vocabulary and adds new concepts from his experiences, his sentences lengthen and become more mature. Most five-year-olds employ all the types of sentences used by adults. Length and quality of sentences is perhaps the best measure of growth in language power.[10] The ease with which the child uses language for self-expression is a good indication of his mental health.

THE PRIMARY SCHOOL CHILD

If there is logic in starting the basic elementary school program at age six, it is that most children by that time have explored their home environment rather thoroughly and are ready for new experiences, social in character and involving participation in the group.

Primary school youngsters have an excess of physical and nervous energy and, if restrained physically too long or too often, they become tense, as shown by restlessness, fighting, or crying. The kindergarten teacher in planning for a good school day intersperses opportunities *to do* with opportunities *to talk*. The first-grade teacher, knowing that young

[10] Dorothea McCarthy, "Child Development: Language," in Walter S. Monroe, ed., *Encyclopedia of Educational Research*, rev. ed. (New York, The Macmillan Company, 1950), p. 168. Also "Language Development in Children," in Leonard Carmichael, ed., *A Manual of Child Psychology*, rev. ed. (New York, John Wiley & Sons, Inc., 1954), pp. 492–630.

children grow restless with sitting and that the span of attention is short, brings together a few children for a brief time in a reading group rather than a larger number for a longer time.

These children are still growing steadily, though not as rapidly as in preschool years. Their large muscles are developing and are in constant use, whereas their small muscles have not yet attained sufficient coördination for detailed tasks in writing. Yet primary grade youngsters may advance greatly in their use of language through appropriate experiences. A group of first-grade children, building a train with large blocks and using it in their play, have many uses for language expression and for reading material of the sort which they dictate and the teacher writes on the board. In such a class one child's first writing was a sprawling sign which he tacked to the end of the train, C A B O O S E. The teacher helped him to write it to serve his own purposes.

With these young children, communication by means of language is only one way of learning; much of their learning is by doing. Promoting the use of language in constant relationship to other activities is therefore an essential part of the language arts program. Observing a turtle, listening to a record of city noises, or playing in the playhouse, for example, furnish excellent opportunity for increasing vocabulary and developing fluency in speaking. It should be remembered that first-hand experience alone may not increase power in language. *Verbal rehearsal* of that experience through sharing or through discussion is all-important.

While these youngest members of the school population act impulsively, and to a great extent emotionally, they will conform because they have a deep need for security and require approval, especially from adults. To them the teacher is the most important person in the school situation. They develop need for group approval with time and with growth in group relationships. They show a growing consciousness of the rights of others in a class in which the group consistently "talks things over" under the teacher's guidance, and they begin to see the need of taking turns in sharing and telling. Their developing sense of responsibility depends considerably upon how much recognition they gain for fulfilling responsibilities.

One group of children were asked to report helpful things they had seen others do. As the conversation was almost ended, Dicky exclaimed, "I picked up paper from the playground all recess and no one even said a word about it." [11]

Youngsters in the primary grades are highly imitative, usually imaginative, often creative. They like to be doing and making, but they have an undeveloped sense of time as well as comparatively uncoördinated muscles and therefore do not respond well to rigid schedules. They seem to be unnecessarily slow and awkward. However, they need the security of regular routine and can work in large blocks of time and in terms of over-all plans. The thoughtful primary teacher sets up a program which gives them opportunity to work in this way. Within this framework she gives attention to small groups and to individuals. Often she works with such groups as they perfect their plans through brief discussions, realizing that in talking things out, children are learning to think and to express themselves. She helps an individual child as he struggles to master a detailed skill like writing a capital letter, or works with the entire class as interest centers around an all-school problem such as plans for "Zoo Day."

While young children are spontaneous and responsive, they may be intolerant of new things, of physical change, or unaccustomed foods, or strange playmates. Through her own storytelling and story-reading, through poetry said to and with the whole group, the teacher presents many new ideas and helps children to interpret new experiences—Marjorie Flack's *The New Pet*, for example, for the arrival

[11] Grand Rapids Public Schools, *Growing by Doing* (Grand Rapids, Michigan, Board of Education, 1951).

of a new baby; or *Everybody Likes Butch* for becoming a helpful member of the group in kindergarten, or the much-loved poem, "The Chickens," for being willing to "scratch" for what they get.

A normal child during these years reveals consistent growth in intellectual traits. His ability to reason grows with his years and his experience. He learns rapidly when materials and activities are adapted to his needs and when he is not pressed for accomplishments for which he is not ready. His interest is in immediate not in ultimate goals. His ability to follow directions increases steadily, provided the directions grow out of situations meaningful to him and are presented in language which he understands. Such experiences, for example, enable him to sharpen his understanding of prepositions and to gain precision in their use. Distinctions between *in* and *on* or *over* and *under* must be related to the reality of his motor experience in order to have real meaning.

Readiness for learning must be investigated carefully. Toward the end of the kindergarten year and in the early weeks of the first grade the teacher watches for interest in reading and in writing. She seeks the "teachable moment" referred to earlier. The school that is realistic about children's growth provides for systematic instruction in these areas only when sufficient maturity is present. Evidences of maturity are sought in such things as interest in looking at books, in writing their own names, or in asking what certain words mean. Children can learn only when they are mature enough to understand and perform the tasks involved.

Again, each step in learning must be built upon another. Materials and activities must be adapted to the stage of development of every child in every group. If a five-year-old in kindergarten has insufficient coördination to outline with a long-handled paintbrush the picture he has in his mind, he probably will not be ready to write with pencils in the first grade. But in the weeks before he is asked to form letters, he will enjoy using large crayons and wide soft-textured sheets of paper on which he can exercise his muscles by making coils of smoke coming out of a chimney or ripples of water on a pond.

Although the attention span of the five-year-old is relatively short, it lengthens as he grows older and persists in activities that interest him. If the attention span does not increase under favorable conditions this may be a danger signal, pointing to questionable health, to limited mental development, to lack of emotional stability, or possibly to lack of challenge in the school program. The teacher may be able to provide the help the child needs, or she may have to refer the problem through her principal or supervisor to a child psychologist, a guidance counselor, or a social worker —whoever is best equipped to help.

Children of seven and eight are still extremely active. They need much freedom and much play while they adapt gradually to school routines. In fact, much of their most effective learning comes through play, in which they explore and plan together. They are becoming good group participants and good listeners. Because they often identify themselves with radio and television characters, the teacher introduces stories which give them opportunities for other kinds of identification—*If I Ran the Zoo,* for example, or *B is for Betsy* or *Eddie and the Fire Engine.* She reads and says poetry in which the children can participate with chanting, with refrains, or with dramatic effects as in "The Tip-Toe-Tale," "Once I Saw a Little Bird," or "The Jumblies."

Children show a wide range of differences in development on entering school. The range, moreover, increases during the elementary years, particularly if the school program is adapted to individual needs. In general, boys lag behind girls in school achievement, the difference being especially obvious in the language arts as girls are usually more facile in expression than boys, verbalizing more easily.

Since children's interest and their thirst for information expand faster than their ability to read, write, and spell, much of their most valuable work is done orally in the primary grades. They can provide the ideas for written material if the teacher will guide their thinking and serve as scribe in recording it. They are interested in "making up" their own stories and in composing poems and songs. They like to keep records of their achievements and pore over them appreciatively from time to time.

Vocabularies expand rapidly during these years and sentence sense develops in both reading and writing activities. Help with correcting unacceptable grammatical usage can be fruitful if it is given tactfully and unobtrusively without making the child self-conscious. Children want to do well and to meet the standards developed by teacher and class together and will make an effort to improve under tactful and considerate guidance. During these years verbs are particularly confusing in a language in which "sing" becomes "sang" but "brang" is unacceptable and "walk" becomes "walked" but "rided" is taboo. Pronouns, too, cause some confusion which can be cleared up through much opportunity for talking and listening and through reading.

Children who are less verbal profit by many opportunities to construct and to manipulate materials for purposes that tie in with their daily experiences, such as building a simple cage for a pet that is kept in the room, or sorting and placing the rocks in the border of the class flower garden. The conversation that goes on normally with such group activities means growth in vocabulary and in the practice of using language for understanding. Boys, especially, may find an outlet for language as accompaniment to these activities which are largely physical. In schools where individual needs are cared for, there is less tendency to find a preponderance of boys failing to make progress in primary classes or lagging behind in the intermediate and upper grades and showing increasing indifference to learning.

Expanding intellectual interests of seven- and eight-year-olds are greatly facilitated by a growing ability to read.

Children find increasing satisfaction in animals and nature. They want to know more about the people and things with which they come in contact. They are capable of considerable vicarious learning through simple stories of other people and places. The wealth of books available to children today makes it possible to satisfy all types of interests—the boy's in animals, airplanes, cowboys, and small-boy adventure, and the girl's in people and in stories of home and family life. The children's growing skill in reading brings satisfaction, not alone through adult approval, but through the sense of power it develops in them. There comes to children at this time a realization of the pleasure in store for them through reading and of the usefulness of books in carrying out their many purposes both at home and at school.

The active, vital interests of these children can be used to promote many types of essential learning. The main problem of the teacher is to know each child well enough to give him the help he needs at the time when he needs it.

THE CHILD IN THE MIDDLE GRADES

Fewer studies have been made of children of the intermediate grades, the nine- through eleven-year-olds, than of children of preschool, primary, or adolescent years. Blair and Burton have brought together many of the better materials about children of this stage of development which reveal certain generally recognized characteristics.[12]

Considered as a group, these preadolescents have boundless energy and have much greater endurance than the younger child. They are less susceptible to childhood diseases and attend school more regularly. They maintain a fairly stable rate of growth. They use their increasing muscular coördination to develop skills in games and in construction

---

[12] Arthur W. Blair and William H. Burton, *Growth and Development of the Pre-Adolescent* (New York, Appleton-Century-Crofts, Inc., 1951).

activities. Their eyes now focus clearly, a fact which contributes to increased reading ability. Some of them become omnivorous readers. Others need constant encouragement through the relating of reading to their immediate interests. In general, their manipulative skills give evidence of their increased muscular coördination. They develop relatively greater skill in handwriting, but if writing tasks become too burdensome and meaningless they may retrogress in quality of writing. They need the challenge of real purposes. The lettering of a simple poster advertising the Red Cross drive may provide incentive for later writing; preparation of a script for a radio broadcast is not beyond the capabilities of intermediate-grade children.

The influence of adults tends to weaken at this age as relationships with other children grow increasingly important. Children tend to resist the patterns of conduct parents and teachers expect them to follow, and shape their behavior after that of other boys and girls of their own age. Knowing this, the teacher helps the class develop group criteria for their activities—for instance, for speaking. Because children now listen to one another, planning and evaluating become important. Simple procedures for group discussion are developed in solving problems such as, "How did the early settlers in this community meet their needs for food, clothing, and shelter?" or, "What kind of program shall we put on for the all-school assembly?"

Relationships to the group become important, especially those of boys to boys and girls to girls. Girls' clubs and boys' clubs develop different kinds of interests. The boy feels that he must succeed in group games well enough to be accepted. It is just as necessary to the girl to be "in" with the other girls. The need for the security which comes from adult approval vies in these children with their need for acceptance by the group. Here stories help the boys to find themselves and shape their own ideals as they read of the valor and achievement of men in story or biography—for example, Robin Hood, Davy Crockett, Daniel Boone, Abraham Lincoln, or Charles Lindbergh.

Children from nine to eleven are eager and alert, intellectually more interested in the world outside themselves than primary children are. Their drive to know and to do is fed by television, movie, radio, and newspaper, and by conversation heard in the home and in the street. Maps, globes, periodicals, and newspapers help them to expand their dawning world consciousness. Tangible connection with other parts of the world, such as having a father or brother serving in a distant land, heightens greatly a child's interest in remote regions. Such an association led one boy to fascinated reading of *Pong Choolie, You Rascal,* a story of a child of North Korea who escaped to the protection of American troops. Here, again, is the "teachable moment" referred to in Chapter 2. Reading at this point may provide for expansion of interests. *The Secret of the Andes* became a joy to a group of fifth-grade children whose teacher had traveled in the Inca region. Better writing becomes important as these youngsters find more real needs to communicate or to record, and they are willing to strive for effectiveness, and even to some extent, for form.

The opportunity to choose their own reading material becomes more and more necessary as interests extend and vary. Many boys develop much interest in mechanics. They are curious about machines, as well as fond of making them, and may succeed in interpreting diagrams and directions of much greater difficulty than their usual reading.

During the middle years many boys tend to lay aside interest in fantasy and seek reality and objectivity. Some girls of this age indulge in an orgy of reading fairy tales and poetry. Others, emerging from the fairy-tale stage into realism, are drawn to a book such as *Daughter of the Mountains* by Louise Rankin, in which the ten-year-old child of Tibet searches for many miles over difficult terrain for her stolen pet. Her endurance and her devotion become as important as the beauty and symbolism of the gold-haired Lhasa terrier, a gift she has received from the mountain monastery.

Most children develop rapidly in these years in their understanding of the physical world and of the operation of natural law. They show increasing ability to see relationships of cause and effect and to form generalizations.[13] Scientific experiments and stories dealing with natural phenomena are among their major interests. Boys who will read little else will enjoy books such as *What Makes It Tick?* by Katherine Britton, *All Around You* by Jeanne Bendick, and *Rockets, Jets, Guided Missiles, and Space Ships* by Jack Coggins and Fletcher Pratt. Interest in science stories reaches its height at about the age of ten. The capacity for logical thinking dealing with concrete objects develops rapidly at this time. Children's magazines which were popular through the fourth grade give way to *Mechanix Illustrated,* and similar periodicals.

Studies of the questions asked by children of the middle grades show that 50 per cent of them can be classified under the heading "social studies," whereas nearly 40 per cent call for scientific information.[14] Choices of reading include many books which expand the social studies interests current in the classroom. Laura Ingalls Wilder's *Little House on the Prairie* and other stories make the study of pioneer life take on reality and vividness.

Children of this age, though they have too imperfect a time sense to understand history as it is frequently taught, often revel in stories dealing with the conditions and people of former times. Concepts of past centuries rarely emerge before the age of eleven.

In addition, boys and girls in the middle grades show a

---

[13] Jean M. Deutsche, *Children's Concepts of Causal Relations* (Minneapolis, Minnesota, University of Minnesota Press, 1937).

[14] Emily V. Baker, *Children's Questions and Their Implications for the Curriculum* (New York, Columbia University, Teachers College Bureau of Publications, 1945).

greatly increased interest in current happenings outside the home. Stories of people of other countries and other social and cultural groups take on new interest. *Blue Willow* by Doris Gates helps boys and girls to understand the migrant child. *Bright April* by Marguerite de Angeli gives insight into the problems of a little Negro girl, and Eleanor Estes's *The Hundred Dresses* reveals the suffering of a Polish child tormented by her more fortunate classmates. Children gain both understanding and a sense of values through such reading. They are eager to increase their knowledge about all manner of people and experience and show increasing objectivity in dealing with such topics.

It must never be forgotten, however, that all studies of children's interests in reading show that young readers place at the very top of the list exciting adventure, mystery stories, obstreperous humor, and the escapades of boys and girls like themselves.

The school program during these years may lay the foundation for permanent interests of great value and at the same time may capitalize upon the natural outgoing tendencies of these children and their eternal "WHY?" Discussions which were personal and spontaneous in the kindergarten and have become a little more planned in succeeding years may be very fruitful at this time because of the interest and objectivity of youngsters of nine through eleven. Children of these ages show a desire to initiate and to plan, to compete intellectually, to reason things out, and to verify facts. They make increasingly clear distinction between the factual and the fanciful and exhibit a tendency to challenge and to prove, if only on such evidence as "My father says so" or "My teacher told us." At this point the books in which "you look things up" become important. Group discussion often necessitates independent research which leads in turn to reporting. These skills may be best developed in the process of using them.

A program that reaches out into life offers these boys and girls opportunity for discussion, letter-writing, and use of important information, gathered by interviews and other oral means as well as by reading.

THE EARLY ADOLESCENT

Adolescent boys and girls rarely are found in the intermediate grades, but make up a rather large proportion of the children in the seventh and eighth grades. In most of these classes one-third of the boys and two-thirds of the girls have emerged from the comparatively slow-growing, physically active, gregarious, and curious-minded period of later childhood into early adolescence. Rapid physical growth, often irregular, creates problems of size and figure which worry these youngsters. Awakening sex interests make for a different social orientation. Self-consciousness about his changing voice may cause the boy to avoid speaking in class. Dress, appearance, and attractiveness to others may be of major concern to the girl when any school activity singles her out individually. One teacher, sensitive to the needs of her seventh-grade pupils in an underprivileged neighborhood, kept a "costume box" of appropriate, attractive used clothing. Through tactful provision of a fresh blouse or a bright tie, many a girl was freed from anxiety about her appearance to do an effective job in a school program.

Play-making offers opportunities to these boys and girls to escape from the limitations of which they are painfully conscious and to live in imagination the heroic, romantic, or vocational roles which their widening interests and more extensive reading reveal to them.

Group sharing of information may take on formality, as in the forum or panel, or the simpler group-planned report. The elements of group dynamics may be developed as pupils experiment with buzz sessions or with role-playing.

Community and civic problems, inter-group relationships, and national and international affairs offer opportunities and materials for study and discussion for these young people. Many of them are idealistic and show a reformer's zeal in attacking social problems. They may be led to read widely in newspapers and magazines and need help in recognizing propaganda and detecting flimsy generalizations based on inadequate evidence. They are striving to build a philosophy of life that they can live by and are eager to understand and use their potentialities in vital ways.

Normally, interests are intense and personal during these years and reactions are often emotional. Some disinterested and withdrawing children at this age may need the help of specialists. Teachers should be alerted to spot the early withdrawing and excessively "good" child who needs help. In general, boys of this age like tales of courage, hairbreadth escapes, and adventure stories with animals or boys their own age as heroes. They find satisfaction in tales of young people who win the admiration of adults as well as of their comrades as they triumph over adversity or win against great odds. Girls read these stories as avidly as boys, adding to them stories of romance. Identifying themselves with the heroes and heroines, they find satisfactions not possible within the restrictions of their own lives. When good books are easily available and when young people have guidance in selecting them, they will read them in abundance; but if better materials are not at hand, they will turn for vicarious experience to comic books and other inferior magazines and to books of poorer quality.

There may be negative aspects also in development during early adolescence. Girls may show varying tendencies to giggle, to weep, to quarrel, to use excessive make-up, or to engage in petty tale-bearing. Boys who are lacking in the masculine association their fathers should provide may take to bullying, to truancy, and to stealing in their desire for excitement and adventure. Clubs and recreation centers that are successful with boys supply this association as well as the vigorous activities boys like. The school should be alert to help all children who reveal emotional needs and should offer all possible security which comes from the teacher, from the child's relationships to other pupils, and from frequent recognition of him in the school as a whole.[15] The program should be so planned as to offer all the help that reading and language can supply.

Participation in community services is especially appropriate for young people of these ages—planning holiday parties for children in institutions, helping to improve a neighborhood playground, spearheading a drive to safeguard street lights, and similar activities. A strong sense of belonging to the group is essential to adolescents. They can analyze and evaluate themselves as a group, and even as individuals, provided *they* feel secure in the group situation.

Human relations pose persistent problems to these children who are straining against home ties and adult control and are seeking a place in their own age group. The teacher who knows her pupils often may suggest books that help many of them work out personal problems such as resentment of parental discipline.[16] Verse-writing and narrative writing [17] serve as emotional release to many adolescents, particularly to those who feel themselves left out of the activities of their companions or who are unhappy in their family relationships. The teacher who recognizes this guides the child in solving his problems through writing, helps with techniques so far as practical, but realizes that the release of emotional tension is of first importance.

Creative and personal writing with some boys and girls is vivid, colorful, and imaginative and shows an emerging in-

[15] Arthur T. Jersild, *In Search of Self; An Exploration of the Role of the School in Promoting Self-Understanding* (New York, Columbia University, Teachers College Bureau of Publications, 1952).

[16] David H. Russell and Caroline Shrodes, "Contributions of Research in Bibliotherapy to the Language Arts Program," *School Review*, LVIII (September–October, 1950), pp. 335–42 and 411–20.

[17] Alvina T. Burrows, June D. Ferebee, Dorothy C. Jackson, and Dorothy O. Saunders, *They All Want to Write: Written English in the Elementary School*, rev. ed. (New York, Prentice-Hall, Inc., 1952).

terest in style. If the young people have not been discouraged during their earlier years by over-concern for correctness, they write freely and with confidence. Both written and spoken language are spiced with the colorful and unconventional diction valued by adolescents, who are not easily persuaded to give it up or to substitute for it the conventional patterns of adult speech and writing.

As boys and girls search for vocations which fit their individual aptitudes, some of them find that what they wish to do requires a higher level of English usage than they have customarily practiced and will begin to put forth real effort to improve. If they have been well taught in their elementary school years, their ears have been tuned to correct usage so that they can improve through individual care and effort.

SUMMARY

Curriculum-building, therefore, involves gearing the various powers and skills in the language arts program to the broad aspects of child development as found in most normal children. Effective teaching carries out such a program by finding the teachable moment for each child's learning of each of the skills involved.

BIBLIOGRAPHY

BAKER, Emily V., *Children's Questions and Their Implications for the Curriculum* (New York, Columbia University, Teachers College Bureau of Publications, 1945).

BAKER, Harold V., *Children's Contributions to Elementary School General Discussion* Child Development Monograph No. 29 (New York, Columbia University, Teachers College Bureau of Publications, 1942).

BLAIR, Arthur W., and BURTON, William H., *Growth and Development of the Pre-Adolescent* (New York, Appleton-Century-Crofts Inc., 1951).

BURROWS, Alvina T., *Teaching Children in the Middle Grades* (Boston, D. C. Heath & Company, 1952).

———, FEREBEE, June D., JACKSON, Dorothy C., and SAUNDERS, Dorothy O., *They All Want to Write: Written English in the Elementary School*, rev. ed. (New York, Prentice-Hall, Inc., 1952).

DEUTSCHE, Jean M., *Children's Concepts of Causal Relations* (Minneapolis, Minnesota, University of Minnesota Press, 1937).

DOLLARD, John, and MILLER, Neal E., *Personality and Psychotherapy* (New York, McGraw-Hill Book Company, Inc., 1950), p. 107.

ERIKSON, Erik H., *Childhood and Society* (New York, W. W. Norton & Company, Inc., 1950).

Grand Rapids Public Schools, *Growing by Doing* (Grand Rapids, Michigan, Board of Education, 1951).

HAVIGHURST, Robert J., *Developmental Tasks and Education*, 2nd ed. (New York, Longmans, Green & Company, 1952).

JERSILD, Arthur T., *In Search of Self; An Exploration of the Role of the School in Promoting Self-Understanding* (New York, Columbia University, Teachers College Bureau of Publications, 1952).

McCARTHY, Dorothea, "Child Development: Language," in Walter S. Monroe, ed., *Encyclopedia of Educational Research* rev. ed., (New York, The Macmillan Company, 1950), p. 168.

———, "Language Development in Children," in Leonard Carmichael, ed. *A Manual of Child Psychology*, rev. ed. (New York, John Wiley & Sons, Inc., 1954), pp. 492–630.

New York City Public Schools, *Chart for Growth in the Language Arts* (New York City Public Schools, Curriculum Division, Brooklyn, 1946).

Ohio State University Laboratory Schools, *How Children Develop*, School Series, No. 3 (Columbus, Ohio, The University, 1946).

OLSON, Willard C., *Child Development* (Boston, D. C. Heath & Company, 1949).

RUSSELL, David H., and SHRODES, Caroline, "Contributions of Research in Bibliotherapy to the Language Arts Program," *School Review*, LVIII (September –October, 1950), pp. 335–42; 411–20.

WATTS, A. F., *The Language and Mental Development of Children* (Boston, D. C. Heath & Company, 1945).

CHILD DEVELOPMENT AND THE LANGUAGE ARTS 41

CHAPTER *3*

Continuity in Language Development

CONTINUITY of experiences is essential to growth in any area
of learning. The wise teacher keeps in mind the stages by
which children develop in language skills through listening,
speaking, reading, and writing. She seeks to have children's
successive activities provide opportunity for learning and for
practice in each of these aspects of the language arts. She
gives careful attention to the needs of each child as an individual and as a member of the group. At the same time, the
teacher realizes that each child progresses in his own way
and at his own rate. A look at several children to see how
each has developed during six or seven years in the elementary school may give insight into the nature of continuity
of growth in the language arts.

Not every classroom teacher will be able to recognize the
children described here as counterparts of those in her own
class, but each will covet for her girls and boys the same
satisfying experiences which Bob, Jean, and George enjoyed.

INDIVIDUAL GROWTH IS VARIED YET
CONSISTENT

No two children are alike. A classroom teacher who has
thirty or more children in her room recognizes that each of
them is a distinct personality to be understood and guided in
experiences suited to his own peculiar needs.

The following are thumbnail sketches of successive activities which helped to provide continuity in growth for three children, selected as types of normal learners.

It Takes Time to Grow

Bob is fortunate in having attended the same school throughout his elementary school life. Now, as a seventh-grader, he is a friendly boy who stops to speak to his last year's teacher when he meets her on the street and visits as though they were old friends. Growth in ability to express himself has been slow but continuous throughout his years in the elementary school. When Bob entered kindergarten, he was very reluctant to talk. He came from a home where children were seen and not heard; where his father had to have quiet when he came home from a day of hard physical work. Bob's teacher spent much time drawing him out, encouraging him to talk about such things as his baby brother, the canary in their classroom, and the trip to the market. By the end of the year when he was able to tell in sequence several things he found interesting about going to the market, she felt real progress had been made.

In the first grade Bob's teacher undertook to develop vocabulary through his experiences. She learned from the material in his cumulative folder that the school had to carry the heavy part of the load for him in his language development. Visits to his home showed he had only one or two picture books. His teacher introduced Bob to the attractive picture books on the reading table, helping him to see that each one was related to something he knew about, such as planes, children, or trips. She made it a point to talk with him about the story when he looked at a book.

Bob was able to recognize his name attached to a large drawing he had made on newsprint paper, and again on a pretty sticker that identified his wraps. When most of the other children in the room were ready to begin reading, Bob still had a limited speaking vocabulary. He showed a lack of confidence in himself and usually did not contribute when the other children talked about their common experiences and helped to develop the reading charts. He did more listening than speaking even when he played. It was difficult to tell from the expression on his face whether he was listening with real attention or out of courtesy to his teacher who always listened to him. By the end of this school year, however, he was working with a beginning reading group and was able to read in a preprimer. When the mothers came to visit school in May, he stood in the hall and gave them directions for reaching the room. Later he told small groups of the visitors how the children fed the goldfish.

Bob's second-grade teacher talked with his teachers of preceding years. She knew that he could not be pushed, that he must be given time. She knew, also, that he must see and handle many real materials and participate in real situations, to stimulate him to oral expression, to give meaning to his reading, and to provide an opportunity for him to listen with a purpose. She gave special attention to finding some real purposes for his beginning writing, which was always prefaced by talking. She emphasized using his name, making captions or titles for pictures, and writing about incidents, observations, or experiences that were real to him. She helped him plan such writing so that only a few sentences were required at any one time.

In the third grade his teacher, who was new to the school, was aware of Bob's slow growth from the materials in his cumulative record folder. She discovered that he had seldom been absent from school. She checked to find out whether eyes or ears might be a cause of difficulty, but found they were not. She realized that some children require a longer time than others to develop and that a child's growth pattern may be uneven. She tried to sum up what she had learned from her own observation. She found Bob reading material on a second-grade level. In writing, he was interested in copying a recipe for raw vegetable salad the children had made, in order to take it home to his mother. He could summarize what the other children had said about how to cross the street safely and was beginning to take from the library books that had many pictures.

About the time he reached the fourth grade Bob made a sudden spurt in reading. He had read a few library books during the summer and had been encouraged by his mother to read some of them aloud to her. He had reached the point where he was very nearly able to read books of fourth-grade difficulty. In school he seemed to enjoy especially the informal type of choral speaking which his group was doing and volunteered to be the cow when the class worked on the poem, "The King's Breakfast." Once he brought from home a volume of a child's encyclopedia to help in answering a question raised by the class. He wrote an acceptable letter to a mail-order house for a pullover sweater with his name on it, bringing the letter to his teacher to check. During that year he gained more self-assurance as a member of the group.

In the fifth grade Bob had a chance to take initiative and responsibility for checking materials in and out of the science corner. He was becoming especially interested in science. He served as chairman of a committee to arrange and label specimens and made several brief talks to the whole group suggesting ways to make the exhibit more attractive and more useful. He did some reading of easy reference books to identify several specimens. He showed a small group how to locate the volume in an encyclopedia which had in it the material that would help with their study of the big trees of California. When the group decided to sponsor a science fair, he was chosen to write a brief statement about it for the school newspaper. He had some difficulties with spelling and with making every sentence a complete thought, but he wrote the entire article. Later he had the help of the editorial committee of the paper in improving what he had written.

The sixth grade was the year when Bob developed real confidence in himself. One day he volunteered to telephone to the junk dealer for an appointment to discuss how and when the class could make the most money from the sale of newspapers and magazines. In this and other efforts he was not always able to interpret correctly what other people had said, but he kept trying until the task was completed. By this time he had accumulated a small personal library and a large collection of comic books. His teacher did not ban comic books, but used his interest in the strip type of illustration to help him develop a picture story from a newspaper account of the leopard that had escaped from the local zoo. At this time Bob was less able than others in his class to do any complex job in the language arts by himself, but with the support of his group, he made definite steps forward.

He had grown steadily though slowly in the years since entering kindergarten. His seventh-grade teacher realized that other teachers along the way had given Bob a chance to be successful by encouraging him while he progressed at his normal rate in developing skills in the language arts. She helped him to achieve further growth by recognizing all that he did well, by guiding him specifically in next steps aimed at using skills in more complex situations, and by assisting him to become self-dependent.

Some Children Seem to Grow by Themselves

Jean, too, is in the seventh grade. How did the experience of the elementary school affect her? She had always been ready and eager as she began each year of school work. Although her school experiences were essentially like Bob's, there is a noticeable difference in the quality of their performance in the language arts. Jean took initiative in expressing her ideas, opinions, and questions. Bob was more likely to wait to be asked. Jean read extensively and intensively, and her writing had a style of its own. Bob did a minimum of writing in relation to school tasks or immediate personal needs.

Jean talked easily in kindergarten, since her parents had always encouraged her to talk. She had something to talk about because her family had taken her on trips and excursions and had provided her with pets, playmates, and play equipment. In addition she had picture books of her own and a library of children's records that she could play for herself. By the end of the first year in school she could talk about an experience, a pet, or a person, and hold the interest of the group. Whereas Bob had only listened because he had little to say, Jean had to be asked to listen because she had so many things she wanted to talk about.

In the first grade the teacher identified Jean as a leader, as a child with ideas and with considerable ability to express them. In her visits to the child's home the teacher encouraged the parents to continue to give Jean worth-while experiences but urged them not to push her too fast nor too far. In a check on her sight vocabulary, the teacher found that Jean knew more than one hundred sight words. Her parents explained that she had been demanding, "What is that word?" since she was four. The child showed in a number of ways—such as looking at books, matching words, and wanting to write her name—that she was ready for reading activities beyond the charts based on group experiences. From preprimers to first readers were easy steps for her, and by the end of the first year in school she had read a number of first readers and several library books for children of her age, and was reaching out for more difficult materials. When the group composed an invitation to their mothers, she could copy it easily and make it look well on the page, with words correctly spelled and manuscript writing quite legible. She could write a simpler invitation of her own correctly and with satisfaction to herself.

In the second grade Jean soon exhausted the supply of second readers, and her teacher borrowed books from the library to extend the child's interests. She also saw to it that Jean had some jobs to do in writing captions or labels, copying the handwritten room newspaper for the school bulletin board, dictating original stories to the teacher, and writing a brief story about the school garden or a pet.

In the third grade, Jean's teacher noted from the comments in the cumulative record folder that the child needed to be challenged and realized that she should be exposed to many situations that required listening, speaking, reading, and writing. She guided Jean into more complex experiences such as locating all the stories about skunks in the available readers when the children were studying these animals, helping other children to find the information to answer group questions, and preparing a story to read to another third grade. She encouraged Jean's initiative in making a weekly newspaper about her own activities and those of her family, and in expressing herself through poetry.

The fourth grade showed Jean continuing to make rapid progress and creating a problem for her teacher in finding experiences sufficiently challenging to keep her busy and happy. She took responsibility for an assembly program in the form of a radio broadcast, acting as leader of an able group from her class; she made a favorite story into a play; and she read both at home and at school a large number of books of various types—poetry, history, travel, fiction, and science.

Jean's fifth-grade experiences revealed an increasing interest in social studies accompanied by wide reading in textbooks, supplementary books, and children's encyclopedias. She made trips to the museum and central library and brought back reports of what she had seen and learned. On some of these occasions she served as chairman of the committee. Through a personal friend she made contact with a child in Austria who was beginning the study of English and exchanged letters with her regularly. Jean's letters were read to the class for suggestions before they were put into final form.

Recognizing Jean as a bright child who found school work

They Learn to Do by Doing.

We'll All Watch. Some of Us Will Talk.

You Can Believe It When You See It.

Informal Play Tests Out Ideas.

Which Story Do You Like Best?

That's My Favorite Program.

It Pays to Listen to the Forest Ranger.

A Sound Recorder Helps to Improve His Talk.

Spontaneous Combustion.

He Makes It *So* Clear.

His Puppet Thinks and Speaks.

The Goblin Scares the Audience.

Have You Tried Yourself Out with a Tape Recorder?

Almost Right—Try Again.

easy, the sixth-grade teacher looked for ways to broaden and deepen her experiences, lest easy successes in limited activities cause her to be too readily satisfied with her achievement. She encouraged Jean to engage in individual investigations that would add interest to class work and help the entire group, and often asked her to assist other children who were having difficulties with reading and spelling. She suggested news articles and other current materials, especially books that would broaden Jean's understanding of other people of the world, and encouraged her to give creative expression to her ideas in poems, stories, and plays.

Some Children Are Neither Fast Nor Slow

George takes things in his stride. As a member of the group, he admires Jean's ability and regards her as a good pal among the seventh graders. He enjoys Bob as a friend and isn't concerned that he needs more time for any school activity than many of the other children. George does not find school work difficult. He speaks easily, listens and is listened to, writes legibly, expresses his ideas clearly, and enjoys reading. The teacher does not need to adjust his activities either by broadening them into new fields, as in the case of Jean, or by simplifying them as she does for Bob.

In kindergarten, George was neither shy nor aggressive. He played with different groups of children rather than alone. His parents had helped him to develop normally. They were not greatly concerned about comparing his ability to speak with that of other children of his own age. Nor did they push him in learning to read, count, or write his name. George was usually ready to listen to the stories the teacher told or read. He would sometimes retell them simply at school or at home. He enjoyed looking at picture books.

When he reached the first grade, George was not among the first children showing readiness for reading. Jean was reading freely in primers before he gave real signs of being interested in books. He liked to help in dictating experience stories to the teacher and would reread these for his own pleasure or to visitors, and to children who had been absent. He was a good listener as a member of a small reading group. When he began to read from a preprimer, he moved along easily and asked for a new book as soon as he finished the first one. He learned to write his name and took pleasure in writing it on everything that belonged to him. As the year went on he learned to copy very brief stories which the group composed and the teacher wrote on the board.

It was in the second grade that George helped to write down ideas when the group made a daily observation of their polliwogs to discover how much they had grown. He was responsible for seeing to it that a brief statement was written as a diary record on the calendar chart. Again, when each child in the group drew a self-portrait and wrote a description, George wrote several lines in manuscript form, telling about himself. He talked for several minutes, describing himself to the group, before writing anything down. He needed help in spelling words and when he asked for them, his teacher wrote them on the board. He copied the words in a brief list which he kept for reference. His teacher listed these same words with others that would be used in a practice period. George was able to begin reading in a second reader about the middle of the year, and he read several books from different reading series as well as a number of books from the library for his own pleasure.

His third-grade teacher read poetry to the children and encouraged them when they tried original writing. George read for himself poems about children and animals, choosing those with broad humor and action. He made several four-to-six-line verses and wrote them in a notebook of his personal writings that the teacher encouraged him to keep. He had learned to listen for rhyming words, for words that sing, for words that are noisy, or for words that try to represent sounds in nature. It was during this year that he began to like to read to the group. He searched through third readers and through books he had used in the first and second grades to find poems on particular subjects such as birds, animals, boys and girls, and other subjects of interest to his group. He practiced reading some of his favorite poems both at school and at home, so that he could share them with others who were having similar experiences with poetry.

When he reached the fourth grade, George discovered that there was more reading to be done than during his previous years in school. Whereas in earlier grades information had usually come through experiences in the classroom and through discussions or telling by the teacher, he was now able to find answers to his questions in science and in social studies from a great many different books. More of his talking and contributions to group discussions were based on what he had been reading. He began to listen critically to statements of other children and asked for proof when another child identified a butterfly as a Monarch rather than an Admiral. At this time he was writing on his own initiative things he wanted to remember—items for his reports, titles and authors of books he had read, names of places to write for materials. He even wrote an exciting story about the pioneers who had lived in his own community. Once he prepared a list of questions and problems that the group had proposed for study.

After a few weeks in the fifth grade, George decided that the language skills he was learning to use made his work easier and helped the other children to understand him better, whether he was speaking or writing. He had used a picture dictionary since he was in the first grade. Now he had some experiences with a simplified dictionary of the standard type, using it to get word meanings. When he found the word *nomad* in his social studies, he looked it up and wrote *wanderer* into the sentence instead of *nomad*, checking the sentence to see whether it would make sense. He developed a personal card file of words he needed to use, arranged it in alphabetical order, and kept it where he could reach for it quickly as he wrote.

His confidence in his use of the dictionary helped him to learn to use the index in locating materials in textbooks in geography, history, and science. Although he was not entirely aware of it when he looked at a table of contents in his readers, beginning in the first grade, he was starting to develop dictionary skills. Another reading technique he learned was the making of a two-step outline as a way of putting down notes from his reading so that he could "talk a report" instead of trying to memorize words.

He shared with his group a recording of Eric P. Kelly's story, *In Clean Hay*. He listened first of all for enjoyment of the story and of the songs, and then when the record was played over again, to note the differences in the voices of the characters, and to discover how the action and the emphasis of the story were shown through spoken words.

It was during this year that George read all the books he could find about butterflies and moths. He became the school's specialist on this subject, and with help, made a one-page bibliography that could be used by other children. This fifth-grade year found him using reading skills for many practical purposes.

When school opened in September and George found himself in the sixth grade, he was interested in children's news magazines that his teacher had spread out on the reading table. Discovering several he had never seen before, he enjoyed looking through them. He was surprised to find there were so many and agreed to keep the group up to date on the highlights in *Boys' Life* each month. He had made a recording of his voice each year that he had been in school, but this year he really became conscious of the fact that one can make his voice higher or lower, louder or softer, more expressive or less interesting, according to his use of it. Every boy and girl added to his own individual record each month, and it was then played back in full. Members of the group listened critically to discover the ways in which each person had improved his voice since the last recording. The children worked in committee groups, listening for clear enunciation, good pronunciation, effective sentences, and interesting ways of expressing ideas.

George made his contribution to a vocabulary card file of new words that the group was learning in relation to the unit, "Why We Have a Pure Water Supply in our Town." These words had come from reading, discussion, observations, excursions, and experimentation, and through the use of flat pictures, slides, and films. Each word was listed on a separate card, together with a definition in the child's own words, and the sentence in which it occurred if it came from a book. The cards were filed in alphabetical order, every child contributing as many different ones as he wished. The group worked out a game with the cards, and George often teamed up with a friend to play it.

Children are Different

These brief sketches of the experiences of three children over a period of seven years spent in the elementary school point up both likenesses and differences in the rate and quality of growth. Under the guidance of an excellent teacher who planned for and with each child as an individual, all three reached each stage at an appropriate time, and each in his or her own way.

Each one grew in ability to gather ideas through listening, reading, and observing; through discussing, examining, or questioning; and through looking at and handling materials. Each showed growth in ability to *express* his ideas through contributing to discussion, through reporting, dramatizing, and writing in activities that were meaningful to him.

To look at the accumulated evidence from the years that each child had spent in school before he entered the seventh grade is to see level stretches where growth seemed either slow or imperceptible. At the same time, there are evidences of experiences or situations which helped to stimulate growth in a steady, continuous way. The teachers were sensitive to the needs, interests, and abilities of each child, so that they could help to extend the "growing edges" as rapidly as was good for each individual, and in as many directions as it seemed wise to pursue.

CONTINUITY OF GROWTH REPLACES GRADE STANDARDS

Through attention to individual needs in such a flexible learning situation, teachers bring about continuous growth in children. They do not think primarily of grade placement of materials, although activities planned are timed to meet the increasing maturity of the pupils, but think rather of next steps in the development of each child in language power. They have a clear understanding of what constitutes growing maturity in each of the language arts and of the stage of progress which each pupil has reached. As is evident from the illustrations just given, children develop in different ways and achieve varied degrees of proficiency at widely different times, but there is discernible in all of them a general pattern of growth in language. Skillful teachers recognize this sequence and guide children toward the desired ends.

It is not easy to measure objectively growth such as that described for the three children whose language arts experiences in the elementary school have been presented, or for all the other children in classrooms throughout the country who are much like them. Over a six- or seven-year period many types of changes can take place in the child as a living, growing personality. These influence his progress in language. He is the same and yet not the same in each successive year of his life.

For the school in which continuous records are kept, the

evidences exist in each child's cumulative folder, including his drawings and paintings, his written expression in the form of letters, his contributions to the school newspaper, his stories and verses, the diary records of his experiences, and many other items. A recording made at intervals of the child's voice as he speaks and as he reads is also available. There are records of books he has read, and observations by the teacher regarding the attention with which he listens to a story, the types of questions he asks, the comments he makes, the kinds of difficulties he encounters, and the materials he brings for the common store of information. Each succeeding teacher adds to the collection of items in the cumulative folder, makes some further evaluation of those already there, and eliminates those no longer significant.

In Chapters 4 through 7, the writers deal in detail with evidences of growth in each phase of the language arts. At this point, therefore, it may be sufficient to give two examples, one in the appreciation of literature and the other in the development of a skill such as spelling.

Appreciation of Literature Comes Gradually

Without growth in appreciation and in ability to interpret literature on increasingly higher levels of maturity, children become adults who still read chiefly at the comic-book stage and who get little genuine value or pleasure from reading. Hence the importance of introducing them to the great wealth of literature available at their level of maturity, by means of which they may come to realize the riches in store for them and may develop such powers of reading and such standards of judgment as may lead to continued reading and intelligent choices of books in the future.

In the primary grades. A child's first experiences with literature should be pleasurable. He may look at a picture book—*All Around the Town,* perhaps—alone or with someone else, or he may enjoy *Peter Rabbit* or *The Three Little*

Pigs, read or told by an older brother or sister or by his parents. Such experiences he is likely to have before he enters school.

In the kindergarten and first grade he listens breathlessly to *The Three Billy Goats Gruff,* chuckling with delight over the "family name of Gruff," showing his pleasure in the repetition of the conversation by joining in with appropriately high or low tones as each Billy Goat in turn meets up with the vicious troll, and registering in the end with a deep sigh his approval of the discomfiture of the villain. Children love the humor of the story and learn to expect just the right ending after the suspense is over. These are the beginnings of literary appreciation.

"Aw, that couldn't happen!" says one boy when Bartholomew Cubbins goes off triumphantly with the king, who is resplendent in the last of the five hundred hats. Then teacher and children start on the long road to distinguishing the real from the unreal in literature. First, it is a matter of fact and fancy; later it takes on renewed significance as the difference between truth to human experience and lack of integrity in dealing with everyday life—matters which ultimately differentiate great fiction from cheap and tawdry writing.

Little children delight in obstreperous humor—*Cicely G and the Nine Monkeys* and *The Five Chinese Brothers.* Gradually, the teacher leads them into more subtle humor with its clever commentary on human experience—in *Winnie the Pooh,* for example, or in *Alice in Wonderland,* in the works of Rose Fyleman or Walter de la Mare.

Another factor in developing a love of literature is to reveal the wealth of it available for a wide variety of purposes and to stimulate a constant desire for more. Many good books give insight into the children's own personal experience and at the same time have universal significance—William Lipkind's *Finders-Keepers,* for example, or *The Elephant's Child, Here's a Penny, Robbut,* or *Flip and the Morning.* Some books will lead young readers into new lands and places such as *One Little Indian Boy* or *Madeline.* Others will take them far into times past like *Mitty and Mr. Syrup, Yonie Wondernose,* or *The Nightingale.* Consciousness of these varied offerings of literature is a part of appreciation and leads to a growing appetite for more.

Enjoyment of poetry should play a large part in the young child's association with literature. Many pupils can recite with pride on the first day of school such Mother Goose rhymes as "Hickory, Dickory, Dock," and "Humpty Dumpty," and should be encouraged to do so. Saying favorite poems together is normally a part of every day's experience—poems, perhaps, from Rose Fyleman, Rowena Bennett, Dorothy Aldis, Robert Louis Stevenson, and all the rest—as the snow falls, as a bird lights on the window sill, as a robin returns, as the circus arrives, or as both children and teacher feel like "imagining" together.

When a child brings a turtle to school, the teacher recalls Vachel Lindsay's "The Little Turtle." [1] Or when Indians are being discussed, she produces Annette Wynn's "Where We Walk to School Each Day." As children use finger paint or crayons and learn the names of the colors, it is appropriate to tell or read Christina Rossetti's "What Is Pink?" As a result, the youngsters may try their hands at making verses that answer the question, "What is pink, or blue, or white?" as one child did when he said, "Snow is white. Falling all the night." Other poems are for a good laugh. The fun the child is having in "Hiding" is very evident to young readers, for what boy or girl could hide under the rug or in the ink well? But Elizabeth Madox Roberts's "Mumps" shows a more subtle kind of humor that is implied rather than expressed directly. This, too, may be familiar experience to some children, and in that sense may seem to them either funny or serious.

[1] Poems mentioned in this chapter can be found in many anthologies indexed in John E. and Sara W. Brewton's *Index to Children's Poetry,* rev. ed. (New York, H. W. Wilson Company, 1951).

Sometimes children tell which of two poems they like the better. In answering, they begin to create a personal yardstick for measuring the appeal of a poem in terms of their own background of experience and interest. Often it is the content of the poem which pleases them. Perhaps it deals with a familiar experience in a new and interesting way, giving them an imaginative awareness of everyday things, like Christina Rossetti's "Clouds." Perhaps it gives a sudden insight into values they have not thought of before, as in Joyce Kilmer's "Easter." Perhaps it carries them far into realms of the imagination, like Rowena Bennett's "Meeting the Easter Bunny." Perhaps it is just for fun, like A. A. Milne's "Three Little Foxes."

It may be the music or the rhyme that appeals to the children or the quiet words for the silence of "Velvet Shoes," or the rollicking, noisy words for "Twenty White Horses on a Red Hill." It may be the pictures as in "Jack Frost" or in Nancy Byrd Turner's "Sing a Song of Wintertime." It may be just the right words to say what the author has to say as in "Choosing Shoes" by Ffrida Wolfe. Whatever it is, children are weaving it into a growing consciousness of the pleasure of reading poetry, which should increase notably as they progress through the grades.

In the middle grades. By the time youngsters reach the middle grades, they should have heard two to three hundred rhymes and poems which will serve as a reservoir to be used in many different ways—for sharing, for choral speaking, for noting likenesses and differences, and as yardsticks against which to determine how much they like a new poem they are meeting for the first time. They will be interested in longer poems, in poems that tell a story with real-life characters, and in situations where characters must sometimes make a choice between two courses of action. They will recognize the fact that ballads reflect the life of the people in the middle ages or of the here and now.

Boys and girls who chant and dance to Vachel Lindsay's

"The Potatoes' Dance" will recognize it as pure fantasy that takes them completely away from the world of reality. Their teacher will encourage them to compile a list of poems that possess this same quality. Nine-year-olds will appreciate Rose Fyleman's "Wishes" and will compare the desires of the child in the poem with their own. They may hear the poem without its title's being given, and by suggesting a name, will show whether they have found the central idea. They will chuckle over some of the wishes and will feel superior to the child who says, "I wish they'd let me sweep the chimneys on rainy afternoons," because they are growing up and do not believe so strongly in fairies as they once did. Eleven-year-olds will enjoy rolling big words under their tongues as they practice reading Arthur Guiterman's "Strictly Germproof." The idea of the bunny, the baby, and the prophylactic pup would be humorous to younger children. But to these older boys and girls, the humor lies in the polysyllabic words that the author uses to express a series of simple ideas. An experience of this sort should lead to a discussion of what makes a poem humorous: the situation? the characters? the wording? the rhythm? a combination of these?

In this period children are growing into an appreciation of poems that rely for their appeal on beauty of thought as well as on beauty of language or of music—Frank Dempster Sherman's "Daisies," for example, or William Allingham's "Fairies." Their readiness for such poetry is conditioned by their teacher's ability to make the poems come alive. Walter de la Mare's "Silver" reflects its color on everything in the landscape. Children are helped to see how other words such as "white" or "gold" might be used to get a similar effect. Fannie Stearns Gifford Davis's "Moon Folly" shows what another poet thought about the moon. How are the poems alike? How different? How have other poets described the moon? Such experiences can lead to the listing of descriptive words about any of a number of subjects such as Christmas, spring, snow, the circus, so that both group and individual poems may result. What and how a child writes is sometimes a good measure of his appreciation of the way poets have used words to convey ideas.

In their reading of fiction, children continue to enjoy humor in these grades—a little less fantastic humor, perhaps, as in *Henry Huggins* or *Homer Price*. The series of poems in *Davy and the Goblin,* in which Robinson Crusoe and the Sole Survivor of the Famous Forty Thieves tell their stories in humorous rhymes are fail-me-nevers in the intermediate grades. Gradually, the teacher may be able by reading aloud *Rabbit Hill* or *The Borrowers* or *Wind in the Willows* to give some children an appreciation of their imaginative power and their gentle, reflective humor.

As the chapter on reading later indicates in some detail, boys of this age branch out into adventure with cowboys and Indians, with Robin Hood and King Arthur, and perhaps with the *Jungle Books.* It is important for them to discover the values in these books and to develop standards against which to measure the kind of breath-taking encounters they are meeting up with in the comics and the cheap juvenile series.

These are years when some girls specialize in the fairy tales and can be led through interest in the stories to appreciate their poetic use of words and their imaginative insight into human experience. Like the boys and their adventures, girls parallel this interest with a tremendous appetite for stories of children like themselves. In this case their own experience of life furnishes an excellent standard against which to measure the truth or falsity of the picture. They can also discover which of these books really help them to know their book characters well and to see them grow and change as children do in everyday life, and which like the Bobbsey Twins or The Hardy Boys are mere stereotypes, the same from one book in the series to the next.

In the upper grades. By the time children reach the seventh grade it should be easier to see evidences of the extent to which literature makes a difference in what they are and what they do. In these years the fantastic may take on an air of reality, so that the child must bring to bear his previous experiences to help him distinguish between the tall tale and the story based on facts. At this time he may meet an unexpected character in Robert Service's "The Cremation of Sam McGee." Service stretches the imagination of the reader to the breaking point when Sam's corpse is put into the furnace and he is returned to life after he thaws out. The reading of such verse, followed by discussion, will bring out a sharing of experiences with tall tales such as those of Baron Munchausen, Paul Bunyan, and others. Boys and girls of this age will draw the conclusion that the bigger the lie, the more apt it is to be believed.

At this age, humor is most appreciated in terms of a situation in which the character does not fit, or in which there is a play on words. For example, in Arthur Guiterman's "The Quest of the Riband," a modern husband sets out to buy some ribbon for his wife in Macy's, but the story is told in language that presents the hero as a knight of old. Young people will be interested to read the poem in order to see how the author secures his effect—with what words? with what misadventures? with what likenesses to the difficulties of everyday life in the age in which we live?

Poetry can take these twelve- and thirteen-year-olds to other times and other places. The reading by the teacher of a few lines from Chaucer's "Prologue to the Canterbury Tales," given the proper setting, may help children to see how our English language has grown and changed over a period of several hundred years. At the same time, the boy or girl whose ear has been trained to listen will discover words that sound much like those in our language today. Perhaps some pupil will attempt to translate what Chaucer says into modern English. Certainly there will be some feeling of interest aroused in how the English language came to be, and how it has changed with the changing times.

Or the group that listens to the Benéts' "Nancy Hanks" will get an understanding of Abraham Lincoln, boy and man, that could hardly be gained otherwise through the reading of several books. The telling of the story by Abe's mother gives it a poignancy that any young person will respond to merely through hearing it read. Why did the authors select these particular incidents to picture the whole lifetime of a famous man? If we were to put our own lives "into a nutshell," what would we say?

During these years there can be an accumulation of poems that are beautifully told. They may picture a single moment and the feeling that goes with it as in Robert Frost's "Stopping by Woods on a Snowy Evening" or A. E. Housman's "Loveliest of Trees." Or they may interpret a mood as in Richard Le Gallienne's "I Meant to Do My Work Today." Or they may develop a character in detail as in Edna St. Vincent Millay's "The Ballad of the Harp Weaver," which demonstrates the love between a mother and her son. The use of a poem of this sort can lead to the pulling-out from experience all the poems, all the books, all the newspaper stories which cause the learner to realize what such a relationship means.

How does the teacher manage to develop such appreciations? She reads aloud often, tells stories and recites poems well, and exposes the children to them continually. She also uses questions skillfully that call for choice or opinion, that emphasize the central idea, the characters or the situation, the language power, and the imaginative insight in the poem or story in terms of each individual's experience. She also gives the children many opportunities to share their favorite poems and books in the same way with their classmates. If a child at each of these school levels voluntarily reads poetry, tries his hand at writing poetry, participates in choral speaking, or buys a book of poems, he has given evidence of what poetry has meant to him. If he himself selects books with zest and standards of judgment suited to his years and experience, he has given the best evidence possible that he is growing in appreciation.

The Teacher Also Must Appreciate Literature

It is obvious that in order to develop in elementary school youngsters a growing appreciation of literature, teachers themselves must be steeped in story and verse for children. They must not only know literature, but they must understand from their own experience both the joy and the illumination which it can give to daily living. They must sense the moments in the lives of boys and girls when the right story or poem can bring pleasure, or uplift, or insight important for each individual child. Back of such knowledge and of such appreciation must be the teacher's own broad experience with literature and her understanding of what it means in her own life through continued nourishing of her spirit upon the thoughts and the experiences which the imagination of the poet or other writer has to offer her. Only by her own appreciation of what makes literature great or pleasurable or significant in everyday life can she hope to establish a similar appreciation in children. Only by her own continuing habit of turning to books for enjoyment and for understanding can she hope to establish similar habits in her pupils.

Spelling Illustrates How Children Grow in Skill

Unlike literature, spelling is one of the elements in language in which growth can be objectively measured. When a child comes to school, he may be able to write his first name, or perhaps to write his full name. During the early part of his first year in school, he will not be urged to go beyond this point. Before the end of the year he should be able to copy some of the simple experience stories he has helped to write. Emphasis is upon vocabulary building, as he hears words spoken and then sees them in writing.

In Grades II and III the child continues to copy material that will be read by someone—his parents, another child, or another adult. In the second year he does some writing that involves using words previously learned, from memory. Then he has occasion to write words that are already in his speaking vocabulary, especially those that refer to concrete objects. During the third year he writes from dictation and does some independent writing that involves spelling. As he studies how words are put together, he notes similarities and differences and any spots where he has made errors. He can now make some generalizations about beginnings, endings, and sequence of letters.

At some point during this primary school period, he works with the group to help appraise their progress, and looks especially at his own ability to spell. Does he have a list of words that he knows he can spell? of words that cause difficulty? Does he have a method for learning to spell a new word? For example, does he try to see it? Say it? Think it? Write it? Check it? Use it? Not every child will need all these steps in learning to spell the approximately five hundred basic words for the primary grades which are found in most lists developed from research studies and used in spelling textbooks. Some teachers may use these words as spelling lists. Others may develop them in relation to units of experience.

In the middle grades the child continues to use the skills he has developed in the earlier years. He does more independent writing. He is now introduced to a regular dictionary instead of the picture dictionary of the primary years, and he learns how to use it in order to check the correctness of his own spelling or of his guesses in spelling unfamiliar or unusual words. He acquires such skills as recognizing alphabetical order, using accent marks, and dividing words into syllables. As he learns how to study, he becomes more independent in seeing where he needs to improve and how he can make progress through asking for individual help when he needs it. In all the writing the child does, he attempts to spell correctly, applying the spelling skills he has learned. Here he especially needs the help of his teacher in checking for correctness when there are many new and unfamiliar words that are called for in writing about personal experiences and in dealing with new topics in science or social studies.

The child in the upper grades should develop more skill in working independently to overcome his spelling difficulties. He should take the initiative in diagnosing his own needs and in using what he already knows about words as he attacks derived forms. Above all, he should develop a spelling "conscience" which makes him realize that word mastery requires continued use and practice until words are spelled correctly. It is only as the child achieves such self-dependence that he accomplishes the major objective of spelling.

As children progress through the grades, how may the teacher know that their skill in spelling is improved?

The primary school child requires guidance in understanding the purpose for which one learns to spell and in spelling those words for which he feels a need. These fall largely within the basic list of five hundred. The middle-grade child develops the tools he needs in perfecting spelling skills such as a basic method for learning to spell each individual word, plus the dictionary skills that will aid him in checking for correctness. At this stage the teacher gives a considerable amount of guidance. The upper-grade child uses the skills previously learned as he becomes independent in finding and using words that will best express his meaning and in seeing that they are correctly spelled.

Together teacher and children, within such a framework, need to set up their long-time and short-time goals. Each teacher then accepts individuals and the group where they are and takes them as far as they can go. As the Denver course of study indicates, the teacher's job is to help pupils (1) to master words that will be used over and over again, (2) to master additional words needed frequently, and (3) to find the correct spelling of words used occasionally.[2] A good source for such words is Fitzgerald's *A Basic Life Spelling Vocabulary*,[3] which includes words commonly written by children and adults. Each child's cumulative folder should contain evidence of the amount of progress he has made toward these goals. Such evidence will include first drafts and finished pieces of writing related to school activities and to his own personal experiences. There may be separate lists of words that he can spell without any help, others on which he is working, and still others that interest him to such an extent that he would like to make them part of his spelling vocabulary.[4]

SUMMARY

The elementary school, then, recognizes an essential continuity of growth in the language arts and provides for each child those experiences best suited to him at his level of development. As the child works happily and successfully in activities appropriate to his stage of growth, he is developing readiness for the next steps. Teachers throughout the elementary school need to be able to identify the sequences of learning in the language arts. They must recognize that no child's growth can be forced, that no learning takes place until the child is ready for each specialized type of skill, and moreover, that learning takes time. There are step-by-step sequences within each of the language arts. How these shall be developed and used in planning a curriculum guide depends upon the individual school and the school system of which it is a part.

[2] Denver Public Schools, *A Program in English—A Guide for Teaching the Language Arts—Kindergarten through Grade Twelve* (Denver, Board of Education, 1953), pp. 313–23.

[3] James A. Fitzgerald, *A Basic Life Spelling Vocabulary* (Milwaukee, The Bruce Publishing Company, 1951).

[4] San Diego County Schools, *Course of Study Handbook,* Education Monograph No. 17 (San Diego, California, Office of the Superintendent of Schools, San Diego County, October, 1948).

BIBLIOGRAPHY

ARBUTHNOT, May Hill, *Time for Poetry* (Chicago, Scott, Foresman and Company, 1952).

Association for Childhood Education, *Sung under the Silver Umbrella* (New York, The Macmillan Company, 1935).

BREWTON, John E. and Sara W., *Index to Children's Poetry*, rev. ed. (New York, H. W. Wilson Company, 1953).

BURROWS, Alvina T., FEREBEE, June D., JACKSON, Dorothy C., and SAUNDERS, Dorothy O., *They All Want to Write: Written English in the Elementary School*, rev. ed. (New York, Prentice-Hall, Inc., 1952).

Denver Public Schools, *A Program in English; A Guide for Teaching the Language Arts, Kindergarten through Grade Twelve* (Denver, Colorado, Board of Education, 1953).

FITZGERALD, James A., *A Basic Life Spelling Vocabulary* (Milwaukee, The Bruce Publishing Company, 1951).

——, *The Teaching of Spelling* (Milwaukee, The Bruce Publishing Company, 1951).

National Conference on Research in English, *Child Development and and the Language Arts* (David H. Russell, Chairman) (Champaign, Illinois, National Council of Teachers of English, 1952–53).

——, *Factors That Influence Language Growth* (Dorothea McCarthy, Chairman) (Champaign, Illinois, National Council of Teachers of English, 1952–53).

San Diego County Schools, *Course of Study Handbook*, Education Monograph No. 17 (San Diego, California, Office of the Superintendent of Schools, San Diego County, October, 1948).

SMITH, Dora V., "The Goals of the Literature Period and the Grade Sequence of Desirable Experiences," in W. S. Gray, *Improving Reading in All Curriculum Areas*, Supplementary Educational Monographs, No. 76 (Chicago, The University of Chicago Press, November, 1952).

THOMPSON, Blanche, *Silver Pennies* (New York, The Macmillan Company, 1925).

PART II

Facets of the Language Arts

CHAPTER 4

Listening

ALTHOUGH listening is singled out for separate treatment in this chapter, it should be developed in a general language arts context and, indeed, in the total "living-and-learning" setting of the elementary school. *When* children listen, *why* they listen, *what* they listen to, are all factors of the total situation. Whether at a given time eight-year-old Phil should *read* the directions for making a model plane, *listen* to a pilot as he demonstrates and explains the instrument board in the cockpit of his plane, or *tell* or *write* of a recent airplane trip depends upon the analysis of needs and purposes engaged in by him, by his teacher, or by his group. During any extensive learning activity he is certain to use all four aspects of language as means of gaining and sharing experiences.

The growth of children in listening is continuously interrelated with their growth in speaking, and after the early years of childhood, with their reading and writing as well. Listening is a forerunner of speaking and continues to bear a reciprocal relationship to it. For every speaker, there must be a listener; the listener, in turn, becomes a better speaker for having listened well to the speech of others.

LISTENING IN A FIFTH-GRADE CLASS

For the purpose of examining the process of listening in a school situation, an account is given here of a group of chil-

dren engaged, under the leadership of their teacher, in studying their listening habits.[1]

With a light touch but with some serious self-examination,
the children produced a booklet entitled, "Our School Room
and Our Listening Habits." In this book they caricatured
themselves and then proceeded with considerable insight to
analyze their listening habits and the school situations in
which listening is important. In their booklet they included a
set of standards for listening which they had developed for
their own guidance. Below are selected pages from their
book:

ONE STARTS
TALKING
AND LIKE
SHEEP

WE FOLLOW
THE LEADER

The noisy one

This is our teacher

She complained of the

Noise!!

So many wanted to tell so much. She said she'd have to get earmuffs.

The next day Beverly brought some earmuffs.

---

[1] Fifth Grade, Longfellow School, Madison, Wisconsin; Muriel De Mars,
Teacher.

How Do We Listen?

We don't listen with our eyes.

Not with our nose.

But with our ears.

> If we listened more and talked less
> We'd get along better!

In a conversation you should

Stop, Look, and Listen

Just as you do at a railroad crossing.

Some people are almost always *Bursting* to say something.

We should give other people a chance to talk.

Our Arithmetic Class

Our teacher tells us to *listen* while she gives directions.
Some of the children write.
Some have private conversations.
Our teacher says, "Tell us all."
Then when she is finished, they say,
"What page?" "How do you do this?"

So and So
Is noisy
When others talk
BUT
If anyone talks
When he stands up
He cries and fusses

Let me talk

WHEN   do we *Listen?*
        We listen when someone talks to us.

WHY   do we *Listen?*
        We listen to learn.

WHERE   do we *Listen?*
        We listen in our schoolroom.

HOW   do we *Listen?*
        With our ears
        With close attention
        By looking at the speaker

Checking My Listening Habits

Do I get ready to listen?
Do I sit comfortably? Slumpy bodies make slumpy minds.
Do I look at the one who is talking?
Do I keep my mind on what is being said?
Do I keep my fingers, feet, and desk quiet?
Do I listen so others will listen to me?
Do I listen so well that I can retell accurately what I hear?
Do I listen to directions so well that I can follow them?
Do I try not to interrupt?
Do I act as if the speaker has something to tell me?
Do I act as if I am thinking about what the speaker says?
Do I get enough sleep the night before so that I can listen?

When the children sent the book to their friend, the curriculum consultant, they enclosed individual letters telling how they made the book and what effect it had upon them. Beverly closed her letter with this paragraph:

In this letter I want to be very truthful so I'll safely say that I think the book helped some of us, maybe not all of us though. It helped two boys in our room quite a bit.

When teachers enlist pupil coöperation in improving listening, the children themselves can sense its importance for learning, can become more analytical about what they hear, can recognize the barriers to good listening, and can suggest ways in which to improve their listening.

REASONS FOR TEACHING LISTENING

The question may be legitimately raised as to why the schools should introduce the teaching of listening into an already crowded program. One reason is that it is the most used of the arts of language. Another is that listening, while it exerts a tremendous influence in life today, is often poorly done. At the same time, evidence suggests that listening habits may be greatly improved through training.

More than twenty years ago Rankin [2] reported that of all the time people spend in communicating each day, 45 per cent is devoted to listening, 30 per cent to speaking, and the rest to reading and writing combined. While one could never determine relative emphasis in teaching by frequency of use alone, these figures reveal clearly the importance of listening in the world today. Miriam Wilt,[3] through classroom observation of elementary children, found that they spent on the average more than two and a half hours out of a five-hour school day in listening. This was almost twice as long as the teachers who were queried in the same study had estimated. Apparently teachers are not fully aware of the proportion of time which they expect children to spend in listening. Perhaps they should consider whether this is a reasonable division of time. Another sobering fact in this study is that, in general, the children listened to their teacher [4] or to one pupil addressing their teacher rather than to each other. How profitable time spent in this way may be is conditioned by the effectiveness of their listening and the value of what they have heard.

With the present extended use of radio and television during out-of-school hours, it is evident that listening is consuming an increasing share of the child's day. Recent studies [5]

[2] Paul T. Rankin, "The Importance of Listening Ability," *English Journal* (College Edition), XVII (October, 1928), pp. 623–30.

[3] Miriam E. Wilt, "A Study of Teacher Awareness of Listening as a Factor in Elementary Education," *Journal of Educational Research,* XLIII (April, 1950), pp. 626–36.

[4] Stephen M. Corey, "The Teachers Out-Talk the Pupils," *School Review,* XLVIII (December, 1940), pp. 745–52.

[5] Paul Witty, "Children's, Parents', and Teachers' Reactions to Television," *Elementary English,* XXVII (October, 1950), pp. 349–55, 396.

———, "Two Studies of Children's Interest in TV," *Elementary English,* XXIX (May, 1952), pp. 241–57.

———, "Children's Reactions to TV—A Third Report," *Elementary English,* XXIX (December, 1952), pp. 469–73.

Paul Witty and Harry Bricker, *Your Child and Radio, TV, Comics, and Movies* (Chicago, Science Research Associates, 1950).

Dallas W. Smythe, "Television and Its Educational Implications," *Elementary English,* XXVII (January, 1950), pp. 41–52.

indicate that children who have access to television view and listen to it approximately three hours a day and that, while television has somewhat reduced the amount of listening to the radio, some youngsters are still spending up to two hours a day with the radio. Although much of this listening is beyond the direct control of the school, there is an obvious need for the school to help pupils develop discrimination in their listening habits.[6] Moreover, it is desirable that the learnings gained from out-of-school listening should be used in the school program whenever appropriate. The group of children in a second grade who regularly listened to a program about zoo animals became an excellent source of information when the class planned a visit to the local zoo.

THE NATURE OF LISTENING

Although listening was the primary means of learning before the invention of printing and although, through the coming of radio, television, and motion picture, it has again assumed a significant place in modern communication, few people have stopped to analyze what is involved in it.

Listening is more than hearing.[7] It involves following attentively the thread of a conversation, the development of an idea, the points of an argument. Like reading, it requires comprehension in terms of the past experience of the listener and often involves critical examination of what is heard. Whenever attention wanders, a portion of what is being presented is lost.

Daisy B. Gessleman, "Television and Reading," *Elementary English*, XXVIII (November, 1951), pp. 385–91.

Robert L. Shayon, *Television and Our Children* (New York, Longmans, Green & Company, Inc., 1951).

[6] See the discussion of radio and television in Chapter 14, in this volume.

[7] John Caffrey, "An Introduction to the Auding Concept," *Education*, LXX (December, 1949), pp. 234–39.

Earl J. Dias, "Three Levels of Listening," *English Journal*, XXXVI (May, 1947), pp. 252–54.

Speaking and writing are sometimes called the expressive phases of language, and listening and reading the receptive ones. This does not mean that reading and listening are more passive for the learner. In comprehending ideas given orally or in print the learner is actively engaged in perceiving these ideas and weighing them against his experience and in deciding upon his actions in response to them. Charles hears Dick talking about losing his baseball glove. He listens carefully to Dick's description of the glove, decides that it fits the glove he saw in the lost-and-found department, and offers to go with Dick to secure it. Thus, while listening, Charles is actively involved in the situation.

Parallels between Listening and Reading

As a means to understanding the processes of listening, many authorities have attempted a parallel study with the techniques of reading which have been analyzed carefully over a period of years.[8] For example, just as clear print and pleasing format make for ease in reading, so children listen more attentively to speech that is easily heard, rhythmical in flow, and free from glaring irregularities in usage or pronunciation. As in reading, readiness for any particular experience in listening is conditioned both by the child's level of maturity and by the listening he has done before. The younger the child, the more intimately must the content which he reads or to which he listens be related to him and his immediate concerns. When children are asked to read or to listen to a new story or to unfamiliar information, they understand more readily if the material is related to some familiar happening or ideas. When children read or listen for a purpose, they get more out of the experience than when their response is undirected. When they use what they have read or heard—by retelling, discussing, dramatizing, or other activity—they remember it better. In listening as well as in

[8] W. Wilbur Hatfield, "Parallels in Teaching Students to Listen and to Read," *English Journal*, XXXV (December, 1946), pp. 553–58.

reading, the natural unit of comprehension is the sentence or the conversational fragment rather than the single word. Unfamiliar words acquire meaning most easily when embedded in sentences in meaningful context. Finally, searching for the speaker's plan or organization in the report he is giving, or discovering transitions and subdivisions of his thought, helps the listener as it does the reader to follow the main ideas presented. Like reading, listening is both analytical and creative. It is at its best when the listener understands and weighs what he hears, adds to it from personal experience, "ponders it in his heart," and does something about it if a problem is involved.

Differences between Listening and Reading as Ways of Learning

While there are many parallels between listening and reading, there are also differences between them. In comparison with the reader, the listener has less control over the conditions under which he listens. The reader often selects the book and varies his rate of reading according to his purpose and his skill. He can reread if need be. On the other hand, listening is usually transitory. The child must listen at the moment when the speaker is talking or lose what is said. A lapse of attention leaves a gap in comprehension, although occasionally, with sound films, recordings, and transcriptions, there is an opportunity to have the material presented again.

Listening precedes reading as a way of learning. Indeed, until children have acquired considerable skill in reading, listening continues to be their chief tool of learning. There is evidence that listening is especially well suited to the building of attitudes.[9] Although research indicates that, for older elementary children, listening may be a less effective means for gaining information than reading, there is a possibility

[9] Phillip J. Rulon and others, "The Effect of Phonograph Recordings on Attitudes," *Harvard Educational Review*, XIV (January, 1944), pp. 20–37.

that what is heard is remembered longer than what is read.[10]

Listening has the advantage of being a shared reaction. Good music or an entertaining story usually is enjoyed more when it is heard in a social situation. One child's sharing of a story with others is worth while if the story is interesting, if the child is well prepared to present it, and if the listening group is not too large. On the other hand, reading has value also when it is not shared. It makes possible intimate personal contact with ideas and experiences over which the individual may linger in reflection or appreciation, rereading and enjoying the content at will. There is no necessary competition between reading and listening. The peculiar values of each and the way in which they supplement each other in the experiences of life should be made clear to children.[11]

Kinds of Listening

The processes involved in listening may perhaps be best analyzed by considering the various types of listening in which children and adults commonly engage. Classification may be based upon purpose, upon situation, or upon the nature of the material being presented. Undoubtedly some of the skills involved differ widely from one category to another, but at present there is almost no research to give guidance on this point. While the following kinds of listening overlap, they serve to bring out important differences:

Passive or *marginal* listening is prevalent today as many children study with the radio on. In fact, there is often a deliberate "tuning out" of what is heard with just enough consciousness of the language or sound to bring the child

[10] Harry Goldstein, *Reading and Listening Comprehension at Various Controlled Rates*, Contributions to Education, No. 821 (New York, Columbia University, Teacher's College Bureau of Publications, 1940).

[11] National Council of Teachers of English, *Reading in an Age of Mass Communication; A Report of the Committee on Reading at the Secondary School and College Levels*, W. S. Gray, ed., English Monograph No. 17 of the National Council of Teachers of English (New York, Appleton-Century-Crofts, Inc., 1949).

back to attention when a favorite radio personality comes on. Similarly, in classroom or home the tone of voice of teacher or parent may flash the danger signal which alerts the child whose attention has been wandering. The way one listens to background music while reading differs markedly from the type of listening one does when evaluating critically a proposed plan for action which affects one personally or professionally.

Appreciative listening is involved when the hearer settles down to enjoy a dramatization, a story, or a poem. The process of developing new or original solutions to problems presented through the spoken word may be termed *creative* listening or the act of entering imaginatively into the experiences, the setting, and the feelings of the characters in a story which is being told orally or produced on screen or stage.

Attentive listening is needed in situations in which accuracy of comprehension is involved, as in directions, announcements, and introductions. Probably there is a different mind set in situations in which the hearer participates, such as in conversation and discussion; this might be called *responsive* listening.

Analytical listening takes place, for example, when the listener weighs what is heard against personal experience and is alert to attempts of the speaker to sway his opinion by the devices of propaganda. This kind of listening must be developed by older elementary and high school pupils in order that they may evaluate what they hear.

CONDITIONS FOSTERING EFFECTIVE LISTENING

Perhaps one of the best ways to study the conditions fostering good listening is to examine the processes by which the young child develops the power to listen for purposes important to him.

Implications from the Child's Preschool Experiences

Almost from birth the child reacts to loud or sudden noises about him. Within the first few months of life he associates familiar sounds with particular situations, reserving "Da Da" for greeting his daddy and "baw" for the appearance of his favorite plaything. Psychologists define the child's first word as a group of speech sounds which are meaningful to him and which he repeats in the same recurring situation. Assurance that a given word is used with meaning comes only when it is used repeatedly in identical or similar situations.

Normal hearing is essential, but it does not necessarily enable children to interpret the world of sound. Children *learn* to distinguish the sound that announces their favorite radio or television program, mother's tone of voice that demands attention, the high whirring drone of passing airplanes, or the low soothing notes of a lullaby. Guidance in listening to all kinds of sounds is comparable to guidance in observing. The better children learn to do both, the more effect each will have upon their use of language.

All normal children delight in the use of their senses. They require only the wise guidance of an adult to fill sounds with meaning. Parents and teachers should recognize the importance of nonverbal sounds to the child who is eager for every kind of sensory experience. The clanging bell, the bird call, the patter of the rain, the splashing of galoshes in the gutter —all hold a fascination for the child. All help to develop an interest in sound and an alertness to differences in sound which stand him in good stead in his growing control over language.

Just as the youngster explores with interest everything in his environment, so he listens avidly to conversations going on about him. Through this listening he acquires language almost unconsciously. When he enters school, his speech reflects the language he has heard. His close identification with his first teachers makes it imperative that they serve not only as worthy models in language but as sympathetic guides to foster his natural interest in the sounds and language he hears.

It cannot be assumed because children listen with understanding to simple commands or to conversation directed to them when they enter school that listening is a natural ability to which the school need pay no attention. One of the reasons why the preschool child grows so naturally in ability to listen is that much of the time he is an individual audience; remarks are addressed directly to him, and the speaker adjusts both the content of his speech and his manner of speaking to the interest and need of the listening child. The youngster is encouraged to ask about whatever he does not understand. His response can be immediate, and the conversation can shift to follow his train of thought.

When the young child engages in talk with playmates, his responses are more or less spontaneous with few adult controls over his use of language. In these early years a great deal of parallel chatter takes place, each child expressing his own ideas without modifying his speech greatly in terms of what his playmate says. However, in his desire to gain response to his remarks, he gradually learns to listen to what the other child says.

The youngster of today has a bigger task in language than children had in former times. He must learn to react to language as it comes to him over the radio, completely divorced from facial expression, gesture, and the personal feeling and tone that are imparted in face-to-face situations. And he must learn to react to language as it is related to moving forms on a lighted screen, as in motion pictures or television.

Climate Favorable for Listening

To a considerable extent, the primary classroom should duplicate some of the conditions under which listening has taken place during the child's years at home. One teacher so organizes the school day as to permit nothing to interfere with her greeting each child personally when he arrives or with bidding him good-by upon his departure. The necessities of the group situation, however, plus the child's increasing maturity, suggest the need for new emphases also in the new learning conditions presented by group activities in the school situation.

In general, listening habits of children will improve throughout the elementary school to the extent that the following provisions are made:

The atmosphere is an accepting one in which the child feels wanted and secure. The teacher regards what each child has to say as important.

The seating arrangement is informal, with young children seated close together and children of all ages seated comfortably. The room is restful, free from disturbing noises and distracting interruptions.

Children who have slight hearing losses are advantageously seated for all types of activities so that they can be near to and see the speakers.

All opportunities that occur during the day are used to encourage children to listen, especially to their classmates.

The children have real purposes for listening. It may be that they wish to hear again a favorite poem or story, or they may be seeking answers to questions about how to care for a pet which is a temporary visitor in the classroom.

The children are prepared for special listening experiences, possibly by a discussion recalling a related story or event, possibly by a picture or even a trip.

The content of material presented is appropriate to the children's interests and maturity. The vocabulary and sentence structure used are neither condescending nor obscure. New terms are explained and new ideas expanded and illustrated.

The length of presentation is kept within the interest span and the amount of time children of a given age can comfortably remain physically inactive.

The speaker, child or adult, is natural in manner, speaks clearly, and watches children's faces and behavior for signs of flagging interest or lack of understanding.

When the teacher presents a story or poem there are frequent opportunities for children to participate by chanting the refrain, by answering interpolated questions, by telling the part with which they are familiar.

From past experience the children have built an expectation of using what they hear. They feel responsible for understanding what is presented, asking questions to clear up any misunderstanding.

Frequent opportunity is given to "talk over" what they have listened to, or to repeat important points covered in order to insure accuracy of listening.

Provision is made for children to give some personal expression to what they have heard—through dramatizations, retelling a story, carrying out directions, or expressing their ideas with paper, paints, clay, or wood.

Children are encouraged to improve their listening habits through setting up standards for good listening and through evaluating the effectiveness of results.

Effect of the Child's Total Adjustment upon Listening

Listening should be considered in terms of the pupil's total development. The poor listening habits of some children are evidence of faulty social development and underlying conflicts. Two types of children with problems that interfere with good listening can be identified.

The first type is the child who withdraws from the situation for whatever reason, through day-dreaming or preoccupation with his own problems. Lonnie, whose parents are separated, is afraid that his mother will be gone when he returns from school and he is not in any frame of mind for listening. Beverly feels unaccepted by the group and often is too concerned with her relationships with her classmates to concentrate on the story or the recording. The teacher keeps bringing each child back to reality by helping him find joy and interest in the pursuits of the group. To the unfortunate child she may be able to give help in solving his personal problems. To the inarticulate child she gives recognition of his ideas, however poorly expressed, and helps him to make his contribution in a more acceptable manner. As his status in the group improves, his listening may also improve.

The second type of child with a listening handicap is the one who is over-eager to talk. He maintains what amounts to a monologue, inserting his remarks whenever there is an opening, with little regard to the ideas expressed in the meantime by other members of the group. Part of this may be because of faulty training, but often such a child is in as great need of sympathetic study as is the withdrawn child. He may be hyperactive for physical reasons, or he may be easily distracted because of emotional pressures in his home situation. The degree of a child's social development is exhibited not only in his ability to express himself easily on occasion but also in his power to suppress his desire to talk long enough to allow others to participate—and then to listen attentively to them.

DEVELOPMENTAL LEVELS IN LISTENING

Instruction in listening will be more effective when the sequence of its development is better understood. Much critical observation by teachers is needed to determine what constitutes normal progress in intelligent listening, what differentiates one level of listening from another, and what are effective methods of teaching listening and of applying standards of evaluation.

Levels of Quality in Listening

One authority has suggested the following levels of listening: [12]

Little conscious listening except as the child is directly and personally concerned with what is being presented

Intermittent listening as the child is easily distracted by people and things in the environment

Half listening while the child holds fast to his own ideas and waits to insert them at the first opportunity

Passive listening with apparent absorption but little or no reaction

Erratic listening, that is, listening for a time but running off at a tangent when a word or idea presented calls to mind a personal interest or experience

Listening, forming associations, and responding with items from his own experience rather than reacting to what is presented

Listening and expressing some reaction through questions or comments

[12] Ruth G. Strickland, *Language Arts in the Elementary School* (Boston, D. C. Heath & Company, 1951), p. 114.

Listening with evidence of genuine mental and emotional participation

Listening with a real meeting of minds

To a certain extent these are developmental levels, perhaps, in the sense that as people become older they listen better, although even adults as well as children lapse into the simpler types on occasion.

Stages of Growth in Listening

A third-grade teacher who makes a survey of the listening habits of children will not be surprised to find a range in levels just as in any other aspect of learning. In Miss B's class many of the children are attentive for as long as twenty minutes during a discussion about a topic related to a class enterprise. These children may even watch to see that they do not repeat what some other child has already said. But John often breaks in with a personal experience called to mind by some statement made, even though it is not related to the point of the discussion. Shy Phyllis can repeat to her mother with great detail what "we talked about in school today," although she takes no part in discussions and often appears disinterested. Blustery Bill, when he finally gets settled, may listen attentively for a few minutes—provided the purpose is strong and the topic appealing. The teacher is concerned about Helen who, although she never disturbs, often seems to be "far away." One or two others listen attentively but seem to accept everything they hear without question. Having identified the children's various responses in listening situations, Miss B. looks for opportunities to help each of them listen more adequately. She also checks to see that what children are asked to listen to during the day is worthy of their attention.

There seems to be some common agreement that by the later primary level most children can be expected to assume their share of responsibility toward the one who is speaking, to ask questions about what they do not understand, to listen and carry out simple directions, and to follow the sequence of events in a simple story. As children set goals for themselves in intelligent listening, their progress will be accelerated. One rather immature second-grade group stated these practices, among others, as the ends toward which they were working:

> We listen to people who have something to tell us.
> We think before we talk. We have something other people would like to hear.
> We look at the person who is talking. We stop what we are doing. We keep very quiet.
> We listen carefully to the rules before we play a new game.
> We wait until the children are all ready to listen.
> We listen the first time; we listen to the *whole thing*.
> We stop and get in line when the fire bell rings.

In the upper elementary grades children will show increasing maturity by their ability to:

> Hold the thread of a discussion in mind
> Watch for transitional phrases
> Listen to content even though it does not affect them directly
> Take notes during a speech or report
> Write a brief summary of an oral report
> Discount bias in a speaker
> Disagree with a speaker courteously
> Indicate by their remarks that they have turned over in their minds the ideas of others
> Reserve judgment in listening to different viewpoints in discussion.

SITUATIONS INVOLVING LISTENING

Listening is not something new added to the program. The school day is filled with opportunities for children to listen. Guidance in these situations will help them increase their listening skills. Some of the most common types of oral language met within the elementary school are described below with emphasis on the listening skills involved. An attempt is made to show how growth in such skills keeps pace with increasing maturity.

Conversation and Telephoning

Conversation is a two-way process. It is an informal exchange of ideas, pleasantries, or experiences by two or more people in a social situation. Only gradually does a child learn to listen to the conversation of others so well that he can fit his remarks into the onward flow of language. In large part this requires practice. Kindergarten and primary classrooms, therefore, offer many opportunities for small-group conversation as children work and play together or gather around the lunch or library table. Class conversations guided by the teacher have their place, also. The children are influenced by the teacher's thoughtfulness as she listens politely to each contribution and, by her own response, gives it value. She asks questions which draw out the child whose responses are meager, sees that all children are included, and introduces new topics when the possibilities of the present one seem exhausted. Older children in the elementary school can set more conscious goals for themselves, including listening as a mark of the successful conversationalist.

When conversation, as in telephoning, is not face-to-face, greater demands are made upon the listener. Not only must he hear and understand the words but he must also be sensitive to those slight changes of pitch, tone, and manner of speaking which indicate the other person's reaction to what he says. Play-telephoning in the primary grades familiarizes the child with this listening situation. Experiences for older children should include the use of the telephone for many purposes, together with opportunities to hold conversations with classmates and adults, strangers as well as acquaintances.

Discussion

Following the train of thought in a discussion is more demanding than engaging in conversation. The child learns to listen to avoid repetition of ideas already expressed, to help make decisions, or to choose between alternate plans proposed. Increasing success in listening to discussion is partly the result of the child's growing maturity and partly the result of carefully guided practice. Among young children discussions center around an immediate plan of action or some happening of interest to them.[13] Only with added years and experience can children be expected to listen to and participate in discussions that do not touch their lives directly. Older children may judge discussions by standards which they help to establish, such as:

Do I listen thoughtfully to others?
Can I tell the difference between two comments?
Do I disagree with another politely?
Can I select from a discussion the ideas most important for our purpose?
Can I restate another person's idea when I think the group has not understood it?
Do I add a new idea sometimes?
Do I listen so well that I can summarize a discussion?

Reports

The sharing period in the early grades tends to be spent in reporting individual experiences and interests. This gradually develops into a time when children listen alertly to material related to a class interest or the results of individual research. Growth in listening is more wholesome when children listen not so much for *how* the child makes the report as for ways the group can use this information. A purpose for listening and a chance to discuss and ask questions afterward are basic requirements. Today the child gives a report which he has prepared with his audience in mind; tomorrow he listens to the report of another. These roles reinforce each other.

[13] Harold V. Baker, *Children's Contributions to Elementary School General Discussions,* Child Development Monographs, No. 29 (New York, Columbia University, Teachers College Bureau of Publications, 1942).

Planning and Evaluating Activities

Daily coöperative planning and frequent check-ups of how plans worked out are characteristic features of the modern elementary school. No better setting can be found in which to improve listening skills, for the children have a real stake in genuine planning. Action will be based upon it, and evaluation will affect subsequent action. As children progress through the grades, their reactions to the suggestions of classmates will become more thoughtful and, presumably, more considerate. At times in all grades the teacher serves as leader. Children are encouraged to assume this responsibility on suitable occasions as they are ready for it. The child who takes the leadership role has the double responsibility of seeing that the comments of all receive consideration and that progress is summarized. Many children should have opportunities to serve as leaders.

Committee work and small-group planning afford a simpler situation both for the listener and the pupil leader. They greatly increase the opportunities for listening critically and constructively to one's classmates. Furthermore, the response to listening can be immediate. In such situations the purpose motivates good listening.

Storytelling and Story-reading

The ability to listen to stories and follow the sequence of events parallels the skill needed when the child reads a story or tells a personal happening in consecutive order. Here, too, ability is dependent upon both mental maturity and experience. The child may develop this ability by listening to members of his family recount interesting events of the day just as effectively as by listening to stories read or told by mother, teacher, or older brother or sister.

In story-reading or storytelling the teacher catches the wandering attention of young children by pictures interspersed with text, by the use of cumulative tales, or by letting the children participate in chanting refrains. Children enjoy listening to favorite stories over and over again. If the level of attention is low, probably either the story or the manner of telling is inappropriate. When children are telling or reading stories, several groups may be formed. Here the more intimate group places less burden on the listener as well as the performer.

Reading around the class and watching the book while classmates reread familiar material cannot be expected to contribute to skills in listening. Being a good audience presupposes that there is something fresh and interesting to listen to. Having children select and carefully prepare stories to read aloud to classmates promotes reading skill on the part of the readers, and listening skills on the part of the audience.[14] Since listening to stories is listening for enjoyment, the atmosphere should be a relaxed, receptive one.

Poetry and Choric Speaking

Listening is the natural approach to the enjoyment of poetry. Because of its structural form, its condensation of ideas, and its imaginative feeling, poetry frequently makes heavier demands on the listener than does prose. It offers the added delight, however, of rhythm and pleasing sound patterns as already pointed out in Chapter 3. Children will listen with appreciation to poems if those chosen are simple and narrative in form, contain humor, and are presented at a time when they enrich a current happening. When a child reads or repeats poetry from memory, he owes it to his listeners to make careful preparation.

Choric speaking develops good listening habits, for the group is striving for a common effect, and children become sensitive to stress or pronunciations which mar the reading. Joy in participation and release of tensions are important goals. In later grades, children may occasionally prepare

[14] Constance McCullough, "How Moral Is Oral?" *Elementary English*, XXV (May, 1948), pp. 286–89.

group arrangements more carefully in order to present poetry or bits of rhythmic prose to a larger school audience.

Directions and Announcements

In a modern school with a program based on children's enterprises, practice in listening to directions or announcements comes through the social situations which require their use. Through developing criteria on how to make effective announcements or to give adequate directions, children may learn to use the same standards in listening to them. If an announcer is responsible for including What? Where? Who? When? and possibly Why? in his announcement, by the same token the listener seeks the answers to these questions. The teacher frequently may wish to analyze her procedure in giving directions to children to see whether it contributes to good listening on their part or encourages them to "tune out" her voice. If young children are to grow in ability to follow directions and understand announcements, it is important that such instructions be given at the time they are needed and interspersed with action based upon them.

Programs and Assemblies

Young children should not be expected to listen to lengthy programs in large auditoriums, especially when the programs are beyond their interest and understanding. Kindergarten children may find even primary-grade assemblies taxing. To be entertained briefly by a parent with musical talent or by a first-grade class with a bit of dramatization offers the opportunity for learning the first lessons in audience responsibility in an informal setting. Plenty of time needs to be taken before and after the listening to enable children to anticipate their role as listeners and to evaluate it afterwards.

A high school acting group in a city famous for its creative drama for children toured six elementary schools with a play entitled *Simple Simon*, for which they planned the settings and the costumes. They produced the play and presented it before groups of children in Grades IV, V, and VI. The experience gave elementary children not only a desirable listening experience but also training in audience behavior, as well as opportunities for classroom discussions and letter-writing.

It requires an all-school emphasis to maintain high listening standards at assemblies and programs. Planning a program with younger children in mind is a worth-while language experience for older elementary school children. Thinking about the probable response of an audience heightens a performance; this concern tends to make children more conscious of their own responsibilities as listeners when their turn comes to be the audience.[15]

Radio

Radios are almost universal in American homes and the amount of time spent daily by children in listening to them is substantial. For various reasons, a relatively small proportion of this radio listening takes place within the school day. The teacher's problem is, first, to give such guidance as she can to the selection of programs; second, to help children set standards so that they may be discriminating listeners and themselves screen the programs they hear; and finally, to encourage children to use in classwork the information which they gain in outside listening. This requires on the teacher's part familiarity with radio programs and coöperation with lay groups which monitor them.

Since the radio is a medium particularly adapted to building attitudes and swaying emotions, older elementary school children should be helped to listen critically to what they hear over the radio. Comparing the various treatments of the same news item is an example of one way to make children sensitive to the means used by news commentators to influence opin-

[15] Josephine Murray and Effie Bathurst, *Creative Ways for Children's Programs* (New York, Silver Burdett Company, 1938).

ion. Out of this they may gain some understanding of the power of the radio.

"Play broadcasting" in the classroom is another device used by teachers to stimulate listening activities. Use of the school public-address system, if there is one, is of course more realistic. The simulation of radio is, however, very real to the children. Another valuable opportunity is the preparation and presentation of real broadcasts over a local radio station. The children taking part in the broadcast feel a great responsibility to keep a satisfied listening audience, and classmates form an articulate part of that group.

Recordings and Transcriptions

Like radio, recordings and transcriptions appeal solely to the ear and offer excellent opportunity for children to develop discriminating listening. Recordings not only hold the same interest for children that the radio does but they have some additional educational advantages. They can be heard in advance by the teacher and can be selected in terms of appropriateness. They can be used at a time convenient for the work in progress. In addition they have a quality of performance which the radio does not have. It is a simple matter to replay a part in order to illustrate or clear up a point. Children gradually evolve their own standards and then apply them as subsequent recordings or transcriptions are played. Longer-playing records, tape and wire recorders, and a substantial library of children's records should be part of the equipment of every well-planned classroom.

An example follows in which a teacher reports the children's interpretation of a listening experience.

The record, "The Children's Prayer," from Hansel and Gretel was played without telling the children the name of the piece. The teacher suggested that they listen and see what pictures the music made them think of.

As they listened, they moved their hands at first and presently were dancing about the room, interpreting the mood of the music. A little later they were given paper and crayons and asked to draw a picture suggested by the music. They made their drawings while the record was replayed.

It was interesting to note how well they had listened. In most instances their drawings were in keeping with the mood of the music. Among the pictures were those showing fairies, angels, leaves falling from trees, a child kneeling to pray at the side of his bed.

When the children looked at the pictures, they talked about all the things they had thought of. Every child entered into the activity with interest and enthusiasm. When they were told the name of the record, many were pleased to learn that they had made pictures in keeping with the artist's title for the selection.

Later, after listening to another record, the children expressed in words the mood of the story or drew the picture which the music evoked. In the subsequent discussion the children noted what words could do that crayons could not.

The tape recorder is a source of interest to children and is proving useful in speech improvement, in oral-reading analysis, and in helping children improve their discussions through listening to the playback of the record. Here is a report of its use in one classroom:

One Monday morning everyone seemed to be bubbling over with something he had seen or done over the week end. The enthusiasm was so great that the children kept asking if they couldn't start sharing time right away. The teacher decided that this was the day for the tape recorder.

The group reviewed briefly some points to remember when speaking before the class. As the children made the various contributions, the teacher wrote them on the board. The children were reminded that they, the audience, should be good listeners. A child suggested that the group list some rules to remember for good listening. These too were put on the board.

The children's contributions were then recorded on tape. This turned out to be the best listening experience the group had ever had, affording opportunities for the speakers and the listeners to find out and discuss where they might improve.

Television

Undoubtedly, television has a powerful appeal to children. Eye and ear reinforce each other. New techniques of teaching are forecast in "How-to-do-it" programs, such as puppet-making, and in science demonstrations combined with oral directions. The alert teacher has an opportunity to improve both the speaking and listening of children as he makes their worth-while out-of-school listening and viewing contribute to the school program. It is likely that the excessive viewing of television which causes concern to some teachers and parents will taper off as the novelty wanes. Teachers need to be aware of the extent and nature of their pupil's viewing so that they can work with parents in better balancing the child's day and can use his television experiences fruitfully. As in the field of radio and sound films, children may be asked to keep a log of their listening outside of school or to make lists such as "What I Like to Listen to" or "What I Don't Like to Listen to." These may then be used as a basis for developing standards of choice in listening.

Sound Films

Sound films, which increasingly find a place in the school program, are another medium offering multiple sense appeal. If the school owns a collection of films, the teacher can preview them and fit them into the school program at appropriate times, so that the viewing and listening may have maximum educational value. Thus, ideally, the film is part of the ongoing program of the class. The formulation by children of questions beforehand, discussion following it, the reshowing of the film or of selected portions of it as the need arises, and the use of parallel reading afterward are techniques commonly employed.

WAYS OF IMPROVING LISTENING

The schools will undoubtedly develop effective methods of teaching children to listen once they have become aware of the importance of listening in life and discover that it can be taught.

The Teacher's Analysis of Her Own Listening

Possibly if each teacher examined her own listening experiences and habits, she would gain increased insight into the factors involved in listening and thus become better equipped to guide children.

In making an analysis of her listening activities, the teacher might ask herself such questions as these: Am I aware of the vast world of sound about me? Am I listening? What did I hear today?

At home: the alarm clock and then the early morning newscast; water running and footsteps elsewhere in the building; bird songs, wind in the trees, and a dog's bark somewhere; the squeak of the milk-truck's brake and the clink of its bottles; the beloved—yet sometimes irritating—early morning talk of one's family!

Then off to work: smooth purr of motors and raucous honks; factory whistles and wheels and church bells; people who go by—a couple chatting, a man whistling, a girl humming, a newsboy shouting, a taxi-driver snarling, a traffic policeman warning!

Sounds everywhere—some natural, some man-made; some welcome, others not; some sought or removed by the flick of a switch, by a "listening look" of expectancy or a frown!

As preparation for guiding the listening of children, the teacher may profitably explore further the factors which condition how effectively she listens to language as an adult. Were recent adventures in listening exalting, sobering, or instructive? Were they adventures in understanding? Assuming that she really heard in a linguistic sense, that is, took in and understood the ideas expressed, why did she listen? Did the purposes influence or control her level of listening? What proof had she that she received the speaker's message? As she compared notes with a fellow listener, she may have been struck with the fact that, in effect, the two had listened to quite different speeches.

Or, to pursue the matter more generally, what gets in the way of the speaker's attempt to communicate with the listener? Perhaps it is lack of background on the part of the listener, or his concern with the worry and tensions of everyday living, or perhaps it is his attitudes or mental set.

Which are communicated more faithfully, the specific facts presented or the general point of view? What effect on listening have the environment, the temperature of the room, the comfort of the chair, the tightness of clothing, the mannerisms of the speaker, the feeling of rapport between the speaker and the audience? Does an adult listen more profitably in situations in which he has a chance to exchange ideas with the speaker? Possibly discussing the shared experience clarifies it for the listeners.

By analyzing the many listening situations in which she is personally involved, the teacher may become increasingly aware of the factors which influence children's listening. Thus she is better able to guide them.

Analysis of Pupil Listening

It is helpful for the teacher to analyze also both the extent of pupil listening and its quality.

Keeping a log of the children's listening experiences during the course of a week and noting group and individual characteristics will reveal the variety of current listening situations and the present levels of listening habits and attitudes. It will also enable the teacher to make plans for further opportunities and appropriate guidance.

The range of listening situations which five-year-olds meet in school is partially indicated by the following excerpts from entries of two different days in a log kept by a kindergarten teacher.

Monday

Listening for his group to be called to bring lunch money to the teacher's desk

Listening at morning lunch to a new grace before repeating it with the class

Listening in order to select songs that other children have not chosen

Appreciating a duet sung by two children

Enjoying accounts of events that took place during the long week end

Attending carefully to the directions for going on an excursion

Listening (as the group walks along the street) to the swish, swish of the leaves, the song of birds, and the radios going in houses passed

Listening to instructions about taking a letter home to mother

Listening for courteous expressions after these had been talked over in the group

Wednesday (Hallowe'en)

Listening to directions for the school Hallowe'en parade

Listening to children in costumes—trying to recognize children by voice without seeing faces

Listening to remarks about costumes made by children in all classes as they took part in the Hallowe'en parade

Listening to judges make awards for the best costumes

Making courteous replies to guests and mothers who came to the Hallowe'en party (Hearing one child say, "Here is a chair," led others to follow suit.)

Enjoying the mysterious and hilarious sounds that are peculiar to a festival—tinkle of bells on costumes, horns, weird sounds

Taking part in a discussion as ideas were expressed about what one should do on Hallowe'en (for example: making people laugh at funny costumes instead of soaping windows)

Older children may readily make listening logs of their own days, which may be used as a basis for discussion and evaluation.

Sensitizing Children to the World of Sound

A first step in making children better listeners is to make them aware of the sounds in their environment. One teacher [16] reports her experience in doing this:

The children in the second grade decided to listen for sounds which occur every day. Before starting the listening campaign, they discussed the things which they might hear—the teacher talking, the principal talking, children speaking, and doors banging. The list, however, was not very long nor impressive. The group decided that they would try to remember something interesting they had heard that day.

At the end of the day their findings were discussed. Both children and

[16] Many of these classroom examples are from unpublished reports submitted by graduate students of Temple University.

teacher were amazed at the number and kinds of sounds mentioned. They had heard train and boat whistles, fire engines, squeaking chalk, scraping feet, children walking and talking in the hall, dropping objects, music in adjoining rooms, barking dogs, crumpling paper, and many other sounds. They decided that every day they would try to find a sound that they had not heard before. The children really did begin to open their ears, and they were eager to report something new.

The class formulated a set of questions which were written on cards and placed around the room:

WHAT DID YOU HEAR TODAY?
CAN YOU TELL ABOUT SOMETHING YOU HAVE HEARD?

Definite Programs in Listening

Teachers who make concerted attack upon listening skills report measurable improvement. Ursula Hogan [17] conducted an experiment with approximately two hundred fifth- and sixth-grade children to try to determine whether listening could be improved through a planned program.

The children were divided into experimental and control groups. All participants listened to a recording of "Miguel and the Pirates" and were then tested with a multiple-choice test of twenty-five items. The questions and choices were read so that only listening was being tested.

Pupils in the experimental group were then given regular instruction and practice in listening. Before beginning the instruction the children developed the following standards:

1. Relax and be comfortable.
2. Try to determine the plan or organization of the talk. Listen for the cue words or phrases, e.g.
   a. "There are three main points. . . ."
   b. "The most important problem is. . . ."
3. Listen for a summary of the talk or discussion.
4. Take notes on informational material.
5. Ask speakers for more information on certain points or for clarification of a point.
6. Compare what is being heard with what is already known about the subject.

[17] Hogan, Ursula, *An Experiment in Improving the Listening Skills of Fifth and Sixth Grades Pupils*, M. A. Seminar Study, June, 1953. University of California, Berkeley, California. David Russell, Sponsor. See also *Language Arts Guide for Yolo County*, Yolo County Schools, Woodland, California.

7. Look up additional information on the subject.
8. Remember to be courteous to other listeners by sitting quietly during the lesson.

The lessons consisted of transcriptions, radio programs, panel discussions, reading by teacher and classmates. Each lesson was prepared in a way similar to a reading lesson. The purpose for listening was made clear; background was developed; evaluation always followed. The control group had similar listening experiences but were not given any guidance or instruction.

At the end of six weeks the original recording and test were repeated and scores compared. The experimental groups showed marked improvement over the control group.

As an additional check on the two groups, a transcription on "John Marsh" was played and twenty-five multiple-choice questions were given. Again the experimental group showed a significant superiority to the control groups.

The teachers of the experimental groups noted a definite gain in the listening skill of their classes. The children followed directions better, were more courteous in listening, stuck to the main points of a discussion more readily, gained in ability to take notes, and asked more pertinent questions.

There was a noticeable improvement in the preparation and giving of talks and in panel discussions. The children seemed to sense the reciprocal responsibilities of an interesting presentation and courteous attention.

It is the opinion of the author of the study, that if teachers were as careful in motivating, conducting, and evaluating listening activities as they are in the other areas of language, it would not be difficult to develop listening to a comparable position with speaking, reading, and writing; for the slow child it would provide an avenue of learning of inestimable value.

Pupil Evaluation of Listening

Pupils must be made conscious that improvement in listening is possible and must become desirous of such improvement. The opening example as well as others described throughout this chapter shows this pupil concern.

One teacher reports that she read to her pupils each day a current article, based on world news, art, science, and the like. After the reading, which she kept to five minutes, she asked five questions about what had been read. The first day only five children out of forty answered more than three questions correctly. On the third day, to increase interest, the children were asked to choose a topic for reading aloud. Gradually scores improved. The last two days two good readers were chosen to bring in and read articles, first to the teacher and then to the class. The children listened eagerly, and responses were largely correct. Only three children out of forty had fewer than three answers right.

Another teacher described the responsibility which her pupils assumed for effective listening. After discussion of what are the listener's responsibilities, the children composed and displayed a chart to guide their listening.

ARE YOU A GOOD LISTENER?

1. Are you polite?
2. Do you get the facts?
3. Do you listen thoughtfully?
4. Do you listen for a reason?
5. Do you use what you hear?

When the group listened to a radio program or had a speaker in assembly or viewed a sound film, three steps were taken: first, the chart was reviewed to set up their objectives; second, the children listened; and, last, they evaluated themselves in terms of the criteria mentioned above. The teacher reported that as a result of this technique, the children seemed to profit more from their listening.

SUMMARY

Listening, then, is a language activity, usually embedded in a social situation, and involving the total personality. The level of listening on which a child operates is the product of his general maturity, his past experiences in listening, his purposes, and the nature of the listening situation.

It is important that children learn to listen well. Studies of the psychological processes involved in listening are being made. The effects of television and the radio are being studied. Teachers are becoming increasingly concerned with providing learning conditions and using techniques which promote pupil growth in listening. Fortunately, listening can be taught.

BIBLIOGRAPHY

ANDERSON, Harold A., "Needed Research in Listening," *Elementary English*, XXIX (April, 1952), pp. 215–25. (Bibliography of research studies).

BAKER, Harold V., *Children's Contributions to Elementary School General Discussion*, Child Development Monographs, No. 29 (New York, Columbia University, Teachers College Bureau of Publications, 1942).

BEERY, Althea, "Listening Activities in the Elementary School," *Elementary English Review*, XXIII (February, 1946), pp. 69–79.

BETZNER, Jean, *Exploring Literature with Children in the Elementary School*, Practical Suggestions for Teaching, No. 7 (New York, Columbia University, Teachers College Bureau of Publications, 1943).

CAFFREY, John, "An Introduction to the Auding Concept," *Education*, LXX (December, 1949), pp. 234–39.

COREY, Stephen M., "The Teachers Out-Talk the Pupils," *School Review*, XLVIII (December, 1940), pp. 745–52.

DAWSON, Mildred A., *Teaching Language in the Grades* (Yonkers, New York, World Book Company, 1951).

DIAS, Earl J., "Three Levels of Listening," *English Journal*, XXXVI (May, 1947), pp. 252–54.

GESSLEMAN, Daisy B., "Television and Reading," *Elementary English*, XXVIII (November, 1951), pp. 385–91.

GOLDSTEIN, Harry, *Reading and Listening Comprehension at Various Controlled Rates*, Contributions to Education, No. 821 (New York, Columbia University, Teachers College Bureau of Publications, 1940).

HATFIELD, W. Wilbur, "Parallels in Teaching Students to Listen and to Read," *English Journal*, XXXV (December, 1946), pp. 553–58.

MACBEAN, Mrs. Dilla W., "Phonograph Records to Stimulate Reading; with List," *Educational Screen*, XXVII (May, 1948), pp. 224–26.

MURRAY, Josephine, and BATHURST, Effie, *Creative Ways for Children's Programs* (New York, Silver Burdett Company, 1938).

National Council of Teachers of English, *Reading in an Age of Mass*

Communication; A Report of the Committee on Reading at the Secondary School and College Levels, W. S. Gray, ed., English Monograph No. 17 (New York, Appleton-Century-Crofts, Inc., 1949).

RANKIN, Paul T., "The Importance of Listening Ability," *English Journal* (College Edition), XVII (October, 1928), pp. 623–30.

RULON, Phillip J., and others, "The Effect of Phonograph Recordings on Attitudes," *Harvard Educational Review,* XIV (January, 1944), pp. 20–37.

SAWYER, Ruth, *The Way of the Storyteller* (New York, Viking Press, Inc., 1942).

SHAYON, Robert L., *Television and Our Children* (New York, Longmans, Green & Company, Inc., 1951).

SMYTHE, Dallas W., "Television and Its Educational Implications," *Elementary English,* XXVII (January, 1950), pp. 41–52.

STRICKLAND, Ruth G., *Language Arts in the Elementary School* (Boston, D. C. Heath & Company, 1951).

WILLEY, Roy D., and YOUNG, Helen A., *Radio in Elementary Education* (Boston, D. C. Heath & Company, 1948).

WILT, Miriam E., "A Study of Teacher Awareness of Listening as a Factor in Elementary Education," *Journal of Educational Research,* XLIII (April, 1950), pp. 626–36.

WITTY, Paul, "Children's, Parents', and Teachers' Reactions to Television," *Elementary English,* XXVII (October, 1950), pp. 549–55; 396.

———, "Children's Interest in TV," *Elementary English,* XXVIII (May, 1952), pp. 251–57.

———, "Children's Reactions to TV—A Third Report," *Elementary English* XXIX (December, 1952), pp. 469–73.

———, and Bricker, Harry, *Your Child and Radio, TV, Comics, and Movies* (Chicago, Science Research Associates, 1950).

WOELFEL, Norman, and TYLER, I. Keith, *Radio and the School* (Yonkers, New York, World Book Company, 1945).

CHAPTER 5

Speaking

As the child comes to school each day, whatever his level of achievement or his age, he can join with the other boys and girls and the teacher in one activity that is common to all of them and essential to their experiences together. He can talk.

A child greets his friend with, "Come on, let's play ball!" His teacher asks the newest member of her class, "What's your name?" One child tells another, "Our science committee is going to work on the exhibit today." Every day from the very beginning of school until dismissal time and at home, too, the bond of the spoken word gives children, teachers, and parents a means of communication that is used so freely, so easily, with so little effort, that its importance is often overlooked.

Throughout his school days and throughout his life, the child will probably use oral communication much more than any other of the language arts except listening. For every word he reads or writes, he will speak and listen to a thousand. He will find in speech an outlet for his emotions, a means of presenting and defending his opinions, a way of making himself a part of his vocational or social group, and a basic tool for all his school work. His speaking will help him to coöperate with other people; at the same time it will help him to maintain his identity as an individual. What he says, and to a great extent how he says it, will be a part of his total personality and will help those who observe him—his parents, companions, and teachers—to understand his actions.

Today modern media, such as the telephone, radio, and television, have increased the importance of speech as a form of communication. Lifting a receiver in order to communicate with another person saves miles of travel and much of the time as well as the effort needed in corresponding. A twist of the radio dial brings news of the happenings all over the world shortly after they occur. Television now reinforces speech with the visual image of its origin. Thus seeing a speaker in a distant place at the moment of hearing him enhances the impact of his words upon one's thoughts and feelings.

Speech is an all-pervasive element in daily living. The child talks while he is building, painting, modeling clay, cutting out pictures, playing in the playhouse, looking at pictures, or working simple puzzles. He talks in planning his contribution to the science exhibit or in describing the trip his group took to the post office. He uses speech as an aid in ordering his thinking. He talks to relieve his tensions, to give vent to his feelings, to control the actions and thinking of others. He needs to talk to gain increased control over his speech mechanism—to use effectively his teeth, tongue, lips, and breath in speech that is meaningful. He needs to talk if he is to develop socially. He is, in many present-day classrooms, as free to talk as he is to move about. He must talk if he is to be in touch with others, if he is to communicate with them in the most efficient manner. At the same time, he recognizes that he must not interfere with what others are doing.

It seems evident, therefore, that every teacher, no matter what her background or training, is a teacher of speech and language. She is responsible for providing the child with every possible opportunity for his development. A good classroom is not a silent classroom.

IF ALL GOES WELL WITH SPEECH
DEVELOPMENT

Speaking, like listening, is a facet of the language arts which has been developing since infancy.

Beginning Stages

When the child comes to the kindergarten or the first grade, he has been talking for three or four years and has been listening and responding to the speech of others even longer. He has already mastered many important oral skills. During the first several years of his life he has depended heavily on talking and listening for his contact with those about him and for his information about the world in which he lives.

Under favorable circumstances the normal child speaks freely and fearlessly when he first enters school. He uses sufficient words to express his wishes and his feelings, and he may even employ with reasonable facility such common phrases as, "Thank you." "Please." "Excuse me." He is full of curiosity and enterprise. His speech is almost continuous, although at first he may use it in communicating with only one or two others.

Behind this first free use of words by the child lie the years of language learning.[1] His home environment, with its affection, sense of security, and familiar surroundings has influenced his learning of speech. Experiences of work and play, contacts with the life of the community, and the every-day observation of people and things have supplied him with material for thinking and talking. If he is like most children, he has gone through many stages of learning in the months and years that have separated his first cries from his first "sharing and telling" experience in school. He has babbled

[1] Charlotte G. Wells, "Factors that Influence Language Growth: The Child's Equipment for Language Growth," *Elementary English*, XXIX (October, 1952), pp. 348–55.

and imitated himself and others. He has found that one word can mean a number of things and can get for him a number of responses. He has learned in some measure how to use language to control those about him. He is growing up in speech as in many other abilities.

He has begun the continuing process of using words in increasingly complex and meaningful phrases and sentences. He has acquired certain abilities in articulation, in vocal inflection, and in adapting his speech to the situations and individuals he encounters. He has been influenced by the speech he has heard from those about him. Now, as he arrives at school, the speech he uses reflects the kind of home from which he has come.

The entire process has been and will continue to be one of learning. Speech is not a skill he is born with, but must be acquired through hearing, through a desire to communicate, through social stimulation and guidance. It may be learned well or poorly, but it is learned.

Later Growth

From his first day in school, the child continues to add to his abilities in speaking.[2] As he has new experiences, he acquires new words with which to talk about them. As he adds to his vocabulary, he learns new ways to put words together to convey what he thinks. His sentences become longer and he begins to use all the kinds of sentences which adults use. Every new experience gives him more words or clearer understanding of ones already known; every new interest makes him eager to find better ways to tell about what he does. His successful contacts with reading and with writing, although they depend in part on his ability in oral language, will also serve that ability.

As he grows older, he becomes more adept at articulation. When he was five, he may have talked about his "fum"

[2] Ruth G. Strickland, "Factors that Influence Language Growth: School Influences," *Elementary English*, XXIX (December, 1952), pp. 474–81.

and his "fingers." Now that he is seven, he says "thumb." When he was younger, he may have spoken of the "wed, white, and b'ue" flag. Now, at eight, he no longer makes such mistakes.

Specifically, one may expect the child who comes to kindergarten to be able to use efficiently those speech sounds that are easy for him to produce and that have acoustic power sufficient to make them easily heard. The sounds *b, p, m, t, d, n,* and the vowel sounds require comparatively simple muscular adjustments and are fairly easy to hear. The young child will probably be able to use these sounds. He will use them, in addition, in place of those sounds that are hard to make or that are more difficult to hear. The difficult sounds of *r, s, z, th,* and *l* may become *w, t, d, f,* and *w* respectively, because it is easier to say *w* than to say *r* or *l,* because *t* is easier than *s,* and so on. Consequently, *"tee fe wady in a wed dwess"* may be a retarded five-year-old's way of saying, "See the lady in the red dress." The meaning is clear to him; his parents will probably understand him because they have learned his system of substitutions; but the teacher, eager to have the child do well and advance rapidly, may consider these substitutions as errors and feel that the child has defective speech. Such sound substitutions do set off a child of nine as different in speech. For the younger child, they are part of a normal sequence in speech development in which he has not yet reached levels of skill that he will, in all probability, achieve later.

The child may, at first, speak more effectively to only a small number of listeners or even to one or to himself. Later, when he is nine or ten, and sometimes as early as seven or eight, he joins in group discussions, in committee consultations about projects being worked out, in social conversation with visitors in the classroom, and even in assembly programs in which he speaks to a large number of people.

His voice, small and perhaps shrill at first, becomes more mature as he grows physically and mentally. He can now be heard by all those in the classroom instead of only by those who sit near him. Further, he learns to make his voice loud or soft, depending upon the situation in which he is speaking. His playground shouts are modified somewhat in the classroom and even more in the conversations of small committees.

His ability to express himself with relative fluency grows also. In his first years in school, he may hesitate, grope for words, repeat sounds and phrases, or even be quite unable to say what he wants to say when he is struggling for recognition or is excited or fatigued. As he grows up in speech, he talks more easily, although he will probably never be entirely free from the hesitations, repetitions, and prolonged pauses that are part of normal speech.

Standards in Speaking

When he enters school, his language mirrors that of his home and neighborhood. If his family and friends speak clearly and with good usage, the child has probably developed language of similar quality according to his maturity level. If the language of the school is not different from the language of the home, he may imitate, unconsciously, the speech of his teacher. If the home pattern differs greatly, the child may be uncomfortable at school and psychologically unable to accept the school's standard of speech. The security of the young child is centered in his home; it is more important to him to be like the people who love him and in whom he feels secure than like the pattern of the school. When he becomes adjusted and feels secure and comfortable at school, he can begin to grow in the direction of the standard the school is working to attain. Young children, under favorable learning conditions, want to do what is expected of them.

To children in the middle and upper grades, the standards of the play group or gang are more important than the standards set by either teacher or parents. Many a boy who has acquired good speech and usage distresses his parents during these years by adopting the modes of expression of the members of his social group. This is an age of keen interest in spicy, colorful slang and even in unauthorized language that is offensive to many people. "Pig Latin" and other secret languages and codes abound. It is all a part of the process of growing up, of establishing oneself as a person independent of adult domination. If a child acquires good speech in his early years and is given help at school with recognizing what is acceptable and of good quality, he can return to it later on when he sees its social value to him as an individual. In school and home situations demanding good speech, he can and frequently does measure up to the standards set for him; at other times, the approval of his own group is his greatest concern.

The elementary school does not strive to develop polished language of a high literary quality. It is concerned with weeding out forms of expression which are on the illiterate level and with developing consistent use of informal standard English. The informal standard level is the one on which most people operate for most of their lives.[3] Polishing of usage which goes beyond that point should be done at the higher educational levels, not in the elementary school.

Thus the child in the elementary grades grows up, speaking constantly but speaking differently with each new experience and each new need for better speech. Not only will what he says change as he matures, but the way in which he expresses himself will likewise become more effective if he makes normal progress.

With suitable help from home and school, the normal child will follow this general sequence in learning and extending speaking. This complex performance called speech will be more than vocabulary or good usage and adequate sentences.

[3] Robert C. Pooley, *Teaching English Usage,* English Monograph No. 16 of the National Council of Teachers of English (New York, Appleton-Century-Crofts, Inc., 1946).

It will be a combination of the mechanical skills of breathing, producing voice, and forming speech sounds with the ability to express thoughts. It will conform to expected usage for a child with his background and will make the expression of ideas something that is relatively pleasant to hear as well as relatively easy to understand. The function of spoken language, which is to present ideas in a way that carries meaning to the listener, will be fulfilled. Stimulated by encouragement to share even the most meager ideas, children will show how they feel, what they think, and what they want, and will grow in the use of language, although at varying rates, throughout their elementary years and throughout their lives.

WHEN ACTIVITIES ARE SPEECH-CENTERED

In order to find specific ways in which speech can be emphasized in the school experiences of children in the elementary school, a committee of teachers from almost every part of this country, from many types of schools, and from the various elementary levels gathered illustrative material that shows the use of speech in the classroom. Although some of the examples which follow have been modified, most of them are probably typical of activities in classrooms throughout the country. Many teachers could supplement them from their own experience. Some will find in the methods used by others ideas that they can adapt to their own situations. In some instances, a plan that is successful with one group will fail with another. Teachers and classroom groups differ, but the need for good speaking is common to all.

These classroom activities could be classified in several ways, but they might best be considered as they group themselves into three types: those that call for speaking in face-to-face situations to one or two others; those that include talking done in larger groups but with a familiar audience;

and those in which the child is in more "public" kinds of speaking situations. In these expanding experiences, the child can be guided to make the improvements he needs, and the group can work together to make effective speaking an essential part of total living.

The three categories into which speech activities have been divided should not be considered as mutually exclusive. They overlap considerably. Furthermore, in any given school day, members of a class group are likely to engage in all three. A visitor to a fourth-grade classroom might, in the course of a day, observe the children talking informally as they enter the room, chatting as they work in committees, or conversing in an interview with the principal (talking by one's and two's); discussing as a class the plans for the day, dramatizing an episode from a social studies unit, or reading aloud to prove a point (speaking in a familiar group); presenting the results of a neighborhood survey to the Parent-Teacher Association or participating in a school assembly program (speaking in situations when the listeners are many and unfamiliar).

Talking to Others by One's and Two's

At times everyone takes part in discussion, conversation, or interviews with only one or two others. Children can have opportunities to participate in face-to-face situations in school as they coördinate their speaking and writing, as they make recordings, as they learn to use the telephone, and as they ask questions, converse, tell riddles and stories, conduct interviews, issue invitations, or take messages.

A class in Washington, D.C. made recordings to give to their mothers for valentines. As each one recorded and listened, he made constant reference to a chart that reminded him to plan what he was going to say, to practice saying last sounds in words very clearly, to speak distinctly, to use an interesting voice, and to have a message especially for Mother. Later when they had a similar experience before Mother's Day, they borrowed the earlier records to compare for improvement in their spoken English.

A group of second-graders in Iowa became greatly interested in a display of birds in a show case in the hall. They sent a delegate to the principal to interview her and obtain information about where the birds came from and how they could find out more about them. As the class instructed their representative and discussed the information later, they learned better ways to inquire and to share information.

The children in a second grade took real pride in telling visitors to their classroom about the important projects which they had under way. Each week a different child assumed the responsibility of a host or hostess. When a new visitor entered the room, the host approached him, introduced himself and asked the visitor to sign his name in the guest book which the children had made. The host then showed and told the visitor about the activities in which the class was interested. It was obvious that the children were developing a good, reasonable set of standards governing the responsibilities of a host.

A third-grade class, preparing for a Valentine Sale, appointed committees of two or three children each to be responsible for making or cutting out the pictures, caring for materials, pasting the decorations on the valentines, making the verses, writing announcements, determining the prices, and handling the sales. The committees met and planned together, discussing the practical problems connected with each task, and preparing a summary of their decisions for a report to the class as a whole.

Members of a fourth-grade class in West Virginia made appointments by telephone to interview citizens of the community in the course of their study of the history of their own county. They decided to remember, when using the telephone, to speak slowly in a clear voice, to listen carefully to what was said to them, and to be courteous.

After the sixth grade in a school in Pontiac had completed their work on a dramatization, they decided to invite the other classes in the building to see their play. So they chose several of their group to give oral invitations to the teachers. The spokesmen for the sixth grade worked out their invitations carefully, trying to make them interesting, easy to understand, and pleasant to listen to.

A seventh-grade boy in a Missouri town liked to be of help to the principal so she asked him to take messages to the various teachers from her office. Although Paul stuttered, he found that the experience of giving verbal messages, when he was in a position of importance and representing authority, helped him to practice the better speech he was learning and gave him a feeling of confidence.

In most of these face-to-face situations, the children in the elementary schools were learning about speech by speaking. They were talking to one person or to a very small group, but they had a chance to find out that speech, as a part of everyday life, can be more useful if there are ideas to communicate and if the speech is interesting, clear, direct, and communicative. From time to time they set up standards toward which to work and measured themselves against them.

Speaking in a Familiar Group

In small group situations, too, speech is a part of the class-room interests and also of activities that extend beyond the school building. Many such situations are common to the activities of the elementary school. Those that seem most useful for emphasis on speech include group conversation, discussion, reports, introductions, reading aloud, dramatic play, dramatizations, pantomime, choric speaking, and story-telling.

Conversing and sharing. Groups of children talk informally as they engage in some common activity in the classroom or on the playground. They share with their friends the interesting experiences they have had over the weekend. Spontaneous talking of this sort develops the bonds of shared interests. From such use of language comes much of the child's preschool growth in speech.

The school continues to encourage this spontaneous use of language. In addition it provides for group conversations around the lunch table, for class conversations, and for times when children can "show and tell" about objects or incidents of personal interest.

Sharing, like all other experiences that involve language, should grow more mature as children grow older. First-grade children may tell about home and neighborhood experiences, or may show a new book or toy they have acquired, or a pair of new shoes. A fifth-grade class may share personal hobbies —building model airplanes or bird feeders, making marionettes, experimenting with a chemistry set, or making a stamp collection. Eighth-grade boys and girls may set up club groups, possibly a current-affairs club for the sharing of interests in current materials gleaned from reading, radio, and television, a photography club, a science club to study and report on civilian uses of atomic energy, and the like. The teacher makes every effort to help young children as well as older boys and girls set up their own plans to use leadership from within their groups. At each level, she assists the children in developing standards appropriate to their maturity and needs.

A California teacher had a group of children in her first-grade class who were unusually exuberant. They found it almost impossible to "take turns" in conversation. One day during conversation time the children, as usual, soon forgot about waiting their turn. This time nothing was said to remind them. Soon everyone was talking at once and a din ensued. When the conversation time was over, several children remarked, "That was no fun—no one could hear." This led to a short discussion about the need for turns and about good conversation.

A first-grade teacher in an Indiana school found the more mature of her children tiring of a sharing period in which all children listened to simple presentations of personal experiences. She encouraged the children to bring in things they were learning about at home or in community experiences that were new to them. Instead of a general sharing period, some of the children might join a group in which a child was showing and telling about a cocoanut someone had sent him, others might talk with a child who had watched street workers cleaning out a sewer near his house, while still others questioned and listened to a boy whose father had taken him to watch a steam shovel at work.

The second grade that decided to make recordings for their mothers for Valentine's Day made up their own stories to tell and tried them out on the class before they made the recordings. Their teacher reports, "The experience . . . gave opportunity for development in every aspect of the language program . . . Children who were busy sharing and planning together with definite goals in mind forgot self-consciousness as they focused their attention elsewhere. They expressed themselves freely because they desired to do so in answer to a felt need. . . . The original stories for mother furnished impetus for some delightful creative thinking and expression which did not cease with the completion of the recordings."

Planning, discussing, and reporting. Throughout the day in modern classrooms, children constantly use oral language as they make plans, discuss problems or topics of interest, or report to others the results of their reading and study. From year to year there is growth in the maturity of the ideas dealt with as well as in the method of handling them.

Younger children discuss home and family life, school happenings, games, and play.[4] Middle-grade children may discuss books, television or motion picture shows, and trips, in addition to local events. Older children discuss national and world events as well as current happenings in their own area, and curricular and extra-curricular experiences at school. Growth is shown in increased use of material from vicarious sources, more reliance on their own thinking, greater interest in matters that are remote in time and place, and more real thinking together. Increasing maturity shows also in ability to speak effectively, to contribute to the subject, and to consider the needs and interests of the group as well as personal interests and concerns.

Planning and evaluating both call for discussion. Younger children participate in planning for immediate interests and relatively brief and simple units of activity while older children can assume a great deal of responsibility for planning the method of attack and the sequence of events for a major unit of study or an important group or school activity. Evaluation may take place at any point. Children need to stop many times in their work to ask, "How are we doing?" "Where are we now in the carrying out of our plans?" "Have we succeeded in what we set out to do?" and "How could we improve on such a project another time?"

Reporting, too, is of many types and shows growth and progression from year to year. The young child's reports deal with his experiences, projects he is working on, or books he has read. They tend to be brief, factual reports that are purely extemporaneous. Older children can learn to plan their contributions, gather material from a variety of sources, organize and outline what they plan to say, and express their own reactions and the results of their own reflections as well as the facts they have gathered. Growth in quality of speech,

[4] Harold V. Baker, *Children's Contributions in Elementary School General Discussion,* Child Development Monographs, No. 29 (New York, Columbia University, Teachers College Bureau of Publications, 1942).

vocabulary, sentence sense, and organization are a part of the maturing process as is growth in understanding of how to locate, check, evaluate, and use resource material.

A first-grade group discussed kinds of trains. They were interested in the appearance and the use of various types of cars and engines. Discussion included the colored signals along the right of way and what they might mean. Pupils planned various ways of gaining information from parents, from pictures and reference books, from trips to the station with a parent—and reported their findings.

In one of the southwestern states, a second-grade group was discussing Mexico, the country from which several of their members had come. The children brought to class many Mexican articles from home. Showing these and telling about them gave the Mexican children an opportunity to make interesting reports. The class discussion which centered about the reports added to the social status of the Mexican children and to the understanding and good will within the group.

When the Association for the Study of Negro Life and History met in the city, a fourth grade became interested in the points made by the speakers and decided they wanted to learn even more about their own people. In the course of their study and discussion they learned that no race can progress far without the aid of another, that an individual or a group can accomplish more through coöperation, and that they could be proud of their heritage. They concluded that discussion was important because it had brought out these points.

A fourth grade studying the postal system had visited a large post office and observed the methods of handling domestic and foreign mails. They found that some of the unanswered questions on their list were such that the local postman might answer them. The class agreed that all who were interested would watch for the postman on Saturday morning and ask his permission to walk a few blocks with him to ask him questions. Some of the district postmen probably resembled the Pied Piper that Saturday morning as the children accompanied them to find out what a man must learn in order to become a postman, how long his route might be, what the service stripes on his uniform meant, and other matters of interest to them. They had discussed the matter of asking personal questions and the need for great tact and courtesy in their interviews. A number brought back careful notes for reports on Monday morning.

A sixth grade which assumed the responsibility for the Student Council discussed the importance of the example they might set for the making of suggestions and reports at Council meetings. They emphasized the importance of making suggestions positive rather than negative and agreed that what was said should be clear and to the point, not just a repetition of something already said during the meeting.

Storytelling and reading aloud. Storytelling is a popular activity with many groups of children. It helps them to learn how to catch and hold the attention of an audience, how to make a story interesting through choice of words and clear, interesting sentences, how to follow a sequence of events or episodes, and how to build toward a climax and a satisfying ending. If they have opportunities to listen to good story-telling by the teacher, by older children, or by members of their own group, they will enjoy making up original stories or retelling some they have heard. Young children like to hear their favorite stories told and retold and enjoy telling them at home to Mother and Dad or to younger children. Occasionally, they like to retell them at school for each other. Their original stories may be rather formless or patterned after those they have heard. There are speech improvement values in either kind of storytelling, though the telling of original stories may call for more thought and more attention to the use of language.

Reading aloud has greatest value when it is done for a real audience of listeners. Sometimes it is used to share with classmates a story or a part of one which the reader has especially enjoyed. At other times, as can be seen from some of the following reports, reading aloud serves to give information which is needed at the time.

Her kindergarten children, a teacher reported, developed more sensitive ears and enriched their vocabularies through listening to a variety of stories, poems, and songs and by retelling, individually and as members of a group, those that were their favorites.

Beth wrote a poem about the class picnic. When, at the teacher's suggestion, she read her poem aloud, the group liked the sound of the words and the rhythm and rhyme so well that they took it home to read aloud to their parents. Some of them tried writing poems of their own. They liked to read their poetry aloud to see if it really sounded the way it sounded "in their heads."

Bert's father had a very special book about Indians. At the time the fifth grade was studying Indians in history, Bert brought the book to school and read aloud some of the most interesting passages. This was almost the first time that Bert had taken an interest in history, but he brought the past to life for the class by the way he read and, some-how, history seemed more real to all of them.

Some of the sixth-graders in a suburb of St. Louis had a chance to hear a professional actor read from good literature. Since not all of the class had attended the performance, those who had gone read some of the passages aloud, not trying to imitate the actor but remembering some of the feeling they got from hearing the lines read well and trying to communicate that feeling and the ideas from the page to their lis-teners.

Dramatic play and dramatization. In dramatic play young children relive spontaneously the life about them, assuming various roles and engaging in appropriate activities. Playing house and playing fireman or policeman are familiar exam-ples. Creative dramatics is the dramatizing of situations or stories in which the emphasis is on the spontaneous interpre-tation of a role, at times several children playing the same role. Dramatic play is often carried on without properties of any kind, the imagination of the child providing all that he needs to play his part. The dramatizing of stories and situations which is done in the kindergarten and first grade is often of this sort.

As children grow older, they appear to need and want some properties or a token suggestion of a costume—a head-band for an Indian, a stick wand for a fairy queen—and they can do an endless variety of interpretations with a few odds and ends from a costume box. Upper-grade children may insist on carrying out an occasional play in great detail with realistic properties and real costumes. Such equipment ap-pears necessary to help some older boys and girls lose them-selves in the role they are playing. Equipment should be kept at as low a minimum as the children are satisfied to have it, so that attention can be centered on the playing of the vari-ous roles.

The speaking parts in creative dramatics are impromptu and unmemorized. A child who has in mind the role he is to play and the kind of verbal reaction it calls for will improvise naturally and creatively, whereas if he memorized a part he would reproduce it stiffly at best, and be completely lost if he failed to remember it.[5]

At Edison School, the kindergarten learned about the grocery store and enjoyed making up a little skit about how some of the foods come to the store. They also acted out shopping and selling and pretended to be the kindly grocer and the mother buying good things to eat. They changed their voices as they pretended to be different people and thus found that voices can be flexible and varied.

Anne's nasal voice was very noticeable until she pretended to be one of the trees in the forest that Red Riding Hood walked through. Then, in creative dramatization, she made noises like the wind and used good vowel sounds, free from nasality. This gave her teacher a way of helping her to hear what better speech would be like.

Although June seemed shy and did not take much part in class discussion, she had a very expressive face and she moved well and easily. So, when the third grade tried to see if they could tell something without words, which they learned was called "pantomime," June did the best job of all. The others asked her about what she had done, and she found herself talking with them quite easily.

The fifth grade in Rushville read a story they liked very much. They wanted to tell it to the fourth grade in their building, but they thought that just telling it would not be very interesting and that only one of their group could participate. So they decided to turn the story into a play. They chose the characters, listened to the voices and speech of those who were to be in the dramatization, picked out the scenes; and then just "made it up" as they went along.

Choric speaking. Simple beginnings of this ancient art may be seen in the way the young children spontaneously repeat refrains or recurring conversations in folk tales, or in the way a group of them chant a phrase or a sentence which has caught their fancy. Such informal activities are much more important than performing before an audience. If public presentations of choric speaking are made by older children,

[5] Corinne Brown, *Creative Drama in the Lower School* (New York, Appleton-Century-Crofts, Inc., 1929).

Isabel B. Berger, *Creative Play Acting* (New York, A. S. Barnes and Company, 1950).

Ruth G. Lease and Geraldine B. Sikes, *Creative Dramatics in Home, School, and Community* (New York, Harper and Brothers, 1952).

Winifred Ward, *Playmaking with Children* (New York, Appleton-Century-Crofts, Inc., 1947).

Carrie Rasmussen, *Speech Methods in the Elementary School* (New York, The Ronald Press, 1949).

they should be only occasional and always as an outgrowth of many satisfying classroom experiences in which the children experiment with assigning solo parts, arranging voices, and producing the effect which they desire. Used wisely, choric speaking promotes appreciation, clear articulation, pleasing tone quality, and the feeling of satisfaction that comes from working together for a common goal.[6]

Teachers are cautioned against using for choric speaking material in which breaking the verse into parts destroys the continuity of thought.

In a Missouri city choric speaking is a favorite activity of the children at the Laboratory school. Their teacher said, "They look forward to it and usually want to spend more time at it than we had planned. Children who are shy, who have deviant speech, or who hesitate to volunteer readily for other reasons, get special help from choric speaking."

Bobby could not say his own name well because he did not close his lips for the "b" sound. After his kindergarten group had visited a dairy, they made up a verse about freezing ice cream and said it together. As the group said, "Beat, beat, beat with the beater," Bobby began to learn how to say the "b" sound.

Such activities illustrate the use of speech in the small group situations common in the classroom. Before the child is expected to talk to large groups and to strange groups, he should be given an opportunity to learn to speak easily and well before his own class.

Speaking before a Large and Unfamiliar Audience

Speaking before a large group is not an easy task nor a frequent one for the elementary child. Activities in which the child speaks as one of a group can often serve to accustom him to an audience.

Choric speaking is a valuable activity for all of the children and may provide individual opportunities, in "solo" parts, for those who are ready to stand alone before a large audience. Singing, not always recognized as an activity re-

---

[6] Carrie Rasmussen, *Choral Speaking for Speech Improvement* (Boston, Expression Company, 1939).

lated to speaking, may provide still other opportunities for emphasis upon good articulation, clear tone, and accurate pronunciation. Group singing brings out vocal volume, since the inhibitions sometimes caused by singing alone vanish when everyone shares in the song. In fact, both singing and speaking situations in which children participate are also frequently enhanced by dramatization, movement, or the use of some original art work.

Appearance in public is occasionally within the experience of the average child in the elementary grades, and his preparation there may enable him, as he grows older and more able to communicate, to speak in public with some facility. He may, of course, take part in a demonstration for a teachers' meeting or a Parent-Teacher Association program. When adults form the audience, they should be helped to understand that the value for the children comes from their planning and from the use of the kind of speech which is natural for them, rather than from excessive drilling for perfection according to adult standards.

The third-grade boys and girls in one school enjoyed giving puppet shows for programs in the auditorium, possibly because puppets enabled them to share in a public program without appearing before the group. Their teacher felt that the experience brought about desirable changes in personal values, developed coördination between thinking and speaking, and helped certain individuals find acceptance in the group.

Another third grade decided to make a shadow puppet show. They chose a story, worked it out, and presented it for a special school program. All of the children helped, and many took part in the production. They made a "public" presentation, but they were not "showing off." Although attention centered on the play itself many speech values were present in the situation. The children remembered that the audience had to hear the lines the animal characters spoke and that one animal had to sound different from another. They worked on their speech as they worked on the play, not in an artificial situation but with a real interest in making something they liked come alive for others.

Four fifth-grade children, a boy and a girl from each of two different schools, took part in making a recording of a panel for the radio program, "Carnival of Books." The author of the book and an adult moderator were also members of the panel. The children, who had previously read the book and prepared questions they wished to ask the author, met briefly with the moderator before the program to lay the general plans for avoiding duplication of contributions and for maintaining audience interest. Later that same day they conducted a panel with the author about the same book before an audience of two hundred members of a metropolitan council of Parent-Teacher Associations. The discussion was informative, thought-provoking, and highly interesting to the adult audience. The children were free from tension and confident in manner. Factors which contributed to their ease before a large, unfamiliar audience were probably (1) the thrill of meeting a real author, (2) the fact that they were not merely presenting their own reactions but also gaining new information and insights about how books are written, and (3) the fact that the focus of attention was on the ideas being discussed rather than on themselves and their actions.

In "public speaking" situations, the child can learn to express his ideas before a group, and, even when he is before a microphone, he can learn to adapt himself to the audience. As he speaks to large groups in public situations, both in school and later, he will have had the microphone experience that is becoming so essential to anyone who must use a public-address system. Thus he prepares for the future as he enjoys the present.

HOW GROWTH IN ORAL LANGUAGE IS PROMOTED

The previous section of this chapter included many classroom examples of speech-centered activities. Not only such activities but the speaking that is an integral part of living and learning together should be made as profitable as possible. Several factors influence the development of effective oral language.

Providing a Favorable Climate

A school which meets the needs of children is almost inevitably a "speech-centered" school, since children who are encouraged to express their ideas and to set up and pursue enterprises which have significance for them will inevitably talk, discuss, contribute ideas, and respond to a sensible measure of freedom in the room by free use of speech. The classroom setting, wholesome personal relationships, and vital experiences are important elements in a favorable climate for growth in oral communication.

The physical set-up of the room can encourage oral language—by informal grouping of chairs or desks, by ease of arrangement, by availability of properties for impromptu dramatization, art materials for making puppets, and machines for recording and playing back the speech of children.[7]

Even more important, however, is the quality of human relationships which prevails. When children feel accepted and respect each other, they are free to learn together under the guidance of a teacher who sees oral language not only as a means of communication but also as a tool for social living.

Something worth talking about is a prerequisite to a worthwhile talk; therefore, teachers consider challenging and interesting experiences with social studies, science and literature, excursions, audio-visual materials, and various kinds of creative activities as basic parts of the classroom setting for growth in oral language. Most teachers would subscribe to the idea that talking needs to be tied closely to real experience. Then new words become a part of the child's vocabulary and the extension of vocabulary, in turn, adds accuracy and breadth to the child's future speaking.

Allowing Time to Grow

Children need time to acquire speaking skills, just as they need time to become ready to read or write. If the school asks too much of them and expects of them more than they can do, it prepares the ground for serious problems in both speech

---

[7] Ruth G. Strickland, "Factors That Influence Language Growth: School Influences," *Elementary English*, XXIX (December, 1952), pp. 474–81.

and personality. Studies of the development of speech sounds indicate that children learn the skills of speech in a rather specific sequence, those sounds requiring finer coördination coming last.

Consonant sounds develop in a definite sequence, according to Davis.[8] Children who are developing normally in speech are able to articulate the sounds represented by the letters at the ages shown in the table below:

3.5 years: *b, p, m, w,* and *h*
4.5 years: *d, t, n, g, k, ng,* and *y*
5.5 years: *f* and *v, z* and *s*
6.5 years: *zh, sh, l, th* as in *then* and *th* as in *thin*
8.0 years: *z, s, r,* and *wh*

Vocabularies grow as the children grow and as they have more need for self-expression to talk about their expanding experiences. Sentences increase in length and complexity as other language skills develop. In addition, the child's discrimination between and among speech sounds, words, and meanings is a developmental matter. The teacher of six-year-olds should not expect to hear twelve-year-old vocabulary and sentence structure from pupils. Rather, she has the task of helping young children to acquire new words, to increase sentence length, to add the refinements of modifiers and connectives, to use the sounds of speech efficiently in oral communication, and to adapt the manner of speaking to the occasion. Such growth is a gradual process.

Introducing the child to reading is often one of the first-grade teacher's most interesting and stimulating responsibilities. Children cannot read sentences that are very different from those they use in their speech; therefore teachers need to consider the readiness of children for the kinds of reading they are asked to do.

[8] Irene Poole Davis, "The Speech Aspects of Reading Readiness," *Newer Practices in Reading in the Elementary School,* Seventeenth Yearbook, Department of Elementary School Principals (Washington, D.C., National Education Association, 1938), pp. 282–89.

Expecting Variations in Growth

All good teachers recognize individual differences. Just as children vary in reading ability, in writing skills, and in general intelligence and achievement, they vary also in speech. Not all of the children in a group will reach the same level of speech proficiency nor of oral language skill at the same time. The thoughtful teacher will bring each child to his best level of achievement through activities that, as part of classroom work, promote attention to speech.

Setting Good Examples

Throughout all of the school day, the boys and girls have one paramount example in speech—the teacher. In everything she says to them—and she must say many things—her voice, her pronunciation, her articulation, her inflections, her simple and clear ways of expressing her ideas influence the members of her class more strongly than she realizes. A group of children on a playground, in a make-believe school during recess, talked with harsh, nasal voices when they were the "teacher" and used their own voices when they were the "pupils." The teacher of that class was vocally characterized very accurately by the children, who just supposed that "all teachers talked like that." The greater the admiration of the children for their teacher, the more likely she is to influence their behavior in speech as in other ways. A teacher with a lisp or an unpleasant voice may be a veritable menace to children if the children leave her sphere of influence with lisps in their own speech or with voices that are harsh and annoying to listeners.

The prevailing mood of the classroom is often set by the voice of the teacher. She can frequently restore calm by speaking softly and in a low-pitched voice. Tension and strain in the teacher's voice can communicate itself to the boys and girls in the classroom and lead to restlessness and fatigue for everyone.

Establishing Goals Coöperatively

To what extent can the teacher expect to influence the children in her classroom to better speech? What should she expect of them? When can she relax her vigilance for clear speech? When can she say, "Well done," and when must she say, "Let's try again?"

No one can answer these questions specifically for any teacher about any group of children. The inquiries themselves stand as constant reminders to the teacher that speech is a never-ending activity for the child and that individual variations exist between and among children. They point up the fact that the speech needs of individuals will vary from time to time and that no two speakers ever face exactly the same speech situation or face it in exactly the same way.

Goals in speech must be realistic and they must be the children's goals if their wholehearted coöperation is to be secured. What did we wish to accomplish in this announcement or dramatization or choric presentation? Did we reach our audience? How can we improve in our next attempt? Throughout the grades such questions should increasingly become a matter of class and individual concern as well as of analysis by the teacher.

In the elementary school, attention must be directed equally toward the content and the manner, the "what you say" and "how you say it." A child who reads aloud with great precision of articulation but with little or no communication of ideas is not maintaining this balance. A child who has good suggestions for group activities but who cannot make the others in the group understand is likewise "out of step" in oral communication.

This balance of content and manner is particularly important for the majority of children who have adequate speech and who need only to make the improvements that enable them to be more effective in oral communication. The transfer of practice from the classroom situation to out-of-school speaking will be facilitated by emphasis on good speech for all at all times. A teacher who requires over-precision in speech from children does them an injustice, since she makes them as "different" in their meticulousness as they might be if they could not be understood at all. The best course lies in making skill in speaking unobtrusive in serving the ultimate purpose of speaking—the interchange of ideas.

The teacher can expect, however, that steady growth in speech abilities will result from a plan that emphasizes speaking well in every classroom activity. Since speech is used so commonly by all people, it should be so used that it will aid communication rather than interfere with it.

Using Normal Activities for Speech Improvement

Good use of oral language will become part of the whole schoolroom experience if, at the outset, the practice periods are part of other activities and if the children themselves select, with the guidance of the teacher, the improvement goals they wish to emphasize. Then everyone will focus attention on the particular point selected, and no one child will feel that he is under critical observation because of his "difference." The children discuss what they should work on next and look forward to other improvements as soon as the first points are mastered, or are well on the way to being under control.

Specific speech needs may be met through group activities. Even such matters as word endings, often emphasized by the teacher in a way that fails to show the children that such things are useful in all speaking, may be attacked by the entire class. A period of special emphasis on "ing" and "ed" endings, for example, may correlate with the learning about such inflectional endings in writing or in spelling and may lead the children to place them, spoken in a natural way, on the words that they use in discussing the problem itself.

As new words are learned, the acceptable pronunciation of them may well be emphasized. When spelling and use and pronunciation are considered together, each reinforces the other and the usual way of saying the word is learned, the more stilted pronunciation or the erroneous one being avoided. Even such simple words as "the" and "a," too often overstressed at the direction of the teacher in early reading, take their proper place and have their proper value in reading and in conversation. And, as the two processes, reading and talking, are shown to be more alike, each gathers strength from the coördination.

Pleasurable group activities, such as choric speaking and spontaneous dramatization, need not be obviously directed toward speech improvement, but can accomplish this end as the children enjoy together the strong rhythms of "The Mysterious Cat" or the humor of "Robinson Crusoe" or the contrasts in "The Pied Piper of Hamelin."

These activities are not usually prepared for public performance, although the group may wish to share with another class in the school the fun they had in getting ready to read the poem or story aloud. At such a time, the explanation of the story and of how the class came to choose it might lead logically to a short expository speech by a member of the group. Further, the fun of trying to sound like someone else, as in puppet shows or characterization in a dramatized story, makes practice on vocal variety an unconscious learning process. Then, too, the listening that must go on as the group chooses the characters or tries out the voices for a choric speaking experience will provide some of the ear-training that is so integral a part of all speech improvement.

Encouraging Good Usage

A child's pattern of grammatical usage is his response to what he learns. Some of the forms used by a very young child may be his own simplification of patterns he has not yet caught or may grow out of his efforts to be consistent with an inconsistent language. The verb forms in the sentences, "Look what I brang you," and "My Daddy gived it to me," are forms a child will probably outgrow as he learns more of acceptable adult speech.

Many of the forms of illiterate speech which children use are learned at home or in the neighborhood and are thoroughly ironed in by constant repetition in all sorts of situations.[9] The way to substitute good usage for poor is to give the child opportunity to hear good usage at school until his ear is tuned to it. His language is an intimate part of him as an individual and great tact is required in motivating him to change it. A child cannot learn to speak differently without some desire on his part to do so. The child who loves and admires his teacher may absorb some of the teacher's forms of expression without conscious effort, but much of language improvement requires thought and effort. Growth is made possible by a sympathetic teacher who offers unobtrusive help and who develops a classroom atmosphere in which it makes a difference whether or not "you say it better." Nothing is achieved by ridiculing or making a child self-conscious. Opportunities for new contacts and situations which call for good speech help a child to stretch on tiptoe and practice the best speech that he can attain. If a child feels accepted and at ease with his teacher and there is genuine group feeling among the children, he can lay hold on the teacher's help and use it for his own upbuilding.

An adolescent may realize that his speech makes him unacceptable in his social group. If so, there are several ways he may react. He may change his speech in order to become acceptable, or he may retire within his shell, resent his position in the group, avoid contributing in any class or school activity, "hate English," and deliberately use illiterate or even coarse expressions to cover up his defensiveness.

When a child is talking, no teacher should interrupt to correct a point of usage. Courteous listening is the teacher's first response, then reaction to the content of what has been

[9] Muriel Crosby, "Factors That Influence Language Growth: Community Influences," *Elementary English*, XXX (January, 1953), pp. 34–41.

said. Last of all, either individually and privately or before the group, she can call attention to a better way to say what the child tried to express, and encourage him to use the better form.

In these days of textbooks and workbooks, a vast amount of reliance is placed by some teachers on the use of written exercises as a means of improving usage. There is value in emphasis on correct usage in written work,[10] but it can only supplement and reinforce oral work, not substitute for it. Not until the form the teacher is striving to have the child accept sounds comfortable to him and the poorer form is less acceptable will he really make the better one a part of his own language usage, and even then he must be given good and honest reasons for doing so.

IF CHILDREN NEED SPECIAL HELP WITH SPEECH

Although most children use speech adequately, almost every classroom group has in it some boys or girls whose manner of speaking seems unsuited to their age and grade level, who are somehow "different" because their speech varies from that of the group in which they are found. These differences in speech may be slight or they may be serious enough to constitute real barriers to the child's acceptance by the group as well as to his school achievement. Some common examples follow:

Jeanne's poor hearing prevents her understanding of questions or comments and makes her replies difficult to understand. She may seem far less intelligent than she really is until her teacher finds out about the hearing loss and its effect on comprehension and articulation and makes provision for her needs. Then the child can become part of the group, contribute her share, and eventually demonstrate her potential abilities in leadership.

Billy's stuttering is a constant problem for him. He does not join in group discussions and refuses to read aloud. He has personality prob-

[10] See the discussion of usage in Chapter 7, pp. 238–39, 248.

lems that may lead his teacher to think him less capable than he really is.

Stewart tries to give his name, but says it so poorly that his teacher cannot understand it; Martha's mother must go to school with her to serve as her interpreter because Martha cannot speak clearly; Dick's voice is nasal and his speech sounds are confused because he was born with a cleft in his palate. Tony has heard Italian spoken in his home far more than English, and his speech reflects the native tongue of his parents. Rosemary is six, but she has such a meager vocabulary that she cannot keep up with the children in her first-grade group.

Although these specific examples may not occur in every classroom, the teacher who observes the speech of the members of her group will probably notice that some have speech that does not serve them as well as it might in school, in social groups, or at home.

Determining What Is Defective Speech

How can one determine whether or not speech is defective to the extent that it will interfere with school work? What is the dividing line between "normal" and "defective" speech? According to one writer,[11] speech is defective when it deviates so far from the speech of other people that it calls attention to itself, interferes with communication, or causes its possessor to be maladjusted. In greater detail, according to still other writers,[12] the speech of a given child may be regarded as defective under the following conditions: if it is not loud enough to be easily heard; if it is partially or wholly unintelligible because of inaccurate articulation; if it is intrinsically unpleasant to listen to; if it is so different in rate, rhythm, pitch, loudness, or individual sounds of speech from that of the average speakers of his age and sex that the differences serve to distract the hearer's attention from what is being said to how it is said; or if it is accompanied by extraneous mechanical or vocal sounds, or by distracting grimaces, gestures, or postures.

[11] Charles Van Riper, *Speech Correction: Principles and Methods* (New York, Prentice-Hall, Inc., 1942).

[12] Robert West, Lou Kennedy, and Anna Carr, *The Rehabilitation of Speech* (New York, Harper and Brothers, 1947).

It seems apparent that the child in the elementary school whose speech is obviously different from that of his classmates has defective speech. One cannot judge all children on the same basis, since their ages, levels of maturity, learning abilities, and personalities vary so greatly. Also, a newcomer may have a regional dialect or foreign accent which may be normal for his background, but which sounds strange in the new setting.

The classroom teacher who has known many children at the level on which she teaches is in a good position to notice those who cannot maintain the same competence in oral language as others in the group. If Alex refuses to speak at all in kindergarten, investigation of the reasons for his failure to talk are certainly in order. If Angela speaks so softly that she cannot be heard by others in her group, her speech problem should be given consideration, whatever its cause. If Pat, at nine, is still unable to produce and use correctly such easy sounds as the "k" sound in "bake" or the "p" sound in "apple," his speech is surely deviant and will attract undue attention. If Terry asks "what?" constantly, does not respond to the speaking of his name when he cannot see the speaker, and seems to be straining to follow the discussion, his hearing should be checked to determine whether or not lack of auditory acuity is the cause of his difficulty. If Donnie stutters in discussion, in oral reading, or in playground conversation, he is in need of remedial help.

Finding Ways to Help

The teacher may evaluate the speech of each child in her group by noting whether the child on the playground is speaking differently from his classmates and by listening to his speech during discussion, storytelling, and other group activities. She may make a more detailed analysis of the speech of an individual child as she listens to his reading.

Differentiating between Speech Problems and Retarded Development

In addition, the teacher may need to discriminate between those children who have specific speech problems and those who are retarded in the acquisition of general speech skills. A child whose speech is so meager that he cannot tell others what he wants or what he thinks may use correctly the few words he does use but may have speech that is so limited that it seems to be defective. Other children are insecure in the classroom situation or may have lacked security at home and may not have developed adequate patterns of speech behavior. Still others will not talk, and the teacher has no basis on which to judge whether articulation and voice are within normal limits.

Emotional and intellectual factors may cause retardation in speech. The child who has been made afraid to talk by older children who tease him or by parents who ignore him, make him be quiet, or threaten him if he interrupts will see little need for and no pleasure in oral communication and may avoid it entirely. The dull child who is slow in acquiring language may continue for years to be inadequate in sentence structure, in vocabulary, or in pronunciation.

The evaluation of speech, the determination of normal limits, is difficult for the teacher who has not given specific thought to speech as an activity that is learned just as reading and writing are learned. Because most children have acquired some facility in speech before they enter school and because speech is so frequently taken for granted, the teacher may not make the same kind of analysis of it as she does of reading and writing. She may even fall into the common error of using speech as the chief indication of intelligence, judging Betty to be brighter than Bobby because Betty speaks so much more clearly.

In order to be more objective in deciding whether or not the speech of her pupils is adequate, the classroom teacher may devise her own system of testing, based on the suggestions in good books on speech. She may turn to the speech therapist, if one is available, or may obtain materials and information on speech tests from the department of speech in the nearest university. Some suggestions appear in the bibliography at the end of this chapter.

Recognizing Factors That Affect Proficiency in Speech

In making a check on the speech of her pupils, the teacher should listen carefully for several factors which affect proficiency. She should analyze such elements as voice, articulation, speed, rhythm, behavior during speech, expression of ideas, vocabulary, and response to the speech of others.[13]

Children's voices vary. In general, they may be high or low in pitch, but the voices of younger children are higher in pitch than the voices of adolescents or adults. Good vocal pitch is suitable to the age and sex of the child, does not differ noticeably from the pitch of the voices of other children of the same age, and varies with the meaning being expressed.

A child whose voice is adequate will have a vocal quality that is relatively pleasant, easy to listen to, not breathy nor husky nor harsh nor unduly nasalized. His voice will be loud enough to be heard in various situations, but will change in volume from one situation to another. It will not be consistently so soft that it cannot be heard, nor so loud and piercing that it overrides all the other voices in the room.

The child whose articulation is suited to his age level will not necessarily be free from sound substitutions, sound distortions, or sound omissions, particularly at the kindergarten or first-grade level. He should be able to use all of the vowel sounds correctly when he enters first grade and will probably be able to do so when he comes to kindergarten. If he mirrors the speech of his family or community in such pronunciations as "jist" and "git" for "just" and "get," if he reflects the speech

[13] National Association of Teachers of Speech, *Guides to Speech Training in the Elementary Grades* (Boston, Expression Company, 1943).

he has heard in such words as "kin" for "can" and "wush" for "wish," he cannot be considered defective in speech, since he is simply following the models he has had. If, however, he consistently substitutes one sound for another in a way that cannot be accounted for by his early experiences in hearing the speech of others, he may be considered to be defective in articulation.

The child who is still in the process of learning to use the difficult consonant sounds may be passing through a particular stage in speech development. He may not need special attention other than a good example in speech on the part of the teacher. The child who lisps or uses infantile sound-substitutions after he has reached the age of eight has defective articulation.

Hesitations and repetitions are characteristic of the speech of the young child. In attempting to master the complicated processes of speaking he often repeats sounds, words, or word-groups. He may pause to call to mind a word that has not yet become familiar. He may speak very rapidly when he is excited or is competing for attention. These "differences" are not really deviations unless they continue and unless they are accompanied by unhappy physical and emotional reactions such as tensions, inconsistent and constantly-changing facial expressions, mannerisms, and undue fidgetings. The teacher may observe that one child uses speech to control the situation and the children concerned in it, while another child makes little attempt to present his point of view or to express himself in the group. She needs to note the behavior patterns that accompany speaking.

Further, the elementary school teacher should judge the status of vocabulary development reached by her pupils. She can note their use of words in speech as well as their comprehension of the speech of others or their understanding of written forms. She may find some children in her group whose vocabularies grow from day to day as they find need for expressing ideas in more complex and in different ways. Others, she may observe, depend on a limited number of words and do not expand their speaking vocabularies to keep pace with their advances in learning and experience.

Finally, the teacher may discover that a child in her class fails to respond to the speech of others, not because he has no response to make, but because he has not heard the comment or questions directed to him. She will find evidences of poor hearing in children who watch faces intently or do not respond unless they are watching the speaker. She will see further indications of hearing difficulties in children who retire from group discussion, who strain to follow classroom conversation, or who give up the struggle of trying to understand what they cannot hear. The teacher will attempt to distinguish between lack of attention and lack of hearing and will give special help to children with either of these problems.

Using Available Resources

When the teacher has completed her analysis of the speech habits of her class, she will probably find that about 8 or 10 per cent of the children would profit by special attention to speech, that about 5 per cent definitely need remedial assistance, and that most of the boys and girls would profit from some emphasis on improvements in skills of oral communication. In other words, some of the children will need speech correction or speech therapy, but all of them will profit by speech improvement.

Although responsibility for the improvement of speech rests primarily with the classroom teacher, many agencies should be enlisted for the aid of the child who has defects in speech or hearing. The recent increase in the number of speech and hearing therapists in public school systems is encouraging, but their services are, at present, restricted mostly to city schools. School psychologists and counselors may help the teacher with some types of speech problems; school nurses, physicians, and dentists can often provide corrective help; administrators are realizing more and more the need for special services to the speech handicapped.

However, in many schools in many towns and cities and in rural schools throughout the country, the classroom teacher must provide such speech training as is given to those children who have defective speech. In such cases, the teacher who has had no special training in the field of remedial speech is at a disadvantage, but can be of most help to the children by realizing her own limitations. She can encourage good speech, provide an example for the children to follow, demonstrate ways of producing speech sounds correctly, discuss characteristics of good voice with children in terms they can understand, and avoid creating problems in speech where none exist. She can promote interest in speech activities and seek help by consulting with specialists, by taking courses, and by careful reading. Since many classroom activities are, in reality, speech activities, she can find frequent opportunity to help children use consistently the new speech skills they learn.

Speech therapists recognize the importance of this "carry-over" when they seek help from the classroom teacher in their attempts to change the speech habits of the child who has defective speech. In the speech class all may go well, and the newly-taught sound may appear in drill, in conversation, and in reading. But the child often leaves his new skill behind him in the speech room unless he can see the relationship between the kind of speech that the therapist recommends to him and the kind of speech that he really needs for his own use. Children who talk better just to please the teacher will not retain their improvements long, no matter how dramatic the changes they make in special speech classes.

Speech correction is essential to any program of education that is to serve the vital needs of all children. Speech is not something "special" to be loosely attached to the "regular" school program; it belongs in the classroom throughout the day.[14] Every teacher should be aware of the difference it makes to a child to be handicapped by a speech disorder and do all she can to help overcome the difficulty.

SUMMARY

This discussion of speech activities and the place of speaking in the elementary school cannot be concluded without a reminder of the continuing use of speaking in the child's further classroom experiences. As he goes on to the more departmentalized work of the high school, and if he goes on to university or college study, he will find that he continues to talk with others about a multitude of topics and that he needs to speak well even outside the walls of the classroom. His business success, his community relationships, his influence on his own children, his recreational activities, his contribution to his times and his society may all be made more effective by the speaking he does. The continuing use of efficient speaking is a means for integrating the individual and the society in which he lives and learns.

BIBLIOGRAPHY

American Speech and Hearing Association, *Speech and Hearing Problems in the Secondary School, National Association of Secondary School Principals' Bulletin,* XXXIV (November, 1950), pp. 3–139.

ANDERSON, Virgil, *Improving the Child's Speech* (New York, Oxford University Press, 1953).

Association for Childhood Education International, *Learning to Speak Effectively* (Washington, D.C., Association for Childhood Education International, 1943).

———, *Storytelling* (Washington, D.C., Association for Childhood Education International, 1942).

BAKER, Harold V., *Children's Contributions to Elementary School General Discussion,* Child Development Monographs, No. 29 (New York, Columbia University, Teachers College Bureau of Publications, 1942).

[14] Wendell Johnson and others, *Speech Handicapped School Children* (New York, Harper and Brothers, 1948), p. 17.

BROWN, Corinne, *Creative Drama in the Lower School* (New York, Appleton-Century-Crofts, Inc., 1929).

BERGER, Isabel B., *Creative Play Acting* (New York, A. S. Barnes and Company, 1950).

CROSBY, Muriel, "Factors that Influence Language Growth: Community Influences," *Elementary English*, XXX, (January, 1953), pp. 34–41.

DAVIS, Irene Poole, "The Speech Aspects of Reading Readiness," *Newer Practices in Reading in the Elementary School*, Seventeenth Yearbook, Department of Elementary School Principals (Washington, D.C., National Education Association, 1938), pp. 282–88.

DAWSON, Mildred A., *Teaching Language in the Grades* (Yonkers, World Book Company, 1951).

ECKELMANN, Dorothy, "The Speech Correctionist Talks with the Classroom Teacher," *Elementary English Review*, XXII, (May, 1945), pp. 157–62.

JOHNSON, Wendell, and others, *Speech Handicapped School Children* (New York, Harper and Brothers, 1948).

———, ed., *Speech Problems of Children* (New York, Grune and Stratton, 1950).

LEASE, Ruth G., and SIKES, Geraldine B., *Creative Dramatics in Home, School, and Community* (New York, Harper and Brothers, 1952).

McCARTHY, Dorothea, "Factors that Influence Language Growth: Home Influences," *Elementary English* XXIX, (November, 1952), pp. 421–28.

National Association of Secondary School Principals, *Speech Education for All American Youth*, XXXII, (January, 1948), pp. 5–222.

National Association of Teachers of Speech, *Guides to Speech Training in the Elementary Grades* (Boston, Expression Company, 1943).

National Council of Teachers of English, Commission on the English Curriculum, *The English Language Arts*, N.C.T.E. Curriculum Series, Vol. I, (New York, Appleton-Century-Crofts, Inc., 1952).

National Council of Teachers of English, *An Experience Curriculum in English*, English Monograph No. 4 of the National Council of Teachers of English (New York. Appleton-Century-Crofts, Inc., 1935).

National Education Association, Department of Elementary Principals, *Newest Practices in Reading in the Elementary School*, National Elementary Principal, XVII (July, 1938), pp. 229–704.

National Society for the Study of Education, *Teaching Language in the Elementary School*, Forty-third Yearbook, Part II (Chicago, Department of Education, University of Chicago, 1944).

POOLEY, Robert C., *Teaching English Usage*, English Monograph No. 16 of the National Council of Teachers of English (New York, Appleton-Century-Crofts, Inc., 1946).

———, "The Language Arts Survey in the Wisconsin Elementary

Schools," *Elementary English Review*, XXIII, (January, 1946), pp. 8–14.

RASMUSSEN, Carrie, *Choral Speaking for Speech Improvement*, (Boston, Expression Company, 1939).

———, *Speech Methods in the Elementary School* (New York, The Ronald Press, 1949).

SAWYER, Ruth, *The Way of the Storyteller* (New York, Viking Press, Inc., 1942).

SCOTT, Louise Binder, and THOMPSON, J. J., *Talking Time* (St. Louis, Webster Publishing Company, 1951).

STRICKLAND, Ruth G., "Factors that Influence Language Growth: School Influences," *Elementary English*, XXIX, (December, 1952), pp. 474–81.

———, *The Language Arts in the Elementary School* (Boston, D.C. Heath & Company, 1951).

TIDYMAN, Willard F., and BUTTERFIELD, Marguerite, *Teaching the Language Arts* (New York, McGraw-Hill Book Company, Inc., 1951).

VAN RIPER, Charles, *Helping Children Talk Better* (Chicago, Science Research Associates, 1951).

———, *Speech Correction: Principles and Methods* (New York, Prentice-Hall, Inc., 1947).

———, *Teaching Your Child to Talk* (New York, Harper and Brothers, 1950).

———, *Stuttering* (Chicago, National Society for Crippled Children and Adults, Inc., 1948).

WARD, Winifred, *Playmaking with Children* (New York, Appleton-Century-Crofts, Inc., 1947).

WATTS, A. F., *The Language and Mental Development of Children* (Boston, D.C. Heath & Company, 1947).

WELLS, Charlotte G., "Factors that Influence Language Growth: The Child's Equipment for Language Growth," *Elementary English*, XXIX, (October, 1952), pp. 348–55.

———, "Speech in the Full School Program," *Elementary English*, XXVIII, (April, 1951), pp. 201–04.

WERNER, Lorna Shogren, *Speech in the Elementary School* (Evanston, Illinois, Row, Peterson & Company, 1947).

WEST, Robert, KENNEDY, Lou, and CARR, Anna, *The Rehabilitation of Speech* (New York, Harper and Brothers, 1947).

CHAPTER 6

Reading

TODAY'S WORLD A READING WORLD

TODAY'S child is born into a reading world. In this country, with universal education well established as a goal, tomorrow's citizen who cannot read will be out of step with his fellow men. Reading is needed at every turn in daily living—at home, at school, in shop and factory, at the polls. In a complex modern society, reading is even more important than formerly as a means of emotional release, as a way of extending experiences, and as a source of needed information.

One person in three in the United States, including men, women, and children, subscribes to a daily or a Sunday paper. Sixteen magazines have a circulation of above three million, and thirty-five more top the million mark. The Book of the Month Club in 1926 had fewer than five thousand members; today, with more than fifty competing book clubs, it has over half a million subscribers, and that in a period when the population has increased only 40 per cent.

Information in the form of handbills, folders, and pamphlets presses upon both children and adults for attention—where to go for a vacation, what bicycle to ride, what to do to be beautiful, what candidates or causes to sponsor, what books or television sets to buy.

Increased Accessibility of Children's Books

In 1920, not one publisher in the United States had a children's book editor. Today sixty such editors devote full time

Elmer Helps Children Learn to Read.

Elmer

Miss Carleton gave
Elmer to us. He is a
desert tortoise. He is
old, maybe 50 years
old.

Elmer
George

That's My Story—What's Yours?

You Write—You Read—You Look.

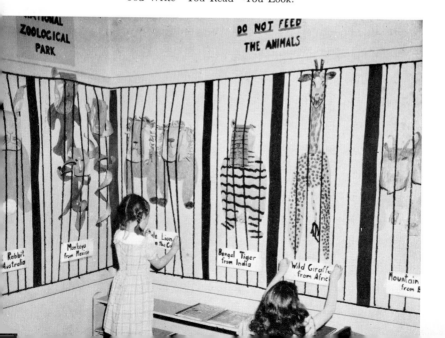

In a Group or by Yourself, You Read.

Research Skills Help Find the Answers.

I Found It Right on This Page.

to studying the market, discovering needs, stimulating writers, and editing books for children. There are several book clubs for boys and girls. Public libraries report increased offerings and a growing number of children served in spite of television and radio. Extension of such services through rural bookmobiles and airplanes makes books available to children in isolated communities. Robin, for example, reads *Patrick and the Golden Slippers* in his isolated lighthouse home, from the packet of books dropped by plane service from the mainland library.

An annual Children's Book Week each November, sponsored by the Children's Book Council,[1] dramatizes the worth and availability of books for children. The *New York Herald Tribune* Spring Festival makes awards annually for the best books of the spring for young people, and the Children's Division of the American Library Association, through the generosity of Frederick Melcher, presents the Newbery and Caldecott medals each spring for the best children's books of the year.

Book review weeklies like the *New York Times Book Review*, *The New York Herald Tribune—Books*, and the *Saturday Review* give space to books for children; and *The Library Journal, The English Journal, Elementary English*, and *Childhood Education* have book review sections in each month's issue. In addition, *The Horn Book* devotes itself entirely to children's books and their authors.

The scouts offer merit badges for wide reading, and the Camp Fire Girls furnish reading lists with every project.

Periodicals for Children

At the same time, magazines for children grow annually in circulation. Some furnish useful information and direction of pastimes. Some offer stories of considerable merit. Others keep children alert to current happenings or guide their reading and activities as scouts or members of Camp Fire. Some

[1] Children's Book Council (New York 19, 62 West 45th Street).

are religious in emphasis. Others promote interest and guide boys and girls in such hobbies as making airplanes, collecting stamps, playing the piano, or working in various crafts.

More than three hundred different comic books, some good, some very bad, sell 86 million copies monthly. Obstreperous humor, childish capers, family discords, and animal antics vie for attention with hair-raising jungle adventures, breathtaking mystery and detective stories, aviation thrillers, and the fantastic activities of "space men." All claim moral values and point to the triumph of right, but at the same time many of them suggest the impotence of the police and the need for taking justice into one's own hands. Meanwhile the hero frequently commits more crimes in the name of righteousness than the villain commits in the cause of evil.

Other comics have attempted to present real heroes, historical events, scientific feats, and the everyday doings of children and adolescents. Still others make comic books out of the classics. The worth of such comics varies with the expertness of the art work and the extent to which mere incident can depict the true values of the story. It is conceivable that the *Life of Buffalo Bill* or even *Robinson Crusoe* could be done in comic strip technique; it is inconceivable that *Alice in Wonderland* could be adequately presented in such fashion.

Need for Standards of Choice

Such quantities and varieties of materials as are available to children today make wise choices in reading imperative. This places upon the school the necessity of developing standards of selection and habits of choice commensurate with growing maturity in reading.

The Little Golden Books and others in twenty-five- and thirty-five-cent editions make it possible for boys and girls to have many more books in their homes. Again, such titles vary in value from excellent to poor, even within each series, so that standards of selection need to be established both among children themselves and through the Parent-Teacher Associations.

The impact of published material makes new demands for reading skill upon both children and adults. Merely finding time to read in the face of conflicting interests is a tremendous problem and is one of the reasons why speed in reading is recognized as important. Increasing use of high-pressure salesmanship in printed materials calls for readers equipped to pass judgment on the authenticity of statements and to recognize the emotional appeal of words. Changing demands and varying materials require skills adjusted to both. Truly, the times set a challenge before teachers of reading.

READING IN THE CHILD'S DAILY LIVING

Teachers, librarians, writers, and book publishers unite in the single aim of bringing children and books together. At no time in history has there been more genuine interest in this problem.

Enjoying Reading

All the ferment in the world of children's reading grows from a conviction that books can enrich the lives of boys and girls. First of all, books bring enjoyment—*King of the Wind* by Marguerite Henry, for the boy who is a lover of horses, *Oley, The Sea Monster*, for those who frequent the natural history museum; *Blueberries for Sal* for the little girl who loves the out-of-doors; *The Three Ring Circus* for the would-be bareback rider. Poems like "The Ballad of John Silver" or "The Pirate Don Durk of Dowdee" delight boys who have reached the pirate stage, and the escapades of the irrepressible *Homer Price* with the doughnut machine are deservedly popular throughout the intermediate grades.

Reading for Information

Books can give boys and girls the information they need to satisfy their curiosity concerning the world about them; Hammond's *Nature Atlas* delights the six-year-old with its hundreds of colored pictures of animals, flowers, birds, and insects. It also provides his high school sister with scientific and readable information for her science class or nature club. The whole range of picture-story geographies, the fascinating *Paddle-to-the-Sea,* a fictionized geography of the Great Lakes, or simple history books like Frances Cavanah's *Our Country's Story* are illustrative of what is available for children. Even the smallest ones can enjoy *The Little Fire Engine, Up Above and Down Below, The Big Snow,* or *The Little House,* all of which interpret their world in terms both clear and interesting to them. Older children learn also that books contain instructions for making things and doing things—for example, Edith Ackley's *Dolls to Make for Fun or Profit,* or Mary Elting's *First Book of Baseball.*

Expanding Horizons in Time and Place

Books can expand the child's horizons in time and space. *Little Pear,* the Chinese boy, becomes a next-door neighbor through reading. Ursli's bell in Switzerland is a symbol of spring and childish aspiration everywhere. Kate is a very human iconoclast in *The Good Master,* and Picken's adventures in Africa or Riki Tiki Tavi's in India bring the jungle nearer the children's own door.

For intermediate-grade pupils, Robin in *The Door in the Wall* by Marguerite de Angeli is as close in his thirteenth-century castle as the infantile paralysis victim down the block, and the spirit of the explorers, Lewis and Clark, still flouts every obstacle through James Daugherty's virile story, *Of Courage Undaunted.*

Understanding Oneself and Others

Books can help boys and girls understand themselves and others. Whether it be *Peter Rabbit* or *Spotty* for the little folks, *Necessary Nellie* or *Lentil* for the middle grades, or *Caddie Woodlawn* or *The Bounces of Cynthiann'* for the older readers, children learn to probe motives and discover answers to their own problems through reading.

Escaping Reality through Imagination

Books of fantasy and invention delight children because of their own active imaginations and offer temporary release from the problems and tensions of real life. *Millions of Cats, East O' the Sun and West O' the Moon, The Five Hundred Hats of Bartholomew Cubbins, Alice in Wonderland,* or *My Father's Dragon* delight the hearts and challenge the minds of children everywhere.

Reliving the Spiritual Experience of the Human Race

Finally, through books children relive the spiritual experience of the human race. They follow Ulysses on his wanderings; they are sold into Egypt with Joseph; they stand with Martin Luther at the Diet of Worms; they follow Joan of Arc to Rheims; they watch breathlessly as Haym Salomon saves the Republic; they listen to Lincoln at Gettysburg; they go with Livingstone and Schweitzer to Africa; they sense the plight of the Negro in *Melindy's Medal* and of the itinerant worker in *Children of the Harvest.* They enter into the delights of music with the boy, Mozart; they create with Irby the original tune for his *One String Fiddle.* They share in the amazing world of the *Goldsmith of Florence;* they watch Gutzon Borglum carving heroic faces out of the solid granite of Mount Rushmore in the Black Hills.

Small wonder that parents and teachers alike are concerned that every child shall develop reading skill sufficient to open these riches to him.

Using Reading in School

Much of the child's educational program tends to revolve about reading. It is true that the changing and expanding curriculum makes learning less completely dependent upon books; nevertheless, the child uses reading increasingly in each succeeding year of his school life. New ways of learning, such as excursions, audio-and-visual aids, group discussion, art and construction activities, expression in dance and music —all these tend to stimulate new uses for and new interests in reading. Likewise, radio and television in the home, when used to best advantage, bring the world much closer to children and offer new incentives to reading.

Said ten-year-old Richard, "The more things I learn, the more books there are to read about them. The more books I read, the more things I find out there are to learn." His world was expanding rapidly, and he was discovering for himself the relation of reading to that expansion.

School editions and school subscription rates bring weekly and monthly news periodicals and science publications into children's hands. These tend now to be graded to several reading levels. A few magazines for children of elementary age can be found in classrooms along with those adult periodicals which appeal to children because of their content and illustrations. Many intermediate and upper-grade classrooms use the local daily or weekly newspaper, which frequently pupils bring from home. In certain cities local editors have arranged at times to supply enough papers daily for class use.

READINESS FOR READING RELATED TO CHILD DEVELOPMENT

When the child goes to school at the legal entrance age of five-and-a-half to six, he may be ready to begin learning to read or he may not. Parents commonly regard entrance to school as synonymous with learning to read and may suffer some anxiety if the reading program is delayed. Part of the school's task is to help parents realize that reading is most happily and successfully accomplished when the child is ready for it.

Age and Maturity

Many factors enter into the child's readiness for reading, or the lack of it. His age and his physical maturity are important. Eye development in some six-year-olds may be insufficient for reading from books. Hildreth [2] quotes Lukiesh and Moss as saying that the visual task of the six-year-old in learning to read is a severe one. The relation between mental age and ability to read has long been a subject of research. Authorities are not inclined at present to say specifically what mental age is necessary, but Anderson and Dearborn [3] on the basis of many studies believe that a "distinct relationship does exist between reading achievement and mental status." Primary teachers generally are now recognizing that numbers of first-grade children lack the mental maturity for reading. Individual or group tests of intelligence, observation of children's adequacy in language and of their performance of simple everyday tasks furnish the evidence. Many school systems have had the courage to delay reading for some children, and to adapt reading activities to the mental maturity of all of them.

Family Relationships

Emotional readiness, which is conditioned by all the child's previous relationships in his family, is perhaps of first importance. Some children before coming to school have been greatly deprived in home relationships, in group contacts, in normal experience. They may, therefore, have emotional

[2] Gertrude Hildreth, *Learning the Three R's* (Minneapolis, Educational Publishers, 1947), p. 182.

Matthew Luckiesh and Frank K. Moss, *Reading as a Visual Task* (New York, D. Van Nostrand Company, Inc., 1942).

[3] Irving H. Anderson and Walter F. Dearborn, *The Psychology of Teaching Reading* (New York, The Ronald Press, 1952), pp. 79–80.

blockings which prevent their entering happily into the life of the school. Actually they may be under-developed because of a lack of fostering love and care. The child who is ready to leave his mother and live and work with a group of children in school is one who has been happy and secure in his home. Jamie, an only child, had been kept a baby in his family. Lela had been frustrated by jealous older brothers and sisters in her efforts to keep up with them. Neither child was ready at six for school experience. If a child has not been permitted and encouraged to do things at home, he may have a very poor opinion of his own ability and thus feel unable to keep up with other children.

Life Experience

Many children come to school unready for reading because of their lack of background in experience. Home and community have offered little for their mental and social growth. Their vocabularies are very meager and their ideas limited. Much stands in the way of such children's having a joyful and successful experience with books.

Children reared in a city slum may know nothing of domestic animals and their ways, of the growth of plants, or of nature's changes season by season. They may even know little of games or pets. On the other hand, children of a backward rural community, though thoroughly familiar with animals and nature, may lack social experience and contact with many material things. In some instances both groups of children may have very meager concepts of home and community life as these are portrayed in modern books for beginning reading.

Rigid ideas prevailing in some families because of religious beliefs, social customs, or family peculiarities may so hedge the child about that his background and imagination are restricted. Without imagination, capacity for sharing the experience of others is sadly limited.

The home which really fosters learning furnishes its children a variety of contacts with ideas and people, establishes real values, inspires its members with enthusiasm for living, and provides them with emotional security.

Attitudes toward Reading

When the child comes to school, he is likely to look forward happily to reading if parents have read to him, or if he has had a real share in a family circle where all are enjoying books. But if he has been ignored by parents and older brothers and sisters who have been absorbed in their own reading, or has been forced to occupy himself with books when he wanted to be playing actively with other children, he may have learned to dislike reading.

There are a few children who have been read to so much at home that they find the process of learning to read tedious and the simple materials lacking in interest. On the other hand, vast numbers of children have been denied the joy of home experiences with books. Those a bit older, because they have had little to read except exciting comics, may find school materials devoid of appeal. Tastes which determine choices of reading materials and understanding which governs the depth and richness of the reading experience are often the products of family life.

The program in reading, therefore, must be adjusted to the background and the capacities of individual pupils. For many immature or underprivileged children, reading from books must be delayed until a background of experience can be developed and until they achieve physical, social, and mental maturity sufficient for approaching the tasks of reading. In some cases, a prereading program is planned to meet their needs, one which follows that offered by the kindergarten.

THE SCHOOL'S PART IN READINESS
FOR READING

The length and the nature of the prereading program ideally are determined by the needs of the group of children involved. In any case, the kindergarten and the first-grade year have reading readiness as a goal of their activities.

The Kindergarten Program

In a good kindergarten the experiences are carefully selected to contribute to the general development of the five-year-old. He learns to live with a group of children of his own age. He learns to play, to work, to share, to adapt, in a situation of which he is not the center, as he probably was in the home. He learns new rhythms and games, and how to enjoy these in a larger group than he has experienced before. He observes growing plants, fish, turtles, and polliwogs. His interest in making and doing is greatly heightened by the presence of other children. He draws and paints, using these activities not only as means of self-expression but also as communication. He uses picture books, listens to stories, and learns songs and verses by sharing them or saying them with others. All this has direct bearing upon his readiness for learning; it contributes to his language growth and thus eventually to reading.

The kindergarten room often makes some use of printed symbols which the child gradually learns to observe in situations significant to him. The teacher shows the story book as she reads it, and if his home experience with books has been limited, he now begins to understand that printed words and lines convey meaning. The notes he carries between home and school he recognizes as messages in writing. He makes some use of symbols himself, recognizing his own name on his blanket used for resting, or on the list of helpers posted on the board. But fundamentally the kindergarten program is one of general development and is not designed to prepare for reading. Neither beginning reading activities nor specific word teaching belongs in the kindergarten setting.

The Prereading Program

The prereading program may follow kindergarten or it may be the first school experience for the six-year-old. It may be a program of a few weeks' duration giving first-grade children time to become acquainted with school, to learn to live together, to sing songs and play games with other youngsters, to share toys, picture books, and stories, before being introduced to reading in charts and books. It may be a year-long program, designed to give fundamental development through work with health, habit training, socialization, experiences, and language.

While time is allowed for the immature child's general development in the readiness program, the teacher is seeking to provide him with many skills that will have specific relation to his learning to read at a later date. Such a child is often severely retarded in language. His vocabulary may be very limited; his speech, infantile or unintelligible. Stories and nursery rhymes, songs and chanting games, all help language growth. Trips to the grocery store, the post office, or the fire station give meaning to words. Actual handling of objects and talking about them develop vocabulary if the words are attached to the objects and used whenever opportunity arises.

Children in this group who have not attended nursery school or kindergarten may have to learn to adapt to school. They may need much time to grow into the habits of attention, of listening, of actually "taking in" that school requires. They must learn to live together. Children who can only snatch and fight, or retreat and cry, must learn to work and play with other children. Intellectual growth is challenged also by group living. The use of materials, such as clay, wood, paints, games, and musical instruments, stimulates the development of unawakened powers.

Many of the prereading activities bear direct relationship to reading. In one classroom children in a play corner were heard naming the articles as they stocked the kitchen cabinet, arguing about whether one should buy oranges or candy at the grocery counter, acting the parts of mother, nurse, doctor, and patient at the clinic. Movies, film strips, and slides, used to supplement direct experiences, often lead to questions and discussion. Pictures and picture books stimulate conversation. The children are exposed to printed symbols in any number of informal ways, but at this stage actual learning of the symbols is not required of them. Prereading books, which are introduced by the teacher late in the readiness program, have a number of features which the children will find later in print. For instance, a series of pictures may be grouped into a sequence, proceeding from left to right and then returning to left on the lower line. In following the order of the pictures, the children are learning to relate ideas in sequence, and also to follow the direction of printed lines in books or charts. The actual holding and handling of books, and the turning of pages, must be learned by some children in this period.

Experience with books is an important part of the prereading program. Every child should have the opportunity to see and to examine fine picture books and to hear stories read and told in his home. However, many children have not had these experiences in sufficient measure. By wise use of books and stories at this point the teacher greatly enriches their imaginations, helps them develop concepts, and influences their attitudes toward reading.

FIRST STEPS IN READING

After home and kindergarten and sometimes a prereading program have promoted general growth, the process of learning to read begins. Whether all children should read during the first-grade year is now questioned in many school systems. Boney [4] reports the happy results of a program in which children are introduced to reading informally without pressure on the slower ones to respond. Some may not begin to read until the second or third year. The experience of teachers and administrators in general is that children vary widely in their readiness for reading and in the rate at which they progress. These differences formerly resulted in a high percentage of nonpromotions in first grade. Today the more common practice is to move the children along regularly and to provide them in each grade with suitable materials and reading activities.

The Use of Experience Charts

First-grade teachers generally agree that the group life and the common experiences of the classroom form the basis of the child's learning. For this reason experience charts are widely used for the first steps in reading. One group of beginners, playing in the park, came forth with spontaneous expressions which the teacher guided into a "story."

Leaves in the Park
Lots of leaves are on the ground.
Yellow leaves! Red leaves!
We pile the leaves up.
We kick the leaves down.
We get hot! We have fun!

The children were not expected to recognize the words in this "story" when the teacher wrote it on the board later, but they repeated the lines with her, and an individual child recognizing his contribution would announce proudly, "That's my part!"

The next step, after enjoying many such stories produced both by the group and by individuals, was to make one the children could read for themselves. "Let's make a story about our dolly," was the starting point. The teacher took from their

[4] Dewitt Boney, *Children Learn to Read* (Champaign, Illinois, National Council of Teachers of English, 1949).

offerings the thoughts essential for a sequence, guiding the sentence form to bring about desirable repetition.

Dolly's Bed

Dolly has a bed.
Dolly has a blanket.
Dolly has a sheet.
Dolly has a pillow.
Sleep, Dolly, sleep.

Chart reading offers practice in necessary skills such as recognition of the left-to-right direction of the line, the return sweep of the eye, the grasping of the thought in terms of a whole line. The chart also makes less demand upon the eyes of little children, as it is written or printed in large characters, and the reader may look at it from some distance. Some matching of lines, words, and phrases leads to sight recognition of a few words with high interest value and marked configuration. The teacher knows that many of the words used frequently in the charts may reappear in the pages of the preprimers the children read.

The Beginnings of Word Recognition

Teachers and parents recognize that the child learns his first words simply by being told what they are. The process by which he keeps in mind the visual image, the pronunciation, and the meaning, is not altogether clear, but he uses such sight words exclusively in the early stages of reading. In chart stories such as *Dolly's Bed* alert children promptly recognize the similarity of the first four lines. They also realize that the fifth line is different.

Several readings by the group of this, their own story, fix in auditory as well as visual memory the place of *bed, blanket, sheet,* and *pillow* at the end of each line and the position of the concluding lullaby. So by a combination of matching and differentiating visual images and by memorizing the position of certain words, they make this brief story their own. An alert six-year-old may single out *pillow* and identify it by its tall middle section. Configuration, or shape and length of the word, is a natural cue for most beginners. Children in the first grade are happily unconscious that they are acquiring these techniques, but they are thrilled to be reading for themselves. Parents and others who call these processes of learning to read "memorizing and guessing" are partly right, but should recognize that they represent a natural way of dealing with printed symbols at first.

As the teacher develops the chart with the children, she works with only a few beginners at a time. Each child must be physically near her; he must have several opportunities for response in a brief period; he must be similar to his fellows in the group in readiness for chart reading. More effective learning will take place if several groups read for a few minutes each than if the teacher tries to hold the attention of a large group. The development and use of experience charts continue through the beginning reading period, serving both for language growth and for actual learning to read. Teachers use charts in all the primary grades,[5] and in many places continue to use them throughout the elementary school.

Initial Use of Preprimers and Primers

Gradually, children move from the reading of experience charts to the wealth of preprimers and primers now available for classroom use. Beginning with the pictures, they develop, through discussion of what the story is going to be about, the necessary vocabulary and concepts for reading it. At the same time, they gain a sense of sequence and orderly progression of events. In the selection of a variety of easy primers, the teacher takes into account similarity of vocabulary and content,[6] particularly for the children who seem to make progress slowly.

[5] Madison Public Schools, *The Use of Charts in the Primary Grades* (Madison, Wisconsin, Curriculum Division, The Public Schools, 1949).

[6] Josephine McLatchy, "List of Common Words for First Grade," *Educational Research Bulletin*, Ohio State University, Columbus, Ohio (September 12, 1951), pp. 151–59.

Use of Notices and Instructions

From the first, incidental uses of reading are part of the classroom environment. Chalk board and bulletin board notices, news bulletins, labels indicating the name or use of objects, simple directions, and many other informal uses of reading stimulate children to read for themselves with appropriate aid. Lists of helpers with duties specified, the outline of plans for a terrarium, a recipe for the Hallowe'en cookies to be made later in the day, the diary record of germinating seeds, an item of school or community interest—any or all of these may be in evidence in a primary classroom. Through the daily challenge of such materials children learn from the beginning that reading is part of everything they do.

Such improvised material lends itself to many uses. The teacher's message, written on the board, often makes use of cues calling for children's reactions. The question or direction with which it ends stimulates discussion:

> Tomorrow is a holiday.
> We will not come to school.
> What will you do at home?

Another type of message may call for action instead of talk:

> Boots! Boots!
>
> Did you wear boots?
> Sometimes boots get lost.
> Look in the basket.
> Find a clothes pin.
> Fasten your boots together.

Children who have been helped to read as far as "Find a clothes pin," are almost certain to supply the meaning of the last line. Thus context clues are developed early in the child's experience in reading.

David H. Russell and Gretchen Wulfing, "Supplementary Materials in the First-Grade Reading Program," *Elementary English,* XXVIII (October, 1951), pp. 347–49.

Beginnings of Word Analysis

Phonic analysis, at one time treated as a basic "method" of teaching reading, is only one of many means of word recognition. When children have learned to approach a printed page as something that has meaning for them, when they are using many sight words freely and making use of picture and context clues in their reading, the teacher helps them develop skill in analyzing words. For beginning readers this is usually no more than encouragement in identifying initial sounds. When they show evidence of comparing words for likeness, the teacher knows they are ready for this step. "That word *Susan* starts like my name," says Sammy. And Sammy's teacher knows that she must create opportunities for him to increase his awareness of likenesses.

Stimulation of Interest through Enjoyment of Many Books and Stories

Meanwhile, colorful picture books with some print and large illustrations are kept temptingly on the browsing table. Much reading aloud by the teacher moves the children to desire to read for themselves. Their own book reading usually begins with simple preprimers carefully selected, and is supplemented for group and for individual use by a wealth of other preprimers and primers and by picture and story books. The teacher encourages the children from the first to read on their own. She gives individuals a chance to read aloud to her and sometimes to a small group for the stimulus of sharing their stories. She helps all children to interpret signs and labels, encouraging those who try to read announcements or news clippings. She notes those who pore over the picture dictionary, matching words in solitary delight, or share with a friend the fun of identifying new words. She approves when a child wishes to take a book home to read to his mother. At the same time, she works with the parents, urging them to tell their children words when necessary, not to spell or analyze them, and to make the home reading activities fun, not drill.

Much reading of stories by the teacher, and much opportunity to browse in picture books for themselves during children's early efforts at reading help to balance the learning-to-read activities. A birthday book for the birthday party (*Birthdays for Robin* or *Manuela's Birthday in Old Mexico*), a circus book for the coming of the circus (*The Circus Comes to Town*), *Katy and the Big Snow* for the arrival of a blizzard, *Journey Cake, Ho!* just for fun, and a poem for every day of the year ("Jack Frost," "Aeroplane," "The Little Turtle," "The Circus Parade") will develop that kind of appreciation and understanding for which reading skills exist. Children will seek to read these books for themselves at the earliest possible moment if experiences with them have been happy. Success in reading is useless unless with it goes the urge to read. Whether children spend excessive time poring over the comics or begin early to find for themselves the rich and pleasurable experiences in good books depends in large measure upon this part of the program.

THE PERIOD OF BEGINNING INDEPENDENCE IN READING

Some children in their first year of instruction show much initiative in reading, seek help from adults in acquiring vocabulary, and devise many ways of their own to get meaning from print. They are demonstrating beginning independence. However, for perhaps the majority of children this stage is attained in the second grade; for some, in the third.

Group Opportunities for Growth in Independent Reading

For most children such independence comes only after much group guidance by the teacher, in which sight vocabulary is extended, and some techniques of word recognition are developed. This stage of beginning to read on their own involves the ability to attack new materials somewhat independently. A paragraph, a page, or a whole story is made to yield its meaning. For many children these skills may be developing only as related to guided reading, while some are forging ahead much on their own.

A good classroom, at any grade level, offers a great variety of opportunities for using reading as a means to learning and enjoyment. Many picture books, story books, and simple informative materials on a variety of subjects are displayed in the library center. Such materials represent different levels of difficulty and a wide variety of interests and can be used consistently in the learning activities of the classroom. James Tippett's *Singing Farmer* may be read independently by many first-grade children when a farm visit is being planned. After a trip on the bus interest will be high in Phyllis McGinley's "B is for Bus" from *All Around the Town* or in Jerrold Beim's *Andy and the School Bus*. Gerald Craig's *Science All About Us* or Harriet Huntington's *Let's Go Outdoors* offer information about many aspects of nature that children will wish to share with one another.

Grouping within the class continues when children are given specific help with a basic reader or other book of which each has a copy. Emphasis is placed upon such elements of word recognition, phrasing, or selection of ideas for a purpose as are pertinent to the children's level of maturity. Oral reading, paragraph by paragraph, around the class or the group, is avoided by the teacher who knows many techniques for stimulating children's responses.

Some teachers make use here of phonic and structural analysis: identifying initial consonants, noting consonant blends, blending consonants and consonant combinations with recognized root or stem words, sensing the uses of beginnings and endings, determining vowel sounds by their relation to the other parts of the word, and recognizing syllables.

It is possible to follow an almost endless series of steps [7] in examining the structure of words, such as identifying small words in large ones (when the pronunciation is identical), breaking down compound words to reveal their make-up, and comparing words for their different types of endings. Children should be helped at each stage of their reading to use all of the means of word recognition they have learned. Many of the skills of word analysis, however, can be developed only with children who have some maturity in reading. They should be presented, therefore, at any grade level in the elementary school where pupils have need of them and are ready to use them in functional reading activities in the classroom.

Teachers observe that long before the advanced stages of word analysis are reached, many children have evolved their own systems of word recognition. They also discover that not all children who are slow in developing independence in reading profit by help in analyzing words. Many teachers, instead of using detailed steps of phonic and structural analysis, find it best to provide a rich and varied program of reading with as much guidance as possible for both group and individual activities. Then they supply specific help in word recognition to those children who seem to need it and give aid to the whole group when new material presents problems of vocabulary difficulty. In any case the primary teacher of today helps pupils to use all the means of word recognition rather than to depend upon phonic and structural analysis alone.[8]

By the third grade individual tastes are emerging and pupils can be guided to cowboy books, doll stories, train books, or circus tales as their interests dictate. They may then share these with each other in movies, puppet shows,

---

[7] William S. Gray and Dorothy S. Horton, *On Their Own in Reading; How to Give Children Independence in Attacking New Words* (New York, Scott, Foresman and Company, 1948).

[8] Alvina T. Burrows, *What About Phonics?* (Washington, D.C., Association for Childhood Education International, 1951).

dramatizations, or other means of promoting creative return and the sharing of enthusiasms.

Individualized Guidance in Reading

Many adults remember learning to read through individual help at home or school. Such learning was usually accompanied by a strong personal drive to learn to read. Mass procedures, developed by schools to teach thirty to fifty beginners, were always felt by thoughtful teachers to be contrary to the nature of little children and were gradually abandoned. Group organization within the class is now the accepted pattern. Children read for a briefer time, under closer guidance, with other children of comparable ability and achievement, in books adapted to their rate of progress. This ability grouping is balanced by many teachers with interest grouping in which children have more choice in the material used, and in which often the group comes together around the present interest, not around the kind of help needed.

Some teachers have tried to abandon group organization entirely, usually where numbers are small. Others continue to use grouping and a common book to get children started, and then encourage individual reading and give a major part of the instructional time to it. Many teachers feel that the most important result of this grouping is the opportunity to know each child better and to help him individually. Recognizing the child's desire to read at his own rate and in the books he chooses as he moves along in the elementary school makes for self-motivation.

One first-grade teacher with forty underprivileged children in her room noticed that those who were able to read ahead of others were not happy. She encouraged them when, on their own initiative, they began to read in preprimers beyond those used in the group. As they worked, she told them the new words they needed. Soon they began to get together in groups of two or three, poring over new or review materials. She helped them as they attempted individually to master the labels, signs, and announcements in the room. She supplied them, too, with many picture books and easy story books. They learned to choose more difficult books which they could read and made progress in knowing when they were ready for them. Interest groups developed when the children found that some of them were enjoying the same books. Individual pupils made astonishing progress. All read more books and with greater interest than previous classes had. They read books from different series without difficulty, so that their teacher began to question the theory that a series of readers must be used because of a controlled vocabulary. She found that children read what was of interest to them and within their range of abilities. Those with special difficulties responded more satisfactorily to individual attention, for the special contact with the teacher seemed to meet a need which these children felt. Pleased with the outcome of individual reading, their teacher remarked, "These children not only *can* read; they *do* read." [9]

THE PERIOD OF RAPID GROWTH IN READING

When children have acquired considerable reading experience, a large store of recognized words, and some skill in attacking new materials, they are likely to do much reading on their own. The stage of rapid growth is marked by the use of many books, increased initiative in attempting new reading tasks, rapid gain in vocabulary based on much reading experience, and familiarity with many materials. At this stage children have increased control of the processes of word recognition, being able to grapple with more varied

[9] For additional accounts of efforts to individualize reading programs see: Ruth Cornelius, "Reading with Six-Year-Olds," *Childhood Education*, XXVI (December, 1949), pp. 162–63.

Melva Harris, "Beginning Reading without Readers," *Childhood Education*, XXVI (December, 1949), pp. 164–67.

forms of familiar words, blending initial consonants with familiar parts of old words (such as *rain* and *train*) and using more varied attacks in identifying new ones.

Many Easy Books Important

Some children may spend three or more years in reaching a stage in which they do extensive and independent reading, although many do so in their second school year. Certain pupils who achieve this independence in the intermediate grades tend to continue reading the story-type materials of the primary grades. Much satisfaction and much experience with easy reading materials may be essential to them. Library habits may be developed at this time with wide use of such easy books as *Ted and Nina Have a Happy Rainy Day* in the Ted and Nina series, *Judy's Farm Visit,* Clare Newberry's *Smudge,* Lois Lenski's *Let's Play House,* Charlotte Steiner's *Kiki Dances,* and Margaret Wise Brown's *Red Light, Green Light.* Some children are ready for Carolyn Haywood's much loved books about Betsy, Penny, or Eddie. Others will try *Mitty on Mr. Syrup's Farm* or such hilarious stories as *Rosie the Rhino* or *Curious George.* At this time also they delight in going back to the simple poetry of the kindergarten or first grade, now reading for themselves the poems they learned originally from the teacher's reciting of them. It is in this kind of reading also that children begin to grasp the distinction between fact and fancy as they contrast, for example, Gall and Crew's *All Round the Year,* with Helen Dean Fish's *When the Root Children Wake Up* or merely compare reality and creative imagination in Dr. Seuss's *And to Think That I Saw It on Mulberry Street.*

Boys and girls at this stage delight in the *Easy Book* shelves of the library, finding many informative books like *The Little Boy and His House* or *This is the Milk That Jack Drank,* which furnish information related to their class activities. In many of these books they are able to find the answers to their questions, and they enjoy sharing these findings with their classmates. The use of the table of contents is developed with some children as they search in available readers or library books for added material on topics of personal or class interest. Notices, directions, and bulletins, written or typed, challenge the children at this stage of progress. The presence of the simpler juvenile magazines on the library table also stimulates wider reading.

Further Help in Individual Reading

In this period also individualized guidance in reading seems to bring good results. In a situation very different from that previously described, a university laboratory school, the third-grade teacher used only interest groupings. Those children who wanted to work on stars, for instance, came together voluntarily. She provided reading material of first- through sixth-grade difficulty. If a child chose a book too hard for him, the teacher helped him until he acquired the information he sought for his group, or until he abandoned the book and chose a more suitable one. Some individuals made as much as three years' gain in reading in this situation. Several who had negative reactions to reading developed real interest. Competition over who was in the "first group" in ability disappeared so far as both parents and children were concerned.

Frances Maib [10] reports trying out individualized reading programs with children at the third-grade level and above, noting the following values: elimination of pressure and tension caused by the attempt of the child to meet group standards, maximum efficiency in the use of the child's time, good results for both the slow and the fast reader, acceleration of speed as a natural accompaniment of increased reading, greater interest as each reader pursued his own concerns in books, and larger amounts of reading done by everyone.

Increased opportunities for individualized reading instruc-

[10] Frances Maib, "Individualizing Reading," *Elementary English*, XXIX (February, 1952), pp. 84–98.

tion present themselves, of course, to intermediate- and upper-grade teachers. The classroom becomes a reading laboratory in which the purposes for reading are established by teachers and pupils together and relate to genuine interests. A great range and variety of books, pamphlets, periodicals, and other materials are provided. The teacher makes careful and practical studies of the abilities and attitudes of all the class members in reading, and time is really given to individual guidance. It is quite natural for the reader to wish to read at his own rate and in relation to his own interests. Moreover, many children need specific individual guidance, sometimes to acquire the most elementary skills, or again to select books to satisfy rapidly developing skills or to further strong personal interests. Emphasis on guiding the individual seems to grow naturally out of group organization within the class, especially when classes are not larger than twenty-five to thirty. Teachers with large classes have rarely undertaken to abandon grouping entirely but can provide at least some experiences on an individual basis.

THE BEGINNINGS OF MATURITY IN READING

The world opens up rather rapidly for children of nine, ten, eleven, and twelve years of age, as their powers, physical and mental, develop beyond those of the primary years. In the intermediate grades they find themselves in a new relationship to reading materials. Because of their increased skill in reading and their own rapidly expanding interests they seek information and new experiences in books. The tendency of their school program is to differentiate into subjects at this point and they have much more to read.

Development of Skills in Use

One glance at the daily routine of the average classroom shows how many and varied are the reading skills required. Pupils at this time begin the use of carefully organized textbooks in many fields. They must learn to use intelligently such typographical aids to meaning as centered topics in large print and subtopics which appear in side headings. They must discover the relation between main topics and supporting details. Their chief problem with factual material is to follow the order of thinking of the author—to outline mentally, and to summarize. The rudiments of this skill are being developed and used in the elementary grades. It is still being learned by students in junior college at more complex levels. Pupils must learn when to read rapidly, as when illustrative anecdotes help explain a generalization, and when to read slowly, weighing each statement with care. Such instruction may come at the point where the reading is first undertaken. It is usually most profitable when applied in the situation where it is needed. For instance, the skills required in reading in the social studies can most economically be developed with the social-studies material at the time of its use. Many occasions are found to use the index and the table of contents and to discover the nature and order of topics in each and its location in the textbook.

Reading around a topic demands selective reading in which the child ignores the organization of the writer's thinking and seeks the answer to specific questions at hand. He must select the pertinent information, reword it in language of his own unless he desires specifically to quote, relate it to his materials gathered from other sources, and organize it for his own thinking, for presentation to his group, or for such a purpose as making the furniture for the corner of a colonial kitchen which his class is reproducing. Using simple material, intermediate-grade teachers guide children in the process of finding the sentences or paragraphs related to their topic, and in the organization of these ideas into a related whole for whatever their current purpose is.

Use of reference books and children's encyclopedias begins for many pupils during these years. They should note how packed with information such content is because of limitation of space and understand what slow, careful reading it demands. Comparison of the presentation of such a character as Miles Standish in James Daugherty's *The Landing of the Pilgrims* with that in the encyclopedia will show pupils concretely what different methods of attack each requires. The reading of maps, charts, and diagrams also needs consideration in connection with reference or supplementary work.

Use of a children's dictionary begins in these years. Children should learn the value of the alphabet as a reference tool. During the intermediate years they can learn to use it in relation to all kinds of reference work, alphabetizing first by the initial letter and then by the second, third, or fourth as needed.

Use of the dictionary is no substitute for building a background of experience and wide reading as aids to the growth of vocabulary. However, it is an important instrument for the development of independence in reading. In the intermediate grades pupils have much use for it, learning how to find words in it, and how to select the meaning appropriate to the context. How to interpret diacritical markings, how to make practical use of syllabication in reading, writing, and spelling may be undertaken with some classes at the intermediate-grade level. Many schools give them additional stress in the seventh and eighth grades.

The development of vocabulary is a major task of the intermediate grades—differentiated vocabularies in various areas of learning and in terms of the interests and needs of individual pupils. The skills of word recognition begun in the primary grades may be developed to a higher level in the reading of these later years. Superior readers will acquire increasing skill through their independent reading. Pupils still reading at lower levels will need to improve their skills and gain increasing independence. Understanding of root or stem and of prefix and suffix are elements in word recognition appropriate at this time.

Intermediate-grade pupils contribute many of the boners

on which collectors pounce with delight. For example, "The farmers in that neighborhood had trouble with their wives," said one sixth-grade boy, mistaking "problems of husbandry" for "marital difficulties." Just as children have acquired a certain sense of security in their knowledge of words, these words appear in new context, leaving the reader helpless. Multiple meanings of commonly used words present special difficulties. Teachers should examine new materials for the kinds of difficulties in vocabulary which they may present to children and be prepared to help systematically with these problems.

Words take on meaning only in terms of the pupils' past experience or that present in the learning situation. If boys and girls are forced to read material completely divorced from their background of experience, mere verbalism results. For example, Jersild, asking pupils of different degrees of maturity to define the word *strike*, found little children saying, "To strike is to hit some one," and intermediate-grade pupils, "A strike is when you don't hit the ball in baseball." Later, youngsters added a new meaning to the word by saying, "A strike is when people walk up and down the street with boards on their backs." It was not until well up into adolesence that some pupils realized that the latter kind of strike represents a conflict between two basic elements in our economic order.[11]

Many boys and girls begin the serious reading of newspapers and magazines in the intermediate grades. At very different levels of skill individuals learn to select material for use in different projects. All those who are capable of reading a news story must learn how its structure controls the reading of it. The ablest may be led to see how an editorial differs from a news story in its demands upon the reader. During these years, also, pupils learn in an elementary way how to

[11] Arthur T. Jersild, *Child Psychology* (New York, Prentice-Hall, Inc., 1940).

evaluate sources of information and the authenticity of materials.

Different subjects of study now present different problems in reading. Arithmetic and science often require careful, detailed attention. Some materials in science afford special opportunity to distinguish between fact and fancy.

The reading of literature during the intermediate grades makes special demands upon children—following clues to predict outcomes in fiction, entering into the mood or music of a poem, enjoying humor, creating a mental picture of a scene described, or sensing a character through action and conversation. Oftentimes, pupils read fiction for its reflection of experience—their own and that of others—or to understand another time or place. Ability to generalize from concrete illustrations, to illustrate generalizations, or to read aloud a passage to prove a point grows from initial experience in the intermediate grades.

Establishment of Personal Reading Habits

Many boys and girls establish at this time habits of reading which last throughout life. At the age of nine, or thereabouts, boys begin to demand thrills and excitement, tales of heroism, real animal stories with a dash of adventure—*Silver Chief, Dog of the North, Misty of Chincoteague, Big Red,* or *Daniel Boone.* Girls turn to mystery, fairy tales, or simple stories of family life such as *The Moffats, Elijah the Fishbite, The Blue Fairy Book,* or *Floating Island.* Both boys and girls seek stories of other children like themselves—*Henry Huggins, Jane Hope, The Wonderful Year,* or *Tom Sawyer.* Substitutes for the comics, competitors for the *Bobbsey Twins,* the *Hardy Boys,* and *Nancy Drew, the Mystery Girl,* are especially needed if standards of selection are to be developed. These also are the years of the children's classics—*The Jungle Book, Alice in Wonderland, Wind in the Willows, The Arabian Nights.* Children capable of reading them should be encouraged in doing so before they outgrow the age of wonder and delight in magic. *Robin Hood* and *King Arthur* come into their own for the abler readers at this time, and fortunately girls like them as well as boys do.

The world of sport is opening up for boys. Simple stories like Marion Renick's *Nicky's Football Team* or informative books like Mary Elting's *The First Book of Baseball* fill a real need. Cowboys and Indians are especially thrilling, and many titles are available, ranging from *Peter's Pinto* to *Smoky, the Cowhorse,* or from *The Matchlock Gun* to Holling C. Holling's *Book of Indians.*

The pirate is equally a favorite—from *Pirates, Pirates, Pirates* to *Treasure Island.* Fortunately, much good poetry about pirates can be used to dispel the idea that poetry is for "sissies;" for example, "If I Were a One-legged Pirate" and others mentioned earlier.

Fiction abounds which will open up historical periods and geographical settings—*The Door in the Wall* or *Adam of the Road* for medieval England, *Children of the Covered Wagon* or *Hello the Boat!* for pioneer days in our own country, *Daughter of the Mountains* for India or *Call It Courage* for the South Seas. Each year brings more and more excellent and simple biographies of our country's heroes such as the Lincoln and Washington of the D'Aulaires, of Genevieve Foster, and of Clara Ingram Judson.

Individual interests and hobbies develop during these years. One boy pores over the *First Book of Stones;* another over *The Tale of the Promethea Moth.* One seeks to know more about television; another, about adventures in space. One girl becomes interested in China through *Sue-Mei's Golden Year;* another, in puppetry through Edith Ackley's *Marionettes, Easy to Make! Fun to Use!* another, in simple biographies of musicians or books explaining the instruments of the orchestra.

The program in reading in the intermediate grades faces the challenge of pursuing interests, broadening horizons, and developing habits of reading in relation to every activity of the school day. It also runs competition with the comics and the cheap juvenile series, which furnishes opportunity for the development of standards of selection on which later years may build.

Importance of Library Skills

It is obvious that such a program demands skills in the use of the library and the establishment of habits of using it which grow from happy contacts with a wealth of books. More elementary school libraries staffed by trained librarians are opened each succeeding year. The highly varying needs for reading of children in the intermediate grades demonstrate daily the importance of such service whether rendered through the local public library or through the school's own library.

THE PERIOD OF INCREASING CONTROL AND POWER IN READING

Obviously, the business of the seventh and eighth grades is to take pupils where they are and to guide them in refining their techniques and maturing their powers and interests in reading.

Different Levels of Achievement to Be Expected

Pupils will vary greatly in their achievement. Some boys and girls will be able to read many adult materials with independence and enjoyment. Ideally, such pupils will have built up a wealth of background in reading experience and a rich store of concepts. They will have a large sight vocabulary and the power and desire to attack new words effectively. They will have developed resources in special skills for coping with different kinds of materials. They will be able to use several sources of reference and to read whole books on a given topic, combining materials into a carefully organized whole. They will have clearly defined personal interests in reading and a well-developed habit of turning to books for pleasure and for information.

Other children, having also had appropriate instruction, will nevertheless be reading as low as the third- or fourth-grade level. For them continued help in acquiring the simpler skills and habits will be a necessity. Their reading materials should be selected carefully in relation to their skill as well as in terms of subject matter. Increased numbers of books with easy vocabulary and more mature interest level are coming from the publishers. Practically every upper-grade classroom needs supplies of these books, in single copies or in small sets. Many older children, constantly baffled by exposure to reading materials too difficult for them, fail to progress, and grow increasingly frustrated in learning. School dropouts may be part of the result.

Pupils, at the upper-grade level, with relatively limited reading skills, need much opportunity to learn in ways other than reading. Visual aids, excursions, discussion, and all kinds of work with their hands will enable them to acquire information, develop concepts, and build vocabulary. These skills relate, in turn, directly to their growth in reading.

Certain books of the Franklin P. Watts Company such as Elizabeth Kinsey's *Sea View Secret* and Allyn Allen's *Lone Star Tomboy* are useful here for their story interest and easy vocabulary. A number of easy books for older children are listed later in this chapter.

Necessity for Building on What Has Gone Before

Appropriate guidance of reading in relation to every subject of study should develop and refine the abilities already exercised in the intermediate grades. Increased use of both summary and selective reading may be expected, with developing power to order ideas and to set them down, when desirable, in outline form. Adult dictionaries and encyclopedias will be used by some pupils, together with government and agency bulletins or technical volumes in fields of special interest. All of the skills enumerated in the description of the intermediate-grade program are important for work in the seventh and eighth grades, as well as the development of critical reading and the use of more advanced study techniques with more highly organized materials.

Development of Critical Reading Desirable

In addition to increased power in study reading, seventh- and eighth-grade pupils should develop skill in the evaluation of what they read, in the detection of bias, of propaganda, or of illogical reasoning. In reading newspapers and magazines, they should learn to inquire, "Who said this? For what reason? On what authority?" The critical reader does not passively accept what he reads, nor thoughtlessly reject it. He examines the author's thought and, in a way, discusses it with him. Boys and girls should understand that freedom of speech and freedom of the press give equal rights to the straight and to the crooked thinker. This places a moral responsibility on the reader to react thoughtfully to what he reads. Even sentences permit of classification into (1) statements of fact, (2) judgments, and (3) sweeping generalizations tending toward rigid classifications introduced by *never, always, all,* or *none.*[12]

Evaluation of Personal Reading Now Important

The amount of reading done by individual boys and girls probably reaches its height in the seventh and eighth grades. In these years they should learn to evaluate their own reading habits. How much do they read? How broadly do they choose in terms of all that books have to offer them? How many differ-

[12] Lee Deighton, "The Survival of the English Teacher," ETC., X, No. 2 (Winter, 1953), pp. 97–106.

ent purposes does their reading serve? How mature are their choices—How true to life the revelations of human experience which their books present? How helpful are these selections in adding to their information on many topics? On one topic of very special concern? Older boys and girls should have cumulative reading cards showing their personal reading choices over a period of years, on which they may make such evaluations under the guidance of the teacher.

Individual interest may cause the older boy or girl to range freely among books for both children and adults. The reader may be developing a greater variety of purposes at the same time that their specificity increases. From an easy biography such as *Booker T. Washington, Ambitious Boy*, he may turn to materials on how-to-do things, such as *The Toymaker's Book;* thence to a story of spirited action, like the imaginative *Train that Never Came Back*, or the more factual *No Other White Man;* to a narrative poem which stirs him to deep feeling, perhaps *North Star Shining;* or to a book that answers his questions about a remote corner of the world, such as *Look Out for the Ostriches.*

In the development of his personal and special interests during early adolescence, the pupil finds a major source of growth in his reading. He may read about a distant land because a father, brother, or friend is stationed there. He may struggle with difficult directions in order to learn to construct a model airplane.

A boy of twelve who had never seen the ocean but had read everything he could find on deep-sea fishing, seized upon the adult books, *The Sea Around Us* by Rachel Carson and Ernest Hemingway's *The Old Man of the Sea* in turn, and later on Eugenie Clark's *Lady With a Spear.*

Recognition of the Place of Reading among Mass Modes of Communication

Reading shares with radio, television, and outdoor sports the time and interest of older boys and girls. Pupils are old enough now to compare and contrast the values of each, to see reading not as a competitor with but as a help to the other forms of communication, as well as having values peculiar to itself.

Appearance of New Problems in Reading Literature

New problems of reading literature may be met in the seventh and eighth grades. For instance, the paragraph in the sense of a structured presentation of an idea may not have occurred in books read at an earlier level. Context clues also assume more specific forms in more mature reading situations.[13] The power of comparisons to clarify and strengthen the presentation of ideas can be appreciated at this stage of development. So also can the emotional power of words— used sometimes for good and sometimes for ill—but always with striking effect.

All that has been learned about visualization in descriptive prose or poetry needs building upon in the upper years. In poetry, too, pupils meet up with inverted order and with the telling comparison, expressed or implied. Both comprehension and appreciation are involved in the development of skill in this kind of reading.

Young people become conscious of literary type as such in these upper grades. They begin to use the terms *biography,* *drama,* and *fiction,* and they need to understand the techniques involved in reading each as an artistic form and as a unit of thought or experience. They need also to discover the process of coming to know a character through what he says, through what others, including the author, say about him, and through what he does, especially in time of crisis.

Again, it must be emphasized that these are but the beginnings of skills to be amplified and made more precise throughout the secondary school. Some pupils will develop a fair degree of proficiency in them by the end of the eighth grade.

[13] Constance McCullough, "Learning to Use Context Clues," *Elementary English,* XX (April, 1943), pp. 140–43.

Others will do well if they achieve a good start on the skills introduced in the intermediate grades.

THE PLACE OF ORAL READING IN THE PROGRAM

In their first attempts at reading it is quite natural for children to respond to the printed words by saying them aloud. Without this spoken reaction, moreover, the teacher would not know whether the child interpreted the symbols correctly —nor would the child know.

Normally, however, the reader begins very early to learn to delay the oral response. He learns to look through the complete sentence or the thought unit of two or three sentences, to ascertain its meaning by identifying sight words, by assuming pronunciations and meanings for the words he does not know, or by asking the teacher for them. With a small group of children seated close to her, the teacher can guide this process successfully. While still in the early stages of reading instruction, the pupils learn to read silently a sentence, a brief thought unit, a paragraph, and finally a whole page.

The reading aloud that accompanies this silent reading is for purposes of sharing, checking comprehension, or proving a point. The teacher by her remarks offers leads to both thinking and emotional reactions. She may say, "How do you think Roland said that?" and a child squeaks out the sentence in a voice that he means to represent fear. Or she may say, "Which part shows that he was disappointed? Read it to us." She avoids set patterns for those leads, encouraging the spontaneous reactions of the children. "Listen to this," says Jerry. "Wasn't he a fool of a puppy!" and reads the part that tells how the puppy kept nosing the bumble bee. "My grandma has flowers like that in her garden and the birds pick at them all day long," says eight-year-old Elsie as she reads, "There were tall sunflowers beside the house, and the young robins ate the ripe seeds for food."

As the children learn to cope with longer units of material, less of the group time is taken for oral reproduction. Discussion, dramatic interpretation, and other types of responses become more important. But insofar as the situation really promotes genuine sharing of thought or emotion through oral interpretation of chosen passages, the foundations of real audience reading are being established.

Through all these types of oral responses, children are expressing appropriate reactions to the material. They are interpreting spontaneously and without self-consciousness the humor, the excitement, the suspense of the story. This emphasis is not upon, "How do we say it?" but upon "What does it mean?" or "How did he feel?" In the course of this kind of reading activity, children who need aid with enunciation and pronunciation may be quietly given the correct sound without interrupting the flow of words.

Reading Aloud to Share Pleasure in Story or Verse

The time comes, even in the first grade, when some child wishes to read a whole story aloud. For the primary child this very rarely means reading to an entire class. The small group with which he reads daily is his natural audience. Only gradually do certain pupils emerge who have the confidence, the power of interpretation, the quality of voice, which can interest a large group.

If a pupil is to read to a group, large or small, he must be ready to do so. To permit the child to read aloud in a halting, mechanical fashion may cause insecurity in the reader and invites inattention and negative response from the listeners. Material to be read aloud should be completely familiar to the reader and should be *new* to the listeners. The teacher's attitude of attention to the thought, rather than to the prowess of the reader, will help to avoid self-conscious display on the part of the individual children who are qualified to read aloud to their classmates.

When the group has enjoyed stories well read by one pupil,

other children will be stimulated to read aloud also. The teacher supplies a number of books with easy stories that have dramatic value and encourages the children to select short stories or the most interesting parts of long ones. She helps to plan for times during the day when stories can be shared and keeps the listening group small, as a rule. Sometimes she has the children who are reading and listening use the cloak-room or a hallway, if the class as a whole is engaged in con-struction or other noisy activities.

Listening to parents and teachers read aloud. Sharing through oral reading should include listening by the children to good stories and verse read to them by parents and teachers. Fortunate children gain their first attitudes toward literature through their parents reading aloud to them in the home. Evans says radio and television "cannot give rise to that feel-ing of family intimacy" which time spent in reading aloud brings about:

> The tension, the hurry, the fuss which characterize so much of life nowadays and lay such a heavy tax on the nerves of children may be at least partly offset by devoting a half-hour daily, preferably in the evening, to reading aloud the literature both old and new which can still thrill the hearts of boys and girls.[14]

All children should have teachers who read aloud to them much and often. Their reading appreciation is always two or more years ahead of their ability to read. Their own eager-ness to share the adventure, the humor, and the beauty of rhythm of verse and narrative often grows out of first sharing through common listening to the teacher's interpretation.

Dramatization and choric speaking. Informal dramatiza-tion and choric speaking, as already noted in Chapters 3, 4, and 5, are outgrowths of oral reading which delight chil-dren. A first-grade group acted out *Peter Rabbit* in pantomime while the child who begged for the privilege of presenting the "play" read the story aloud. Fifth-grade children, book in

---

[14] Clara Evans, "On Reading Aloud," *Elementary English*, XXVIII (Feb-ruary, 1951), pp. 82–85.

hand, read from *Sleeping Beauty* the speeches of the furious uninvited godmother, the distraught king and queen, the triumphant prince. As the lovely princess, reclining on two chairs, (the only prop thought necessary) could not read her part in this position, a member on the sidelines read it for her.

Many of the beloved stories of childhood lend themselves to oral reading by the group. Some of these are *Pelle's New Suit* with its repetitive dialogue; the nonsensical conversation of the Hare and the Hatter in the "Mad Hatter's Tea Party"; and, for the older and abler readers, the poetic, somewhat archaic language of *Robin Hood* and his outlaw band; or the magniloquent pronouncements of a thundering Zeus in any collection of myths and legends.

Choric speaking begins with the youngest ones when they spontaneously join in the tale of "Little Miss Muffet," "Chicken-Licken" or "A Visit from St. Nicholas," as told or read to them. They like to make the imitative sounds of "Koorookoo, Kookoorookoo" by Christina Rossetti and to chant the verse and beat out the rhythms of "Ding, Dong, Bell"; or they may prefer the eerie lines of "Overheard on a Salt Marsh" by Harold Monro. As they come to read verse for themselves, they can interpret "Hickory Dickory Dock," "Hot Cross Buns," or "Polly Put the Kettle On" according to the mood and tempo of the verse. Later they like Vachel Lindsay's "The Potatoes' Dance" with all its opportunities for change of pace, "Father William" by Lewis Carroll for its counterpoint as well as its nonsense, and the lovely simple prose of *In My Mother's House* by Ann Nolan Clark, which lends itself to group chanting.

For older children the ballads are a rich field of interest and expression. These require reading aloud or group speaking for any measure of interpretation. Modern ballads such as "Red Iron Ore" from Carl Sandburg's *The American Songbag* vie in interest for older boys with such long-time favorites as "John Gilpin's Ride."

Reading Aloud to Report Information

In a classroom which is organized around vital interests there is much information to be shared through reading. Careful guidance can make this a profitable and interesting part of the group activities. Routine reading of reports prepared from reference material or oral reading of the material itself may be very deadly. A contribution from the daily news may indicate a child's interest, but he may not be able to read it well. Recognition of the interest back of the child's contribution is important. The teacher, however, has him read the selection aloud to her first in order to discover whether he can hold the attention of the group before she permits him to read it to his classmates. The same values often may be served by helping him work out the meaning of the material and prepare to tell the important points to the group, particularly those matters that help to solve a problem on which the class is working.

One sixth-grade teacher helps the pupils recognize clearly the points in their study where more information is needed. She works with them on the most interesting and helpful ways of presenting such additional material. Often in her class a child, thumb in book, talks out parts of his contribution and reads brief parts aloud. In other cases, two or three children plan to present reports by reading aloud brief selections in sequence. "My part will explain how the coal was formed in the earth," says John, "and then Stewart will read about what made it hard."

In this class during one morning's planning period a girl read the directions her grandmother had written out for making soap; a boy read the reply received to his letter asking what material the visual aids center could furnish to their colonial room exhibit; a third child read a description of a loom which he had copied from the tag in the museum; still another contributed a news clipping about a pioneer family in the community.

ATTENTION TO THE DIFFERING NEEDS
OF CHILDREN

The range of children's interests and abilities is nowhere more obvious than in their reading. Clear recognition of these differences and specific ways of meeting them are essential to the reading program.

Helping Every Child to Grow at His Own Rate

It is the right of every child who can learn to read to do so through a series of happy experiences with materials always at his own level of difficulty. This principle needs especially to be put into practice in the intermediate and upper grades. Schools tend to recognize more clearly that primary children must have their reading activities adjusted to their needs than they do with older boys and girls. Every child should have consistent guidance whether he is learning to read rapidly or slowly and should never feel any stigma attached to his reading status because of his rate of learning. The gifted child should have the stimulus of strong group and individual interests that encourage him to read widely as well as intensively. He should be encouraged to use the public library, to acquire his own collection of books, and to develop the skills he needs for pursuing a topic in several sources.

Children in the upper grades should have their reading abilities carefully analyzed, and regular group and individual guidance should be provided in accordance with their needs. They should receive help in the skills they need for their reading in content fields, for developing appreciation of good prose and poetry, and for evaluating critically the material found in books as well as in newspapers and periodicals.[15] Those whose reading abilities are at a low level should have

[15] David H. Russell, "Reading for Critical Thinking," *California Journal of Elementary Education,* XIV (November, 1945), pp. 79–86.

John J. DeBoer, "Teaching Critical Reading," *Elementary English Review,* XXIII (October, 1946), pp. 251–54.

the materials and the guidance by which they can profit.

Group reading, in texts and supplementary sets, should be evaluated carefully in terms of its purposes, whether the building up of a common background of information or literary acquaintance or the development of specific skills in interpretation.

Social studies, science reference books, mathematics texts —all require specific skills for their use. Such reading should be balanced, for all children, against a great variety of activities in which they read alone for individual ends such as selecting and preparing stories to read to the group, seeking information in a variety of books concerning topics of group or personal interest, or reading for sheer enjoyment in materials that have something to offer of adventure, humor, or characterization.

At the intermediate-grade level this means, on the school's part, careful study of each pupil's reading ability, particularly through informal procedures such as reading silently or aloud with the teacher. It means the grouping of pupils on the basis of the kind of help they need with individual attention and encouragement for each child. It means supplying material at every level of difficulty at which children are working, and this not only in reading classes, but in social studies, science, arithmetic, music—in every activity in which books are used. It means organizing many learning activities which are not based on reading, or which involve a minimum of reading, so that the children of low reading levels and those of high reading levels can work together freely during part of their day.

Providing a Wide Range of Reading Material

Again, to recognize children's needs in reading means supplying a wide range of materials suitable for all levels and for a variety of interests. It means helping every child to learn the varied uses of reading, to range freely in the realms of science, history, and other areas of personal concern. It means supplying him with widely varied literary materials, selected to meet his special needs and interests. It means offering him the opportunity to appreciate the humor, pathos, or excitement in a story, to escape into the world of fancy, to identify himself with characters in literature, thus finding release for those emotions he may not express in action, or to come to know himself better because he sees himself in story characters or compares himself with them.

Materials to stimulate good readers. At the same time, caring for pupils of superior reading ability and lively interests requires materials not always found in the classroom. These may be literary selections considerably beyond the average level of maturity of the pupils in the class. They may include difficult books on topics of personal interest, adult reference materials, or even government reports for special research on the part of gifted pupils.

The child who has learned to read freely and well should have much freedom of choice among well-selected materials, but should have consistent guidance in broadening his range to include all types of material, in interpreting thoughtfully the materials he reads, in using reading in relation to his life and school activities, and in appreciating poetry and prose that have real literary quality in accordance with his own measure of insight and imagination.

In factual reading he should not be limited to encyclopedic materials written in summary form, with the consequent temptation of copying or repeating without understanding, when there are hundreds of books written with great skill and illustrated beautifully, in which he may learn about the world in which he lives.

Special materials for weak readers. The child who has insufficient ability to read easily and freely at the intermediate-grade level should likewise have a variety of reading activities and materials, especially those which combine maturity of interest and simplicity of vocabulary and sentence structure. Guidance of his progress in reading should be continuous and consistent. Under no circumstances should he be required to cope with materials too difficult for him, whether these be poetry and stories, or whether they be materials prepared for social studies, science, arithmetic, language, spelling, or other areas of learning. Nor should he be limited to books chosen with the development of skills in mind. There should be many easy books and many highly illustrated books from which he too may make individual choices, such, for example, as *One Horse Farm, Travelers All*, the *Picture Book of Astronomy*, or *The First Book of Indians*.

The child with limited reading ability will need many types of graphic materials: maps, globes, charts, newspapers, periodicals, slides and films with captions. Some of these will meet his needs because of their high interest value. Boys, for instance, of low reading ability, sometimes show real interest in materials which help them to make things such as model airplanes. These books or periodicals often supply pictures and diagrams which enhance the value of the material.

Books are now being produced with appeal to the interests of older boys and girls, but with texts couched in simple vocabulary, with straightforward sentences and clear-cut organization,[16] such as the Aviation Readers by Henry J. Lent and others; the Core Vocabulary Series by Huber, Salisbury, and Gates, including *The Ranch Book, Rusty Wants A Dog*, and *Smoky the Crow;* the Landmark Books, including *Christopher Columbus, Mr. Bell Invents the Telephone*, and many others; the Real Book Series such as *The Real Book about Pirates;* and the First Book Series including *The First Book of Stones, The First Book of Presidents*, and other titles. There is much more of this kind of material, which teachers and librarians find useful. There is still need, however, for additional publications of high interest value simply written. Many ingenious teachers write materials for use in their

[16] Donald Durrell and Helen Sullivan, *High Interest-Low Vocabulary Reading List* (Boston, Educational Clinic, Boston University, 1952).

classes. Some of these appear in published form.[17] Some pupils of fifth- and sixth-grade level write materials for themselves, put them into some kind of permanent form and share them with other children. Utah teachers, working with original materials growing out of state-wide community exploration, edited the children's original reports and stories and produced reading for social studies classes.[18]

Finding Basic Causes of Retardation [19]

Many children with special difficulties in reading profit from the kind of help which the classroom teacher, with a reasonable pupil load, can give them. Such help begins with careful study of the causes of the pupil's difficulty. Comparison of reading age and mental age is only a beginning. All those factors which have affected and are affecting the child's growth and development have a bearing upon his reading performance. Therefore the teacher studies a variety of sources of information for clues to the real causes of his retardation and to the necessary measures for improvement.

Some sources of information and assistance may include the following:

1. Cumulative school records including results of standardized diagnostic reading tests
2. Pertinent data from physical examinations
3. Interviews with parents
4. Informal reading inventories for the analysis of abilities and techniques in silent and oral reading
5. Interviews with children
6. Interest inventories

[17] Marie Hatten, *Arthur Denny's Dream* (illustrated by her fourth grade at Fairview School) (Seattle, The Seattle Public Schools, 1953).

Grand Rapids Public Schools, *Our City* (Grand Rapids, Michigan, Board of Education, 1952).

[18] Utah State Department of Public Instruction, *Utah's Land and Early People* (Salt Lake City, 1947) and *Meeting Community Needs in Utah* (1949).

[19] Prepared by Cecelia Unzicker from original studies made at Teachers College, Columbia University and State Teachers College, California, Pennsylvania.

In addition, the teacher may intensify her study of the child and make use of further resources:

1. Interviews with previous teachers
2. Study of the home culture and family relationships
3. Study of the child's immediate environment
4. Study of his speech, writing, play acting, painting, drawing—all his forms of expression
5. Study of his ability to listen and observe
6. Referral to a specialist for diagnosis and correction of physical disabilities, such as faulty vision or hearing, or for study and help with emotional disturbances
7. Referral to a reading clinic for special kinds of assistance

Rarely does the teacher employ all these means in studying a child. In one case she analyzes the difficulty and promptly finds ways of doing something about it. In another case, however, she finds that prolonged study is required and the use of many sources of information before the real cause of difficulty can be discovered. She becomes more adept in selecting resources, and, in determining the sequence in which to use them, gains experience in analysis and tries out many procedures. In some instances she sees at once, when a child shows signs of eye strain in reading, that he needs the services of a specialist.

Guiding Individuals in Programs for Reading Improvement

Examples follow showing how information obtained from available sources led to the detection of difficulties among individual children whose reading improved when blocks to their learning were removed and appropriate help provided.

Utilizing data from physical examinations. James was in the third grade, yet he could not read well in books on the first-grade level. He seemed highly intelligent in most respects; his use of language was excellent. He often looked at pictures in books and talked about them freely. He was interested in the content of stories he had learned by listening. However, continued observation revealed his actual repulsion toward words in print. When the teacher called his attention to visual symbols for the words in his speaking vocabulary, or indicated in books material related to ideas already familiar to him, he turned his head and slipped away to engage in another activity.

No difficulty in vision had been revealed in the screening test at school, but the parents were advised to have a more thorough check of his eyes. The specialist found a functional disorder, and James' visual reëducation followed. Later, when a program to improve his reading was undertaken, James showed no aversion to print. In this case it would have been futile and dangerous to undertake any kind of reading program while the basic difficulty remained undetected and uncorrected.

Building an interest in reading. John would have nothing to do with books. His personal history showed that his physical development had been slow and that his mother had pushed, bribed, and threatened to get him to do better work in school. Her older children had been unsuccessful in reading, and she was determined that her young son should improve upon their records. As a result of this treatment John was rebellious. He did not want to read, and no one could make him do so. At this time he was in the third grade and could not read a primer nor write his name. There was a typewriter with large type in the room which he was invited to use. This was something new, and he liked it. He was taught to insert the paper and set it in position. He pecked off letters and was fascinated to see them on paper. When he was able to spell some words, his teacher suggested that he write a story and put it on the bulletin board for the boys and girls to read.

"What story?" he asked.

"We will write about something that really happened. You

tell it to me, and I will write it with my pencil. Then you can type it out on the typewriter with your name at the end and pin it up on the bulletin board."

John was silent for a few minutes. Then he said, "I can make up a story about my dog," and composed the following sentences:

> I am going downtown to get my dog.
> He will be little.
> He will be black and white.
> I will teach him to do tricks.
> I will teach him to jump through a hoop.

After the teacher had written the story out for him in longhand, John laboriously copied it on the typewriter. He worked for two days trying to complete it in correct form. On the third day he came in crying and announced, "I can't put my story on the bulletin board. My mother didn't take me downtown to get my dog."

The teacher called the mother, and when she came to school and saw John's story, she was astonished. She gladly talked with the teacher about ways of working together to help her son, promising to take him to town that very afternoon to buy his dog so that his story could be posted on the bulletin board.

John became a happier child and much more responsive. He wrote more dog stories and worked willingly to find needed sentences, phrases, and words which the teacher supplied in a card file. His first primers were selected because dogs appeared in the stories. He progressed to first readers and finally into easy second readers during that year. He developed interest and confidence and realized that he could translate print into ideas that interested him. The process was slow and sometimes painful, for him, his mother, and his teacher.

Relieving home tensions. David was a charming boy, coöperative and eager to do good work at school but quiet and retiring in comparison with other boys in his fifth grade. He seemed to listen attentively, but he had little to say. When he was spoken to, his face lighted up with a winning smile, but his usual expression was one of strain or worry. He worked doggedly at every school task. His face puckered, his teeth clenched, and his fists tightened when he was trying to work out a simple test sheet that others were doing with ease. When working in groups or with others, as for instance in locating informational material for discussion purposes, he made random efforts, and finally gave up, leaving the completion of the task to others. Then he appeared to be much chagrined, defeated, and exhausted.

His achievement in all subjects but art was decidedly below expectation for a boy of his ability. His lowest grades were in arithmetic and reading. His comprehension in reading seemed better when he read alone and simply for pleasure than when he worked with the group or attempted any type of planned reading activities for which all children were held responsible.

The teacher worked mostly on building a warm relationship between herself and David, trying to communicate to him that she liked him just as he was. She had made guesses but was not too sure about the causes of his frustration.

Early in the year she was invited to David's home for dinner. She knew the father to be a prosperous business man and the mother an attractive and competent member of the school Parent-Teacher Association. David greeted his teacher happily and cordially. Almost at once the father focused attention on the sister—two years younger than David—an outgoing and composed child. Her father talked about her excellent record in the third grade, her ability to learn quickly and to read books that were too difficult for David. All this went on in David's presence. At the dining table the father quizzed the children on arithmetic problems involving several steps in thinking. Ann gave the answers immediately while David, lost in his confusion, could utter no sound. The teacher made efforts to tell about David's accomplishments in art and to point out how well he got along with other members of his class group, but she saw that the evening was a strenuous and disappointing one for David.

When the children had retired, the teacher managed in talking with the parents to indicate that David probably was frustrated in his great need for winning acceptance by his father. She pointed out that David also was intelligent, although his abilities seemed to be different from those of his sister. The father admitted that in his anxiety to have David able to take over his business some day, he might be ruining David's chances of becoming his best self. The parents frankly recognized the seriousness of the situation and agreed to work with the teacher to set up conditions in which David could gradually release his creative energies and find real satisfactions. As tensions were removed, David's reaction to a program in reading development improved, and his progress became more and more pronounced.

Interviewing and informal reading inventory. Betty's teacher observed that she was not contributing in committees responsible for reading and reporting in the social studies. She was of normal chronological age for the seventh grade and was a happy, well-adjusted child.

Betty knew she was reading less well than others in her classroom and when she and her teacher talked things over, she gave the reasons for her difficulty. Because her family had moved often, she had been in no one school for a long period. Many of the schools she had attended had offered much less opportunity than the present school. She was unaccustomed to engaging in reading for functional purposes. She did not recall that she had ever received help in learning to read, such as working in a small group with the teacher. She now felt pressed to keep up with her group whenever reading was undertaken. The teacher in some individual work found that all the ideas she gained in reading appeared to her of equal importance. She failed to recognize the wholeness of the selection because she could not single out and see the subordinate ideas in proper relationship to the main topic.

In a second period of individual work with Betty, the teacher observed and analyzed her silent reading of a selection from the social studies text. This informal inventory corroborated the first analysis. It also revealed that she was coping with many words that lacked meaning for her. The teacher gave Betty several periods of special help stressing the skills she needed in the books she was using in the social studies. She taught her how to clarify the problem she was reading to solve and how to break it down into its subordinate parts. She helped her to find specific information by using the index and then locating the appropriate pages. She showed her that studying chapter and section headings would help her to locate pertinent information. She guided her in the building of a simple outline and showed her how to place information under the proper subpoints. She taught her how to report from the outline and then how to get along without it. She helped her with the use of a simple dictionary to find the meanings of unknown words and guided her in checking words for their various meanings by observing their use in conversation and in print. Intermittently Betty checked her progress by trying again to work with a committee in joint study and reporting. She, her classmates, and her teacher all felt she had improved noticeably.

The interview and the informal reading inventory were the chief means of discovering Betty's difficulties and deciding what to do about them.

Building language abilities. When Helen was in the seventh grade, she was fourteen years old. Her intelligence quotient on an individual test was 90, and she was reading, according to the reading examination, on the fourth-grade level. She had repeated the first grade and the fourth. A Slavic dialect was spoken in her home. Her father worked two or three days a week as a coal miner. The home with eight children was operating on a limited budget. Nevertheless, she was well nourished, was dressed neatly and becomingly, and seemed alert and interested. In art and music she showed some achievement and satisfaction. She progressed least in language expression and reading. Most of the time she said very little, using a word or phrase, often inaccurately pronounced, to convey a thought, instead of expressing herself in sentences or complete thought units. She communicated mostly by gesture, facial expression, painting, singing, and laughter, with only a word here and there. A careful check revealed, in fact, a second-grade level of speaking vocabulary.

The teacher felt that Helen's retardation in oral expression was basic to her retardation in reading, so she began giving her more opportunities to talk. Because Helen liked to sing, she was helped to learn the words of a song and to pronounce them distinctly. Later she sang this song for the class. The teacher drew her out in class discussion and helped her to talk distinctly and to express complete thoughts. When the class planned a program as the culmination of their study of South America, Helen was chosen to make the opening announcement to the parents. Guidance was given her in preparing her simple speech, and she experienced success in this effort as she had in the singing and in the class discussion.

In helping her with her reading, the teacher used first a book of simple legends because the dramatic quality of the stories appealed to the child. Each selection was first read silently. Difficult words were analyzed and special attention was given to pronunciation of them. As she read these stories and felt her success in mastering them, she wanted to read them aloud and did successfully read them to a fourth-grade group.

Similar procedures were followed in guiding Helen's reading at successive levels. She was well along in reading on the fifth-grade level when school closed for the summer. Her interest in reading was growing and she was taking library books home regularly. She was talking oftener and more spontaneously and had effectively expressed herself to a group on a number of occasions. Her behavior suggested clearly that her level of intelligence was higher than the initial testing had indicated.

Making a direct attack on reading skills. It is obvious that such methods of attack on the general problems of reading will open the way for specific attention to the child's habits of studying words, to his attention to meaning as opposed to word calling, to his techniques for organizing and remembering what he has read. Careful diagnosis frequently brings to light children who are normal in all other respects but who fail to read comprehendingly because of inadequate approaches to the act of reading itself. Often such pupils are intelligent far beyond their ability to read. Their difficulties are due in large measure to inadequate teaching, to frequent absence from school, or to inability to keep up with the class in an approach to more complex reading tasks before they have acquired rudimentary skills necessary to success in them. Helping intelligent pupils to develop simple reading skills pays large dividends, for it makes possible rapid progress under their own direction.[20]

Helping the Slower Readers in Class Groups

Sometimes the teacher finds that all the children in the class, or at least a number of them, are reading a year and a half or more below what might reasonably be expected of them because conditions for learning have, for some reason, not been good. In such cases she organizes activities which call for group participation. Much depends on the size of the class. As frequently as possible individual help, along with group guidance, should be given.

In providing programs for groups of children needing special help, the teacher seeks to relate the reading to all of

[20] Guy L. Bond and Eva Bond Wagner, *Teaching the Child to Read* (New York, The Macmillan Company, 1950).

William S. Gray and Dorothy Horton, *On Their Own in Reading; How to Give Children Independence in Attacking New Words* (Chicago, Scott, Foresman and Company, 1948).

the language arts and to other areas of the school curriculum. She attempts to build readiness for reading and to help children experience real satisfaction through increased competency. Dr. Hildreth in *Helping Children to Read* describes concretely how one such group improved in reading, applying intensively to individual pupils the principles set down in this chapter.[21]

Diagnosing Needs of Individuals

As in the previous description of diagnostic procedures, survey and diagnostic tests in reading may be used as first steps in analysis. The cumulative records of the children supply important information. Other sources help to reveal particular needs. Group needs can be determined early, such as the need for social recognition, for improved oral expression, for broader experiences, for better ways of working together, for challenging interests, for desirable attitudes toward reading, and for more and better opportunities to read. These are over-all needs, and often there is a combination of many of them which should determine the direction of the program. At the same time, special needs in improved methods of attack on words, use of context clues, and the search for meaning in sentences, in paragraphs, and in whole selections will demand attention if children are to become more proficient readers. Adaptation of speed and techniques of reading to the purpose in hand is of great importance. In a few cases of extreme difficulty the teacher should have help from a school psychologist or other person specially trained in educational diagnosis. For such children a series of "case conferences" involving teachers, principal, psychologist, school nurse, supervisor, and others may be profitable in getting at causes of difficulty and in enlightening the school personnel involved.

[21] Gertrude Hildreth and Josephine Wright, *Helping Children to Read* (New York, Columbia University, Teachers College Bureau of Publications, 1940).

Motivation through broad units. Often in the upper grades such help can best be given in a situation in which reading is motivated through instruction built around interests in social studies, science, the arts, or physical activities. Possible topics might be the making of a newspaper, a study of deep-sea diving, a class party, a study of the library, the operation of a mock radio station, or a study of sports. The teacher then considers the possibilities in each of these choices for excursions and visual aids to build and extend experiences and develop concepts, for opportunities in oral and written expression, for promoting real purposes for reading, for specific teaching of reading skills, and for encouraging adequate use of the dictionary and library reference tools.

Providing materials and stimulus for reading. In the course of any such program children should have time in school to read books of their own free choice every day. This is especially important for a group that has not achieved up to its potentialities in reading. The classroom should be provided with many books of this type, the collection should be changed often, and those not selected by children exchanged for other books as frequently as necessary. Some school systems make definite provision for supplying collections. Others work in close collaboration with the public library to provide sufficient variety in books for individual reading. Teachers find that children make remarkable gains in reading power through provision for books and for the reading of them. Schools with their own children's libraries and librarians are particularly fortunate.

Reading should be so organized that each child is reading materials appropriate to his instructional level. This level is often about one-half year below his grade score on standardized tests. Careful guidance is here given to help the child build skills in analyzing words, in recognizing sentences, in actually securing the ideas from the printed material and making some simple, practical organization of them in his thinking. He is helped to recognize the wide variety of reading materials that is available for different purposes. If basic readers are used in this program, the accompanying manuals may offer some useful suggestions as to procedures.

Helping children gain satisfaction from reading. Children who have been relatively unsuccessful profit by much praise for every small gain and for their efforts regardless of how meager the results may be. They require consistent assurance that they can succeed. They are helped by real evidences of their success, such as charts and graphs showing total group achievement or the achievement of each individual as measured against his own record. These graphic materials should never be used to discourage any child. Comparison between individuals is destructive. Posting the type of graph or chart which compares one child with another defeats the purpose. Pupils profit by opportunities to share their accomplishments with other children whose approval means much to them. They greatly need the understanding, encouragement, and praise of their parents. Therefore, the teacher draws the parents into the program early and thereafter keeps them advised individually as to the kind of help and support their children should have at each stage of growth. She furnishes to the parents of each child evidence of progress as often as possible.

Studying the results. The teacher evaluates individual progress for the sake of her own guidance by every means available. She observes the daily reactions of the children to reading, their choice of books, the number of books they read, their enjoyment and use of the ideas gained from reading, their ability to read for specific purposes, and the like. She uses comparable forms of the standardized test given at the beginning to measure progress at later stages.

Providing Expert Help for Some Children

Reading difficulties are sometimes so severe that regular classrooms are not equipped to cope with them. Such cases should be referred to specialists for complete diagnosis and special treatment through either group or individual procedures. The school system is fortunate which has access to a reading clinic. Reading difficulties of a severe nature and of long duration may seriously affect other aspects of the child's life. Diagnosis often requires complete medical examination, psychological testing, sometimes even psychiatric examination, and always close study of reading behavior by clinically trained teachers. Diagnosis should be followed by carefully planned treatment of the specific difficulties in intensive individual or semi-individual situations. Since few children belong in this category, caution needs to be exercised. There are different causes and degrees of difficulty. It is wise to find out as much as possible about the child before deciding that he needs special diagnostic and remedial treatment.

SUMMARY

Any consideration of reading must recognize the necessity of consistency in the over-all program. Basic plans for reading development may fail of results unless seen in perspective. A program of reading readiness in the primary grades based on clear recognition of children's differences in maturity may result in fewer remedial cases at the intermediate level.

Study skills such as the use of the dictionary, developed in the intermediate grades, point back to the first-grade child's learning to look for the word by its picture and forward to the eighth-grade pupil's using the alphabet to the third order to locate an author's name in the card catalog.

Appropriate and excellent books in adequate quantities for primary and intermediate children support the junior high school goal of wide and discriminating reading.

The senior high school student learning to cope critically as well as responsively with adult materials is using the approach to reading through thinking which his teachers fostered throughout the elementary school.

Moreover, the all-inclusive view sees reading in relation

to the other language arts and as pervasive in a vital school program. This requires that the whole school staff look at the reading program and that all evidences of growth in reading be sought, not only the results of standard tests. Continuity in growth in reading for every child at every point in his school experience is the logical aim.

On the basis of the program presented in this chapter, it is possible to set down a series of questions, the answers to which may give an adequate evaluation of the teaching of reading in any school:

1. Are the level of reading ability and the specific reading problems of each pupil known to the teacher?
2. Does the teacher have adequate supplementary knowledge of the child's health, home background, intelligence, interests, and social and emotional status to diagnose his difficulties adequately?
3. Do the materials for reading in the classroom cover the same range of difficulty and interests as those revealed in the study of the children themselves?
4. Is individual help given to each pupil either separately or in groups?
5. Are superior readers stimulated to read widely and intensively at a level commensurate with their ability?
6. Are weak pupils given a similar chance to read widely and for enjoyment at their level of ability?
7. Are pupils mastering such important skills as adjusting their speed and technique of reading to the purpose for which they read and the nature of the material read?
8. Are basic skills carefully defined and taught in relation to use?
9. Is reading related to every activity of the school day? To the personal interests of the pupils?
10. Are reference skills and use of the library developed in connection with study reading? With personal reading?
11. Are appreciation and enjoyment of literature given their place in the program?
12. Do personal habits of reading receive careful attention with adequate evaluation of breadth, maturity, and standards of selection of materials read?

BIBLIOGRAPHY

ADAMS, Fay, GRAY, Lillian, and REESE, Dora, *Teaching Children to Read* (New York, The Ronald Press, 1949).

ALMY, Milly C., *Children's Experiences Prior to First Grade Reading and Success in Beginning Reading* (New York, Columbia University, Teachers College Bureau of Publications, 1949).

ANDERSON, Irving H., and DEARBORN, Walter F., *The Psychology of Teaching Reading* (New York, The Ronald Press, 1952).

ARBUTHNOT, May Hill, *Children and Books* (Chicago, Scott, Foresman and Company, 1947).

BETTS, A. E., *Foundations of Reading Instruction* (New York, American Book Company, 1946).

BETZNER, Jean, *Exploring Literature with Children in the Elementary School,* Practical Suggestions for Teaching, No. 7 (New York, Columbia University, Teachers College Bureau of Publications, 1943).

BOND, Guy L., and WAGNER, Eva Bond, *Teaching the Child to Read* (New York, The Macmillan Company, 1950).

BONEY, DeWitt, *Children Learn to Read* (Champaign, Illinois, National Council of Teachers of English, 1949).

BURROWS, Alvina T., *What About Phonics?* (Washington, D.C., Association for Childhood Education International, 1951).

CORNELIUS, Ruth, "Reading with Six-Year-Olds," *Childhood Education,* XXVI (December, 1949), pp. 162–63.

DEBOER, John J., "Teaching Critical Reading," *Elementary English Review* XXIII (October, 1946), pp. 251–54.

DEIGHTON, Lee, "The Survival of the English Teacher," ETC., X, No. 2 (Winter, 1953), pp. 97–106.

DURRELL, Donald, and SULLIVAN, Helen, *High Interest–Low Vocabulary Reading List* (Boston, Educational Clinic, Boston University, 1952).

EVANS, Clara, "On Reading Aloud," *Elementary English,* XXVIII (February, 1951), pp. 82–85.

GANS, Roma, *Guiding Children's Reading through Experiences* (New York, Columbia University, Teachers College Bureau of Publications, 1941).

GATES, Arthur I., *The Improvement of Reading* (New York, The Macmillan Company, 1947).

Grand Rapids Public Schools, *Our City* (Grand Rapids, Michigan, Board of Education, 1952).

GRAY, William S., and HORTON, Dorothy, *On Their Own in Reading; How to Give Children Independence in Attacking New Words* (Chicago, Scott, Foresman and Company, 1948).

HARRIS, Melva, "Beginning Reading without Readers," *Childhood Education,* XXVI (December, 1949), pp. 164–67.

HARRISON, Lucille A., *Reading Readiness* (Boston, Houghton Mifflin Company, 1936).

HATTEN, Marie, *Arthur Denny's Dream* (Seattle, The Seattle Public Schools, 1953).

HILDRETH, Gertrude, *Learning the Three R's* (Minneapolis, Educational Publishers, 1947).

HILDRETH, Gertrude, "Reading Programs in the Primary Grades" in *Reading in the Elementary School,* Forty-Eighth Yearbook, Part II, National Society for the Study of Education (Chicago, Illinois, University of Chicago Press, 1944).

———, and WRIGHT, Josephine L., *Helping Children to Read* (New York, Columbia University, Teachers College Bureau of Publications, 1940).

KIRK, Samuel, *Teaching Reading to Slow-Learning Children* (New York, Houghton Mifflin Company, 1940).

LAMOREAUX, Lillian A., and LEE, Dorris May, *Learning to Read through Experiences* (New York, Appleton-Century-Crofts, Inc., 1943).

LUCKIESH, Matthew, and Moss, Frank K., *Reading as a Visual Task* (New York, D. Van Nostrand Company, Inc., 1942).

McCULLOUGH, Constance, "Learning to Use Context Clues," *Elementary English,* XX (April, 1943), pp. 140–43.

McLATCHY, Josephine, "List of Common Words for the First Grade," *Educational Research Bulletin,* Ohio State University, Columbus, Ohio (September 12, 1951), pp. 151–59.

Madison Public Schools, *The Use of Charts in the Primary Grades* (Madison, Wisconsin, Curriculum Division, The Public Schools, 1949). (Pamphlet)

———, *Learning to Read in the Madison Public Schools* (Madison, Wisconsin, Curriculum Division, The Public Schools, 1945).

MAIB, Frances, "Individualizing Reading," *Elementary English,* XXIX (February, 1952), pp. 84–98.

Maury Elementary School Faculty, *Teaching Reading in the Elementary School* (Danville, Illinois, Interstate Publishing Company). Pamphlet.

MONROE, Marion, *Growing Into Reading: How Readiness for Reading Develops at Home and at School* (New York, Scott, Foresman and Company, 1951).

National Education Association and Affiliated State Education Associations, *Skippy and the 3 R's; A 16mm Motion Picture Which Shows How a First-Grade Child Learns the Fundamentals* (Washington, D.C., National Education Association, Division of Press and Radio Relations, 1954).

National Society for the Study of Education, *Reading in the Elementary School,* Forty-Eighth Yearbook, Part II (Chicago, University of Chicago Press, 1949).

———, *The Teaching of Reading,* Twenty-Fourth Yearbook, Part I, (Chicago, University of Chicago Press, 1925).

———, *The Teaching of Reading: A Second Report,* Thirty-Sixth Yearbook, Part I (Chicago, University of Chicago Press, 1937).

OLSON, Willard C., *Child Development* (Boston, D. C. Heath & Company, 1949).

ROBINSON, Helen M., *Why Pupils Fail in Reading* (Chicago, University of Chicago Press, 1946).

Russell, David H., *Children Learn to Read* (New York, Ginn and Company, 1949).

———, "Reading and the Healthy Personality," *Elementary English* XXIX (April, 1952), pp. 195–200.

———, "Reading for Critical Thinking," *California Journal of Elementary Education*, XIV (November, 1945), pp. 79–86.

———, and Wulfing, Gretchen, "Supplementary Materials in the First-Grade Reading Program, *Elementary English*, XXVIII (October, 1951), pp. 347–49.

Utah State Department of Public Instruction, *Utah's Land and Early People* (Salt Lake City, 1947).

———, *Meeting Community Needs in Utah* (Salt Lake City, 1949).

Witty, Paul, *Reading in Modern Education* (Boston, D. C. Heath & Company, 1949).

CHAPTER 7

Writing

IMPRESSION precedes expression; intake precedes outflow in all aspects of language learning. A baby listens and responds to words adults are saying long before he says those words himself. His ear is tuned to the distinctive sound symbols of individual words and to the way they are strung together in sentence chains—to the varying rhythms, intonations, and inflections that carry varying meanings. As he begins to talk, he can often express his whole meaning in the use of a single word. "Daddy" may mean, "Here comes my Daddy," "There is Daddy," and "I want my Daddy," without the use of any supporting words. It will take the child several years to learn to use sentences with all the kinds and arrangements of words which adults about him employ.

Similarly, a child watches the process of writing long before he does any real writing. When he is mature enough to hold a pencil, he may scribble in imitation of adult writing and perhaps interpret to an adult his concept of what he has written. One very independent little girl scribbled a lengthy letter, stuffed it into a used envelope, then dropped it into the mailbox, confident that grandmother would receive and enjoy her message. Children can grow into writing through motivation that stems from their own interests, but more direct teaching and conscious learning are necessary than in learning to talk.

ASSESSING THE CHILD'S REAL NEEDS FOR WRITING

Most children of elementary school age have relatively few real needs for writing in their out-of-school life, but writing becomes a necessary tool for school experience with the beginning of the primary years. Some children learn to write memoranda and simple messages quite early if they are called upon to do so in connection with errands and with answering the telephone in their homes. If they belong to clubs or organized groups, they may have occasion to write notes, plans, and messages of various sorts. Whether they use writing for personal correspondence such as letters to friends and relatives, invitations, and notes of appreciation depends upon the letter-writing habits of their families. Some families teach children from an early age when it is appropriate to write letters and notes and what kinds to write. In many homes, perhaps the majority of them, there is no such guided learning. At school, children need writing for assignments and reports of various kinds, for records, plans, news bulletins, sharing of experience, and creative expression. Some of their needs for writing are associated with school routine and are means to a variety of ends, and others are concerned with individual expression of ideas, interests, emotions, and imaginings.

Guidance in learning to write is constantly geared to the maturity of the child and his emerging needs for the various skills of written communication. Some of the learning is incidental to other experiences as the teacher helps the children to achieve their purposes. Some of it is the result of direct teaching. When the need for a skill arises, the teacher guides the learning through planned lessons and provides the practice that is necessary for the development of the required skill. For example, in securing their parents' permission for certain educational trips, all children may need help with letter-writing early in the year. Later, some will be able to do their writing independently after the class has set up the plan and designated the essential items to be included in each letter. Other children will need additional teaching and careful supervision over a longer period of time.

Home Activities Leading to Writing

A number of activities carried on by children during their preschool years stimulate interest and develop skill which is later utilized in writing. The interest in scribbling and in dabbling with crayon and paint helps develop muscular skill and eye and hand coördination. Large muscles develop before the smaller ones concerned with fine coördinations, so that any work of this kind is good muscle training. Cutting with blunt scissors, building with blocks, and working with clay and other plastic materials also serve this purpose, so that the child gradually learns to make his hand do what his mind wants it to do. An X-ray picture of the wrist of a six-year-old shows cartilage where bony structure will appear in an adult wrist. There is still unfinished development of a number of kinds, and muscular activity which is suited to the child's developing powers is important to his growth at each stage.

Mothers often encourage a little child to dictate or to scribble a message to go in a letter to grandmother or to daddy while he is away, and they read to a child the part of a letter that is directed to him. Through such experiences a young child gradually becomes aware of what writing is and the purpose it serves. He learns that his own ideas and the words he says can be put into black marks on a white page and shared with others who can interpret them. His interest in scribbling shows his desire to lay hold on the process and use it for himself. The experience of dictating messages helps him to learn to put his ideas into words so that they can be written for him. His interests in expression and in sharing are expanded to take in this new form.

Your Name Says It's Yours.

A Third Grade's Idea of a Dictionary Box.

Here's How You Use the Dictionary Box.

This Is *My* Autobiography.

All Kinds of Dictionaries Help with Writing.

Words—Words—Words—Make a Vocabulary.

A Newspaper Calls for Teamwork in Writing.

Kindergarten Experience as Background for Writing

Many of the activities carried on in the kindergarten lead directly toward writing. The development of muscular skill and coördination continues and is gradually refined through many types of guided activities. Play with blocks, finger painting, crayoning, cutting, and working with clay and wood all help to build eye-hand-mind coördination. Many toys and puzzles help with this also. The child grows in ability to express himself orally through the many opportunities for conversation that occur in the daily planning, sharing, discussing of activities, reporting on work accomplished, and evaluating individual and group experience. The interests and activities in which the child participates serve to build vocabulary, clarify meanings, expand his background of experience and help him put his concepts into words—all of which is prerequisite to written expression. Written messages which pertain to the children come to the teacher from other classrooms and from the administrative office. She reads some of these to the children and helps them to understand and respond in the appropriate way.

WRITTEN COMMUNICATION IN THE KINDERGARTEN

The transition from receiving messages to sending them is a natural one.

Opportunities for Written Communication

Kindergarten children have many opportunities to dictate messages for the teacher to write. Perhaps they plan a trip to a nearby farm and need to make arrangements with the farmer in advance. Perhaps they need to send an invitation to their mothers to come to a school party or to share in their activities. Again, they may write invitations to other grades or responses to invitations received. Sometimes they dictate a note of appreciation for services rendered the group or a note of congratulation or commendation for an assembly program they have been permitted to share. Dictating letters to classmates who are absent or ill helps the children learn how one writes a letter and what goes into the writing.

Observation of Writing Form in the Kindergarten

Children of kindergarten age learn a great many things from the experience of dictating material for the teacher to write. They do not master the techniques of composition at this age—that comes later—but they are introduced to some of the basic problems of composition. In the early stages of dictation the child merely talks along, and the adult takes down what is said as best he can. As the child gains in experience and becomes interested in the process, he makes some effort to formulate sentences and give them forth in form to be written. He takes some pains to express his thinking clearly and concisely. The teacher serves as scribe as well as guide, explaining to the child from time to time just how she is writing what he says and why it is done this way. Thus she calls his attention to simple elements of conventional form, presenting them as matters of convenience and also of courtesy and consideration for those who are to read the material.

In writing a letter the teacher points out the elements that are essential to its form. There are some forms of greeting and leave-taking that are suitable for face-to-face contacts and other forms that are suitable for written contacts. When a child meets his friend on the street, he says, "Hi!" or "Hello, John," but in a letter one says, "Dear John," instead. "Good-by" at the close of a letter is said differently also. When the greeting has been written and the children are ready for the message, the teacher may say, "What shall we say to John? Who has thought of a good sentence to write first?" If the children's ideas pour forth faster than the teacher can write, she may say, "Wait just a minute. I can't write quite so fast.

Mary, tell me your sentence again so I can put it down just right. Now I am ready for your sentence, Tom."

The children are not expected to know what a sentence is, but they come in time to associate it with a group of words expressing an idea. Perhaps the teacher pauses at the end of a sentence to say, "We are asking John a question in that sentence, aren't we, so I'll put a question mark at the end." The teacher adds punctuation as it is needed, using the correct name for each element as she calls attention to it. Enunciation problems which might cause difficulty with spelling at a later time can often be caught and worked on in the course of dictating. The child in a second grade who said, "How do you spell *'smorning*? I want to write, 'It rained 'smorning!'" might have been helped earlier in this way.

Basic vocabulary and ideas of form are introduced casually and as a matter of course at points where they fit and carry their own meaning. Children begin to see the need for starters and stoppers and for occasional signals along the way. Dictation provides opportunity for the introduction of ideas that will become a part of the children's working knowledge at a much later period in their school experience. When that time comes, they will have some concept of the meaning and value of the element and will more readily master its use than they would if the idea were entirely new to them.

Creative Writing in the Kindergarten

Creative writing has a place in the kindergarten also. Young children enjoy telling about home and family experiences and those in the neighborhood. They like to make up simple, fanciful tales based on stories they have heard or out of their own imagination. Telling stories from pictures, a practice in some schools, has less of value because interest is at a lower level than when children deal with their own experiences. If the teacher writes these spontaneous stories as they are given, the child's satisfaction and appreciation of the worth of his own thinking are immeasurably increased.

Five-year-olds have their own individual ways of expressing themselves which are fresh and interesting, and some of what they say has values often found in good prose and poetry. Sensory impressions may be expressed in combinations of words that are colorful and vivid. The little child who complained, "My hands are all rusty," and the one who remarked as she rode the elevator at nursery school, "The elevator oozes down. It's my favorite slow," pictured very clearly the chapped hands and the enjoyment of slow motion. Children enjoy making up chants as they play and work. Compiling a scrapbook of the children's own stories and verse encourages them to want to dictate material for the teacher to write. "Fun in the Snow" shows what one kindergarten did:

Fun in the Snow
by
The Afternoon Kindergarten

Today we went up to the bank.
It was windy. It was a stormy day. It was sleeting.
The sleet came down slanting sidewise.
It made hard ice all over Tower Hill.
It made a crust on the snow.
When we stepped on it, we went right down through.
It made a sound like crickle, crackle, crickle, creet, creet, creet.
Pieces of broken ice scattered all over.
They slid down the hill.
Two dogs followed us. They could hardly walk in the snow it was so
    deep.
They shook their heads because the sleet was so wet.
They didn't like it. But we did.
We had fun.

As children dictate, they learn to choose vivid, meaningful words and to sharpen the edges of what they say so that their meaning is clear. The joy of seeing their material carefully reproduced on a page and having the teacher read it back to them helps the children build interest in both reading and writing and eagerness to learn the processes for themselves.

Listening to the teacher read stories and poetry about their own experience or related to it helps children to sense the power of words and the ways in which they are fitted into sentences. Such experience builds readiness for reading and writing long before the children are mature enough either mentally or physically for the labor of recording their own stories.

WRITING IN THE PRIMARY SCHOOL

The same motives for writing, the same needs for increased power in expression, and the same demands for conventional form as an aid to the reader follow the child into the primary grades.

Needs for Writing in the Primary Grades

During the primary school years the child has an increasing number of needs for writing. He learns to write his name in order to identify the pictures he makes and his personal belongings. As other needs arise, he is taught to manage his writing equipment and to form the words he needs to use. The process develops slowly in the first year and more rapidly in the second; by the end of the third year the child is probably writing with a fair degree of skill and independence. Needs for writing include notices to parents, letters of appreciation, and requests for materials and for services—to a museum or transportation company for materials, to the principal for help with a project, to parents for various kinds of assistance. There are lists of materials to be gathered for use; records of facts discovered, of interests, and of reaction; work assignments of various sorts; and certain types of creative expression. Specific needs vary with the experiences being carried on in the classroom, but genuine uses for writing are found in almost every activity.

The Place of Skills in the Primary School

As the child learns to manage a pencil, the teacher finds ways for him to help produce the written material he needs and wants. A note to mother may be dictated by a child or by the group; the teacher writes or duplicates the necessary copies, and each child signs the note he is to take home. Later he learns to insert the greeting, "Dear Mother," as well as his name, and possibly adds pictorial decoration. A still later step is for the child to make his own copy of the material he has dictated to the teacher. Dictation in these early stages has great value for children. Through it they are introduced to the concept of the *sentence* and learn to use the term. They acquire some rudimentary ideas about punctuation and form and reasons for the conventional patterns that are commonly used. They learn very gradually not only *how* to write but *when* and *for what purposes*. Certain types of writing come to be thought of by the child as expressions of courtesy, thoughtfulness, and friendliness; other types of writing are also means of getting things done and of achieving goals that cannot be conveniently achieved through face-to-face contacts.

As the child gains in ability, he is encouraged to write independently, turning to the teacher for any help he needs with placement on paper, handwriting, or spelling of words. He takes hold with interest and confidence when he knows that the teacher is standing by, ready to give him all the help he requests. As he develops independence in writing and spelling, the child also grows in interest in using writing for various personal and practical purposes and in satisfaction in the power he is achieving.

An Example of Sequence in Learning

An example of sequence in learning can be shown in the development of a little classroom news sheet in a first grade. In September the teacher and children together selected the news items, composed the sentences, planned the arrangement of the pages on the blackboard, and made the illustrative sketches. Then the teacher transferred the material to paper and duplicated it for the class. A month later, the children were adding the illustrations to the duplicated copies of the news sheet, inserting the date, or filling in items of material. By March, individual children were doing the writing. They took turns serving as "editor," which meant selecting and composing the news items with the help of the group. They worked hard to write well enough to produce the master sheet which was to be used on the duplicator to furnish copies for all members of the class.

Varied Techniques Providing for Differences in Rates of Growth

Dictation should not end when the child has achieved ability to put material on paper for himself. Many children will be ready to write brief factual notes using content that has been worked out by the group before they are ready to attempt putting their own creative thinking on paper. In practical writing, a child can return to his facts or his purposes when he becomes confused or has difficulty in writing, and can reconstruct his wording. A story he has developed in his imagination may be lost while he struggles to spell a difficult word or to remember how to write a q or an x. Some children who have good ideas for writing become so fatigued with the combination of mental concentration and physical exertion that they end a story weakly rather than put forth the effort required to pull it through to its climax and a smooth conclusion. At such times, the teacher takes over the role of scribe as the child tells the final portion of his story aloud.

Oral language precedes written language and is needed as an accompaniment at many points. Through informal talking and discussion in class the child gains a certain degree of familiarity with content and facility in the use of oral language before he attempts to write. He can put on paper only material that has become warmly familiar through first-hand experience or through being lived with in imagination. An account, for example, of what he found most interesting on a trip will be greatly improved if he has relived the trip in class discussion and thought about it for a few days before attempting to reproduce it in writing.

Care must be taken in matters of sentence structure and vocabulary not to push the children beyond their normal stage of development. "At the lowest age-levels it will be enough to aim at securing good sense and continuity in the child's own style without attempting to teach adult modes of expression." [1] Primary-grade children cannot be expected to arrange their sentences in their minds before starting to write them. That ability comes with greater maturity, and with adequate command of the vocabulary and idiom necessary for expression. Children should be encouraged to think first and write afterward, but too great emphasis on planned writing at too early an age usually robs the writing of all its freshness and naturalness. Writing something that to the child is worth writing and doing it as freely and easily as he talks are of first importance.

Personal and Creative Writing in the Primary Grades

Some children enjoy making up fanciful tales from a fairly early age and begin to put them into written form as soon as they can write. One group of first-graders enjoyed the visit to school of a pet puppy named Snowball. They made up a story about his visit. Intermittently throughout the year they added to the collection of stories some that were partially true and some that were wholly imaginary. Here are two of them:

Snowball Visits the First Grade

Snowball followed Tommy to school again one day. When Snowball arrived at school, he saw all the boys and girls, but they did not see Snowball. He crept quietly into the room. Snowball sat in one of the

[1] A. F. Watts, *The Language and Mental Development of Children* (Boston, D. C. Heath & Company, 1947), p. 120.

chairs. Then Snowball went up to the chicken pen and he saw four fluffy yellow chickens. He went sniff, sniff. Then Snowball said, "Woof, Woof!" The children turned around and they saw Snowball.

Tommy said, "Go home, Snowball."

The teacher said, "It is just about time to go home so let Snowball stay here until it is time to go home."

Snowball went up to Tommy and sat down beside him. He sat there quietly and listened to the first-grade lessons.

Snowball Chases Cars

One day Tommy's father was driving to work. Snowball happened to see him. Tommy's father got all the way down the driveway. Snowball started chasing the car. Tommy's father did not see Snowball. Snowball jumped on the running board of the car. He was a little bit scared. Father was speeding up because he wanted to get to work on time. Snowball had about decided to jump off when Father speeded up too fast.

Father got to the office and parked the car. He got out and heard, "Woof, Woof!" He looked around and saw Snowball and said, "There's Tommy's puppy." He picked Snowball up.

Tommy's father called up home, and everybody came down on the bus to get Snowball. Tommy held Snowball all the way home.

For Mother's Day these same children decided to make up stories for their mothers. Twelve children worked together to dictate their story which was one of several duplicated to give to all the mothers at a party.

For Mother

On Thursday Tom and Don were cleaning the attic. Susan was trying to help the boys. She was cleaning out the toy box and found her old doll. Don was making up the attic bed. Just then Tom had an idea for Mother's Day.

He called Susan and Don and they all sat down on the attic floor. Tom said, "Mother's Day is Sunday. It is close now. Why don't we make her a Mother's Day present? She wants a hat box."

"Yes, Yes!," said Don and Susan.

They got their boards and nails and tools. It was a nice big hat box. It would hold two hats. They put on a lid with hinges. They covered the lid with pink paper and the sides with blue wall paper. They lined it with flowered wall paper. To make it slick they painted it with shellack.

"She will be surprised when she sees this on Mother's Day," said Susan. Just then Father came up to the attic. He saw the hat box. They told him it was a secret.

Susan said, "Father, would you please take us down town and buy Mother a hat?"

He said, "Yes."

Then they wrote some poems to put in the box.

This is Tom's poem.

> Mother's Day is coming,
> It's the spring of the year
> Mother's Day is coming,
> Everyone should cheer.

This is Don's poem.

> A hat box for you, dear Mother,
> Open it up
> And you shall see
> A great surprise
> It will be.

Susan had Don write something for her. He wrote:

> Dear Mommy,
> I love you.
> Susan

Mother was very happy when she saw the hat box and her new hat.

Emphasis on Positive Values

At all levels of instruction, but especially in the primary grades, positive values are more important than error counting. The sincere interest of teacher and children in whatever each boy or girl has to say is the most significant element in stimulating individuals to write. Relating writing to first-hand experience is all important. Winnie the Pooh, seeing the pine cones lying all around, hummed a hum, the kind of hum one hums hopefully for others. Children can be led through directed observation to see with the eye of the imagination and to express what they have seen in ways that interest others. Much reading aloud to children of both poetry and prose dealing with everyday experiences helps them to recognize an apt expression, an experience well shared by the author. *Time for Poetry* and *Very Young Verses* are especially useful anthologies for this purpose. Such stories as *Roger and the Fox* and *Shawneen and the Gander* help second- and third-grade children to sense the power of words to reproduce experience.

Journeys into the neighborhood in search of sounds and smells described by Mauree Applegate arouse an interest in sensory expressions.[2] A feeling for sequence carries over from such stories as *The Three Billy Goats Gruff*. Experiences described in readers help develop a pattern for the order of events in sharing a trip to the peanut butter factory, and the simple nature study materials of Webber and Tresselt give evidence of the need for grouping ideas in making reports to the class.

While their writing should never be merely imitative, young children can learn to appreciate effective methods of expression from the poems and stories they read and from informative materials which are clear and interesting to them.

Handwriting in the Primary School

The first writing at the primary level should be short bits used for some purpose clear to the children. It should be real communication from the beginning, not practice on letters and strokes. When need for improvement is evident, the elements to be practiced can be drawn out and worked upon and then fitted back into use again. Far less practice is needed to develop a particular skill when a child sees for himself his need for it than when he practices it to meet an arbitrary adult requirement.

The value of manuscript writing. Manuscript writing is the form of handwriting best suited to younger children and is a valuable tool in many situations in life for people of all ages. It fits the children's stage of muscular development because it requires less of fine coördination and sustained effort than cursive writing does. A child can learn to write the words he needs from the very beginning. He does not require prolonged practice on letter forms before he can fit them into

[2] Mauree Applegate, *Helping Children Write* (Scranton, Pennsylvania, International Textbook Company, 1948).

See also Board of Education, City of New York, *Developing Children's Power of Self-Expression through Writing*, Curriculum Bulletin, 1952–53, Series No. 2 (New York Public Schools, 1953).

words and sentences. Manuscript writing is used by the teacher in charts and is closely comparable to the print in the child's books. Thus he is called upon to learn only one form for both reading and writing. Legibility is the first need; children gain speed and ease as they have occasion to use writing. Helps for the formation of letters should be made available to the children to assist them in diagnosing their own difficulties

Addition of cursive writing. From the point of view of independent writing, the third or fourth grade appears to be the best time to introduce cursive writing. Some schools still add the cursive form during the second year. Children of this grade, however, are just beginning to find real satisfaction in independent writing, and the adding of a new burden at this time appears unwise. If they can be encouraged to use their manuscript writing to serve new purposes and new needs so that they grow in power to put their ideas on paper for themselves, they can develop considerable ease and confidence in writing. If, however, the desire to write is interfered with by the adding of a new form of handwriting at this time, many children may lose the enthusiasm and interest they are just beginning to show. The gains in attitude, interest, and writing power are well worth the delay in introducing the other form of handwriting. This is shown in the photographed material on pages 250–253 which traces the growth of a child from Grade I through Grade VIII. It is quite probable, also, that children should be allowed to use whichever form they wish once they have learned both. In fact, in some schools, in this country and in England, children use only manuscript writing throughout elementary and high school.

Children can help to evaluate their own writing. They enjoy keeping a folder or portfolio of their written work. Often a child will get out an earlier production to compare with his latest one and take both of them to the teacher saying, "Don't you think I write lots better than I used to?" Children enjoy analyzing and noting their progress toward goals they

Carol t

I like to pick tulips.

They are so pretty.

Wilmette, Ill.
April 5, 1950

Dear Miss Reynolds,
I am so sorry
you are not here at
school. This afternoon
we are going to dye eggs.
I wish you are here right
now.
Your friend
Carol Tideman

Writing of Some Wilmette, Illinois, Children in Grades I and II.

'Lloyd Wright.

We saw a hamster in kindergarten. It went across the bars like we do.

Wilmette, Ill
April 5, 1950
Dear Miss Reynolds,
I am sorry you can not come. Please send a letter. I know all the children would like to know how you are coming along.
from Lloyd Wright.

Writing of Some Wilmette, Illinois, Children in Grades I and II.

222

Caryl Aschbacher

I went to

the circus. The

clowns are

Caryl Lynn Aschbacher.
I see the rabbits in the flowers.
I see an Easter flower.
I see the Easter eggs.
The school is full of Easter eggs.
The rabbits are dying the eggs.
In the church the children are
singing songs.
A pretty mother is in the church
with a pretty hat,
and she has a flower
   in her hat.
I see the Easter flower.
My family is in the Easter
      parade.

Writing of Some Wilmette, Illinois, Children in Grades I and II.

Ronnie T.

I saw a hamster in school. A little boy owned it. It can do

Ronnie Turner
An Easter Story
There are 6 more days till Easter. The Easter rabbit is hard at work. He probably is painting Easter eggs. I can hardly wait till he comes. I dont think you can wait either. Do you! I lik to hunt for jelly beans. I find a basket of Easter eggs on my table.

have accepted and understood. They can learn to compare their handwriting with a standardized handwriting scale to judge the quality of their work and the points at which they need to improve. They find satisfaction in working for self-improvement if the need is clear and the goals are reasonable and attainable.

Spelling in the Primary Grades

Spelling is incidental in the first grade, but most children learn to spell certain words from using them in their dictation and copying. Learning to spell becomes more systematic in the second grade and is of continuing importance. Crucial words of greatest frequency in ordinary usage and of suitable difficulty for children at different grade levels appear in available spelling lists and textbooks based upon extensive research. Teachers should check the spelling needs of children against such lists to see that a well-rounded experience is offered to them. They should give opportunity for pupils to test themselves from time to time and to do remedial work on such common words as cause them trouble. Simple graded lists in alphabetical order, prepared and mimeographed by teacher and pupils, have proved useful for reference in many primary grades as an aid to an independent attack on spelling. Care, however, is necessary to see that no child is pushed beyond his capacity to learn while more capable students have an opportunity to far exceed the others in the number of words they make their own.

Since most of the spelling words that adults know have been learned outside of systematic spelling instruction, the goal of first importance is helping each child to acquire an effective method of learning the words he needs to use. This calls for a study on the teacher's part of the individual differences in children, and the way they learn and remember spelling. A visual approach and emphasis meets the needs of most children. Some require more emphasis on the sound image of the word; they should be encouraged to write the syllable "in" as they hear it in "into" or "interest" without thinking its separate letters. For some children the kinesthetic impression is most important. They need to get the "feel" of the word as they write it. Children who have difficulty need to interweave all forms of sensory impression—visual, auditory, speech motor, and hand motor—in order to master spelling. It is true that an important task of the elementary school is to help children to master the spelling of as many as possible of the common words of English, but the development by each individual of an *effective method* of learning spelling is of first importance.

When children in the late first or in the second grade are doing simple independent writing, they can help themselves if picture dictionaries, packets of words related to a topic, and the like, are available for ready reference. Or, the child may start to write the word, leaving space for its completion until the teacher can give him the personal help he needs.

Capitalization and Punctuation

Capitalization and punctuation are learned as they are needed. Children do not require special drill in the filling of blanks and other types of exercises. If they are encouraged to give thought to the way they would *say* what they are writing, the use of capitals as starters for sentences, periods or question marks as stoppers, and commas or other forms to indicate partial stops becomes simple and natural. Capital letters for the pronoun *I*, the names of persons and such titles as *Mr., Mrs.,* and *Miss,* the name of the school, the town, and the state are an obvious necessity in the primary grades. Names of months and days appear constantly as plans and records are made and special days observed. When the community is explored, the names of streets and buildings offer special problems in capitalization. The learning of rules is frequently more confusing than helpful at this stage. Reference sheets which show form and usage are valuable for self-help, or children can learn to refer to textbooks in reading or language and thus become independent in meeting some of their needs.

WRITTEN COMMUNICATION IN THE MIDDLE GRADES

Children whose writing moves through easy and comfortable stages in the early grades feel a growing sense of power. They usually like to write and do so very willingly. There are many uses for writing in the school and out-of-school life of the middle grades. Situations arise constantly which afford many opportunities for writing and some genuine demands for it.

Needs for Writing in the Middle Grades

Intermediate-grade children couple with an interest in themselves an increasing concern for the rest of the world, their curiosity extending beyond the community to state, nation, and world, even to the universe and all the fascinating questions which space presents. In the broadening program of the school they depend more and more upon books and reading to explain first-hand experience and to extend their knowledge and understanding vicariously. Assimilation of all this material becomes a major problem. Writing it out in words that are one's own, reflecting upon it, and reacting to it personally are significant elements in learning. Research indicates that problems of sentence structure encountered in such activity cause greater trouble at the intermediate-grade level than at any other. Confusion arises when words which children think they know bob up with new meanings and strange forms. Verbalism and repetition of the words of the book must be guarded against. Grappling with the expression of these new ideas and experiences is imperative if real growth is to take place.

These are also the years of the Cub Scouts, the Brownies, and the Bluebirds. Organizations demand minutes and reports. Upper-grade children in the six-year elementary school assume leadership in the school and are faced with many duties which involve writing. Sometimes they produce a school paper or write reports for the school council.

Writing in the middle grades is of two basic types: practical writing which is designed to serve a specific purpose and will be used and reacted to by others, and personal writing in which the individual has more freedom to be himself and to follow his own impulses and ideas.[3] The writing of business letters, reports, and records, the filling out of forms, and the writing of notices and other kinds of publicity are all practical tasks for which there is a definite purpose. Friendly letters, gift cards, diaries, and reminders are less formal and more personal. The writing of original stories, poems, plays, dramatic skits, jokes, and riddles calls for creative imagination and original thinking and is a personal matter. The content of practical writing is gathered from appropriate sources and must be organized to suit the purpose which the writing is to serve. The content of creative writing may be inspired and colored by outside influences, but it is reworked in the writer's mind until it is his own.

Steps in Writing Procedure

All children need to be encouraged to give thought first to the content and then to the form of their writing. A sensible and logical progression of steps for them to pursue in the middle grades is the following:

1. Put down what you want to say. Get your meaning on paper. You may need to decide in advance just what you want this piece of writing to do for your readers and to gather material to fit your purpose. It may help to jot down, briefly and in order, the points you want to make for the main events in your story or report.
2. Read it over to make sure that it says just what you want to say and in as clear and interesting a manner as possible. Does it begin and end well? Have you used interesting words? Have you made your reader see what you see?

[3] Alvina T. Burrows, June D. Ferebee, Dorothy C. Jackson, and Dorothy O. Saunders, *They All Want to Write: Written English in the Elementary School*, rev. ed. (New York, Prentice-Hall, Inc., 1952).

If the material is to be for personal use only or to be read to the class, this will suffice. If it is to be read by others or used for any other purpose, there are three more steps to take.

3. Look it over carefully for form. Is it arranged so that others can read it with ease? Are the traffic signals placed so as to aid smooth and accurate reading of your meaning? Is your composition arranged on the paper in convenient and readable form? Is the spelling correct? Does every sentence begin with a capital letter and end with an appropriate mark of punctuation? (Middle-grade children can be guided into increasing use of self-help materials at this point. Dictionaries and the models in their textbooks, in handbooks, or on guide sheets will help them to help themselves at many points.)
4. Take it to the teacher for final proof reading and any correction essential to clarity and effective expression.
5. Make a final copy that will serve your purpose and do you credit—one that you will be satisfied to have others read.

Most written work that is to be used for any practical purpose at the elementary school level needs to be talked over before the writing begins. Talking clarifies thinking and helps the children to see both the significance and the possibilities in what they are doing. It helps them to plan the form and the wording of what they are to write so that both can be of as high quality as possible. Later, when the children bring their material to the teacher for a final proofreading, she has opportunity to help them see their problems of usage and improve them wherever necessary. Guidance at this stage while both the material and the purpose are fresh in the children's minds is worth far more than red penciled corrections handed back to them the next day. Now it really matters—tomorrow it is hard to rebuild interest to the same pitch. Such procedure respects the child's individuality so far as expression is concerned, and enables him to achieve a product of which he can be proud.

Goals to Work Toward in All Writing

The basic goals in written as well as oral language are four rather obvious ones. The first is *ease* in writing. If a child can approach his task with confidence and a sense of adequacy, he can put his energy into making his writing serve his purpose and often find pleasure in doing it. *Clarity* is intimately associated with ease. *Suitability* in writing is highly important for all social purposes, and *originality* adds flavor and interest for both writer and reader.

Ease. Ease in writing is closely related to ease in speaking. A child who talks easily and confidently and has a background of wide experience on which to draw will not find it difficult to compose sentences that say what he wants to say. Ease and confidence come also with legible handwriting, command of simple spelling, an extensive and useful vocabulary, and at least rudimentary knowledge of how to put ideas into understandable conventional form on the paper. By the time children reach the middle grades almost all of them have the muscular coördination and physical strength to do any writing they need to do. The range of ability in composition, however, is wide. Some children are keenly interested in independent writing and can manage with ease any task they have occasion to do. But there are always a few children who cannot compose, write, spell, and carry on all the complex mental and physical labor of getting their ideas down on paper. If they can dictate what they want to say and then copy what the teacher has written for them, or sometimes if they are allowed to use the typewriter, they can turn out a product that gives them satisfaction. This is a legitimate intermediate step for those who are slow in gaining independence. It keeps the standards of quality in both thinking and writing at as high a level as the child is capable of at that moment and gives him time to develop confidence and skill before taking over the whole process. Abundant experience in writing is necessary to the attainment of ease for pupils at all levels of performance.

Clarity. Clarity is first of all a matter of clear mental concepts and well-formed ideas. No child is ready to write until he has had adequate experience, developed whatever knowledge is necessary, and thought and talked the subject through until it has become a part of him. He cannot write clearly out of meagerness of knowledge or experience nor out of hazy, half-formed ideas. Clear thinking is essential to clear writing at all times. Clarity in writing is dependent also upon the child's choice of words, the way he fits them together in sentences, his handwriting, his spelling, and his knowledge of how to place his thoughts on the paper so that others can read them.

Many types of practical writing require careful planning in order to achieve clarity. A request for information or service must have in it all the elements of information that are essential if the request is to be granted. An invitation must make clear the time, place, occasion, degree of formality, or any other information a guest may need in order to accept. Analysis and planning preparatory to writing, and checking and evaluation of first drafts should be done under the guidance of the teacher.

That clarity is dependent on knowledge and experience as well as on ability to do careful, accurate writing is well illustrated in a composition which is guaranteed to be authentic. The child's writing is above reproach; the problem lies in the fact that he has had little experience with either the bird or the beast he chose to write about in response to his assignment.

A Bird and a Beast [4]

The bird that I am going to write about is the Owl. The Owl cannot see at all by day and at night is as blind as a bat.

I do not know much about the Owl, so I will go on to the beast which I am going to choose. It is the Cow. The Cow is a mammal. It has six sides—right, left, and upper and below. At the back it has a tail on which hangs a brush. With this it sends the flies away so that they do not fall into the milk. The head is for the purpose of growing horns and so that the mouth can be somewhere. The horns are to butt with, and the mouth is to moo with. Under the cow hangs the milk. It is arranged for milking. When people milk, the milk comes, and there is never an end to the supply. How the cow does it I have not yet realized,

[4] Edward Weeks, "Peripatetic Reviewer," *The Atlantic Monthly*, CLXXXV (June, 1950), p. 78.

but it makes more and more. The cow has a fine sense of smell; one can smell it far away. This is the reason for the fresh air in the country.

The man cow is called an ox. It is not a mammal. The cow does not eat much, but what it eats it eats twice, so that it gets enough. When it is hungry it moos, and when it says nothing it is because its inside is all full up with grass.

Suitability. The matter of suitability is even more important in writing than in speech. The weight carried by a written record and the permanency of it make it particularly important that thought be given not only to the message to be conveyed but also to the emotional overtones and attitudes it portrays, the response it may produce in the reader, and the social consequences of the response. Children need to learn that expression which might have little consequence in a conversation between friends could bring entirely different and perhaps highly unfavorable response when said in the more impersonal setting of a business letter or even of a personal letter. Facial expression, friendly attitude, and the very way in which words are spoken tend to heighten or tone down the emotional reaction of the hearer. Words that are spoken are passing things—one speaks and the sound is gone. If the speaker senses unfavorable reaction in his listener, he can modify the reaction through explanation, apology, or a change in his own approach, but that is not possible when the words are set down on paper. The permanence of a written record is both a value and a source of responsibility. The record is available for further reference, which makes it highly useful, but that very fact makes it doubly necessary that the content and form not only serve the writer's purpose but do him credit. Children need to learn to think of these paper messages as highly important to their own reputations and to take pride in sending out messages that speak well of them.

Suitability of usage for a given situation is an important factor in the development of language power. As Volume I of this series points out,[5] there are recognized social levels in the use of English. Children learn early when it is appropriate to use the greeting, "Hi!" "Hello!" or "Howdy!" Other more formal contacts, they discover, require "How do you do?" There are social levels in which "ain't" is more comfortable usage than "isn't." The opposite is equally true. Some understanding of the social implications of usage can be developed in the middle grades. Since the United States prides itself on the mobility of its social classes, power to express oneself on a level higher than that to which he is accustomed may be a vital factor in social and business success.

It is difficult to motivate children to give up unacceptable usage that is characteristic of their families and neighborhoods. The school has the child not more than 17 per cent of the total year, whereas the home and neighborhood influence him all of the rest of the time. Besides, the child's security and happiness are closely tied up with his home and the people in it. He does not want to be different nor to risk separation from those who love him most and in whom his security is centered. Efforts to improve usage in a child's speech will bring little result until the child himself wants to improve and until his ear is tuned to the better forms so that they "sound right." The book material the child uses, on the other hand, may be predominantly better in usage than his speech. He becomes accustomed to patterns of usage in print which he does not carry over into his speech, at least beyond the teacher's presence. In writing, the child can become accustomed to higher standards and may learn to write better English than he speaks. Filling in blanks probably does not aid him much; improvement comes through many experiences in doing real writing that is important to him.

[5] Commission on the English Curriculum, National Council of Teachers of English, *The English Language Arts*, N.C.T.E. Curriculum Series, Vol. I (New York, Appleton-Century-Crofts, Inc., 1952), Ch. 12, "The Modern View of Grammar and Linguistics," p. 278.

Writing serves many purposes, and children must learn to fit content to purpose. A factual report will differ from a report of one's personal reactions to a book he has read. The formality or informality of writing determines how much of himself he can put into it. A major task of the middle grades is to help children learn to differentiate between situations and needs and to suit the techniques they use in both writing and speaking to those needs.

Originality. Children who are free and uninhibited have their own fresh and lively ways of saying what they are thinking. Originality and creativeness need to be preserved and fostered. Often a teacher can help a child whose writing is dull and uninteresting by saying, "Tell it to me just the way you are thinking it. Now let's write it the way you talk. Your reader will enjoy it more if it sounds just like you—just as if you were talking to him." Children should be taught to respect their own thinking and their own expression of it and to be themselves in writing as well as in face to face conversations. Such an attitude need not prevent clearing up any gross errors in usage that stand in the way of clarity.

Need for Personal Encouragement in Writing

Writing can become important to children if they are encouraged to use it as a means of expressing their own thoughts and feelings. A teacher who accepts what children write, and does so with sincere interest and without overdoing praise or undermining with criticism, will find children growing in interest in writing. If they are encouraged to be themselves in their writing, to say what they think, believe, or imagine, most of them find real satisfaction in the task. The more they write the easier it becomes to put their ideas on a page. When the writing itself ceases to be a heavy task, they can give more thought to style and to creating the effect they want to create. Children will try hard to write beginning sentences that catch and hold interest and to build up the sequence of events in a story so that there is an interesting climax. The example which follows was written by a fourth-grade girl:

The Mystery of the Mysterious Egg

Once upon a time there lived a man who liked children very much. He gave a party for every holiday in the year for the children in his neighborhood.

This story takes place at an Easter party he gave. It was the morning before the party and the man getting things ready was hiding colored eggs, high, low, and right in the middle for an Easter egg hunt. He was just finishing when the children started coming.

When all the children had come, they started. First they played a few games and then they ate cookies, cake, candy, and ice cream. Then they went outside and were very excited when the man announced the Easter egg hunt. The children looked all around and finally they had found all the eggs they could and brought them to the man and the man counted them. The man finally after counting them several times announced that there was one missing.

They looked high, low and right in the middle and couldn't find it. Then one girl came up to the man and children and opened her hand—peep, peep—a little chick. She had solved the mystery of the mysterious egg. The man gave her her prize and everybody lived happily ever after.

The End.

Poetry writing comes more slowly with most children. They will often dictate poems long before they are able to write them for themselves and often will prefer to dictate their poetry even after they have learned to write stories quite satisfactorily.

The poem which follows was written by a fourth-grade boy:

The Breeze and the Leaves

I love the autumn breeze . . .
Playing catchers with the lovely leaves,
   I whisper softly
  Come down lovely autumn leaves,
    And play with me.
They toss and tumble through the air,
You would think they were at a jolly fair,
   I whisper softly
  Come down and play with me,
    Lovely Queen of all the leaves.

Ronald

Therapeutic Values in Writing

For many children there are therapeutic values in writing. Through reproducing and reflecting upon experiences which trouble them, they are better able to accept and to live with them, relieving fears and tensions as they write. One teacher found that all of the stories written by a fifth-grade girl expressed in one form or another her deep antagonism toward her small brothers and sisters and her resentment toward her mother who made her care for them. A third-grade boy expressed such violent jealousy of a small sister who claimed most of his mother's attention that the teacher helped the mother to understand the problem and find ways to add to the boy's sense of security. A child may express his deepest feelings and longings in a story or poem. He may leave his own inadequacies and infirmities and the restrictions of his environment behind him and do or be in imagination what he truly longs to be. The lonely child, in his stories, has many friends; the restricted child has freedom to do as he wishes; the shy, insecure child is bold and strong; the child who is uncertain of his mother's love has a parent who cherishes him. Free writing can help teachers understand children. It can also help children to work through some of their problems, thus gaining in confidence and appreciation of their own potentialities and the worth of their own ideas.

Most children will write stories very willingly if there is a comfortable working relationship in the group, and they feel at ease with the teacher and their companions. No child will expose his real thoughts until he is sure of the way they will be received. If the teacher accepts them sincerely and is generous in her attitudes and in her help, the child will bring her more and more material, and his writing will express his own personality.

Skills in the Intermediate-Grade Program

The skills of writing take a long time to master. They are complicated, and attack on them begins only after the child enters school. Moreover, in life outside the school, he receives much less practice and help in written than he does in oral expression. The middle years are, for the average child, crucial years in the mastery of simple essentials of usage. Much practice on them should be given to all pupils in relation to the needs revealed in their speech and writing. Contractions, for example, should be mastered once and for all by many children. Such mastery takes little mental power. The writing of contractions demands clear visualization and continuous practice in use. Possessive forms can wait on familiarity with contractions, for they demand insight into the *meaning* of possession—an intricate problem for many children.

Spelling. In spelling, research shows that it is the easy words the intermediate grade pupils misspell—the three kinds of *there* and the three kinds of *to*. Children should not be pushed into intricate spelling until they show need for the words in their own writing, but should be helped to gain permanent mastery of such often-used words as Fitzgerald's *Crucial Core Vocabulary* based on the writing of pupils in Grades IV–VI.[6]

In the intermediate grades pupils add to the devices for seeing and hearing words learned in the primary grades, *syllabication*, with special attention to the second half of longer words, which they tend to slur over in their haste to get to the end of the word. Attention to the most common suffixes aids both reading and spelling. The plural of such words as *baby* and *valley* needs to be learned. Use of the dictionary as a source of reference for spelling and meaning becomes increasingly important during these years. Teachers should remember, however, that unless children know how a

---

[6] James A. Fitzgerald, *Basic Life Spelling Vocabulary* (Milwaukee, The Bruce Publishing Company, 1951).

word begins, they cannot look it up in the dictionary. It is more reasonable to look up *circumference* under *sir, ser,* or *sur* than it is to try *cir.* Pupils in the intermediate grades may be aroused to a lasting interest in words and to a sense of responsibility for spelling them correctly in all written work. The methods of attack on new words learned in the primary grades should become habitual during the middle years.

Handwriting. Carelessness and poor handwriting are the most frequent causes of mistakes in spelling. Teaching handwriting during these years is largely a matter of individual diagnosis and effort toward improvement on the part of the pupils themselves. The program in cursive writing begun in the primary grades should be maintained for those children who prefer it to manuscript writing.

Grammatical usage. Concerted attack on individual items of usage in the intermediate grades helps greatly in clearing the way for more mature elements of speech and writing in later years. Crucial matters of literacy should come first. Niceties such as the distinction between *can* and *may* have no place in the program of pupils still saying *I seen it* and *I done it.* Labeling the parts of speech has proved in one research study after another, both in this country and in Great Britain, to be futile so far as its effect on speech and writing is concerned. Intermediate-grade pupils should have practice in the *use* of language, not in the classification of forms. This does not mean that the teacher may not refer to a word as a verb or pronoun and that some children will not use the terms after her. It means that instruction will be focused on improvement in the pupils' own speech and writing. Children may note how useful it is to have words which can substitute for names, so that Mary does not have to say, "Please pass Mary the cream for Mary's oatmeal." They can learn readily that both the name and the substitute are unnecessary—as in *My mother—she.* They must remember to name themselves last in a series. They can discover that they often make mistakes when talking about two persons which they do not make when speaking of one: "He went." "I went." they say, but frequently, "*Him* and *me* went." They know how to write, "My mother read *me* a story." or "My mother read *her* a story." but they put the two together as, "My mother read *she* and *I* a story." The rule is a simple one: Say what you would say for each one separately. Practice in combining such sentences is more effective than filling in blanks.

The value of concrete, descriptive verbs can be demonstrated again and again in the children's own writing and in the stories they read. It should be noted constantly.

Certain verb forms cause trouble for children. Attack upon such problems in their own writing should be in proportion to the cruciality of the usages. Distinctions between *lie* and *lay* and *sit* and *set* are unimportant for children who still say, "He *has went*," or "He *come* to my house yesterday." The four verbs most used in the English, besides the verb *to be*, are *see, do, come,* and *go*. Misuse of them is evidence of illiteracy. Special attention, therefore, should be given to them. Fundamentally important also is the use of *was* or *were*, *is* or *are*, or *have, has,* or *had* with such verb forms as *begun, rung, written,* and *frozen* in the making of statements. A list of crucial usages against which children's speech and writing may be checked in the intermediate grades appears in Dr. Robert Pooley's *Teaching English Usage,* published by the National Council of Teachers of English.[7]

Diction. In a unit on Our National Parks, a group of children applied the word *wonderful* to food, bears, glaciers, and weather. They used *cute* to describe flowers, a cottage, a guide, and a donkey. The search for synonyms for overworked words is important in the intermediate grades to stimulate concrete and effective expression.

Sentence sense. Development of sentence sense at the intermediate grade level can be related to this problem. Build-

[7] Robert C. Pooley, *Teaching English Usage* (New York, Appleton-Century-Crofts, Inc., 1946).

ing sentences by adding descriptive modifiers to such a base as *horse ran* or *boys rode* is a game children enjoy and one which helps them understand both the base of a sentence and the effective use of words. Reading aloud the resulting sentences shows the interesting variety of pictures presented.

Research indicates that run-on sentences, fragments, and garbled expression occur more frequently in Grades IV–VI than at any other level of the school system.[8] Perhaps the burden of new ideas and information has been too great for assimilation. Clear thinking is the only adequate basis for clear sentences. Reading aloud what they have written and listening to their sentences helps children to sense completeness, to discover omissions, and to detect elements lacking in clarity.

Capitalization. Problems increase in capitalization as children broaden their contacts with the rest of the world. Geography introduces distinctions between directions and sections of the country. Names of specific mountains, lakes, rivers, and oceans need capital letters, whereas general terms do not. States of the Union and countries of the world must be capitalized. Whatever problems of capitalization grow out of the daily work of the classroom should be emphasized.

Punctuation. Children at the intermediate grade level commonly have much conversation in their stories. They should use their reading texts and library books to discover how the printer paragraphs and punctuates conversation. As sentences grow more firm, the series appears. As they grow more complex, there is need to join or to separate modifiers within the sentence by the use of commas. Simple appositives will be common. The use of the comma before *but* connecting parts of the sentence will be needed, and sometimes before *and* when necessary for clearness. Individual children will vary greatly in the maturity of their expression and hence in

[8] Mata V. Bear, "Children's Growth in the Use of Written Language," *Elementary English Review*, XVI (December, 1939), pp. 312–19.

the amount of punctuation they will need. Some will do well to confine themselves to end of sentence punctuation. Self-help should be stimulated by reference to reading and language books and by the compiling of home-made usage handbooks by the children themselves as they analyze their need. A guide prepared directly in relation to such need is the *Handbook of English for Boys and Girls,* which grew out of a committee report of the National Conference on Research in English.[9]

THE IMPROVEMENT OF WRITING IN THE SEVENTH AND EIGHTH GRADES

When pupils enter the seventh and eighth grades, they are approaching adult status in thought and expression, so that the problem of grappling with the adequate communication of those ideas is a major one.

Emphasis on the Same Principles Used Earlier

The principles governing the teaching of writing in the middle grades are equally applicable to Grades VII and VIII. The motive for writing comes from real needs arising from the daily life of boys and girls at school and at home. Clarity, ease of writing, suitability for the occasion, and originality of expression are still the goals in early adolescence. Selection and organization of materials in terms of the purpose of the writing become increasingly important as pupils deal with more and more complex problems and ideas. Skills must be developed in use as needed for real communication. Constant encouragement from the teacher and a growing sense of responsibility for the improvement of their own writing should help children gradually to achieve more power of expression.

[9] Delia E. Kibbe, Lou L. La Brant, and Robert C. Pooley, *Handbook of English for Boys and Girls* (Chicago, Scott, Foresman and Company, 1939).

The Inevitability of Wide Differences in Achievement

Under good teaching, individual differences in performance increase with the years. Hence teachers in the seventh and eighth grades must expect a wide range of achievement in written expression among the boys and girls in their classes. Skillful guidance of the gifted and never-ending patience with those less facile in expression are especially necessary in early adolescence, when young people are examining themselves critically and developing attitudes of self-confidence or lack of it which profoundly influence their future.

In general, boys and girls in the seventh and eighth grades have progressed a long way in writing ability. Some of them write with ease and maturity of expression. If their writing experience has been reasonably satisfying, many of them are genuinely interested in original composition and in imaginative writing of varied types. Some are concerned with style in writing and can set individual goals for their own improvement. Both a seventh-grade teacher and the children in the class cherished the following story written by a student the first day of school after the midwinter holidays. In the writing, which was preceded by a discussion of New Year's resolutions and what one expects of the New Year, the children were striving to develop originality and humor and to lift themselves above their usual humdrum way of saying things.

'44 Can Help with His Pins

It was December 31, 1943 and Father Time had called his years together for a family council. He did this every year in the past and all the old years decided what to do for the New Year. The years before "1492" gave him a man to discover America. The years before 1776 gave him the Declaration of Independence for the Americans. The years before 1914 gave him the Panama Canal.

So now this large family was deciding about what to give 1944.

"Years," began Father Time as he stepped up onto a platform, "You know a little boy is going to bounce in here very soon now—namely 1944—and we must have a present for him."

"A juke box would be definitely super!" suggested 1943.

"He'd look so cute riding around on a bicycle built for two!" sighed 1890.

"Give him a spinning wheel. That's something useful," contributed 1785.

"But those are silly things to give him," said Father Time. "I was thinking that what 1944 in the United States needs most is a *victory*."

"Now, hold on, Father Time," objected 1812. "A victory would be swell, but victories don't grow on trees. You have to fight and work for them. I know from experience."

"I know, too," assured Father Time, "but I have a plan. We all have some scrap metal, paper, or rubber. 1939, you have plenty of rubber, since Goodyear discovered a method of vulcanizing it during your time. 1765, you must have a lot of copies of *Common Sense,* and you years that have metal inventions, and old newspapers can donate those too. I hate to give it up, but I am donating my scythe. And 1944, himself can help, too. He can donate his safety pins."

Mary Jackson

In an effort to develop original creative thinking, an eighth-grade class was encouraged to write imaginative stories built about inanimate objects. Two examples serve to illustrate results. All of the stories were ingenious and colorful though the quality of writing differed materially within the group.

My Secret

So many people have looked at me and wished that I could talk that I have decided after all these years to talk and tell you my secret.

I am a big long room of a house located at the corner of Eighth and Jackson Streets in Springfield, Illinois.

My first owner was a preacher. Then one day he sold me to a tall bony man. This man looked so sad I wondered if I could ever get used to him tramping over my floor. His name was Abraham Lincoln and he was trying to be a lawyer but he was almost a failure at it.

His little boys tracked mud in on my floor and sometimes the chickens and ducks would come in too. In fact I was a mess most of the time, except when Mrs. Lincoln would decide to have a party. Then I knew I was really in for a beating. She was a society lady, and sometimes she would invite three hundred people to one party.

But the time I liked most was when Mrs. Lincoln and the boys were upstairs, fast asleep. Then Mr. Lincoln would have some men come over and they would close my doors so no one could hear them talk. Then they would sit in front of my fireplace and plan what was best for our country.

One day Mr. Lincoln left me and never came back, so people said.

After a while some folks came and cleaned my walls and my floor, and took out most of the furniture; then they put a rope across my doors.

Now people walk in very quietly and stare at me as if I were dead, but that is my very own secret. I'm still alive and so is Mr. Lincoln.

Late at night, after all the sightseers are gone and everything is quiet, Mr. Lincoln gets his friends together and they come back to me. He says he can think better in his own living room.

Mr. Roosevelt comes with him lots of times. They are very good friends, for you see now they are not a Democrat or a Republican, they are both Americans. They have lots of big plans they would like to share with you; but that's their secret, and I musn't tell.

But I have told you my secret, so when you come to Springfield and visit me, don't be sad and gloomy and look at me as if I were a monument. Please be happy, for I am the happiest room in the world.

Carl

Stiffy and Me

I spoke to Stiffy, the stalk of hemp next to me, in low tones because we were ripe now and the cutters were coming to cut us down. I started to speak and, all of a sudden, we were sliced by a sharp knife, dragged up by a rake, and thrown into a big wooden cart. On the cart the driver, a little Negro boy, sat on us the whole way to the mill where we were made into rope. It just happened that Stiffy and I got in the same rope, we were lying right together, too.

Then we were shipped to America where we were sold to a hardware store. We lay on the counter for days before we were bought. One day an old cowboy came in and bought us. He took us out to his ranch where he made a lasso out of us. The next day he tried us out (we did all right for beginners). One day I felt mean so I gave a steer a rope burn on purpose.

Several months later we were taken to the rodeo. That day we worked pretty hard (we had some pretty stiff and sore hands) but we won 3 blue ribbons and one red one. The thing that put us on the favorite hook was yet to come.

One day Texas 8 Ball Tex, terror of the town, came riding wildly down the main street, shooting all the ladys veils off and shouting like mad. That's one thing our master won't stand for and that's disturbing the ladys. So our master jumped on his horse, grabbed us and took off. After we had chased 8 Ball a long way we came within lasso range. Stiffy and I were tense, and we sensed that our master needed our help. Then he raised us and threw us toward 8 Ball. We strained toward him, then settled around his neck and pulled.

Now we sit on our masters favorite hook and we're only used on special occasions.

Bill

Some of the compositions written by young adolescents are highly dramatic and fanciful, and some show an emerging philosophy. The paragraph which follows was written by a boy in the eighth grade.

Guess What!

I ruin lives and people without killing. I never forgive and seldom forget. I gather strength with age. I am really a parasite that lives on good and bad alike. My victims are as numerous as the stars in the sky and often as innocent and defenseless. I am handled badly, being tossed carelessly from one person to another. I in myself mean no harm, but I am what people make me. In fact, I think it's too bad that I, and others like me, even have to exist.

My name is — — — — — — — gossip!

Taylor

Consistent Help for Poor Writers

On the other hand, one finds in the seventh and eighth grades some boys and girls who are almost completely inarticulate, who do not know a sentence from a fragment, and who write in short jerks with little mastery of spelling or mechanics. For these children especial sympathy is required and patient help with matters long since mastered by others in the fourth or fifth grades. For them much oral discussion should precede writing to give clarity and order to their ideas. Much personal help should be given them in proofreading and improving what they have written.

The Growing Importance of Practical and Expository Writing

The need for practical writing increases during early adolescence. As the activities of young people expand both at home and in the classroom, many occasions for writing arise. Travel calls for both business and personal letters. New social experiences make similar demands for gracious invitations and courteous acceptances and expressions of appreciation. Clubs and other organized activities demand notices, inquiries, and minutes. Many adolescents who listen to radio and television programs write letters for information or offerings of varied sorts together with expressions of approval for programs they especially enjoy. Hobbies and collecting demand letters of request and the keeping of records.

Writing book notes for all to share is a common activity of these years, when the recommendation of a fellow student is often worth much more than that of the teacher. Attracting the attention of the reader by a novel presentation, by use of vivid words, by recreating characters, scenes, or events, so as to capture the reader's interest and persuade him to read the book is an absorbing task for many seventh- and eighth-grade pupils. Use of proper form for a bibliographical entry and for mention of a title in written context can easily be mastered by the average student during these years.

Real motives for writing. Much writing with real motives for expression is imperative if seventh- and eighth-grade pupils are to develop a sense of responsibility for clear, interesting presentation in complete and acceptable form.

At the same time, the school program itself calls for an increased amount of carefully organized expository writing. Class and individual work in the social studies demands taking notes, making outlines, writing reports, keeping personal and group records, writing business and friendly letters and invitations, and responding to those received. All of this necessitates clear statement and accurate handling of factual material as well as acceptable use of various forms of writing. Work in science requires exactness of expression in recording observations and accurate stating of facts. The defining of problems and their solution call for preciseness in thinking and in the use of words. In all of these experiences children can learn to use written expression with increasing skill and ease.

Selection and organization of ideas. Material must be gathered from several sources and woven into a unified plan of presentation. With the effort to expand more complex ideas comes a need for paragraph structure. Larger topics must be broken into their contributory parts, and each part developed before discussion of the next is undertaken. These are difficult tasks with which seventh- and eighth-grade students need much guidance in the classroom in the initial stages of thought and organization.

The resulting plan of presentation must be their own—not merely a reproduction of what is in the book. Facts and ideas must be digested and made to serve the purposes of the pupils' own thinking. Problems of plagiarism which often arise during these years are due not to dishonesty but rather to lack of guidance in assimilating and organizing material and in the use of proper conventions for acknowledging sources. An excellent description of how one teacher and librarian worked together to help seventh-grade pupils solve the problem of wasteful copying of the encyclopedia appears in Volume I of this curriculum series under the caption of "Coöperative Use of Fingers and Heads in Reference Work." [10]

Disciplined use of words. Summaries of findings of reports and of class discussion demand disciplined use of language along with clarity of thinking. It is not too early in these years to emphasize for average students or above the problem of the effect of language upon the reader or listener—the difference between fact and opinion, the backing-up of generalizations with evidence, and the quoting of legitimate authority. Stereotyped expressions can be avoided, and also rigid classifications marked by such words as *never, always, all,* or *none.* The emotional appeal of words can be studied by older boys and girls, and the power of figurative language to influence thought and feeling.

Problems of sentence structure. Problems of clarity, completeness, and variety in sentence structure need special emphasis at a time when pupils are grappling with more and

---

[10] Commission on the English Curriculum, National Council of Teachers of English, *The English Language Arts,* N.C.T.E. Curriculum Series, Vol. I (New York, Appleton-Century-Crofts, Inc., 1952), pp. 238–39.

more complex ideas. Again, the base of the sentence built up by use of concrete words and varied modifiers requires practice on the part of boys and girls. Learning classifications is not the aim so much as power in the expression of ideas.

Increased modification of ideas leads to greater use of the comma to give clarity to the sentence. (Semicolons are rarely needed by junior high school pupils.) Modifiers must stand next the words they modify. The word for which each pronoun substitutes must be made clear.

Matters of usage. Certain items of usage which have been introduced in Grades IV–VI will have become habitual for many students in these grades. If they are not, mastery of these simpler skills becomes an important task of both teacher and pupils. Research indicates that a few unacceptable usages repeated many times make up the bulk of the problem at this level. Again, Dr. Pooley's *Teaching English Usage* indicates what these are. Individuals can make their own handbooks of usage, containing those elements with which they have continued difficulty. Self-help devices of this kind should lead to a personal sense of responsibility for improvement. Putting one's own manuscript into proper form before asking. anyone else to read it should be emphasized constantly as in Grades IV–VI. Often the best way to do this is to read aloud what one has written, because the ear may catch errors which the eye misses.

Handwriting and spelling. Handwriting in these grades is largely a matter of self-diagnosis and self-help from materials provided. With the increase in vocabulary due to a broader curriculum and wider social experience, correct spelling of new words in each subject of study and in the personal writing of individual pupils should be watched with vigilance. Formation of plurals of certain words causes trouble, as do distinctions in meaning indicated by the spelling of such verb forms as *choose* and *chose* or *lead* and *led*. Again, as in Grades IV–VI, first emphasis should be upon the simple, everyday words which pupils commonly misspell, upon the curriculum words for each unit, and upon those needed to record the personal experiences and widely varied thinking of individual pupils. Learning effective methods of attack on new words is all-important.

GROWTH IN WRITTEN EXPRESSION

It is always enlightening to watch the progress of pupils in writing throughout the elementary school, to see how language power and thought power progress together, to discover the relationship of both to growing social and intellectual maturity, and to sense the increasing control over vocabularly and sentence structure which comes with added experience and with grappling with the expression of that experience in writing. What is especially needed to clarify the whole process is to follow the same child from kindergarten up, noting his gradual maturing from year to year.

Growth of One Pupil from Grades I to VIII

That guiding children's progress in written expression can be a stimulating and satisfying experience for the teacher is evidenced by the following series of papers showing the growth of one pupil from the first grade through the eighth. Most of the examples are of writing which served some practical classroom need. It is interesting to note the growth from year to year of firmness and flow in handwriting, though all of it shows the same individual characteristics which appeared early in the child's writing. Growth in sentence structure is also interesting to trace. From simple, schoolbookish expression in the early grades, she has moved to free, colorful, expressive writing which tells something about the personality of the writer, her sensitiveness to qualities in other people, her interest in them, and her sense of humor. Ability to handle written form also shows growth from level to level; there is free and confident use of punctuation though there is still some confusion with regard to spelling.

Dear Mother,
Come to our Doll
Show on Monday
at 1 P.M.
Love,
Sue

Grade I
September, 1945

Little Fox

Little Fox has a Tom Tom
He likes to play on it.
He beats the Tom Tom
for Indian dances.

Grade 2
1946

Sue   Hornstein

Samples of the Writing of a Baltimore Girl from Grade I through Grade VIII.
Note the growth in handwriting and in power of expression.
250

How the Mexicans Dress

In Mexico, the children dress like their parents do. The women and girls wear rebosos and gay colored skirts that are very long. The men and boys wear serapes and sombreros. The sombreros of the rich men and boys are made of felt. The sombreros of the poor men and boys are made of straw. The women and girls wear blouses. The men and boys wear gay sashs.

Grade 3
October · 1947   Sue

What am I?

When the early settlers came to the New World the Indians taught the people how to use and cook me. I am very important to eat because I make you so very strong. I come in a can or in the form of an ear. I hope you will eat me and like me. Who am I?

I am the corn crop.

Sue Hornstein

Grade IV
1948
(First use of ink)

Samples of the Writing of a Baltimore Girl (con't.)

251

The Friendly House

I live on Dorchester Road. I am a big brick ~~thing~~ A whole family lives in me. A girl, a boy and their mother and daddy. I really don't know what they would do with out me. If it rained, and they didnot have me they would surely soak, and if it were ninty-nine out side and they diden't have me they would scortch to death. I do think they are grateful to me because I am so helpful. Beautiful flowers make me the prettest house in the block.

Sue Hornstein
Grade 5a
Feb. 9, 1949.

Riddle For The King

During the winter I was in a play called "Riddle For The King." It was an entertaining dramatization about a girl and a boy who lost a day. Rose Ellen and David met many strange charters including The King of the Year. I played the part of Jestr which was written as one of the funnist parts in the play. We had a verry appreciative audience which made ~~this~~ put forth our best efforts for a good proformace.

Grade VI - 1950

Samples of the Writing of a Baltimore Girl (con't.)
252

Book Review

The story was about Francis, Joan & a slight and somewhat spirited person whose father was sending her to England for a year. But now her fear at leaving America has a goatee of cheer. There's the story of fascinating section of English bard, and what they will be like, and the appearance on shipboard of Aunt Esglos't girl who had hide, & that girl who are sharp too! There Pop's going to put her wants for her if she should go for throuft. Francis to experience with "hands across the sea" see for herself better in-tune and no central hoosing. Francis's shockers are endgrowed as well as spirit. It isn't just that class what uniform this looks like or socks — but the pulling hospitality of "who was asked his a thank's";

The story was about completed is called "Francie," by Alan.

Grandma Stages Comeback

In the gay flapper twenty's a silent screen star, named Gloria Swanson enjoyed great popularity. Almost lost, many years later sound movies came to life she retired a wealthy women. Becoming a grandma, Miss Swanson lived a quiet and happy life. This kind of life became boring over a long period of time and, the queen of silent movies began to remember the "good old days" when she was a screen star. Paramount Pictures gave Gloria Swanson the opportunity, every star dreams of, in "Sunset Boulevard," a picture showing the era that she knew so well, in forgotten talents were revealed. Currently she is appearing in a Broadway show, and is wanted by many television programs. At fifty-five, famous Grandma Swanson had proved that good showmanship recognizes no age.

1951

Suzy Johnstein
7A

1952 - Grade VIII

Samples of the Writing of a Baltimore Girl (con't.)

There appears to be real interest in writing and enjoyment of it. The examples are typical of the grades they represent and show the kind of growth which many children achieve under stimulating guidance.

Growth in Handwriting by Two Persons

On pages 255 and 256 are samples of the handwriting of two persons, one left-handed and the other right-handed. The first example was written by a fourth-grade child and copied by the same individual at age 22. This girl wrote with her right hand and had achieved legible writing at age nine though it is imperfect in a number of ways. The general style of writing is the same at age 22 but more consistent and flowing. The second example is of the writing of a left-handed girl in the sixth grade and at age 22. Again there is distinct similarity in the pattern of writing, though the adult has given up efforts to achieve a righthand slant and is writing a legible, uniform backhand slant, which is the natural pattern of writing for her. It is interesting to note in these examples, as well as in daily contacts with adults, that each person uses an individualized form of handwriting which has become easy for him regardless of the style which the school has taught. Legibility, ease, and enough speed to meet individual needs are the only practical goals for the school to set in handwriting.

SUMMARY

Children who do their writing under guidance and with help that is suited to their needs have many opportunities to practice good writing. Proofreading with the teacher, where necessary, gives them opportunity to see and understand their mistakes and what to do about them. Making a final copy gives them practice in writing a good hand. There is little or no practice on drill material to hand in to be graded, but a constant teaching-learning situation in all written work, which bears fruit in interest in writing and in high standards

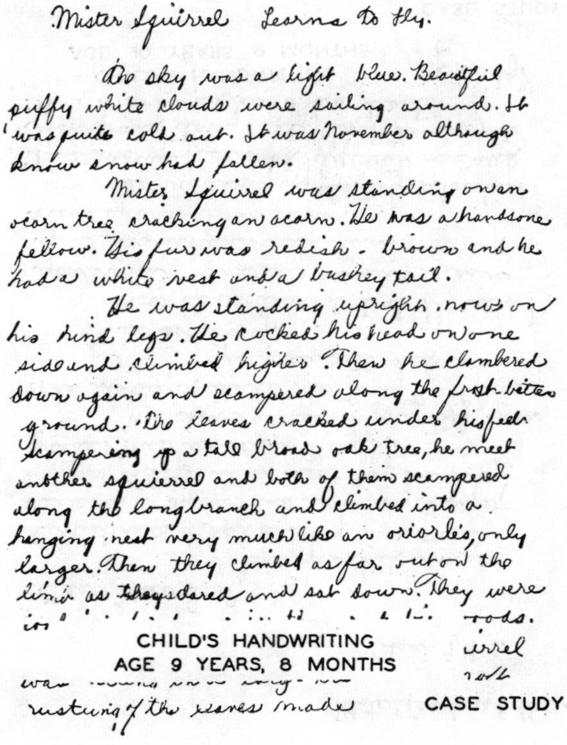
Mister Squirrel Learns to Fly.
The sky was a light blue. Beautiful puffy white clouds were sailing around. It was quite cold out. It was November although know snow had fallen.
Mister Squirrel was standing on an acorn tree cracking an acorn. He was a handsone fellow. His fur was redish - brown and he had a white vest and a bushey tail.
He was standing upright. nows on his hind legs. He cocked his head on one side and climbed higher. Then he clambered down again and scampered along the frost-bitten ground. The leaves cracked under his feet. Scampering up a tall broad oak tree, he meet another squierrel and both of them scampered along the long branch and climbed into a hanging nest very much like an oriorle's, only larger. Then they climbed as far out on the limb as they dared and sat down. They were

CHILD'S HANDWRITING
AGE 9 YEARS, 8 MONTHS

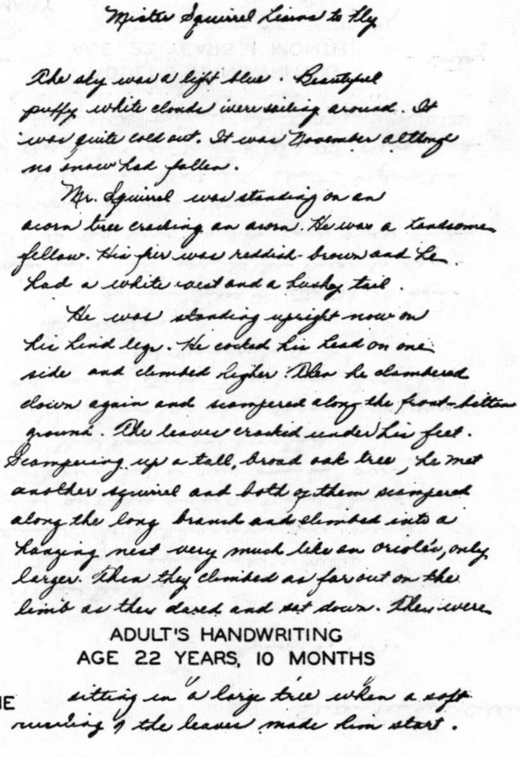
Mister Squirrel Learns to Fly
The sky was a light blue. Beautiful puffy white clouds were sailing around. It was quite cold out. It was November although no snow had fallen.
Mr. Squirrel was standing on an acorn tree cracking an acorn. He was a handsome fellow. His fur was reddish-brown and he had a white vest and a bushy tail.
He was standing upright now on his hind legs. He cocked his head on one side and climbed higher. Then he clambered down again and scampered along the frost-bitten ground. The leaves cracked under his feet. Scampering up a tall, broad oak tree, he met another squirrel and both of them scampered along the long branch and climbed into a hanging nest very much like an oriole's, only larger. Then they climbed as far out on the limb as they dared and sat down. They were
sitting in a large tree when a soft rustling of the leaves made him start.

ADULT'S HANDWRITING
AGE 22 YEARS, 10 MONTHS

CASE STUDY 15 - ARLENE

State Teachers College

Jan. 9, 1939.

Dear Miss Sage,

I hope you had a very nice Christmas. I had a very nice one. I received a radio and so many things! There are so many things I would. His name is Ronald.

We have a club again this year. The name of it is The Busy Bee Club. I am the vice-president and the secretary.

How do you like it at the school you are in? It would be nice to visit your school. Won't you come over and visit your schoolroom.

This morning we are studying about Exploration. Then found things out about them, what they discovered and whom. Ilunid

Sincerely,
L. Coily,
or

CHILD'S HANDWRITING
AGE 10 YEARS 9 MONTHS

State Teachers College

Jan. 9, 1939.

Dear Miss Sage,

ADULT'S HANDWRITING
AGE 22 YEARS 1 MONTH

CASE STUDY 11 – ROSEMARY

at all times. Children learn to take pride in good writing and to recognize quality in the writing of others. For all children, writing should be a source of increasing satisfaction as they note and evaluate their own growth. And for teachers, the opportunity to watch young people expand and grow in power of expression should be especially satisfying.

BIBLIOGRAPHY

APPLEGATE, Mauree, *Helping Children Write* (Scranton, Pennsylvania, International Textbook Company, 1948).

BEAR, Meta V., "Children's Growth in the Use of Written Language," *Elementary English Review*, XVI (December, 1939), pp. 312–19.

Board of Education, City of New York. *Developing Children's Power of Self-Expression through Writing*, Curriculum Bulletin, 1952–53, Series No. 2 (New York Public Schools, 1953).

BURROWS, Alvina T., FEREBEE, June D., JACKSON, Dorothy C., and SAUNDERS, Dorothy O., *They All Want to Write: Written English in the Elementary School* rev. ed. (New York, Prentice-Hall, Inc., 1952).

COLE, Natalie, *The Arts in the Classroom* (New York, The John Day Company, Inc., 1940).

DAWSON, Mildred A., *Teaching Language in the Grades* (New York, World Book Company, 1951).

FITZGERALD, James A., *A Basic Life Spelling Vocabulary* (Milwaukee, The Bruce Publishing Company, 1951).

———, *The Teaching of Spelling* (Milwaukee, The Bruce Publishing Company, 1951).

KIBBE, Delia E., LABRANT, Lou L.; and POOLEY, Robert C., *Handbook of English for Boys and Girls* (Chicago, Scott, Foresman and Company, 1939).

McKEE, Paul, *Language in the Elementary School* (New York, Houghton Mifflin Company, 1939).

National Council of Teachers of English, Commission on the English Curriculum, *The English Language Arts*, N.C.T.E. Curriculum Series, Vol. I (New York, Appleton-Century-Crofts, Inc., 1952).

National Elementary Principal, Bulletin of the Department of Elementary School Principals, Twentieth Yearbook, *Language Arts in the Elementary School* (Washington, D.C., National Education Association, 1941).

National Society for the Study of Education, Forty-Third Yearbook, Part II, *Teaching Language in the Elementary School* (5838 Kimbark Avenue, Chicago 37, Illinois, National Society for the Study of Education, 1944).

POOLEY, Robert C., *Teaching English Usage* (New York, Appleton-Century-Crofts, Inc., 1946).

RAGLAND, Fannie J., Compiler, *Children Learn to Write,* Pamphlet Publication No. 7 of the National Council of Teachers of English (Champaign, Illinois. The Council. 1944), 78 pp.

SMITH, Dora V., *Evaluating Instruction in English in the Elementary Schools of New York* (Chicago, Scott, Foresman and Company, 1944).

————, "Making a Curriculum in the Language Arts; a Report of the Commission on the English Curriculum of the National Council of Teachers of English," *Elementary English,* XXVII (November, 1950), pp. 421–24.

STRICKLAND, Ruth G., *English Is Our Language, Guide for Teaching Grades 1 and 2* (Boston, D. C. Heath & Company, 1950).

————, *The Language Arts in the Elementary School* (Boston, D. C. Heath & Company, 1951).

TIDYMAN, Willard F., and BUTTERFIELD, Marguerite, *Teaching the Language Arts* (New York, McGraw-Hill Book Company, Inc., 1951).

WATTS, A. F., *The Language and Mental Development of Children* (Boston, D. C. Heath & Company, 1947).

WEEKS, Edward, "Peripatetic Reviewer," *The Atlantic Monthly,* CLXXXV (June, 1950), p. 78.

PART III

The Program in Action

CHAPTER 8

Early Childhood

PART I was concerned with the place of the language arts in
the lives of boys and girls and in the world in which they live.
It revealed something of how children grow and of the
intimate relationship between the pattern of their growth and
the development of language power. It emphasized the social
nature of language and the need for an environment rich in
stimulation and affording ample opportunity for actual communication in pursuit of purposes real to the child.

Part II showed how ability to read, write, speak, and listen
is consciously and systematically developed in connection
with the total program of the school. Because, within the
larger setting, specific attention has to be given to each of
these skills in turn, separate chapters were devoted to them.
It is obvious, however, that all aspects of language power
develop together in relation to one another and to the purposes for which pupils communicate.

Part III, therefore, presents a series of closely integrated
programs illustrative of these intimate relationships. Some
of the programs use the language arts themselves as a point
of departure. Others emphasize all-school activities or those
related to various subjects of study, giving opportunity to
develop language powers in a functional situation.

261

A YEAR IN KINDERGARTEN

A year in the kindergarten for four- and five-year-olds in the University Schools of Ohio State University will illustrate the program at that level.

Daily Conversation and Sharing

Five-year-old Sue Ellen paused in her job of replacing the front of the cage for the hamsters. She had something to tell the student teacher and Eddie, who had been holding the chicken wire for her. Chuckling with glee, she reported,

> Last night I called Roger on the telephone. I asked him if he could eat lunch with me some day. He said, "I could eat with you Sunday, Monday, Tuesday, Wednesday, Thursday, Friday, Saturday, and Sunday." He is going to have lunch with me tomorrow.

Her enjoyment of her friend's language play had carried over into her busy day, and she enjoyed repeating it.

Lynne displayed dry twigs with cotton bolls attached when a group gathered around the teacher for sharing and telling. She talked freely and easily.

> When we were going down to Florida, we saw some cotton growing and Mother said, "Why don't you get some of that cotton?" Dad got out of the car and went across the street and got this cotton.
> I'll show you the seeds. They are hard to get out. These are the branches it grows on. They're like bushes.

Four-year-old Kip, showing his silky-haired brown Cocker, said briefly and a bit formally, as if over-awed by the "fives", "This is my dog. Her name is Penny. She is a girl dog."

In a corner Karen transferred the hamster tenderly to Roger's hands, warning, "Hold Wiggly very carefully. Don't squeeze her."

Intent on painting the doll bed she had made of wood, Lindabeth, tongue between teeth, heard nothing and saw nothing but the task before her. So things went in the big kindergarten room of the Lower School where forty children, (fifteen four-year-olds and twenty-five five-year-olds) worked together with the kindergarten director, two graduate assistants, and sometimes one student teacher.[1] All day long the busy hum of activities was accompanied by the steady flow of conversation. There were times, of course, definitely set aside for conversation and discussion, such as the planning period which opened the day. At this time the children gained experience in learning to take turns, to give attention and consideration to the ideas of others, to coöperate in promoting the happiness and success of the group, to share with others, to plan coöperatively, and to make decisions and judgments.

Varying Activities in the Kindergarten

At this time the children also made their own choices of activities which they announced for recording in the "planning" book. In the work period immediately following they constructed and painted objects of wood, modeled in clay, painted at the easel, drew with chalk or crayons, worked with puzzles or with scissors and paper, or engaged in dramatic play. Dolls, household equipment, blocks, trucks, and figures representing animals and people familiar to small children supplied needed properties. Small lengths of lumber and odd pieces of cloth also were utilized to meet the needs of the moment. Play related to home and community living was most in evidence, perhaps because the girls were very active in initiating and directing construction activities with blocks, around which much of the dramatic play centered. When kindergarten teachers participated in their dramatic play, the children often acted out familiar stories such as *Ask Mr. Bear* or *Monkey See, Monkey Do.* Toy pistols and guns, which stimulated a limited kind of dramatic play, proved a distracting influence, and children were asked to keep them in their lockers to use only during out-of-door activities.

Much discussion went on, too, after clean-up, which was

[1] The University Schools, Ohio State University; Cecile Swales, Kindergarten Director.

accepted as a regular and necessary part of the work period. Individual undertakings—pictures or objects made of wood or clay—were submitted to the group for suggestion, criticism, and approval. Ruthie, showing a pot holder, offered her own evaluation as well as an explanation of the process.

See this is where I made a little mistake. But Daddy helped me fix it and I made it all myself. I don't know what you call it but it has nails sticking up and you put the things over and under, and under and over until it's done.

Opportunity was given at this time also for individuals to recount experiences, tell original stories, and perhaps simply announce proudly, "We are getting a new baby."

Jules, offering his bright new copy of *Peter Pan,* said, "I thought some people would go to see the movie, so I brought this book so you can read it."

An informal thirty minutes of music devoted to singing, rhythms, and "playing" songs extended the sharing period. At other scheduled times stories were read or told, poems were enjoyed, and books brought from home were shared with the group.

Books were available and accessible at all times to the children. They helped to choose those which were brought from the library to the classroom to be looked at and read during story hour, and almost daily some child brought one of his own to share with the group. Each child checked out a book on Friday for week-end reading.

Animal stories were always productive of discussion about the ways of animals and how they grow. Among the most popular were *Make Way for Ducklings, Flip and the Cows, Come to the Zoo,* and *Tim Tadpole and the Great Bullfrog.*

Boys and girls of other lands came in for their share of interest. Such books as *Captain Joe and the Eskimo* would start the children talking about other people who live differently from us. Experiments with globe, light bulb, and the like to discover "Why it is day here and night in China" always followed a reading of *Ting Ling* and *Mee Too.* A good basis for discussion of race relations was found in *Two is a Team,* and for understanding and accepting of differences among ourselves in *The Smallest Boy in the Class.*

Such books as *The Golden Flute, Time for Poetry,* and *Very Young Verses* were always at hand to supply poetry effectively classified so that the teacher could easily find the poem for the occasion. Children developed favorites, of course, and would often join in the "saying" of the poem as it became familiar.

Fulfilling Broader Aims

The planning of the kindergarten program which resulted in continuous opportunities for language arts was, of course, in terms of broader aims of education. These were considered by the Lower School staff to be desirable personality adjustment and consistently good mental, social, physical, and emotional development. Every phase of the program was planned to foster desirable attitudes; to furnish experiences which would help children to become increasingly coöperative, self-reliant, resourceful, and self-directing; and to promote growth in their use of language as fundamental to these purposes. Each day provided opportunity to talk over problems and to make decisions, to choose and handle materials, to carry out one's ideas, to express one's self verbally as well as to listen to others, to feel increasingly adequate in meeting the experiences of the day, and to coöperate and to share with others. The schedule was adapted, so far as it seemed necessary, to the different needs of the older and younger groups, but whenever possible both shared the same experiences.

For example, the four-year-olds had their play time during the five-year-olds' work period, and the "fives" played while the "fours" worked with materials. The groups were together daily for rest. Other experiences they shared were assemblies, trips, movies, listening to recordings, and discussing such group concerns as desirable behavior on trips. Before school in the morning the two groups also mingled and made friends.

For other activities the double room arrangement—one large one and a much smaller one with a communicating door—made possible a separation of the groups with opportunity for more individual help and freedom.

In the large room the equipment included a jungle-gym, piano, record player and records, large hollow blocks of various shapes and sizes, a doll and housekeeping corner, easels, magnets, magnifying glasses, a hamster cage, a clay table, work benches, and bulletin boards. In the small room were tables where children could draw, work with puzzles or scissors and paper and paste, or look at books undisturbed by the noisier, more vigorous activities. The small room also provided space for the child who needed additional rest or isolation from the group or for five or six children who wished to work independently. Open lockers, one for each child, were located in three different sections, two on opposite walls of the big room and one in the small room, to help prevent congestion and disorder at times of arrival and dismissal.

After the early morning discussion and planning came the work period. Later there was a lunch of milk or orange juice, which the children helped serve, and a rest of fifteen or twenty minutes on rugs on the floor. The remainder of the morning was spent in free play out of doors in suitable weather and in an indoor basement playroom at other times. The schedule was flexible so that rearrangement of individual and group activities was possible whenever the demands of group living made change necessary or desirable.

Problem-solving

Problem-solving situations arose daily. Children were helped to find answers to their questions and to solve the problems they encountered through manipulation, exploration, experimentation, and conversation or discussion. With the aid of the science teacher an empty aquarium was converted into a home for goldfish and snails, whose needs were discussed as the work proceeded. The presence of two hamsters raised the question of the kind of home best for them and of their need for air, light, food, and water. The possibility that there would be baby hamsters was also considered. When questions about fire, air, rain, snow, fog, and other natural phenomena were raised, the children were aided in performing simple experiments which helped them to answer their own questions.

Magnets and a magnifying glass stimulated much interest and discussion. Soaking lima beans, examining them, and planting pumpkin seeds saved from jack-o-lanterns furthered understandings about living things and their relations to each other. A large land turtle, three baby goats, and a pheasant, brought in at different times, stimulated observation and discussion.

Introducing Letter-writing

The hamsters were checked out every Friday for a week-end visit. Written invitations for such visits were posted and reservations made in advance.

Dear Mrs. Swales:
   Eddie would like to have Taffy and Wiggly home this week end (May 1–2–3) if they will be available. If they are not, then any future week-end will be fine.

Sincerely,
Marian Cox

It was the special responsibility of the "hamster helpers" to have the cage clean and in readiness for the trip. Many books came into use to answer children's questions, especially through their pictures. *All Around You, The First Great Inventions,* and *The First Book of Bugs* proved helpful.

Letters dictated by children were written to absent members of the group. Thank-you notes, letters to former teachers, requests for help, and other such situations emphasized the need for writing in everyday life. Letter form became familiar from the many times the children participated in dictating, reading back, folding, sealing, addressing, stamping, and mailing the letters. One such letter told of the misadventures of Wiggly.

Dear Karen:

We are sorry you have the chicken-pox. Wiggly got lost but Susie's brother found her in the basement.

We hope you will come back soon.

The Kindergarten

Letter-writing was now common practice with the fives. As Natasha said, "You do the writing, but we tell you the ideas."

Relating Other Activities to Language Development

Number concepts developed out of daily experience, and words were used to indicate size, shape, and spatial relations. The daily counting of the children present and checking of absentees for the attendance record, daily reference to the calendar for the same purpose, reading the thermometer, counting out doilies, napkins, straws, and bottles of milk or glasses of juice for the lunch table, and building with blocks of various sizes, stimulated and encouraged a feeling for numbers and developed the vocabulary needed in dealing with them. In work with footstools, book holders, boats, and other construction activities there was some need for measuring and some use for the terms *feet, inches,* and *yards.*

Musical activities included singing, rhythms, dramatizations, listening to recorded music, and playing instruments. There were songs related to stories, songs of the seasons, songs about pets and play activities, and the songs that accompanied games and simple dances.

Discussions centered often around safety and health. The dangers of running in the halls, the need for care in crossing the streets, and the use of slide, swing, and teeters were all given emphasis in both small-group and large-group conversations. The reading of *Curious George* often led to talk about fire-alarm boxes and ways of putting out fire. This discussion usually ended in plans for a trip to the fire house.

It was followed also at later times with various experiments at school with fire and air.

The need for good breakfasts, for mid-morning lunch, and for rest, the reasons for concern about ventilation and light in the room, the importance of good posture, and other such aspects of healthful living were discussed.

Short trips were taken about the neighborhood: sometimes to Mirror Lake on the campus to observe signs of fall and again in the spring to note changes in nature; sometimes to nearby stores for needed materials or to the fire station to see the engine and hook and ladder or to question the firemen about what happened in case of fire; and sometimes to the Archeological Museum to see the log cabin and the older types of cars and bicycles. The stuffed animal exhibit was also a favorite. A University bus supplied transportation to the University Farms at a time when many baby animals could be looked at, touched, and talked about.

Questions raised on this trip led to later trips to a dairy and a visit to one child's home to see "where the baby goats live."

During the winter quarter when trips are inadvisable because of the weather, such movies as *Farm Animals, Bear Twins, Shep the Farm Dog,* and *Three Little Kittens* were shown regularly. The children created their own continuity with conversation; little need was felt for the captions. Weekly responsibilities were assumed by each child in turn in caring for the hamsters, feeding the fish, watering the plants, helping to prepare the tables, serving the lunch, and laying out the rest mats. A feeling of belonging to the school as a whole and a sense of sharing responsibilities was encouraged through participation in all school activities such as attending assemblies, taking part in the Christmas program, contributing to the Red Cross, collecting clothing for European children, and aiding in the magazine, paper, and other all-school drives.

Constantly Evaluating Growth

Throughout the year the teachers attempted to key all the activities to the stages of growth evidenced by the children. Evaluation went on continuously. Anecdotal records were used for study of the child's growth in language arts as well as in all other respects. Conferences with parents were often based on these records. The teacher on one occasion showed Karen's father three selected recordings revealing successive steps in her development. Each was a student teacher's record of the child's report to a group. The first was made when she was four, early in her first year in kindergarten:

I used to have a dog but it ran away and got dead.

The second record was made after Christmas the year she was five.

This is a dress my aunt sent me. This is really a petticoat. It's an extra dress you can wear separately with a belt. This one is a sun dress.

The third item was recorded in April after she was six. It was an experience recalled from the summer before.

When we were in Minnesota there was a pony called Cinnamon. He was cinnamon color and he could pull two people almost to the pond—but not all the way because he got tired.

From her shy single-sentence contribution couched in words that even her four-year-old group had regarded as "babyish," Karen had advanced to a free and spontaneous sharing of personal experience. Her report on the pony revealed mastery of vocabulary and recall of previous experience, which meant definite steps forward for her.

The daily living together, the opportunity to choose, to do, and to see results, to work together and to work alone, to have adult help and guidance, or, on occasion, to do without it, gave each four- and five-year-old the opportunity to grow in terms of the objectives shared by teachers, parents, and the children themselves.

BOOK-MAKING IN THE PRIMARY GRADES

The staff of the Lafayette School in Norfolk, Virginia, planned a language arts program in the primary grades which grew out of the daily activities of the classroom and interrelated in normal fashion the skills of reading, writing, speaking, and listening.[2] Fearing there was a tendency to give undue emphasis to reading at the expense of oral and written expression, they developed a program which began with the teacher's recordings of the children's oral expression, the children's reading it back to her, and finally the children's writing of their own experiences. Making books of their own compositions for permanent record and sharing them with others in the library along with "books" by other "authors" spurred the children on to much personal and creative writing.

Dictating to the Teacher

In the first grade during group conversation periods, as six-year-olds shared personal possessions, related incidents and experiences, or told simple stories, the teacher jotted down what they had said on paper. At the end of the telling period she read these stories back to the group saying, "Today you have told some good stories. I wrote them as you told them. Listen while I read them to you." The children listened eagerly for their own contributions. She always ended by saying, "Soon you will learn to write and read your own stories."

From time to time the teacher varied her method of recording. Sometimes she made a caption over an article brought in for the sharing table, such as, "See Mary's New Birthday Doll." Sometimes she printed simple sentences for the news corner which announced that Ned had a new baby sister or Johnnie had the measles.

[2] Lafayette School, Norfolk, Virginia; Alice D. Edwards, Principal, and Staff.

Group experiences such as a trip to the farm, a movie, or a special school event were developed into stories by the group and recorded by the teacher, first on the board and later on charts. Through these experience charts the teacher introduced the children to their first steps in reading skills, in matching words and phrases, in moving the eyes from left to right, and in recognizing familiar words as they appeared in new situations.

Early in the first year children began to show a readiness to write down experiences for themselves. Some asked for help in writing a sentence or a word to go under a picture, or attempted to copy stories from the board or from charts. Shy children, otherwise reluctant to talk, would often tell about the pictures they had made. The teacher encouraged them by writing what they told on large pieces of paper and posting them with the children's drawings on the bulletin board.

Writing names of their possessions, their pictures, and notes to go home, and writing a "Thank you," "Happy Birthday," "Dear Mother," and "Come to school" on invitations and letters were additional opportunities for developing written expression.

At the end of the first year some children could make and record simple stories of a few sentences; others could copy words or phrases from the board, while many were still at the telling stage. Sometimes a child would come to school with a story which he had dictated to someone at home. The teacher encouraged this carry-over into the home by saying after a trip, "When you go home today tell your Mother what you saw at the park. Give her a pencil and a piece of paper and have her write just what you say. Tell her that is the way we make stories at school."

One day Patsy came to school with a story dictated at home. "My brother wanted to write this another way," she said, "but I said, 'If you do not write it as I tell it, it will not be my story; it will be yours.'"

When You Varnish a Doll Bed, You Can Tell About It.

You Be the Mother, I'll Be the Neighbor.

Be Careful, He's Our Only Hamster.

Cocky's School Visit Brings Questions and Answers.

This Is the Best Story Yet.

Your Own Painting Gives You Something to Talk About.

Let's Show and Tell.

Patsy's Story

Yesterday Miss Dee took us to the park. We saw the monkeys playing in the cage. One baby monkey was hanging on his mother's back. He wouldn't get off. I like the duck pond best. The peacock was the queen of the park she had a crown on her head. I tried to catch some feathers, but they floated away like magic.

Individual stories grew in length and interest. One day Mary Ann, in Grade Two, wrote pages about her trip to the circus. The following is a part of her story.

The Circus Clowns

I went to the circus Saturday at ten o'clock. A clown came out with a bouquet of flowers in his hand. He laid the flowers on a chair. He grabbed a boy and he put his hand down the boy's shirt and brought up a rubber ball. One clown came out with a Ford. They called it the 1951 Ford. When the clown was driving it a firecracker went off. Then he cranked the car up and water started to fly up. Then the clown took a bottle of water and drank it and spit it at the car and the more he did it the more it would fly up. Then some clowns came out dressed like Scotchmen. One of the clowns tooted his horn and one of the Scotchmen's shirt fell off. He ran off the stage. One clown took his shirt off on purpose. He had bells all over him, they were on his back. Some clowns were dressed up like doctors and nurses. I enjoyed the circus clowns.

Using the Arts in Book-making

The need of illustrations and music to accompany the records gave the arts a place in the program. The first stories were picture books of drawings. Chart stories, invitations, or story books never seemed complete without drawings, paintings, block prints, or designs for illustrations and decorations. Children experimented with all types of material and art media for book covers. They used finger paints, tempera paints, and crayons; they designed cloth, wallpaper, wrapping paper, and even newspaper. Freedom in use of these materials developed maximum creative abilities. A peek into the classrooms on any day might find a first grade choosing songs to go with a spring dance they had just made up, a second grade using simple hand puppets to dramatize a fable, a third grade making papier maché animals of their favorite fairy story, "The Musicians of Bremen Town."

Initiating the Project

When the children realized they could make books for their own purposes, all kinds of written expression began to appear—good chart stories, picture books, big books, little books, story books, and poem books. Some were class books or individual books and some were school newspapers. A brief description of how these were made may help others see what a dynamic experience book making became for the whole school.

It was Monday morning and the first-graders were coming into the classroom one by one. Everyone seemed to be carrying some treasured possession. Johnnie had a toy car. Mary was hugging a doll and Billy had a black cat in his arms. The teacher greeted each one with a cheerful "Good Morning. I see you have brought something to share today." The children began to gather informally in groups. Three little girls went to the play corner. One boy picked up a picture book and two boys ran for the block corner. Forest hurried over to the science shelf to feed Flip, the goldfish. The teacher walked quietly around the room observing the children, listening to their conversation and making notes on a pad. Finally she called the group together for their regular Monday morning sharing time. On the board written in big manuscript letters was a simple three-line message which she read to the children:

> Good morning, boys and girls.
> Do you have something to share?
> Do you have something to tell?

Hands shot up and eager voices cried out, "I have, I have." Ann told about the new baby kittens she had found in the closet. John showed his new shoes, and Janice her new doll. Tommie excitedly told about his trip to the zoo.

Like the boys and girls in the kindergarten, these children

showed a tremendous interest in the farm, stimulated by such films as *Farm Animals* and *Shep the Farm Dog*, the telling of favorite stories like the *Wooden Farmer* and *Cock-a-Doodle-Doo*, and the reading of rhymes from the *Singing Farmer*. As this group planned a trip to the farm, their discussion periods became more clearly organized, centering largely around that experience. Plans were made to go just before Easter so the children could see some baby chicks and other animal babies like the ones they had seen in the films. Simple letters which said, "May I go to the Farm?" were written by the teacher. All this time the teacher recorded on charts their class plans, the rules of behavior they adopted, the questions they wished to ask, and stories which developed from their discussions. After the trip, class storybooks telling of the experience were written in group fashion, and a few children made storybooks of their own. These first books were simple ones of a few illustrated pages with brief sentences and with paper backs.

The following are two of these first attempts at dictation:

The Baby Calf

We saw a baby calf.
He was just one day old.
He could walk.
His mother was sick.

Donnie

Baby Chicks

Some chicks were black.
Some chicks were yellow.
They didn't have any mother.
They were hatched in an incubator.

Lucy

Before the end of the first year, children were dictating all kinds of stories and eventually wrote for themselves such stories of personal experiences as the following with as much help in spelling as they requested.

Tip

Tip is a collie.
Tip is black and white.
Tip is not my dog.
But we have fun.

                        Ruth

In one classroom a combined group of first- and second-grade children dictated what they called their poem after a walk around the school grounds. The spontaneous expression of the children as they talked about their experience is reflected in many of the lines.

Our Sunshiny Walk

It was a nice day.
The sun was shining bright and gay.
All of us were happy so we took
A little walk around the school.
Pretty trees were growing on the ground.
Grasshoppers were jumping
In the grass having lots of fun.
Down by the lake we stood in a row
And watched the blue flies
Flying up and down.
Splash! went the water
When we threw in a rock
And the blue flies flew far away.
Under a tree we found some toad stools
And acorns and sycamore balls.
We watched the little ants going
In and out of their holes
And listening to the crickets in the grass.
A big brown bird flew over our heads
And five airplanes too.
But they were going fast.

Relating Speaking and Listening to the Program

The second-grade teacher, building on the background of the first year, expanded the children's experiences, extended their interests, and planned for the development of language arts skills on a higher level.

Many opportunities for oral expression came in the course

of the school day, such as telling out-of-school experiences, describing a fire, an accident, a television show, or an animal seen at the zoo; giving directions for playing new games, for using equipment or conducting an experiment; discussing new school safety and playground rules; taking messages and making announcements to classrooms; and planning excursions into the community to learn about the services rendered by the milkman, breadman, and postman. There were also opportunities for use of oral expression from other areas of the curriculum, such as reading, social studies, art, music, arithmetic, and science. Through these speaking situations the teacher taught writing skills. As she helped the children formulate and dictate invitations to a party and letters to people in the community, she called attention to correct forms, punctuation, and capitalization. Neatness and legibility of handwriting improved as children strove to write letters good enough to be mailed, or stories interesting enough to be recorded.

Listening skills were developed similarly through speaking situations. As the first- and second-graders shared personal experiences, made daily plans for classroom activities, listened to, told, and dramatized stories, recited rhymes and poems, and took part in group games, rhythms, and play, they gradually developed a group consciousness. Under the daily guidance of the teacher they learned such social amenities as when to talk and when to keep still, how to take turns, and how to listen with courtesy to others. They also learned how to speak so that others would understand and listen, how to stick to the story or subject, how to tell a story in sequence, and how to discuss simple topics or problems on their level of experience.

Stimulating Individual and Coöperative Writing

Individual and coöperative group compositions and stories continued in the second grade. The amount of writing done depended upon the interest and maturity of the children.

Story-writing was the favorite activity of many children. They wrote every day and about everything. Others were content with an occasional story or a contribution to a coöperative one. The children began to recognize needs for writing, spelling, and punctuation skills as they wrote stories and made books. The teacher encouraged them to use the class picture dictionary and to make word files of their own. Some children wrote the words they had asked for in note books for future reference. As they used them over and over in their stories, the words became part of their writing vocabularies. Although stories continued to be the main form of creative writing, a few simple poems and rhymes began to appear.

Rain

Rain, rain falling down
Cool wet rain
Rain, rain falling down
Down, down, down.

The children were not content to keep their precious manuscripts in simple paper-backed books, so under the guidance of the teacher, they made scrapbooks of their own with heavy cardboard covers.

Taking Pride in Books

As they set up more and more books, the children learned the names for the parts of books, such as Title Page and the Table of Contents, and included them in their own volumes. Writing skills improved as youthful authors strove to improve their stories so that they could record them in the books. Stories were always read and checked and errors corrected under the guidance of the teacher before they were copied into the books. With the making of their own books came a new respect and regard for those made by others. Some of the favorites of the second-grade children were *Let's Play House, The Little Family,* and *The Little Airplane* by Lois Lenski. *Millions of Cats* and *Nothing at All* by Wanda Gag; and *And to Think That I Saw It on Mulberry Street* by Dr. Seuss. These were favorites because the stories were simple, interesting, and written in a manuscript style similar to their own writing. The children learned to read many of them for themselves.

When the care and preservation of books was discussed, the children's own books were referred to as of equal importance with library books. A special shelf was provided for them in the school library, and they were checked out for reading just like regular library books.

By the time the children reached the third grade, bookmaking had become a natural activity of the school day. Building on the experiences provided in the first and second grade, the third-grade teacher included in her program such speaking and writing experiences as relating in organized form incidents and anecdotes from individual reading, creating realistic and imaginative stories and verse, making puppet shows, preparing a radio program, reading to others, giving short talks, and participating in choral speaking.

At this time the children began to show some skill in evaluating their own expression. Gradually, as they listened to and shared in classroom discussions, gave planned oral reports, and related facts and information gained through listening to the conversation of others at home or at school and on television or radio, they learned to evaluate the effect of their own language on others.

Writing and Collaborating in the Third Grade

The children were able to write more independently as they improved in handwriting and spelling skills. They began to group themselves into committees of twos and threes to write a make-believe story, to record group experiences, or to compile stories already written. One group of three girls wrote a book telling how the class made an aquarium. Another group recorded in an illustrated book new safety rules set down by the safety patrol. Two boys described in simple sentences some concepts they had gained from new science books.

This method of working together became more popular

after the children were told that it was called "collaborating."
They were also told that people who wrote stories were called
"authors" and people who made the pictures, "artists." Several
library books were used to show the children names of authors
and artists who worked together, like Munro Leaf and Robert
Lawson in *The Story of Ferdinand* or Alvin R. Tresselt and
Roger Duvoisin in *Follow the Wind* and *White Snow, Bright
Snow.*

Developing Skills

The teacher encouraged the independent writing begun in
the second grade by giving help freely and promptly when
needed. She worked with small groups who needed special
assistance with spelling or word usage, while other children
engaged in independent activities. Sometimes she helped a
group set up books for recording stories. At other times she
had children read stories with her for aid in making corrections.

Special attention was given to children who still needed
help in setting down their thoughts. Very often the teacher
acted as scribe for those who became tired or discouraged
before they had finished their work. Words which the children
asked to have spelled were listed in alphabetical order in individual dictionaries or in the class word file and were later
added to individual spelling lists. Sometimes a child had difficulty in finding a word in the class word box. He was urged
to repeat the word after the teacher to get the initial sound,
sometimes repeating several familiar words beginning with
the same sound. Capable children were encouraged to look
up words in pictures and beginners' dictionaries which were
on the book shelf. At other times the skills of word attack,
word usage, and spelling were taught from the words asked
for during the day.

One group decided to make Christmas cook books for gifts.
Favorite recipes brought in by the children were written on
the board, read, and filed under alphabetized headings ac-

cording to kind, such as bread, cake, or meat. Typewritten copies of the recipes were made for individual books. The children had the responsibility of making their book covers and pasting in the recipes in alphabetical order. It was very interesting to observe the maturity and growth of the children during this project both in clarity and organization of ideas and in ability to alphabetize.

Emerging Interest in Creative Writing

Creative writing, which was spasmodic rather than continuous, became more personal.

Third-grade Billy, for example, felt his lost tooth was quite a joke. He wrote the story, expending great care in getting quotation marks in the right places.

My tooth was out and I couldn't find it. I was out doors playing football, Harry called me over to him. He said, "I see something." "What is it?" "I'm not going to tell you." "Please tell me." "No, I will not tell you." Then he said, "It is somewhere over here." I looked for it. I couldn't find it. So I gave up.

Mother came out doors to wash clothes. I was in the house and Mother called to me, I ran. Then I went back in the house. Then Harry came over and we played football. Then I saw something. I ran to it. Guess what I saw. I saw my tooth! Then that night I put it under my pillow. The next morning I saw some money.

With some children, it was necessary to stimulate writing by suggesting titles: Our Picnic, Helping Mother Make Cookies, Jack Frost's Fun, or My Secret Wishes.

Realizing Therapeutic Values through Writing

Sometimes the pupils revealed their innermost thoughts in this kind of writing in such a way that Miss Blair could help them greatly. For example, Elsie, a third-grade child, wrote:

Dear Magic Fairy,

I would like for you to grant me three secret wishes.

The first wish is a bicycle at Christmas.

The second wish is that I could talk like a girl and not like a boy so that people would stop teasing and asking about it.

The third wish is that we would have more homework every day.

A visit to the child's home disclosed that it was her mother who had made her conscious of her deep boyish voice. Elsie, who liked to sing, had to be constantly reminded that she must use a softer voice. Miss Blair talked to Elsie about the quality of her voice. She told her that it didn't really make too much difference what kind of voice one had if he used it in the right way. "You really have a lovely husky voice," she assured her, "like many of the stars in the movies and on television." She asked Elsie to listen to the women on the television programs to see how many had very deep voices, which they had learned to use well. When the time came to choose two narrators from the class for the Christmas play, Elsie was chosen as one because she had a good speaking voice which was easily heard.

The making of books and recordings of class activities proved fruitful, year after year in this school. The children continued to develop their books in the intermediate grades. A nucleus for work in composition, the class and individual books seemed always to offer new and fresh incentives to the children.

CHAPTER 9

The Middle Grades

By the time children reach the intermediate grades they are usually capable of more sustained effort in activities which involve clarity of purpose, more highly developed habits of work, and organized effort toward a clearly perceived goal. Illustrations of such programs come from widely separated schools in Phoenix, Arizona, and in Richmond, Virginia.

OUR RESEARCH PROBLEM: A SIXTH-GRADE EXPERIENCE

Scissors, paper cutters, and a store room of discarded magazines in the hands of an eager, resourceful sixth-grade class —this seemingly simple combination at Whittier School in Phoenix, Arizona,[1] created a library of valuable current materials.

The program had its inception in a conviction that libraries of important reference data ordinarily are lost through the habit of throwing away current informative periodicals.

A simple workshop problem of organizing and filing current materials launched the class on a continuing series of activities that encompassed all phases of the language arts. As the research unfolded, it provided satisfying work for every member of the class. Each pupil felt a sense of being an important contributor to the project because it afforded an opportunity

[1] Whittier School, Phoenix, Arizona; Ann Sutcliffe, teacher, and Mildred S. Kiefer, supervisor.

for individual preference in the jobs to be done. The project went ahead happily—so much so that observers wondered if the children realized they were working hard. Boys and girls stood as much as an hour at a time at the pasting table and refused to be relieved. They felt that they were doing something worth while for all the classes of the school. At the same time their remarks showed that they were getting more out of their tasks than they were giving to others.

Among the values the pupils themselves were most conscious of reaping from the undertaking were interviewing adults on specific topics, working under observation of visiting groups of teachers and students, carrying on discussions with school district officials, and making new friends through the project.

Initiating the Project

This reference library problem grew out of a letter to the sixth grade from the supervisor of intermediate grades, asking for help. She explained that she had several hundred magazines and other kinds of material that people had given her from time to time for use in the schools. The room in which they were stored was needed for other purposes and had to be vacated.

In accordance with plans made in advance with the principal and teacher, the supervisor suggested to the pupils that they examine, classify, and catalogue the materials for use in classroom study. She asked them to let her know what they thought of the suggestion.

That called for class discussion of such questions as, "Where shall we store the magazines? Where can we do the work, and who will provide the needed materials and pay for such things as proper paper, glue, brushes, tape, and a filing cabinet?"

The class named a committee of three pupils to call on the principal. The committee presented the supervisor's letter, stating that they would like to carry out the project but they needed storage space for the magazines, a work place, and materials. The principal took them to a storage room, provided a key, sent to the classroom tables and chairs for the project, and approved obtaining materials through the regular school channels. Committee members returned to the classroom and made their report to the other pupils.

The class decided to go ahead with the plan. That called for drafting a letter to the supervisor. A pupil went to the blackboard and wrote what the others contributed. As the class composed the letter, individual pupils made corrections in spelling and changes in sentences as they saw where improvements were needed.

A chairman for the project, elected by the class, was delegated to copy the letter and send it to the supervisor. Following is the letter:

> Whittier School
> May 10, 195–

Dear Miss Kiefer,

We discussed your letter in class and decided that we would like to help you with your problem. Our class thinks that the materials would be very helpful to our school. Many times in our own class we have not had enough materials to finish our studies.

There are many problems facing us so we cannot go ahead. They are storage space, materials we will need like proper paper, paste, tape, and files, the method to use in mounting and filing, and enough space in which to work.

Today a committee talked these things over with Miss Sutcliffe. She took some of the problems off our hands. She will provide storage space, a file, additional work space, stools and tables. Miss Sutcliffe suggested that we invite Miss James (the library supervisor) to tell us how to classify and mount the material.

The problem remaining is, who is going to furnish the supplies we need to do the work? Can you help us get them?

> Yours very truly,
> Juanita Beaver
> For the Sixth grade

Planning the Procedure

Teacher and pupils planned together from the start. The pupils' activity was directed by repeated questions: How shall we proceed? What shall we do next? What jobs need to be done and who will do them? How much time each week shall we devote to the problem?

It was decided to limit the work on the problem to three eighty-minute periods a week. The teacher's remark that some record of work and procedure would be needed as the activity broadened, brought forth from the class a suggestion that they keep a diary. The pupils agreed to keep a record of the activities in which they participated, on large sheets of paper attached to an easel. A guide for writing the diary entries was then set up.

How to Keep the Diary

Decide what facts it is important to keep a record of; record these in order, grouping those which belong together.

Write in complete sentences.

Begin each sentence with a capital letter.

Keep a group of sentences about the same thing in a paragraph.

Indent to show the beginning of a new paragraph.

Always write names with a capital letter.

At the end of a line divide words between syllables only.

Two questions, "What materials and pictures shall we keep from these magazines?" and "How shall we mount and catalogue them?" broadened the scope of the problem. In the discussion the children thought the teachers and pupils could best answer the first question.

Arranging Interviews with the Teachers

They decided to arrange for interviews with the eighteen teachers in the school. Eighteen chairmen were selected, and each named another class member to constitute the committee for the undertaking. A notice placed on the teachers' bulletin board, they thought, would help in arranging time for interviews. Three pupils volunteered to prepare the notice, which the class decided should contain the project plan, the teachers' names, and a place for them to insert the date and time when they would see the committees.

Interview plans provided a lesson in oral language. Four points were set up for inclusion in the interviews: (1) a personal introduction, (2) explaining the purpose of the visit, (3) asking for lists of subjects studied or topics wanted, and (4) requesting copies of current periodicals received by the classes to add to the project files.

Several pupils who recently had enrolled in the school did not know some of the teachers or the rooms in which they taught. Floor plans for both upper and lower floors were worked out by a committee, showing the location of the various rooms, and labeled with the teachers' names and room numbers. The Parent-Teachers' Year Book was used for the correct spelling of names and other information. Thirteen of the eighteen interviews were completed within twenty-four hours after the time the notice was posted.

Sorting the Topics

The next step in the program was the listing of class topics desired by each teacher. The pupils were not familiar with some of the topics submitted, and they referred to their dictionaries for correct spelling and meaning of unfamiliar words and terms. The list, which contained more than 150 unorganized topics, would not be workable unless it was arranged in alphabetical order. The class, therefore, organized itself into groups and classified the subjects under principal alphabetical divisions with subtopics. An index thus was set up for filing all the articles, pictures, and materials found in the search.

Spelling assumed a prominent place in the program, inasmuch as pupils readily saw the importance of spelling correctly all the words used in their records. Not only did pupils select their own spelling words, but eventually they assumed responsibility for self-imposed "assignments." The most able pupils set for themselves the task of learning about twenty words per week; slower learners usually chose about ten words. This differentiation grew out of the coöperative nature of the undertaking in which there were many individual needs for spelling. Among words regularly used and spelled by the sixth-graders were: *interview, examine, classify, catalogue, duplicate, material, articles, record, mount, gross, research, checked, method, altogether, teachers, pictures, identify.* Frequently, the pupils studied the spelling and use of the varied forms of such verbs as *clip, cut, mount,* and *paste.* Misspelled words appearing in the diary, letters, newspaper articles, and other compositions were posted in review lists for special attention. The results which followed the functional use of many new words far surpassed former attempts to "build vocabulary" by more traditional, formal methods.

The topics requested by the teachers posed some difficult problems for sixth-graders. For instance, they were asked to gather pictures of the seven basic foods. For research and reference work the pupils decided to seek information in their health books and in the encyclopedias and also to ask the school nurse for posters, pictures, leaflets, pamphlets, and charts.

Learning to Select and Mount Material

For proper mounting of materials the class called in the supervisor of elementary school libraries to offer suggestions and to give a demonstration of proper methods of preserving and mounting the materials. She recommended rubber cement or gaylo paste for mounting pictures and thermofilm for finishing them. Four sizes of paper were used for standardizing the mountings. Single-page articles were mounted in the same way as pictures. Lengthy articles covering several pages were put into a booklet made of oak tag covers, stapled, and bound with masking tape. To preserve choice pictures, the librarian recommended the laminating process, which could be done by special machine at the administration building.

At this stage of the project the pupils could hardly wait to get at the job, acting as if they thought the room where the magazines were stored was a treasure room to be entered only by a committee chosen to select representative magazines for starting the clipping and mounting process. The five boys selected thought themselves fortunate to be in charge of the "store house" and eagerly reported that the room was stacked to the ceiling with magazines. "Golly," said the chairman, "there must be six hundred of them." More than twenty different publications appeared on the list.

The class plunged into the work of clipping and mounting pictures and articles with even more eagerness. As guides for making selections, they drafted two wall charts, one for evaluating pictures and the other for judging reading material.

In deciding "what makes a good picture" the pupils set up criteria including: color, simplicity in detail, clarity, boldness, and size.

For judging reading material they were guided by six points:

Will it be useful?
Is the subject in our index?
Is it interesting?
Is it easy or difficult?
What is the grade level?
Is it up to date?

Arrangements were made with the art teacher for a series of small-group instruction periods on neat and appropriate mounting, so that each member of the class could learn all the skills essential and share in all the tasks of the program. The instruction included accurate placement of pictures on background with specific margin requirements and deft pasting methods. The pupils also learned upper- and lower-case lettering for labeling file envelopes and booklets. Ruler measurements were required to insure good lettering.

A committee excursion was made to a photographic laboratory to learn whether the use of foto-flat for mounting pictures would be practical for the class. The laboratory operator demonstrated its application and explained its merit. The research diary recorded:

We found out the cost and size of foto-flat. The operator showed us how to use it. The sizes are 8 x 10 and 11 x 14. We could get a dozen

8 x 10 sheets for 35¢. We could get a gross of 11 x 14 for $5.75, or a dozen for 60¢. The teacher took some pictures for demonstration purposes. The operator put one of them on a piece of paper and fixed the foto-flat under it. Then she heated her photo iron. She used the iron to go over the picture. She used it again but it didn't stick because the iron wasn't hot enough. She tried it again. Then she told the committee to remember that "Haste makes waste" and added, "It pays to do it right the first time."

Organizing the Class and Clarifying Individual Tasks

To keep the program moving smoothly and efficiently the class was organized with a chairman, co-chairman, board of advisors, and committees for sorting, clipping, mounting, and filing. The board of advisors was composed of apt pupils who could help their classmates by answering many routine questions and by screening materials.

The actual work of each pupil was checked by means of a folder plan. The pictures and clippings of each pupil were placed in a separate folder and evaluated according to requirements set up by the class. The plan provided a gauge of the reading abilities of the pupils and afforded opportunities for making corrections of written work and for discussing them.

Reading levels of the pupils were cared for in the wide selection of periodicals, which ranged from *My Weekly Reader* of third-grade level, *Junior Scholastic,* and *Science Newsletter,* through such popular magazines as *Life* and *Travel* up to *Fortune, Holiday,* and *American Artist.*

A record was kept of the working periods like this one for January 22, 1951:

Today we worked for one hour. Group One examined *Science News Letter* magazines. They reported that the magazine has many articles on astronomy, forestry, and animals. Group Two examined *Weekly Readers* of the third and fourth grade level. Group Three looked at *Fortune* magazines for pictures.

The diary of February 5, 1951 read:

Today we examined *My Weekly Reader, Young America,* and *Current Events.* We examined and clipped 164 articles and pictures. We worked from 2:30 to 3:30 P.M.

Almost at the start of the clipping and mounting, the class was faced with the problem of pictures and articles which were printed on both sides of a page. A boy discovered a striking collection of pictures of poisonous snakes so printed in *Life* magazine. "The fourth grade would like all these pictures for their snake study," he said. "That means we will have to try to get another issue."

Plans were discussed for keeping a record of additional issues that would be needed and methods of obtaining them. A chart labeled, "Watch for These Magazines" was placed on the blackboard, and on it were listed those issues which were most urgently wanted.

Committees went to classrooms in the building to ask for such copies. The teachers permitted lists to be written on their blackboards. Posters were placed on the school bulletin board with an appeal such as this: "We Need *Life*—May 27, 1947." Other appeals were made in articles in the school newspaper. Through these efforts the class was able to obtain as many as five or six copies of the issues they needed.

Explaining to the Superintendent

One workshop day the children were surprised with a visit from the superintendent of schools. Enthusiastic explanations followed his, "What's this I hear about your work at Whittier?"

One volunteer explained, "It all started when we got a letter from our supervisor." Another, pointing to the diary on the easel, described the series of activities that were carried out after the letter was received. A third went to the index chart and explained how the pupils had arrived at the alphabetical list of words.

"Why are you doing this?" the superintendent asked.

"Because it will give us more material for our school. Sometimes we need more references than we have."

The pupils showed the superintendent some of the mounted pictures and articles they had prepared. "How do you know the teachers and boys and girls will want these materials?" he asked.

"We have interviewed the teachers to find out what type of pictures and articles they would like," they said. "We have talked to the boys and girls, too."

"What do you call this problem you are doing?" the superintendent asked. This question took the pupils by surprise. Then came the reply, "Magazine Survey." The superintendent suggested, "It's a research problem, isn't it—isn't that what you are doing?" Then he remarked that the teachers might like to see various types of materials to determine how suitable they would be for their grade levels.

Following the Superintendent's Advice

After he left, the class decided to submit the material for examination to the teachers. As they planned interviews with several of them, they selected and put into folders articles on subjects taught in their classrooms, such as "Birds" in the fifth grade, "Sea Life" in the fourth grade, and "The Farm" in the first grade.

The results of this activity are reflected in the following paragraphs from a letter the class wrote to the superintendent:

We wish to thank you for the suggestion you made about making folders of material, showing them to the teachers, and getting their opinions about it. When we showed a folder to a fifth grade teacher she thought it had some wonderful material on hamsters in it. She liked it so much that we let her have it.

We are holding Open House every Thursday morning at 10:40 till 12:00 o'clock for people who are interested in our research problem. (That is what you called it.) Last Thursday a group of students from Tempe College visited us. We are also inviting teachers and our parents to visit us while we work. We would like it very much if you could come and visit us during our open house.

Improving through Pupil-Teacher Planning

Workshop periods proved more absorbing to the class as the program continued. Interest and enthusiasm never lagged even though the project extended over many weeks. Class members begged to take the research problem materials with them for "home work."

Teacher-pupil planning reached new heights in the workshop activity. Much of it was done with the pupils unaware of the teacher's part in their efforts.

"How can we improve?" was a guide for the beginning of each work period. Mistakes and faults of the previous session were analyzed and corrected before pupils went on to the next step. The research problem developed from a single phase of examining magazines to a complex classroom activity in which groups of pupils were cutting, sorting, mounting, labeling, binding, and filing materials.

Because of this complexity, the pupils saw the need for individual responsibility and set up a work code. It proposed: Work independently. Think about yourself and the task before you. Think before you act, and keep your voice down. The rule, "Think before you act," was suggested after pupils found that they had ruined a picture or article by failing to look on the other side of a page to see if it contained material which they preferred to what had been used.

Promoting Individual Interests

The pupils' workshop attracted so much attention outside the school that they decided to hold an open house every Thursday morning, as explained in the letter to the superintendent. Parents and teachers of Whittier school were invited and Arizona State College students made several visits to the open-house program.

Instances of almost amazing reader interest occurred repeatedly as the work of the pupils progressed. In one of the sessions a Tempe College student who was specializing in ornithology observed that a boy was so much taken up with "Bird Lore" that he seemed oblivious to the class visitors. Suddenly he proposed to the teacher, "Let's not tear up this magazine. The whole thing is about birds. Let's give the fifth grade the whole magazine for use."

This incident opened a much greater interest for the boy in

bird lore. The Tempe student discussed birds with him for a long period and gave him a personal copy of the "Arizona Bird Guide," which the pupil prized very highly and used in his individual bird studies. A similar interest in astronomy was fostered in another boy in the class.

Using the Language Arts in a Functional Setting

As has been mentioned previously, the mechanics of the research project provided a functional setting for all phases of the language arts program. Oral activities included many discussions, announcements, and scores of interviews and talks, both planned and extemporaneous, when parents and other visitors attended the work sessions.

The writing included preparing bulletin-board notices for teachers and articles for the school newspaper, keeping the diary, drafting charts, making the alphabetized index, and writing numerous letters on program activity and problems.

The reading phase included development of much-needed but often ignored skills: locating information through table of contents and index; using special aids such as atlas, encyclopedia, dictionary, graphs, maps, and charts; skimming, analyzing, choosing, and organizing material; and finally, comprehending what was read, to the end that not only the sixth-grade pupils profited but the whole school as well.

It should be emphasized again that oftentimes the by-product, in the form of concentrated, absorbed reading, undoubtedly resulted in more actual pages being read and a higher level of comprehension than was formerly accomplished in teacher-assigned tasks.

The following paragraph from a letter to the Curator of Fossil Reptiles, American Museum of Natural History, New York City, is an example of the scope of the letter-writing:

In the fourth grade at our school the children are studying prehistoric animals. During the study the teacher found a copy of the Dinosaur Book which was produced in 1934. We understand that you helped to write this booklet. Since we cannot find the address of the oil company that puts it out we would appreciate it if you would send us their address or any copies that you might have of the booklet. If the booklet is not available, we would accept anything similar that the museum might have.

The following letter to the supervisor of the Phoenix Elementary School Libraries is another example of how letter-writing functioned in the program.

We have some very interesting pictures in our room. We would like to have them laminated if possible. Miss Sutcliffe will send them down in a folder before we come so you can look them over. We would like to come down March 29, about 9:30 A.M. because while down there we would like to be shown through the Administration Building, after we laminate the pictures. Do you think you could arrange that for us?

The high point in the picture-mounting activity was reached when the supervisor of the school libraries demonstrated to the class the lamination process at the administration building. More than a score of selected pictures that the class wanted to preserve were processed. All the specimens were in color and included a wide variety of subjects such as Indian Art, Desert Flora, Arizona Birds, and Poisonous Reptiles.

Photographing the Project

It was a red-letter day for the pupils when a member of a photography class selected their reference library project for a series of pictures.

"What shall we show?" and "Who will be in the picture?" were the big questions before the group in a planning period. One pupil wrote on the blackboard suggestions made by her classmates. They decided the shots should include the supervisor writing the research program proposal to the class, the boy reading the supervisor's letter to the class, the school principal being interviewed by a pupil committee, a committee interview with a classroom teacher, the recording of the research-problem diary, examination by pupils of the alphabetized index, and finally a group shot of sorting, examining, cutting, mounting, and filing.

They planned a telephone call to invite the supervisor of

libraries to join them in the pictures. They felt that she should demonstrate the mounting processes. A boy was selected to make the call, and all members of the class joined in drafting the plan of conversation.

Although all the pupils naturally yearned to be in the pictures, they decided that only those who had participated in the particular activity in question should appear in each shot.

Involving the Whole School in Culminating Activities

The culminating activities of the problem were planned in such a way that all the intermediate-grade classes and all of the teachers in the school could participate. Each class was invited to the workshop and a review of the entire program was presented to the pupils. For example, the visiting pupils were given an introductory greeting and a brief summary of the project. The collections of the pictures and articles that they would be able to use in their study next year were exhibited to them, and the use, care, and placement of the files were explained.

Eight assemblies were held and more than 250 pupils were instructed in the research program. All the 6-2 pupils took part in planning and conducting the assemblies. Their efforts were met with spontaneous and overflowing enthusiasm from the classes. Many of the visiting pupils were so excited about the materials in the files that they started to voice preferences for study for the next year.

When the principal arranged for a staff meeting to place the research problem before the teachers, the 6-2 class named a committee to represent them in explaining the project, exhibiting the reference file, and presenting the research library to the school for the use of the teachers and the pupils.

The contribution of the thirty children in the 6-2 class reached monumental proportions, with files containing 1415 selected pictures and articles for the school library. Of this number, 180 pictures were 12″ x 15″ in size, and 544 were 9″ x 12″; there were 280 booklets and 411 selected articles.

Evaluating the Outcomes

It can truly be said that this activity scored high in the final evaluation given it by teachers, pupils, and others involved in its development. It provided opportunities for teacher-pupil planning and for the pupils to accept the responsibility for carrying out decisions once made, in terms of the capabilities of all the members of the group. Finally, it provided the best possible situation for developing and using the various language arts skills in ways that had meaning for the pupils. It demonstrated the superiority of the functional approach over the drill approach to learning. Moreover, and perhaps most important of all, it provided for learning in an atmosphere of joy and enthusiasm, with pupils working for what they recognized as worth-while purposes.

INTEGRATION OF THE LANGUAGE ARTS IN AN
ALL-SCHOOL PAGEANT

The sixth-grade children in Phoenix, Arizona, profited notably from doing something *for* the children of the grades below their own. In Maury School in Richmond, Virginia, the fourth-grade pupils, who were the oldest in the school, were the leaders in an all-school project in which they planned and worked *with* the children of the lower grades in an undertaking which gave a sense of unity to the experience and efforts of the entire school.

The children of the Maury School [2] work throughout each school year on some major activity around which all subjects of study and the contributions of pupils from the youngest to the oldest can be interwoven for a common purpose. Each year such an undertaking culminates in a pageant. The teachers, working as a committee, develop the theme—on this

[2] Maury School, Richmond, Virginia; Etta Rose Bailey, Principal, and Staff.

particular occasion, friendship among the children of the world. They discuss the theme with the children, who work out under their direction during classroom planning periods, a series of statements which develop in terms of their own ideas. The next step, again through class discussion, is for the children to decide with the aid of their teachers which particular aspect of the theme each class can best present.

In this instance, the title agreed upon was *The Children of the World*. Youngsters at every grade level could grasp and contribute to the idea. They talked about what the children of the world want and what they need most. They sought to find out what American boys and girls can do to help them secure these things. They spoke of friendship, of warm, inviting homes, of work, of freedom from fear, of enjoyment of nature, of freedom to move about, to think and speak, and to pursue their own desires. In the final pageant, these were summarized by the staff in a selection for choral speaking:

> To be friends with all the children of the world
> To work and love the working
> To make homes that are happy and good
> To play in the sun and the wind and the sand
> To trace the rainbow through the rain
> To be free as the eagle is free.

Presenting the Children's Case to the United Nations

As a framework for the pageant, the pupils chose to present the needs of the children of the world to selected delegates of the United Nations, represented by members of their own group. Each class chose and developed in detail in tableaux, in creative dramatics, in choral speaking, in the dance, or in song whichever aspect of the theme they thought they could do best. The art and music supervisors worked with them from the beginning to give unity of mood and movement to the whole pageant, the music supervisor improvising the music which helped tie together the various scenes. Great care was taken in planning the color schemes and designs of the costumes jointly by the children, the art supervisors, and the teachers. These were ultimately made by the mothers, who planned them so that they could be modified and used as best dresses for the summer.

As the pageant opened, the delegates from the United Nations took their places on the simply decorated stage. More than one hundred children came in singing "We Are Climbing Jacob's Ladder" as they passed in review before the delegates. Then, with dignity and poise, these boys and girls, with simple properties arranged in the center of the room, lived through the ten scenes representing their plea for the children of the world.

For example, a fifth-grade girl introduced Scene I with the words: "The Children of the World want to be friends. When some are hungry, we want to share our food with them. When they need clothes, we want to clothe them. When some are oppressed, we want to free them." Then followed dances, interpreting children of different nations in these situations and American boys and girls coming to their aid. One boy's interpretation of a dictator was especially dramatic.

Revealing Homes around the World

Again, a child introduced home scenes around the world, saying, "The Children of the World want to live in happy homes with their mothers and fathers." Quickly and easily children brought out simple stage properties from the side lines: a rocking chair and an evening paper for the child who was the father, a chair and a story book for the mother in the same informal group; in one scene a table spread with a colorful cloth and a small amount of food; in another a chair and some handwork for mother. Then the children, in simple costumes, grouped themselves informally in these three settings on different parts of the stage. In the first, a small child in a pink nightgown leaned against the mother's knee where a story book was opened wide. Seated on the floor and propped against her was a second child dressed for the night; over the back of the chair still another leaned drowsily with a toy in her arm. Father rocked and read. The second group, obviously from a foreign land—father, mother, and two children—quietly took their places at the table and sat with bowed heads. The third family group was made up of the mother with her work in her hands and two children who played at her feet. Choral speaking and singing provided the mood and the atmosphere for interpreting the theme, one girl ending the scene with a beautiful song by Teresa Del Riego, an English-born woman of Spanish descent:

> "All things come home at eventide
> Like birds that weary of their roaming
> And I would hasten to thy side
> Homing." [1]

Presenting Other Needs of the World's Children

Throughout, the poetry used represented many nations; for freedom, E. V. Harburg's lines from *Bloomer Girl:*

> "River it like to flow
> Eagle it like to fly
> Eagle it like to feel its wings against the sky.
> Possum it like to run
> Ivy it like to climb
> Bird in the tree and bumblebee
> Wants freedom in autumn or summertime.
> Free, as the sun is free
> That's how it's got to be
> Whatever is right for the bumblebee
> And river and eagle is right for me.
> We've got to be free
> The eagle and me." [2]

For the mood of safe-keeping, a Czechoslovakian folk tune was used, and Paderewski's "Starlight, Silver Bright"; for the wonder of the universe, Lizette Woodworth Reese's "Glad That I Live Am I."

At the end of the ten scenes, an older child sang the stirring lines of John Addington Symond's "These Things Shall Be":

[1] *Homing.* Copyright Renewed Chappell and Co., Inc. Used by permission.
[2] *The Eagle and Me.* Copyright, 1944, by DeSylva, Brown, and Henderson, Inc. Used by permission.

"These things shall be, a loftier race
Than e'er the world hath known shall rise
With flame of freedom in their souls
And light of science in their eyes.

They shall be gentle, brave, and strong
To spill no drop of blood, but dare
All that may plant man's lordship firm
On earth and fire and sea and air.

Nation with nation, land with land
Unarmed shall live as comrades free
In every heart and brain shall throb
The pulse of one fraternity."

Voting by the Delegates

In response, the delegates of the United Nations cast their votes, saying each in his own tongue, "These Things Shall Be," as the Children of the World went out singing, "We Are Climbing Jacob's Ladder."

Using Reading, Dramatics, and Other Language Arts in the Project

There could be no better example of how the language arts can permeate every phase of the life of the school—both in planning and discussing and in creative and imaginative experiences which the children will remember as long as they live. Choral speaking, music, poetry, pantomime, and dramatic play all contributed to the success of the pageant.

Exhibits outside the assembly room displayed books of all types which the pupils had read to become acquainted with the children around the world. The notes they had taken were there, their sketches drawn for costumes and staging, and the books which they themselves had written to summarize what they had learned. Every room from the kindergarten up had had a part in the pageant.[3]

[3] Based on an account by Helen K. Mackintosh, "The Children of the World," *School Life*, XXIX (November, 1946), pp. 9–11.

CHAPTER **10**

The Upper Years

WHETHER young people in the upper grades are in elementary
or junior high school, they are at an age when strong motivation and real purposes are necessary if they are to make
progress in the language arts. Often they are leaders in the
school. They find themselves in situations which call for
independence, initiative, and ability to work with others.
The demands made upon them for skills in reading, in listening, and in oral and written expression grow more complex
daily. The activities in which they engage must seem worth
while to them, and where possible, should render a service
to the school or to the community. Thereby pupils develop
increased maturity in the use of language, ability to evaluate
their own achievement, and a consciousness of power in
working with others.

Three examples of such teaching follow—one from a
highly favored group in Cleveland, one from an average
class in Minneapolis, and one from a slow-learning group.

HERE'S IRELAND

As St. Patrick's Day approached, an upper-grade class in
Cleveland became interested in the contributions of the Irish
to American culture.[1] They had read in the newspaper that
the Irish in Cleveland were planning a cultural garden in

[1] Major work class, Willard School, Cleveland, Ohio; Grace McNealy,
teacher.

Rockefeller Park and wondered what men and deeds might be commemorated in it. The teacher saw in this interest a chance to pursue further the idea that America is a nation of nations and owes much to those who brought their cultures with them from overseas. She hoped also that such a study would heighten the children's appreciation of their own country as a land of liberty and opportunity. The whole project proved rich in occasions for interrelating the language arts with music, art, history, geography, and travel.

Introducing the Project

A survey of class nationalities showed that although only two pupils had Irish names, their family trees contained fourteen Irish grandparents hidden in their ancestral branches. Forty per cent of the class had at least one Irish ancestor.

Making Plans

Discussion of the possibilities of the project brought out these questions to begin with:

1. What have the Irish given to the world that is worth while?
2. What have the Irish contributed to American progress?
3. What men and deeds might be commemorated in Cleveland's Irish Cultural Garden?

Each pupil chose the question for which he wished to find the answer. Groups were formed according to these choices. Before long the class felt the need of knowing something about the history of Ireland, its geographical divisions, its problems, and its contribution to literature and the arts.

One group sought an answer to the question, Why is Ireland called the "Emerald Isle"? Another investigated what Ireland has to offer the tourist. They learned something of the periods of Ireland's history and her problems of today and yesterday. In her golden age, they found monasteries rich in manuscripts, in medicine, and in poetry from the days when she was known as the "Isle of Saints and Scholars." They discovered she was one of the world's richest storehouses of fairy tales and hero stories.

Learning Skills in Use

Throughout all of this study there was need for library reading, and for the use of children's encyclopedias and of poetry and fiction. The pupils learned how to select and organize material for presentation to others. Some decided to liven up facts by dramatization of St. Patrick, for example, and the Christianization of Ireland. Many records were kept of the information thus found. All were carefully proofread for errors in spelling, punctuation, capitalization, and grammatical usage before being filed in library file folders. As the pupils grew in maturity of expression—particularly as they grappled with setting down in their own words new ideas and concepts gained from their reading—they needed much help with clarity of expression and sentence structure. This unit was particularly rich in vocabulary development and in recognition of the colorfulness of language and the musical rhythm of the sentences used by the Irish storytellers.

Lists were prepared of the kinds of problems in grammar and in mechanics of writing which were met by individual pupils throughout the project, and special help and practice were arranged for groups having similar difficulties.

The children wrote letters to the Department of the Interior for recordings and pamphlets of the radio series, *Americans All—Immigrants All*. They wrote also to steamship companies and travel bureaus for illustrated materials on Ireland, specializing among other things in the legends which surround Killarney.

They explored Irish story and song, dramatizing Seumas McManus's "The Plaisham," and using recordings of such familiar songs as "Killarney," "The Harp That Once through Tara's Halls," and other melodies of Tom Moore, "The Lake Isle of Innisfree" by William Butler Yeats, and Samuel Lover's "Rory O'More" and "The Bells of Shandon." They listened to the radio on March seventeenth and chose as their favorites: "The Irish Spinning Wheel," "Father O'Flynn," and "An Irish Lullaby" by A. P. Graves, which were rivaled closely by the "Londonderry Air."

The more gifted pupils in the class became acquainted with the Abbey Theatre and William Butler Yeats, with John Millington Synge and Lady Gregory. They reveled in Padraic Colum, in James Stephens's *Irish Fairy Tales*, in Eleanor Hull's *Cuchulain*, in T. W. Rollefston's *The High Deeds of Finn*, in *The Donegal Wonder Book* by Seumas McManus, and in Joseph Jacobs's *Celtic Fairy Tales*. What these stories mean to the children of Ireland, they learned from such modern fiction as Hilda Van Stockum's *Cottage at Bantry Bay*, Maura Laverty's *Gold of Glanaree*, and Rose Sackett's *Cousin from Clare*.

Irish dances were demonstrated in the physical education classes and Irish music and song by a special glee club of Irish Singers. One girl discovered the Gaelic alphabet, cutting from green paper and mounting the Irish greeting "Cead mile failte"—"A hundred thousand welcomes."

Studying the Irish in the United States

Others investigated the contributions of the Irish to the United States and those of the United States to the Irish, who sought and found freedom here when their liberties were curtailed.

Stereotypes of the Irish were also examined and "the stage Irishman" characterized in contrast to the evidence of literature and history.

The resources of the public and school libraries were used freely both in the field of literature and in history, such books as *Ireland Beautiful* by Wallace Nutting, *Ireland's Story* by Charles Johnston and Carita Spencer, and *One America* by Joseph S. Brown and Francis J. Roucek proving especially valuable. Pupils were delighted to find among Americans of Irish descent notables in all walks of life—Augustus St. Gaudens and James A. McNeill Whistler in art, Charles and William Mayo in medicine, Father Flanagan in social work, and Samuel S. McClure and P. F. Collier in journalism.

Presenting the Program

In the end, the pupils planned a program to which they invited not only the other children of the school but distinguished Irish leaders in the community. The ending— The Irish in America—and the song "God Bless America" centered in a tableau of the Statue of Liberty welcoming other peoples to our shores.

PROGRAM

1. Address of Welcome—"Cead mile failte"—Gaelic for A Hundred Thousand Welcomes
2. The Irish Cultural Garden
3. Ireland Beautiful (Illustrated with Map and Pictures)
4. The Geography of Ireland
5. Irish Traits and Characteristics
6. Song—"Rory O'More"
7. Dance—The Irish Jig
8. The Gaelic Language
9. The History of Ireland
    a. Pagan Ireland
    b. Dramatization of the Introduction of Christianity—St. Patrick at Tara
    c. The Golden Age of Ireland
    d. Invasions of Ireland
    e. Ireland's Problems
10. Song—"The Kerry Dance"
11. Ireland—The World's Story Book
    a. Ancient Literature (A group in costume representing important characters told the story of Cuchulain)
    b. Folk Tales
    c. Thomas Moore—Best Known Irish Poet
    d. The Gaelic Revival
    e. Songs
        (1) "The Leprechaun"
        (2) "The Harp That Once through Tara's Halls"
        (3) "Believe Me if All Those Endearing Young Charms"
12. Dramatization of "The Plaisham," adapted from McManus's folk tale
13. Irish Art
14. The Irish in America
15. Song—"God Bless America"

In sending out invitations and in receiving and introducing guests, the class had much practice in the language arts of guest-host relationships. Correct spelling and letter form were also stressed. Planning and carrying out the program, the pupils demonstrated the techniques of group discussion and learned the value of the many skills of oral expression and dramatic presentation.

BOOK WEEK IN THE UPPER GRADES

The theme of Book Week for 1952 was *Reading is Fun*. A junior high school class in Minneapolis Ramsay Junior High School decided to find out whether the statement is true.[2] Their teacher felt the need for some activity which would broaden the interests and reading experiences of the group and give the pupils a chance to share their enthusiasms with each other. She hoped also to help the pupils recognize the place of reading in the enjoyment of leisure, to give them practice in using the library, and to assist them in developing standards for choosing and judging books for their own personal reading.

Introducing the Unit

The opening discussion grew out of the display of Book Week posters and book jackets which greeted the pupils on coming to class. What kinds of books do different people think make reading fun? Which books represented in the book jackets had they enjoyed? Soon a list of many kind of books was drawn up, and the boys and girls divided themselves into groups according to their choice of topic—adventure and mystery, sport stories, science fiction, teen-age-girl books, hobbies, and the like.

[2] Ramsay Junior High School, Minneapolis, Minnesota; Marion Allen, teacher.

Planning the Procedure

Next, pupils discussed how to find the books they wanted in the library catalogue and on the shelves, in useful reading lists such as *Leisure Reading* and *Books for You* by the National Council of Teachers of English, *Gateways to Readable Books* by Ruth Strang and others, *Books for Reluctant Readers* by Anita E. Dunn, Mabel Jackman, and members of the staff of the Albany State Teachers College in New York, and similar lists loaned to them by the librarian. After several class periods in the library with the help of both teacher and librarian, each pupil prepared a list of books on his topic and began reading the ones in which he was most interested.

During this time each of them developed a notebook in which he wrote evaluations of the books he read and the criteria on which he would judge them. He pasted in it clippings from newspapers and magazines in his home library about books and authors and forthcoming Book Week events.

In the beginning some reading was done in class and some at home. When each person had read one book, the pupils met together in groups to decide how they could best share their reading with others. Some retold humorous, thrilling, or unusual incidents; others discussed standards for judging their books; some dramatized stories; others put on a panel or a radio program. The group studying books that have been made into motion pictures arranged to have sections of the film, *Two Years before the Mast*, shown at the school.

Most of these reports were on individual books or authors. Eventually, each group was to present to the class a brief program representing the area of reading on which it was working—the best to be woven into a Book Week Assembly for the entire school. Each group also was to file in the school library a composite list of the best books in its field for use in other classes. Each was to prepare a poster and one exhibit case of books for the hall during Book Week.

Learning the Techniques of Group Work

This scheme necessitated many small group meetings within the class. Much time can be wasted in such meetings unless they are preceded by careful discussion of how to carry on the planning. The following check sheet was prepared by the pupils for use at the conclusion of each period. Next day the group chairmen presented to the class as a whole a report of strengths and weaknesses in procedure.

SAMPLE CHECK SHEET—TODAY'S CLASS PERIOD

I.	Yes	?	No
A. Did the discussion show progress toward the goal?			
B. Did everyone seem to understand *what* we are trying to do?			
C. Did everyone seem to understand how we are trying to do it?			
D. Did the meeting show evidence of preparation for today's task?			
II.			
A. Was everyone equally interested?			
B. Was interest maintained, or did it lag?			
C. Was there evidence of group unity?			
D. Were individual interests subordinated to the common goal?			
III.			
A. Was participation general or lopsided?			
B. Did contributions show that those who made them were listening to what others had to say?			
IV.			
A. I was satisfied with the group work.			
B. I received benefit from it myself.			
V. Comments:			

Meanwhile, the class had decided upon standards for judging the group contributions: (1) originality and variety in presentation; (2) wealth of material presented; (3) evidence of careful preparation and organization of material; (4) enthusiasm and animation of the performers.

Reporting in Groups

The sports fans presented their report in three sections: (1) why junior high school pupils should be interested in sport stories such as Howard M. Brier's *Phantom Backfield*, Philip Harkins's *Southpaw from San Francisco*, Jackson V. Scholz's *Gridiron Challenge*, Caary P. Jackson's *Shorty Makes First Team*, and John Tunis's *The Kid from Tompkinsville* or *All-American*; (2) how to tell a good sport story from a poor one (in this pupils were helped by Miss Scury's article in the *Horn Book* for October, 1952); [3] and (3) what sports heroes one can become acquainted with through biography. They introduced these men to the class and let them tell their own stories: Babe Ruth, Lou Gehrig, and Joe Louis.

Next, the group on science fiction broadcast from space— from Mars, from the moon, or from some other planets— telling of their experiences in getting there. Franklyn M. Branley's *Lodestar, Rocket Ship to Mars*, Robert A. Heinlein's *Farmer in the Sky*, Leslie Greener's *Moon Ahead*, and similar titles proved useful. At the end, they presented their reading list to the class with some ideas for their evaluation from August Derleth's article in *The English Journal* for January, 1952,[4] which the teacher helped a superior reader among the boys to summarize.

Books about teen-age girls were popular with a group of girls who presented a program on *Find Yourself in Books*. Among the most liked were Betty Cavanna's *A Girl Can Dream*, Adele L. DeLeeuw's *With a High Heart*, Mary Medearis's *Big Doc's Girl*, and Mary S. Stolz's *Organdy Cupcakes*. The talks were grouped around such teen-age problems as deciding what one wants to be, getting along with the family, and dating.

Another group introduced books that have been made into

[3] Colleen Scury, "A Score Card for Reviewers," *The Horn Book*, XXVIII (October, 1952), pp. 348–51.

[4] August Derleth, "Contemporary Science-Fiction," *The English Journal*, XLI (January, 1952), pp. 1–8.

motion pictures—among them, *Alice in Wonderland, Tom Sawyer, The Yearling, Two Years Before the Mast,* and *Lassie Come Home.* They tried to decide why these particular books had been filmed, what kinds of people would like them, what happens to a story when it is filmed, and why. Finally, they discussed what a book has to offer that a moving picture has not and what a motion picture has that a book cannot furnish. The aim was to recognize the values of each.

Historical fiction, biography, sea stories, adventure, and mystery were also presented. Finally, groups concerned with nonfiction, chiefly mechanics and hobbies, gave their reports. In the latter groups the tendency was to show evidence of interests opened up or models made from the reading of such titles as Jeanne and Robert Bendick's *Television Works Like This,* Ruth M. and Albert N. Halls' *Home Handicraft for Girls,* The Eastman Kodak Company's *How to Make Good Pictures,* Richard H. P. Curle's *Stamp Collecting,* Winifred Mills's and Louise M. Dunn's *Marionettes, Masks, and Shadows,* Elsa Z. Posell's *This is an Orchestra,* or Ben Hunt's *Whittling Book.* After each report, a display of the books mentioned appeared in the library, and pupils who had become interested through the reports were allowed to take them out. The class also made a trip to the public library to see what new books of the year were displayed at the Book Week Exhibit.

Evaluating the Unit

In the end, the pupils evaluated the group presentations and selected the best for the school's Book Week Assembly. They also recorded for future study those aspects of English in which the class as a whole needed help. They returned to the original theme of the unit, *Reading is Fun.* "Is it?" they asked, and different pupils told what they had learned to convince them that it is.

During the project, each pupil had participated in group planning, had helped in oral presentation of the group report, had given at least one oral talk of his own, had participated in class discussion, and had written evaluations of the books he had read. Each had also written up in his notebook standards for judging the books read. Each had learned and practiced the library skills inherent in the use of the card catalogue, making a bibliography, and finding books on the shelves. Each had learned the spelling of words involved in the unit, such as *stories, science fiction,* and *bibliography*. Each had been introduced to the form of bibliographical entries and the capitalization and punctuation involved. Each had read at least three books and had handled or heard about many more. One pupil read as many as twelve. Altogether, the unit proved useful in stimulating an interest in reading, in developing standards of evaluation of books to be read, and in opening up a broader array of purposes for reading than the pupils had been conscious of before.

A COMMUNITY PROJECT FOR SLOW LEARNERS

Sometimes slow learners in the upper grades who have struggled with little interest and less success through an academic program ill-suited to their needs have learned to protect themselves by saying as little as possible. How to motivate the simplest expression either orally or in writing is the teacher's greatest problem.

Accepting the Challenge of a Practical Project

A group of girls and boys who were in this frame of mind acquired an industrial arts expert for their homeroom teacher.[5] At the same time the Community Chest made available twenty-five dollars for any group of boys and girls who would be willing to do the planning and the actual labor of rehabilitating the home of an elderly couple who lived in the vicinity of the school.

[5] George P. Phenix School, Hampton, Virginia; Theodora N. Neilson and Randall G. Parker, teachers.

Here was something worth talking about. Interest in the project was guaranteed to loosen tongues and to make organization of the class, the assigning of tasks to individuals, and the keeping of written records necessary. The pupils made a trip to the home, talked with the man and his wife, and immediately saw the things to be done. There were weeds and tin cans to clean out of the yard. Doing that job was a good start. The front steps and the roof were broken; the two-room house was weatherbeaten and unpainted, inside and out. There was outdoor work for the boys and indoor work for the girls.

Organizing and Planning the Work

The pupils needed to discuss what things they could reasonably plan to do in two hour-and-a-half periods each week, and what should be done first. They planned to take pictures at the very beginning and as the work progressed. When the group returned to school after their first visit, everyone had suggestions to offer. With their teacher they began to lay out the various jobs, to get committees to work on finding costs of lumber, paint, nails, screws, and other materials. They needed to decide, too, who would work together as well as how everyone would have a part. While the discussions went on in their homeroom, other teachers became interested. Different children took responsibility for summarizing in a diary record the important agreements reached. This diary was kept daily as the project developed.

Introducing the Skills

Sentences were short, but to the point. Lists were carefully made in orderly fashion. Spelling of simple words was studied: *woman, roof, repaired,* or *curtains.* These were the words which these young people would need. In addition, the common demons such as *where, their, already,* and *too* were emphasized as they are in any unit in which they inevitably appear.

A very few matters of usage such as *John* DID *the repairs on the roof* were considered. Clear and accurate pronunciation was emphasized with words such as *washed*, not *worshed* and *helped*, not *help* in sentences like *Mary helped with the curtains.*

The principal came in every few days for a report, which the pupils took turns giving, with the entire class helping in the preparation of it.

Reading of a few simple books and magazines was fostered as pupils looked for instructions on how to do this or that or for ideas on home furnishing.

An interest in spelling, handwriting, reading, and oral expression developed with a suddenness that was almost overwhelming for their homeroom teacher. A daily expense account gave practice also in arithmetic.

Increasing Self-confidence

When the group found that twenty-five dollars was not sufficient, they made plans for a sale which brought in an additional ten dollars. The comments of people in the community, the response of the elderly couple, and the reaction of their schoolmates and teachers, gave these children a prestige they had never before enjoyed. The photographic record of progress also helped them to keep in mind their final goal.

Reporting to the Community

When the house renovating project was completed and the yard had been cleared of trash, when the steps and roof were repaired, and the house painted outside and in, when the curtains were washed and mended, the blinds repaired, the furniture upholstered, and additional furniture improvised, the pupils planned an Open House to give the community a chance to see what had been done. They wrote the invitation, which was printed in the school paper and sent to interested guests. They planned the program, pointing out records they had made of the progress of the enterprise. They practiced receiving and introducing guests and pronouncing their names clearly and accurately.

Evaluating the Results

From an apparently diffident and hopeless group, these slow-learning pupils developed into a well-motivated and self-confident class. Their opportunity for success in a realistic situation caused them to attack the learning of skills with a drive that brought about greater accomplishment than they had made throughout their previous school lives.

PART IV

Building and Appraising
a Language Arts Program

CHAPTER 11

Factors Which Facilitate a Good
Language Arts Program

EVEN at the risk of repetition, it seems well to recapitulate at this point the factors which facilitate a good language arts program. The description of various schools in action has already revealed what some of these are. The comprehensive discussion of each of the language arts in turn, which appears in Part II, has added further details to point up the problem, and the preliminary consideration of the growth of children and their need for language in today's world has presented a basic philosophy for further examination of the program as a whole. After the recapitulation, two considerations remain —first, to discover how home and school can best work together toward the desired ends, and second, to consider what means are available for determining how nearly these goals have been attained.

LANGUAGE FUNCTIONS IN THE TOTAL
SCHOOL PROGRAM

It has been demonstrated often in this volume, as it is in life, that the language arts are avenues to all learning. Knowledge, skill, ideas, standards of value, and interaction with other people are all gained through the medium of language. At each level of schooling, therefore, language is both end and means to ends. Not only does the child use his language as an aid to learning, but he has much to learn about the language itself in order to use it with increasing effectiveness and understanding.

The Language Arts Are an Integral Part of School Living

Children listen, speak, read, and write throughout the school day, in relation to all the activities of school living and as part of their work in every area of the curriculum. Young children, for example, in studying life immediately about them, whether they are visiting the post office, planning a school garden, or experimenting with air compression, are constantly listening, talking, reading, and perhaps writing. Older pupils, while exploring the problems of conservation, studying their own folk backgrounds, or setting up a page for the school newspaper, are led to seek and share information, explain processes, interpret printed materials, clarify ideas through oral discussion, organize and write summaries, or creatively express their ideas in verse, fiction, or dramatic form.

In music, art, and organized games, in social studies, science, or health activities, even in arithmetic, the language arts are essential to all learning. Although at times there may appear to be no listening, speaking, reading, or writing going on, language is still being employed as the children think—in words. The child working out an arithmetic example on paper, for instance, may be saying to himself, "Nine fours are thirty-six. Two to carry makes thirty-eight. This eight isn't very plain. I'll erase and write it over." Usually such thinking takes place faster than words can be vocalized, yet key words tend to pass through the mind.

In the past, children's listening consisted of their paying attention to the teacher or to some other adult; the school program did not provide for their listening to one another. Today's teacher knows that a child learns much through communication with his fellows and that his social attitudes and behavior are conditioned by his opportunities to mingle with

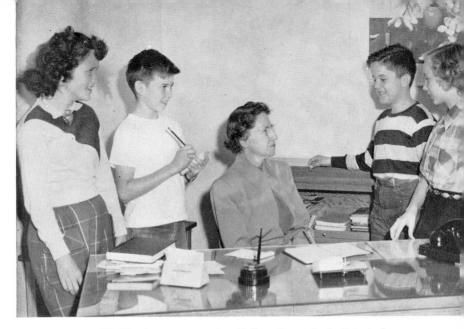

We Use Our Language Arts Skills to Persuade the Principal.

A Daily Diary Keeps Track of the Highlights.

Sixth Graders Interview a Teacher.

Selecting, Cutting, and Pasting Are Part of the Job.

Mimeographing the Newspaper Calls for Planning.

Summing Up What We Know about Aviation.

Listening, Speaking, Reading, and Writing Are Part of Playing.

It Takes Many Skills to Prepare a Report.

children of his own age and to share his ideas with them. Listening has become a recognized phase of the language arts, largely because school workers realize that radio, sound movies, television, and recording instruments have become exceedingly important in children's lives.

Older children, as they make plans, give progress reports, discuss the problems that constantly arise in a group project, or explain and interpret their final results, make an increasingly organized use of the language arts. A Pennsylvania teacher's summary of a fourth-grade enterprise shows typical opportunities for a special sort of listening and speaking.

Archie's grandfather was invited to school to tell some of the stories which Archie was constantly repeating. Thus began the children's intense interest in pioneer days in our community. They searched their readers and library books for pioneer stories; they interviewed older residents in the town; they planned and took a trip to the museum in an adjoining county seat. Parents were induced to look through files of old newspapers and yellowed histories of the county. An amazing amount of information was reported as the result of these investigations.

Words were not enough. The children wanted action. Committees were formed and out of their planning came many enterprises. Original plays based on happenings in local pioneer times were worked out. The girls dressed dolls in typical pioneer costumes while the boys made models of carts, wagons, and simple machinery of the early days. An exhibit was developed as children brought relics from home. One boy brought an old diary that his great-great-grandmother had kept during her trip to her new home "in the West." At the end of their study, the children arranged an assembly and exhibit for their parents.

As pupils progress through school, they use reading increasingly for study as well as for recreation. They use an almost endless variety of materials—textbooks, reference books, pamphlets and circulars, old letters, inscriptions on monuments, and labels in museums. In exploring the factual materials and building up a background of information, they develop interest in the poetry and in the stories and plays that relate to the area they are studying. They begin to see for themselves the relationship between study and investigation on the one hand and recreational reading on the other.

Writing begins with the dictated label or letter in the

kindergarten, and use of it increases through the primary grades. The children write notes to their mothers and to classmates who are sick or have moved away, keep simple diaries of on-going activities such as the raising of rabbits, or express in personal writing the emotions stirred by experience or by reading. Sherry in Grade IV wrote about snow.

The snowflakes look like hundreds of stars floating down to earth. When the sun comes out it makes snow look like stars twinkling in the sky.

More specific and more varied needs for writing occur as school experiences grow more extensive. Children in the upper grades read several parallel references, select relevant ideas, take notes, and develop outlines in preparation for writing reports.

They become more adept at organizing their materials so that others may learn from them easily. One group made a chart as a result of their study of the United Nations. In this activity they used the same skills of reorganizing and summarizing ideas which are employed in outlining. Sometimes a child prepares a list of questions to aid his listeners in learning the salient points to be made in his report. Said Samuel, in introducing his science report, "This is a tiger lily from our garden. You can see the parts of a flower that we have been reading about in our science books. Here is a big chart that also shows the parts. As I talk and point out the flower's parts on the lily and on the chart, think about the questions I have put on the chalkboard." The following are examples of the dozen guiding questions Samuel had written:

1. Which part holds the pollen that bees carry to other flowers?
2. Where do they get the nectar?
3. Where do seeds form?

The Language Arts Have Subject Matter and Values of Their Own

By no means all of the activities in the language arts develop out of the other curricular areas. Reading, speaking, writing, and listening have a place in the school program in and of themselves. Conversation and dramatic play go on in the kindergarten. Children of this age love to listen to stories and poems that fit their level of interest. Storytelling and play-making, which are natural interests of young children, are used for their values in improving voice quality and enunciation, as well as in widening vocabulary. Later, throughout the elementary school years, there should be much reading for sheer fun and many opportunities to enjoy stories and poems which have particular appeal to the child and seem to him worth sharing through oral reading, dramatization, and retelling.

Interpreting poetry has a special appeal for most children. They like its rhythm and the clarity of its word pictures. Choric speaking, if it is well handled, may not only provide enjoyment, but may help to modulate voices and clear up careless enunciation.

Children who live in a world of books, who read abundantly for themselves and frequently listen to the teacher's reading or telling of stories, tend to develop their own creative powers. Creative writing is the outcome of rich experiences at home and at school as shown by eight-year-old Rickey's response to the blinking lighthouse near the shore.

> I saw a lighthouse
>   Out all night
> Blinking, blinking,
>   Blinking out its light.
> It looked out
>   Over all the sea,
> But kept its eye
>   On me, on me.

The effective teacher learns to bring an infinite variety of language arts activities into the experiences of her pupils. She is constantly trying to develop appreciative listening, creative speech and writing, informative reading, and the enjoyment of literature because she recognizes their power to enrich the child's living. She realizes that each of the language arts merits a special place in the curriculum in addition to its services in all other areas of the school program.

The Language Arts Are Intimately Interrelated

When a child visits the airport, he learns with all his senses. His eyes are dazzled by the gleam of sun on aluminum wings, he is deafened by the roar of motors, and his breath is taken away by the wind as planes sweep down the runway. Fascinated by these whirring creatures, he learns more about them not only by observation and by asking questions, but also by reading and looking at pictures in books. He may even write a letter to a pilot of his acquaintance to learn more about unsettled issues which have arisen in class discussion. All the language arts work together to build concepts and round out understandings.

The language arts aid and reinforce each other as the child develops skill in their use.[1] The words he uses first are those he hears used in his presence. Later, reading will further supplement his vocabulary. In the course of learning to read, the pupil acquires visual images of words which are important to his learning to spell. Power developed in spelling extends to his ability to write. His growing control of sentence forms in his oral expression carries over also into his writing. In numberless ways, the abilities learned in one of the language arts are carried over and applied in others.

The Language Arts Develop in Step-by-step Sequence Geared to the Needs of Individual Children

The sequential relationships among the language arts are most important in the child's early years. First comes listen-

[1] Sterl A. Artley, "Research Concerning Interrelationships among the Language Arts," *Elementary English*, XXVIII (December, 1950), pp. 527–37.

Virgil Hughes, *A Study of the Interrelationships among Selected Language Arts Areas and Abilities*. Unpublished doctoral dissertation, College of Education, University of Missouri (Columbia, Missouri, University of Missouri Library, 1950).

National Conference on Research in English, *Interrelationships among the Language Arts* (Sterl A. Artley, Chairman), (Champaign, Illinois, National Council of Teachers of English, 1954).

ing. The baby of a few weeks is aware of sound and soon learns to take notice of his mother's voice, the opening of the door that signals her approach, the swishing sound of the milk in the bottle approaching his lips. Many weeks before he speaks his first meaningful word, he understands words addressed to him. Eventually he learns to say his first word.

By the time the child enters school, he is reasonably proficient in speaking and listening. Here, after a reading-readiness program adapted to his background, he learns to read. Still later he learns to put his ideas into writing. Thus he completes at least the initial skills in the language arts cycle: first listening, later speaking, then reading, and last of all writing.

Not only is there a natural order for the development of the four basic language arts, but there is also an orderly sequence for the development of each of them. A baby babbles before he uses words. A first-grade child dictates sentences composed of words and ideas that are familiar to him before he attempts new words and ideas that expand his vocabulary, his knowledge, and his experience.

A teacher who is deeply interested in the progress of every child studies the language development of each in turn to help him to utilize the background he has already built in taking his next steps forward. No two children at any grade level have exactly the same degree of language achievement. Growth is rapid and substantial when the teacher helps each child to understand his own individual needs and motivates and guides him in reaching for the next higher goal.

Importance of sequence in developing skills. It takes time and a carefully developed sequence in learning to insure consistent growth in proficiency in the language arts. In each of the areas, certain basic skills are essential to competence, and it is usually necessary to take time to teach the techniques involved and to provide sufficient practice for real learning. Although the need for learning a specific skill is likely to arise in any area of the curriculum and proficiency may be gained through using it all through the day, most skills will be well learned only if a certain amount of direct teaching is done, and time can be set aside for that purpose when it is needed.

The skills required at a given time may be very specific and may permit of direct attack, such as clarity of enunciation, slant in handwriting, ability to grasp the central thought of a paragraph or selection, proper sequence in telling an incident, or precision in the use of synonyms. On the other hand, an activity may demand the use of a complex galaxy of skills such as are called for in recording an original play for deposit in the school library, in summarizing for the class log the growth of the mineral-fed vegetables in the window garden, in running a campaign to create interest in rearranging play space in the schoolyard, or in making an objective appraisal of class procedures in discussion.

As pupils employ the language arts in carrying on such enterprises, new and different problems in communication constantly arise and the teacher attempts to be ready with appropriate help for each child so that he can consistently develop the skills for which he is ready. Such an approach is obviously different from the traditional program of class instruction. Each child contributes his share in solving real-life problems and, therefore, benefits from the opportunities for genuine use of the various areas of the language arts. The curriculum reaches out into the community and into the world at large and offers the children real reasons for listening and reading, real stimulation to speak and write.

Since there is a developmental sequence in which learnings take place, there may be distinct danger in attempting to teach skills only as the need and opportunity arise. The teacher can direct her program in such a way as to make her pupils feel a need for a skill at the time when she knows they are ripe for learning it. Otherwise there may be gaps in the children's learning and elements may be taught too soon or too late and out of relationship to other skills. The skillful teacher, however, is able to synchronize time of need with understanding of the developmental sequence in learning.

When specific need arises and a skill is taught at the best moment, opportunity for practice may have to be created. Mr. D. supplied his fourth-grade pupils with envelopes and taught them to address the Parent-Teacher Association communications to their fathers and mothers each month, when he thought it was time for them to master the writing of superscriptions on envelopes. When children first make use of a beginning dictionary, they must use alphabetical order of the second place. The teacher not only demonstrates that *bird* follows rather than precedes *bear;* she sees that the pupils have opportunity for practice with additional words. When the seventh grade explores the origin and use of synthetic textiles and suggests that they write for samples and printed materials, their teacher has them make a survey of all possible sources so that every pupil may have the chance to write a letter. At this point a discussion takes place as to whether the advertiser's purposes are in any degree served by furnishing his expensive advertising material to a class. The children decide to raise this question frankly in each letter. Much careful wording and rewording of questions take place before these letters are written. In this connection the teacher sees that all skills of letter-writing used in the past are reviewed, and the new ones involved are carefully developed. The seventh-graders are surprised at the time and effort it takes to write a letter in terms of the new standards they have set for themselves. They are not averse to seeking out spellings in the dictionary, practicing addresses on the chalkboard, or even writing preliminary pencil copies of their letters for the teacher's judgment and help.

Differences in Children's Backgrounds and Rates of Learning. Just as children vary from approximately eight to seventeen months of age in the time for speaking their first meaningful word, so do they vary in their rate of vocabulary growth and mastery of sentence forms. Children entering school differ in their ability to use the mother tongue, not only in quantity of words and completeness of sentences, but in the quality of their speech as shown by articulation, choice of words, and the clarity of their sentences.

The kind of physical and social environment in which the child grows up is an important basis for individual differences. Poverty, inadequate diet, little association with interested adults, and a lack of enriching experiences will result in relatively meager development in speaking. The child whose parents have given him every possible manifestation of love and provided him with varied experiences and abundant opportunity to discuss them will be more advanced. A farm child has words in his vocabulary unknown to the city child; a boy who has experienced the long winters and heavy snows in northern Minnesota may use words different from those of a boy who has grown up with the red clay banks and warm winds of South Georgia.

Several other factors help to determine individual differences. The sex of the child is one, for girls tend to develop in language faster than boys of the same native ability. Bright children are usually superior to dull in their ability to express ideas. Acuity of the senses may likewise be a factor since a child handicapped in sight, hearing, or any other phase of physical development is thus deprived of certain experiences that give language meaning. The only child, who associates with adults much of the time, may be expected to be advanced over one growing up in a large family, especially if the brothers and sisters are still immature in their use of language. Personality, too, is a factor. For instance, an aggressive child may have some advantage over a shy one because of his encountering forces and objects which the latter misses through timidity. Language growth is correspondingly affected.

Children grow best when they are given opportunity for continuous progress in language skills. Cook's study shows that promotion of a weak pupil gives him fresh opportunity to learn, in a new setting, skills he has formerly failed to master.[2] When children who were considered "failures" were matched and half of them promoted and half not, those promoted improved more in English skills.

SCHOOL ENVIRONMENT INFLUENCES LANGUAGE GROWTH

There are several factors which have a direct influence on growth in language, just as they have an important effect upon many other aspects of the school program. Among these factors are the classroom environment, the organization and operation of the school, and forces outside the school which affect the children.

Importance of the Classroom Environment

The classroom itself is highly important to growth in the language arts. If the room is attractive and welcoming, a pleasant place with many centers of interest, the child will want to talk, to write, and to read. The young child may be a bit less ready to listen, but through sharing and participating, as well as through maturing, he grows in inclination and ability to do so.

"Classrooms should be workshops and studios where children seek coöperatively and creatively for learning," says Strickland.[3] Certainly movable furniture, whether desks or tables and chairs, should be considered fundamental to a good language program.

"The room is right for children to work in" is the first criterion set up in *The Place of Subjects in the Curriculum.*[4]

[2] Walter W. Cook, *Grouping and Promotion in the Elementary School,* College of Education Series on Individualization of Instruction No. 2 (Minneapolis, University of Minnesota Press, 1941).

[3] Ruth G. Strickland, *The Language Arts in the Elementary School* (Boston, D. C. Heath & Company, 1951).

[4] Effie G. Bathurst, Paul E. Blackwood, Helen K. Mackintosh, and Elsa Schneider, *The Place of Subjects in the Curriculum,* Bulletin No. 12 (Washington, D.C., United States Office of Education, 1949).

This brief bulletin describes and pictures a fourth-grade classroom with its functional equipment and its varied activities and carries a running comment in which an observer notes the learnings in the "subjects" including the language arts.

The importance of centers of interest. Perhaps no two classrooms should ever look alike. The upper-grade room at Hickory School is largely the result of teacher's, parents', and pupils' planning and action. A sawbench, a tool chest, and a rack of scrap wood in the enclosed entranceway indicate that much of the equipment is improvised. Two sewing machines in a corner are used by both girls and boys. This corner has boxes of scrap material, yarns, and also a variety of needles, tape measures, buttons, and the like. Costumes for plays, as well as more utilitarian garments, can be quickly devised. A rough table, its legs painted bright orange, and its top covered with plain green linoleum, holds the big dictionary, the globe, an atlas, and a set of encyclopedias. In the science corner a terrarium with a snake, some snails, and other fauna is flanked by rocks containing excellent fossils from a nearby road bank.

Daily and weekly papers are found in the "news corner" with the portable radio. The bulletin board in this corner displays local as well as world information: "Tom J's cow has a new heifer calf."

Adjoining the bulletin board is the "library." *Meph, the Pet Skunk,* published in 1952, is shelved beside a dog-eared version of *The Story of Mankind,* first issued in 1922. *Pinocchio* and *Paddle-to-the-Sea* appear to be equally used. To supplement the nature and science texts in the room there are such helps as *Traveling with the Birds* and *The Grasshopper Book.*

Some of the books have been brought from the children's homes. Most have come from the county library by bookmobile. Folding camp chairs with gingham tie-ons are grouped around a plain oak table that has been sanded smooth and varnished by the eighth-grade boys. In the center of the table are current copies of children's weekly and monthly magazines.

The Art Center consists of a tall corner cupboard with all kinds of supplies, including a zinc tub of clay also collected from the same road bank. Murals made on wrapping paper decorate the walls.

"The Swap Shop" of this room is a unique feature. It contains a growing cotton plant, seeds of which came from Georgia. There are postcards from the seacoast of Maine and a tiny fan from Japan. These articles represent correspondence with other children and in some cases with adults. The boys and girls of Hickory sent appropriate articles when inviting correspondence. Thus the "swap" idea.

For younger children Rainwater [5] suggests a somewhat more standardized equipment. She believes that, "Rooms that are set up in centers of interest stimulate interest and initiative and provide for independent work." She suggests the following equipment:

1. A reading center—with a table with attractive books, plenty of light, and comfortable chairs.
2. A home living center—with a doll and all the equipment of home —much of it made by children; children assuming responsibility for all of it.
3. A science center—an aquarium or terrarium—set up and stocked by children with guidance of the teacher. Other specimens of plant and animal life added from time to time, a magnet, a magnifying glass, and a prism.
4. Art and craft centers—with materials and equipment for painting, crayoning, working with clay, weaving, and woodworking.
5. A small garden near enough for children to reach quickly from their room.
6. A music center with xylophone, marimba, or autoharp
7. A globe and maps
8. A bulletin board

To these one should add a record player for recordings of songs and stories and access to a film projector and a radio.

---

[5] Cleo Rainwater, "How Children Become Independent," *Children Can Work Independently*, Bulletin 90 (Washington, Association for Childhood Education International, 1952).

Centers of interest change from time to time as the interests and activities of the group change. The important point is that materials are ready at hand for the children to carry out their purposes and evaluate their achievement without constant direction and guidance from the teacher. Children can learn to plan and utilize their time fruitfully if the environment is set up to stimulate thinking and self-direction.

The teacher as example and guide. The teacher is the most important element in the school setting. Her own use of oral language, the way she speaks, listens, reads, and writes sets the pattern and standard for the children. If her voice is pleasant, soft, and expressive, the children's voices will take on in some measure the same characteristics. If her voice is harsh, nasal, or unpleasant, these qualities will tend to appear in the children's voices or be reflected in the tensions they develop. If her manner of speaking to the children is courteous, considerate, and thoughtful, they will speak to each other in a similar manner. If she listens to their ideas with respect, they will tend to do likewise. Her reading aloud of poems or stories sets the standard for their oral reading. Children will do some imitating, too, of the writing on the board or the writing which the teacher does on the margins of their papers.

The place of textbooks. Textbooks in the language arts, in small groups or larger sets, are used in most American schools —readers in sets, language texts, spellers, and handwriting manuals. The purpose of writers and editors is to meet the interests and needs of the largest possible number of children in the country as a whole. Materials have been selected and edited for this purpose, and developmental sequences in the learning activities are based on the known facts about child development and how children learn. A general order for introducing activities and for developing skills suited to maturity levels is presented. Since the purpose of the text is to serve, not to determine, the curriculum, the book-per-child-per-subject concept of its use can be injurious. The materials of any text may be too easy for the fast-learning child and too difficult for the slow-learning one if the book is selected to meet the needs of the middle group of pupils, as is likely to be the case. Children within a class vary too much in maturity, ability, achievement, interests, and needs to warrant undiscriminating use of texts.

The reading abilities of children at any grade level cover a range of several years. To meet this range it is necessary to use books of several levels of difficulty. Many schools buy small sets of readers of a number of series and levels of difficulty as well as many single copies of readers for individual work. In this way the slow-moving, the average, and the fast-learning pupils can each work with appropriate material and progress at rates that are most profitable for them.

In one third grade, various groups of the children were able at the beginning of the year to read primers and readers ranging from Grade I to Grade V. The teacher requested one partial set of each grade level from the series just adopted. All her pupils thus had new and fresh reading materials. The better readers were interested in reading the easier books quickly and passing on to the next in the series. The slower readers were able to use the primers, then the first readers, and eventually the second readers. The room was supplied, of course, with other supplementary sets at several levels of difficulty and with a variety of individual copies. There were library books covering a wide range of difficulty; a number of these provided challenge for the most able readers. Many school systems now use the multiple adoption plan of selecting texts so that several series of readers are available in small sets to each classroom. Some schools select a series or two of basal readers and supply additional copies or partial sets of so-called supplementary books.

Language textbooks are probably best used as sources of reference. They are designed to reach into the entire curriculum so as to take advantage of the situations where speaking, listening, and writing arise. Skills and learning activities are arranged in developmental sequences so that children can progress naturally and gradually toward competence and independence. The children can learn to check the text for help in any language skills they need. In most texts there is a development lesson introducing and explaining the skill, with follow-up exercises for practice and for evaluating actual use. Standards, models, and inventories give further aid. Whenever the textbook sets up topics, these should be considered illustrative and not prescriptive. What the children talk about, listen to, or write about should be determined by the on-going activities of the classroom and the interests of the children. The teacher's knowledge of a book, a story, or a poem for every occasion and her enthusiasm for wide use of many resources helps children to see where the values in textbooks lie and to supplement them with many other enriching materials.

The place of the spelling textbook in a classroom where the program is geared to practical and individual uses of writing has to be determined by the time and ingenuity of the teacher, and by her over-all knowledge of how children learn to spell and what words are of most practical value. Many teachers prefer to teach the spelling of words currently needed in connection with the children's various learning activities; they do not depend on a spelling book. There are advantages of timeliness and motivation in this because words are being learned for actual use. However, experience has shown that in this way relatively important words are sometimes omitted. If the daily list is made by teachers and pupils, it should become cumulative and the teacher should regularly check a standard list for grade placement and for relative importance of the words taught. If the teacher depends upon the spelling text or on a printed list, she can supplement to meet current needs. Spelling textbooks tend to be based on research findings regarding the words most used by children; so the basic list will fall quite naturally into any unit of interest. By either plan, the teacher must so arrange the work that each child is dealing with words that have meaning to and use for him, and that his current list is within his ability to master. Emphasis should be placed on learning a method of attack on new words and a sense of responsibility for learning spelling, since the school can not teach all the words individuals will need in later life.

Handwriting guides and self-help materials are useful for individual practice at all grade levels. Some children attain legible writing at an early age with very little practice other than the practice they gain in doing practical and creative writing to suit their own purposes or their classroom needs. Other children need a great deal of guided practice over several years. Writing guides used to meet individual needs can be helpful; but used for uniform drill for all children, they can result in waste of time and deadening of interest in any kind of useful writing.

The Organization of the School as a Whole

Continuity in the language arts is secured not only through the experiences of the classroom and through the way in which the teacher herself works with children, but it is also influenced by the organization of the school itself. The self-contained classroom in which one teacher has responsibility for guiding the child's total program obviously contributes to continuous language growth. This plan of organization, commonly used through the sixth grade, in many instances is coming into use again in the seventh and eighth grades. In a self-contained classroom the teacher can know the child's problems, can see his successes and failures, and can help him consistently throughout the entire day. This makes for steady growth in the language arts as well as in the total program. In a highly organized, subject-centered program such as departmentalization tends to produce, the teacher's opportunity to work with the child in terms of his needs is fractionalized. In *Fourteen Questions on Elementary School*

Organization the following are the reasons given by cities planning to modify their current seventh- and eighth-grade departmental organization:

Highly departmentalized organization makes it impossible to meet the social, personal guidance, and growth needs of the age group involved. It makes relatedness in learning difficult and fosters a subject-centered approach which does not provide the variety of experience necessary in a balanced school program. Teachers tend to be prepared to teach subject areas and too often do not have the child-development point of view.

. . . . children are too young at this stage in their development to adjust to or even profit from contact with so many varying and diverse adult personalities.[6]

The bulletin also reports that forty-seven cities out of fifty-two queried stated that in policy they were committed to the self-contained class unit as the basis of organization within the elementary school.

While the report pointed out that not all of the school systems adopting the policy had been able to put the plan into complete operation, they seemed to be moving toward the self-contained unit as rapidly as possible.

This movement away from the platoon system and departmentalization has apparently covered a considerable number of years. Not all schools reporting gave an answer to this question. At least five schools mentioned having dropped some previous form of organization 20 to 25 years ago, five spoke in terms of 15 to 20 years, seven in terms of 5 to 15 years, and five of changes made during the past several years. The chief reason given for dropping other plans of class organization for the self-contained class unit was the fact that such set-ups contradicted the accepted philosophy of education.

In junior high schools at the present time there is at least

[6] Effie G. Bathurst and others, *Fourteen Questions on Elementary School Organization,* Pamphlet 105, United States Office of Education (Washington, D.C., Superintendent of Documents, 1948).

partial departmentalization in the seventh and eighth grades though there is effort in some schools to set up a core program or large area groupings. The movement toward less departmentalization is significant for all phases of a child's development and especially significant for the language arts. The teacher who is responsible for a group of children during their entire school day can work on the language arts from the time she greets the first child who comes into the room in the morning until she says "good-by" to the last child in the afternoon. Continuous study of children's needs and consistent guidance can bring about highly satisfactory results.

The Impact of Forces Outside the School

It is obvious that the home and the neighborhood in which a child grows up are vital influences on his language development. Meeting children's needs requires conferences, home visits, constant observation culminating in anecdotal records for each child, and coördination of community agencies for purposes of rounding out the educational program. Through such means teachers can do much to learn just where a child is, determine the direction and rate of his growth, and plan what learning activities should come next. There are many suggestions in the following chapter for home and school coöperation.

Innovations in modern living have a powerful impact on the language growth of children. The radio, talking movies, and television are among these. When better programs prove attractive to children, their background is enriched and widened to world proportions, their vocabularies are extended, and their diction improved. Teachers have a great responsibility to keep abreast of current attractions in these media and to interest children in the more desirable ones. Pupils can be helped to evaluate radio and television programs, comics, and moving pictures, so that they will have standards and motivation for choosing the better ones. Teachers and parents have many resources available to guide them in helping children to become more discriminating.[7]

Increasingly, school systems are making systematic use of audio-visual aids and are discovering their educational values. Recordings of storytelling and of poetry-reading can be used to motivate clear, effective speech as well as to add interest to the literature itself.[8] The delightful films dealing with farm life, animals, and other aspects of nature provide content for class discussions in the primary grades, and films dealing with social studies, science, and literary content are available in large numbers for the middle and upper grades. In the schools where equipment is not available, teachers can still do much to help children listen discriminatingly and appreciatively when at home, can direct them to programs in which diction is especially good, can encourage them to retell or dramatize good things the radio or television set has brought in, can lead them to write creatively when good programs stimulate original ideas, and can help them find reading materials paralleling programs which have aroused great interest. The mass media of today can be made timely and effective aids in setting up a vital and constructive language arts program.

On the reverse side of the picture is the fact that many programs, shows, and comics are inferior with the result that the children's concepts, diction, vocabulary, interests, and standards of behavior may be unfavorably affected. Here it is

[7] Paul Witty and Harry Bricker, *Your Child and Radio, TV, Comics, and Movies* (Chicago, Science Research Associates, Inc., 1950).

Edgar Dale and John Morrison, *Motion Picture Discrimination; An Annotated Bibliography* (Columbus, Ohio State University, Bureau of Educational Research, 1951).

Josette Frank, *Comics, Radio, Movies—And Children* (New York Public Affairs Committee, Inc., 1949).

Robert L. Shayon, *Television and Our Children* (New York, Longmans, Green & Company, 1951).

Charles A. Siepmann, *Radio, Television and Society* (New York, Oxford University Press, 1950).

[8] *Educational Film Guide*, Dorothy E. Cook and Katharine M. Holden, comps. (New York, H. W. Wilson Company, Annual).

Filmstrip Guide, Katharine M. Holden, comp. (New York, H. W. Wilson Company, Annual).

that the teacher, parents, and community must work together to encourage productions of a higher quality. A description of such efforts is found in Chapter 12, "Coöperation of Home and School in Promoting Language Growth."

THE COMMUNITY PROVIDES CHALLENGE AND OPPORTUNITY

There is nothing new in the concept of the teacher as a pivotal figure in the teaching-learning situation, but there is need to re-examine the role of the teacher in creating a school-community climate as a framework within which a language arts program operates. The right environmental atmosphere can foster in boys and girls those values and skills which are fundamental in building decent, harmonious, and constructive relations with other human beings.

Community Life and Education Are Closely Related

One of the fruitful ways in which to approach the problem of the relationship of the school-community climate to children's learning is through candid camera shots of some of our schools in action. As each of the following pictures is studied, it is possible to identify the forces which are at work shaping the attitudes, understandings, and skills of teachers and children. Through seeing others at work it is sometimes easier to see oneself.

A Pennsylvania Dutch school. Gorman's School is a one-room building located in the rolling hills of the Pennsylvania countryside. It is square and sturdy like the boys and girls who live in it. Forty seventh- and eighth-graders from farms near and far drive up in school busses every day. They come early and leave late because there is work to be done and fun to be had.

First, the fire must be stoked. A big, friendly furnace dominates the room. It is painted silver with a crown on its top. It has a personality and a name of its own. It is called

"The King." On windows and walls are bright Pennsylvania Dutch designs and scenes which the children paint from time to time.

Furniture is moved out or regrouped as needs of the children dictate. At the back of the room an old-fashioned, round dining room table is placed near the door. Here the children meet for committee work or a chat. Here, also, when it is covered by a clean cloth, the teacher and occasional visitors enjoy luncheon.

When the day ends early for the children, as it must when the county teachers' study group meets in Gorman's School once each month, everyone helps to tidy up and make a welcome for the visitors. Then the teacher must remind the children many times that school is over for the day, as they are loath to leave.

Once each year, Gorman's School puts on an operetta in the county firehouse to raise money for supplies and materials. Knowing that the religious convictions of the group prevent youngsters from dancing, the whole school faces the problem of what to do about the dances which are an essential part of the operetta. Finally it is decided that adaptations may be made which make them acceptable. Home goes a note written by each child to his parents explaining the adaptations that have been planned.

On the night of the performance, the house is sold out. Staid bearded farmers and their plainly dressed wives enjoy the operetta. A sum of five hundred dollars is raised through the efforts of forty boys and girls and the interest of their parents. Now, they will decide together how to spend this money. School is fun.

How has the language arts program helped the children of Gorman's School meet their needs? The teacher knows that creating an environment which will challenge boys and girls to action is important. She knows that when there are real problems to be met the children understand the purpose in learning the skills of communicating. In writing letters to parents, each child was acutely conscious of the fact that if his parents' permission to participate was to be obtained, if support for the operetta was to be secured, his letter must be effective. Each child strove to present his ideas with clearness and exactness, a real effort was made to present the facts in an interesting and forceful manner, and to meet standards of correctness which the class had set up to guide letter writing. In meeting a real problem, the boys and girls of Gorman's School learned, in addition to the many language skills necessary in letter writing, the power of one form of communication in establishing rapport and coöperation with other people. The writing of letters was, of course, only one small part of the language arts program in Gorman's School. But it serves to emphasize the importance of environment, of felt needs, of real motivation, and of working together as a stimulus to learning the arts of communication.

A second picture of American schools at work describes conditions quite different from those of Gorman's School, but nonetheless significant in stimulating an effective language arts program.

An Appalachian community school. High in the foothills of the Appalachians is a valley of unusual beauty and fertility. The early pioneers who settled in this valley elected to remain here while their companions continued their search for a passage through the mountains and the blazing of the Wilderness Trail.

Today the descendants of these original settlers are the "first families" of the valley. Five or six families own much of the land. They are determined that the beauty of this valley shall not be desecrated by pleasure seekers from the populous East who would make a playground of its trout streams, golf course, swimming holes, and picnic grounds. A few villages may be found in the valley and a number of small farms. Truck gardens are numerous. Nearly every resident, whatever his occupation, has his own kitchen garden. Often the crops are so bountiful and the labor supply so meager that the gardens are left unharvested. Food lies on the ground until it rots away.

The children do not fare well in this valley because the landowners do not feel that education should cost much. Old frame school buildings are in sad need of repair. Little play space is provided. The children and teachers of one school have tried time and again to correct the sanitation problems of their school. Through a mistake, the sewer of an adjacent village empties in the middle of the school grounds. After many futile efforts to interest community members in this menace, some sixth-grade pupils proposed in all seriousness to invite the adults of the village to "visit and smell awhile." The public health nurse reports a high incidence of tuberculosis and many nutritional ills. The village dentist reports that many youngsters of thirteen have lost all or nearly all of their teeth. While food is abundant, the poorer families need education in health building through proper diet and healthful living. In a world of wealth an impoverished people is being produced.

Teachers Grow as Well as Children

Every school provides challenge for a teacher who is concerned with utilizing all of the motivating power that is available in the school-community setting to make the learning of children vital and valuable. When teachers and administrators work together, drawing upon all the resources that are available, they find motivation for growth in the language arts in even the least promising environments. If parents can be drawn into the study of children's needs and can help with the planning of improved opportunities and resources for their children, the gain is even more spectacular and more permanent.

Coöperative curriculum building. One summer the principal and faculty of the valley school attended an in-service curriculum workshop at the county seat. The superintendent, the supervisor, and the state university provided the necessary encouragement, resources, and supervision which resulted in a plan for action by children and adults to improve the quality of the school-community environment. When September rolled around, the children, led by their teachers and other professional personnel, began a campaign of interviews, speeches, demonstrations, radio skits, articles for the local paper, and conferences with community agents, which resulted in improved conditions and a richer, more satisfying development of all who participated. The effectiveness of the language arts program in this school grew out of a real need and resulted in a better school and community for all.

The action program was the result of coöperative curriculum building in which the children and teachers took the initiative in arousing the community to action. The superintendent induced the state university to establish a summer workshop in the community rather than on a campus one hundred miles away. The closeness of living together for eight weeks, planning ways and means of attacking mutual problems, resulted in a group solidarity that bore results for the professional staff, the children, and the community.

The picture of the valley community indicates the essential place of in-service training in any program of education. What was the role of language arts in this situation? The teachers arrived at their summer workshop well oriented to the community problems they were eager to attack. Their needs centered in developing and sharing techniques of communication for themselves and for their children. They were concerned with acquiring skill, for example, in teaching boys and girls how to write a good article for the local paper, how to write an appealing radio skit, how to interview people, and how to collect, organize, and present facts in such a way as to stimulate concerted action in meeting community needs. Like the situation at Gorman's School, this workshop itself presented felt needs, real motivation, and coöperation as a stimulus to learning the arts of communication. In addition, it reflects a quality of in-service education made possible by the school administration and the state university when they coöperate to help teachers help themselves.

These two pictures of education at work serve as illustrations of the ways in which achieving a good language arts program stimulates and is stimulated by the improvement of teaching and coöperative curriculum building. At Gorman's School the children with their teacher were realizing, in some measure, the fruits of a vital approach to learning the arts of language in meeting the needs of the community.

Growth in a stimulating environment. An effective language arts program never "just happens." Effort and skill play major parts in creating an environment which encourages children to develop through experiences in the four areas of language: listening, speaking, reading, and writing. Such a situation at its best includes a teacher who knows how to help children satisfy their language needs, one who is encouraged to participate in administration and supervision and who has a share in creating the framework within which she lives with boys and girls.

A language arts program requires rich and varied materials. Foremost among those available to the teacher and children are a wealth of experiences which are present in day-by-day living together in and out of school. These experiences involve problems to be solved which are themselves materials of instruction. Another important resource is a wealth of literature, new and old, available in homes, schools, and libraries. Bookmobiles, which are now penetrating even into remote areas, are assisting greatly in making this possible. And, finally, there is need for an ample supply of films, radio and television programs, recorders, transcripts and records, and other audio-visual materials.

Language power grows in an environment where creativity not only in language but in other art media is prized. The environment must be one in which the in-school and out-of-school life of the child are joined together by strong, real, functional bonds. Evaluation procedures must be consistent with the values and aims of the language program and must motivate growth in power.

The teacher is a key factor in creating a climate for learning good human relations. The current widespread efforts to effect changes in the education of teachers reflect this conviction. The potentialities of education as a powerful social force will be realized only to the extent that teachers are prepared to fill increasingly demanding roles as citizens and teachers. Using and teaching the language arts are important factors in developing them in both aspects of their task. With teachers increasingly able to fulfill their roles, it is imperative that administration and supervision share the responsibility for creating a school-community climate conducive to the best development of sound human relations. The quality of the language arts program will in large measure determine the effectiveness of relationships practiced in and out of school. To this extent every school-community is a new frontier.

INSTRUCTION IN THE LANGUAGE ARTS IS RELATED TO GOALS

A great deal has been said and written about the schools in recent years—some of it favorable and sympathetic, and some of it highly critical. It is clear that most citizens have definite and positive convictions about what the schools should achieve in the language arts. They want their children and their employees to speak, read, write, and spell accurately and efficiently, and they hold the elementary schools responsible for demonstrable achievement in these skills. But they want far more than that. The Curriculum Commission of the National Council of Teachers of English believes that the teaching of the language arts should be pointed toward the achievement of ten major goals, all of which are applicable to the elementary school as well as to high school and college.[9] Experience in the language arts should help each child to progress as far as he can toward the achievement of these goals:

1. *Wholesome Personal Development*

Children grow in confidence and in the sense of their own worth and their power to learn and to achieve when they are accepted and respected members of a group. They can learn to face their own weaknesses and work to overcome them if they are secure in the knowledge that their contributions and their efforts are recognized and appreciated. Language and personality development are closely related, especially during the child's early years. Opportunity to plan and work with others and freedom to pursue their own purposes and interests are especially important for wholesome growth. Formal lessons, exercises, and drills cannot achieve this goal. It can be approached only through normal and friendly but challenging and stimulating social relationships under the guidance of a teacher who is genuinely concerned with meeting the needs of each child.

The solving of problems, whether they deal with subject matter, ways of working, or personal behavior, helps children to think objectively about themselves and others, helps them to understand human beings and why they behave as they do. Real experience gained through trips out into the community and the vicarious experiences of audio-visual materials and literature enable children to enter into the thinking and the emotional reactions of others and to add to their own background of mental pictures, intellectual concepts, and basic understandings.

[9] National Council of Teachers of English, Commission on the English Curriculum, *The English Language Arts*, N.C.T.E. Curriculum Series, Vol. I (New York, Appleton-Century-Crofts, Inc., 1952), pp. 41–54.

2. *Dynamic and Worth-while Allegiance through Heightened Moral Perception and a Personal Sense of Values*

The nation as a whole is in the midst of a period in which values are shifting, and some people appear to be discarding those allegiances which have been considered a fundamental part of the American way of life. The strengths and values that are to be found in worthy home membership are revealed in many of the stories written for children. The kindergarten or first-grade child who has listened to stories and pored over picture books that portray simple childhood experiences, as in Ethel Wright's *Saturday Walk* or Lois Lenski's *The Little Family*, or has searched with Danny for a very special present for his mother's birthday in *Ask Mr. Bear,* has added a little more depth to his appreciation of his own family and his place in it. In Laura Ingalls Wilder's books children of the middle grades have followed the hardy pioneers in their westward journeys as they carried on their warm and wholesome family life in spite of hazards and the constant need for new adjustments. In them boys and girls have learned a good deal about the strengths that lie in human beings which can be drawn upon for their own upbuilding as well as that of others. Good triumphs over evil in many of the children's stories, from the folktale, "Snow White and Rose Red," to Ruskin's story of *The King of the Golden River*. Simple biographies which are being made available in quantity show children how greatness is achieved through high purpose, courage, and steadfastness in working toward worthy goals.

3. *Growing Intellectual Curiosity and Capacity for Critical Thinking*

Anyone who has attempted to answer the question of a four- or five-year-old child is aware of the fact that children of this age are interested in everything, that their curiosity is as insatiable as that of the Elephant's Child in Kipling's story. The task of the elementary school for most children is not building intellectual curiosity so much as it is feeding it and guiding it into worth-while channels. There is real danger today that children who live with radio, television, and moving pictures, which give them a taste of this and a few minutes' worth of that, may become too satisfied with a smattering of surface knowledge and never learn to dig deep for fundamental knowledge and understanding. The units of interest that are carried through in great detail in elementary classrooms and that utilize all of the language arts in serving their ends may help children to find satisfaction in greater depth and breadth of knowledge and in the application of that knowledge to their own day-by-day living.

Critical and analytical thinking begins with the problem-solving of kindergarten and primary children in the real situations that arise in classroom living. This is gradually extended under teacher guidance to the material in books and radio and television programs. Helping children learn to think clearly, to attack problems intelligently, and to exercise judgment in an increasingly mature manner is fully as important as teaching them to read intelligently or to write or speak coherently.

4. *Effective Use of Language in the Daily Affairs of Life*

The informal, wholesome classroom living which is essential to other aspects of personal growth is essential to language growth also. Effective communication requires not only clear speech and writing, but in addition, understanding of how other people think and react. There are many opportunities even in the primary grades to help children to understand psychological reactions to words and the problems that can result when individuals carry different meanings and different pictures in their heads and therefore react differently to identical words.

Children can learn very early that conformity to accepted patterns of grammatical usage and spelling are as important as the use of commonly understood letter forms in writing; they soon understand that marks on a paper or sounds expressed verbally have no value unless the person who sees or hears them can put the same meaning into them that was intended by the speaker or writer. They learn, too, that good communication oils the machinery of group living and that it affects the individual's own reputation, his friendships, and his work and play experiences.

5. *Habitual and Intelligent Use of the Mass Modes of Communication*

Young children need definite recommendations for programs on radio and television which are good for them and to which they should give attention. They need guidance in how to look and to listen and what to overlook and forget. They need help also to fit what they see and hear into the total pattern of their previous experience so that association deepens understanding and helps them to sense values. Older children need experience in listening and viewing under guidance so that they, too, stow away clear and usable concepts and go on to books, interviews, or other sources of self-help to clarify points that are imperfectly understood. In detecting propaganda and bids for their attention they need to know how to evaluate both the purpose and contribution of the various types of programs.

6. *Growing Personal Interests and Increasingly Mature Standards of Enjoyment*

Elementary school children are beginning to set up their own personal yardsticks against which to measure values in many areas—radio and television programs, movies, comics, books of all sorts, and people with whom they come in contact, as well as the values that can be bought with the money they earn or receive as allowances. Many of the interests of these children are concerned with sensory enjoyment; they want to explore, to experiment, to make and do things. Their curiosity and their zest for living are vivid and intense.

Experience in the classroom and the community should help children to develop interests which can be utilized during their leisure time when they can make their own choices. Given a wide selection of well-written books that fit their level of ability and their interests, they will read widely and with increasing appreciation for books and reading. Too often, schools fail children at this point. They teach them *how* to read but do not give them opportunity or guidance in becoming readers—and a reader is a person who reads, not a person who can read but does not choose to do so. Books can be used to deepen existing interests and to create new ones. They can deepen children's understanding of people and why they behave as they do, and of activities and events and what their outcomes and consequences may be. Wide reading of books that present life realistically and wholesomely helps children to look at life with increasing insight and increasingly mature judgment. This growth is reflected in their choice of films and radio and television programs as well. Fanciful materials that are vivid and artistic help them to set increasingly high standards for their own creative writing as well as for their enjoyment of art, music, and literature.

7. *Effective Habits of Work*

One of the major tasks of the elementary school is to help children develop the techniques they need for the performance of essential tasks. They learn during these years how to use many self-help materials such as dictionaries, handbooks of writing, encyclopedias, atlases, and the like, and for what purposes to use each of them. They learn to set their own goals realistically and to work for them persistently and consistently.

Growth in independence and in the power to do well what one does is a source of great satisfaction and pride during these years. Children enjoy saving samples of their own work to compare with other samples from later dates as a means of noting progress. They will put forth great effort to achieve goals which they have been encouraged to set for themselves, if the goals are not too remote or so difficult to achieve that they can see little progress along the way. The old adage needs an additional word for children: "Nothing succeeds like *observed* success." Each new area of interest in social studies or science can call for new goals in planning, in study of techniques, in reporting, and in evaluating. Children can be led to enjoy stretching on tiptoe to new personal and social goals.

8. *Competent Use of Language and Reading for Vocational Purposes*

Actual selection of a vocation does not take place for most children until after the elementary school years. Consequently, preparation of language skills for a specific vocation would not be found at this level. But all children should strive to reach those common goals in the command of language and reading which are essential to a good personal and social life. They need to learn in writing letters, in bearing messages, and in all types of written or face-to-face relationships that both *what* one says and the *way* he says it are fundamentally important. Consideration for others is expressed through clear speech and clear writing which require a minimum of time and effort on the part of hearer and reader. Children need help during these years to recognize the effect of their communication on the attitude of others and to take pride in presenting themselves and their ideas in the best possible light.

Middle- and upper-grade children become interested in the reading of simple biographies. They can be led without preaching or moralizing to become aware of the qualities of character and personality that stand out significantly in the stories. In books such as the Landmark Books they can learn to see the effect of the strengths and the weaknesses of men on the course of history. As they set their own sights and begin to think of their own possible roles in the adult world, they can be helped to see the values in competent handling of language and reading.

9. *Social Sensitivity and Effective Participation in Group Life*

All types of experience with language and reading can help children to understand people and their motivations and the forces in their lives that make them what they are. Kindergarten children begin to learn how to participate in group living. They learn to take turns, to wait until someone else has finished talking before expressing their ideas, to listen and react to the ideas expressed by others, to put their own interests into the background for at least a brief time to consider the interests of others. Discussion, planning, and sharing periods at this level are carefully guided by the teacher. Children of the fifth and sixth grades can take responsibility for sessions devoted to planning, discussing, reporting, sharing, or evaluating and can learn to be leaders as well as participants. Under good guidance, they can analyze and study group processes and develop fairly mature methods of procedure.

Literature available to children helps at this point also. Seven-year-olds can understand the problem of *The Hundred Dresses*. Nine-year-olds can appreciate the longing of the little girl in *Blue Willow* for a real home. Sensitivity to the feelings and needs of others grows rapidly through facing real problems as they arise in school and also through the vicarious experience of entering into the problems of the people in books.

10. *Faith in and Allegiance to the Basic Values of a Democratic Society*

A fifth grade, studying life in New England, was deeply stirred by the teacher's reading of Esther Forbes's story of

Johnny Tremain. Undoubtedly, they missed some of the significance of the patriotic fervor of John Adams, Paul Revere, and the others whose lives touched that of the young apprentice, but they gained some concept of the lofty ideals for which men are willing to make sacrifices. *The Little House on the Prairie* helped them to understand the struggles and the satisfactions experienced by people who pioneered to add to the greatness of our country. There are many books for boys and girls which set forth that story of growth and upward striving and do so with authentic pictures and demonstrable ideals. Again, many of the Landmark Books, which are written by historians and authors of high reputation, help children to appreciate the problems and the glories, the strengths in ideals and aspirations, and the weaknesses in human frailties and mistaken ideals which are all a part of history.

Immediate Goals of Specific Units

The goals which have been outlined are general goals toward which every teacher works at all grade levels. The specific goals for any unit of work are set up to fit the content to be studied, the interests and aptitudes of the individual children who make up the group, the on-going sequence of development in skills, and any other pertinent factors.

Planning a Mother's Day party in a first grade may call for goals such as these:

Learning to compose a simple invitation
Learning to weigh and evaluate one's own ideas and those of others
Learning how to greet guests and make them comfortable
Speaking clearly and loudly enough for the mothers to hear
Selecting, preparing, and reading simple stories for the mothers to enjoy

Specific goals for a sixth grade's study of pioneer life might include some of the following:

Improving in the writing of business letters requesting materials or information
Gaining greater skill in leading and participating in group discussion

Developing new techniques in the use of the card catalogue and in-
dexes in the library

Improving in outlining and note-taking

The specific goals are planned to meet immediate needs or to
capitalize on readiness for new learning experiences. They
cannot be set up in advance by courses of study, textbooks, or
any type of general requirement. What one group can
achieve in the fourth grade may be too difficult for another
group or too immature for a third. The classroom teacher,
through her study of the children with whom she is dealing
and the general goals toward which she is working, assumes
the responsibility for making the decisions as to next steps.
Goals must always be adjusted for each member of the group
as well. What one child can achieve with reasonable effort
today may be far beyond the power of another child. It is
both a challenge and a source of satisfaction to a teacher to
make the necessary adjustments to meet the immediate needs
of each individual in the group.

In teaching the language arts one may teach also philosophy, ethics, history, government, science, or any other area
of content. Attitudes, skills, knowledge, standards, and ideals
are all both aims in themselves and concomitants of other
aims. All good teaching in the language arts results in the
development of individual personalities in the direction of
their highest potentialities.

SUMMARY

The three factors, then, which facilitate a good language
arts program are, first of all, the integration of the language
arts with one another and with all the learning activities of
the school program. Stimulation of growth in language comes
from the normal activities of the school day—a growth which
in turn contributes directly to the success of these enterprises
themselves. At the same time, the language arts have a specific contribution to make to the enrichment of personal liv-

ing among boys and girls through informal conversation, dramatic play, creative writing, and the enjoyment of poems and stories imaginatively conceived and related to personal experience. The sequence of the learning in either case must be adjusted both to the rates of learning among individuals and to the sequence which is natural to the subject itself.

The school environment, in the second place, may either stimulate or discourage reading and expression. The equipment itself, the development of lively centers of interest, the enthusiasm and friendliness of the teacher, her own command of language, and the richness of her background in literature are important aspects of this environment. The development, especially in the primary and intermediate grades, of self-contained classrooms makes for effective learning in the field of the language arts.

Finally, the community itself should furnish challenge and opportunity for growth in language power. Real motives for reading and expression can be generated through consideration of community problems of concern to everyone. As pupils grow in power to use language in the solution of these problems, they gain a real sense of the importance of the language arts in life outside the school. Out of such common interests of school and community comes that kind of coöperative curriculum planning which means joint consideration by teachers, pupils, parents, and community of the major aims of teaching the language arts for both school and life beyond the school.

BIBLIOGRAPHY

ARTLEY, Sterl A., "Research concerning Interrelationships among the Language Arts," *Elementary English* XXVIII (December, 1950), 527–37.

BATHURST, Effie G., and others, *Fourteen Questions on Elementary School Organization,* Pamphlet No. 105, United States Office of Education (Washington, D.C., Superintendent of Documents, 1948).

———, BLACKWOOD, Paul E., MACKINTOSH, Helen K., and SCHNEIDER,

Elsa, *The Place of Subjects in the Curriculum,* Bulletin No. 12 (Washington, D.C., United States Office of Education, 1949).

COOK, Walter W., *Grouping and Promotion in the Elementary School,* College of Education Series on Individualization of Instruction, No. 2 (Minneapolis, University of Minnesota Press, 1941).

DALE, Edgar, and MORRISON, John, *Motion Picture Discrimination: An Annotated Bibliography* (Columbus, Ohio State University, Bureau of Educational Research, 1951).

Educational Film Guide, Dorothy E. Cook and Katharine M. Holden, comps. (New York, H. W. Wilson Company, Annual).

Filmstrip Guide, Katharine M. Holden, comp. (New York, H. W. Wilson Company, Annual).

FRANK, Josette, *Comics, Radio, Movies—And Children* (New York, Public Affairs Committee, Inc., 1949).

HILDRETH, Gertrude H., and others, *Educating Gifted Children* (New York, Harper and Brothers, 1952).

HUGHES, Virgil, *A Study of the Interrelationships among Selected Language Arts Areas and Abilities,* unpublished doctoral dissertion, College of Education, University of Missouri (Columbia, Missouri, University of Missouri Library, 1950).

KENDALL, Glenn, and others, "Community, A Curriculum Resource," in California Elementary School Administrators' Association, *Vision for the Elementary School Administrator,* Twenty-Fourth Yearbook (The Association, Thompkins School, Oakland, 1952, pp. 59–77).

KIRK, Samuel, and JOHNSON, George O., *Educating the Retarded Child* (Boston, Houghton Mifflin Company, 1951).

National Conference on Research in English, *Interrelationships among the Language Arts,* (Sterl Artley, Chairman) (Champaign, Illinois, National Council of Teachers of English, 1954).

National Council of Teachers of English, Commission on the English Curriculum, *The English Language Arts,* N.C.T.E. Curriculum Series, No. 1 (New York, Appleton-Century Crofts, Inc., 1952).

National Society for the Study of Education, *The Community School,* Fifty-Second Yearbook, Part II (Chicago, University of Chicago Press, 1953).

National Society for the Study of Education, *Teaching Language in the Elementary School,* Yearbook XLIII, Part II (Chicago, University of Chicago Press, 1944).

RAINWATER, Cleo, "How Children Become Independent," *Children Can Work Independently,* Bulletin 90 (Washington, D.C., Association for Childhood Education International, 1952).

SHAYON, Robert L., *Television and Our Children* (New York, Longmans, Green and Company, 1951).

SIEPMANN, Charles A., *Radio, Television, and Society* (New York, Oxford University Press, 1950).

STRICKLAND, Ruth G., *The Language Arts in the Elementary School* (Boston, D. C. Heath and Company, 1951).

WERTHAM, Fredric, *Seduction of the Innocent* (New York, Rinehart and Company, Inc., 1953–54).

WITTY, Paul, and BRICKER, Harry, *Your Child and Radio, TV, Comics, and Movies* (Chicago, Science Research Associates, 1950).

WOELFEL, Norman, and TYLER, I. Keith, *Radio and the School* (Yonkers, New York, The World Book Company, 1945).

WOFFORD, Kate V., *Modern Education in the Small Rural School* (New York, The Macmillan Company, 1947).

CHAPTER 12

Coöperation of Home and School in Promoting Language Growth

IT IS in the home that the child has his first experiences in communicating his needs, in establishing verbal rapport with his parents and often with brothers and sisters, and in acquiring status among them. Early home experiences with language influence for good or ill much of what happens when the school begins its work. Only as the child's language development keeps pace with his urge to be a part of the group can he maintain satisfactory relationships with other children. He is eager not only to speak and listen, but to write or to read the ideas of others. These new experiences form much of what he thinks and talks about when he goes home from school.

The patterns of communication which the child develops are influenced by the people, things, and activities in the home. One home may have all the newest technological means of communication—television, radio, and telephone. There may be books and magazines that the family shares. Mother and father may spend time talking with the child or discussing current happenings. The child may hear a story or radio program before he goes to bed each night. In other homes, mothers and fathers are at business every day, and it is necessary for each member of the family to assume a share of the home duties with little time to discuss experiences and radio programs or to tell a bedtime story. A language other than English may be spoken in the home because the parents have recently come from another country. This situation needs careful handling so that its assets may be preserved while its handicaps are overcome.

THE IMPORTANCE OF MUTUAL UNDERSTANDING OF THE ROLE OF HOME AND SCHOOL IN LANGUAGE DEVELOPMENT

From whatever kind of home the child may come, he brings to school ideas to communicate and a desire to have a place in his new environment. The parent is the key person in the home; the teacher, in the school. At home, it is the parent who listens to the child telling about his experience, who shares a trip with him, answers his many questions, and gives him a pattern for communicating his thoughts. It is by means of observation, firsthand experiences, and language interchange that new ideas are acquired and new words become a part of the child's vocabulary. As an experience is retold, new words are used and their meanings clarified. At school, experiences that provide the opportunity to increase the speaking vocabulary, to organize ideas, and to speak understandingly are shared by the teacher and the class together with those which the child brings from his home.

How Home and School Share their Knowledge of the Child

Joe, aged six, lived in a suburban community in a cottage with his father, mother, and two older sisters. He was a very good-looking boy with large blue eyes, rosy cheeks, and blond hair. Naturally, he was the joy and pride of the entire family and all of his wishes were anticipated. His first tooth, which appeared at two years, was the cause of a real celebration in the home. He did not talk until he was three years old. He walked at twenty months of age. Joe was very anxious to go to school, and each morning for two long years he watched his sisters go down the street.

At last, the first day of school arrived for Joe. He was up at an early hour and urged his mother to hurry because the teacher had told him on registration day at school that she would be looking for him on Monday. His mother was concerned about Joe's school experience because of his delayed development in talking, walking, and acquiring teeth. In her first conference with the principal, she told of his late physical and emotional development. The teacher needed this information in planning her program, so a conference was arranged between the teacher and the parent, who was invited to visit the classroom to discuss home experiences as well as prospective ones in school, and to meet other children. All of this helped Joe to have a feeling of security and adequacy in the larger group of which he was to become a part.

When the child enters school, he brings with him the habits, attitudes, and spoken language which he has acquired at home. He has been a member of a small family group where his responses have followed the patterns of the home. In school he becomes a part of a large group, where he must learn how to listen, to speak clearly, to follow suggestions, and to participate in group experiences.

What parents can learn from visiting the school. In order that both parent and teacher may understand the factors which influence a child's life in school, a conference is frequently arranged for the first week in the term in which the parents of all the children in any one room may meet with the teacher. Many parents are conscious of the fact that children are not alike and that they differ in innate capacity and in the degree to which their potentialities have been developed by their environment. From such awareness they learn to accept the fact that, in varying degrees and at different rates, children will learn in school to read understandingly, to write legibly, to speak clearly, and to listen more effectively. Parents can also be helped to appreciate the sequences in language development which children follow at their own rate and to the extent of their capacities.

What teachers can learn from visiting the home. The teacher invites the parents to visit the classroom so that they may see their child in his school setting and observe his performance in a group. This experience aids them in understanding both their own child and others, as well as providing a means for becoming acquainted with the school program as a whole. The parents, in like manner, are glad to have the teacher call at their home to see the child's room, his books, and his toys and to discuss what he does, what his interests are, and how he feels about many things.

In such a visit the teacher discovers the sense of security a child feels or does not feel in relation to his parents and to other children in the home. She senses the attitude of the home toward the school and understands better the child's feeling as to what he may expect and what will be expected of him. She learns the part played by books in the child's home and which ones have become treasured possessions after parent and child have selected them at the store, shared and discussed the stories together, and ultimately have found a cherished place for them on the child's own bookshelf. During the visit the teacher also learns something of the parents' ambition for the child and the extent to which they are able or eager to give him a wealth of worth-while experiences. Many of these factors have already been shown to have a significant effect on the child's progress in reading and language.

Such a visit also provides the opportunity for the parents and teacher to discuss the types of home assignments that are given. Although home study of the traditional kind may have been dispensed with, it is essential to interrelate home, school, and community activities in the well-integrated development of the child. Conversation with the parent can clarify why the teacher has asked various members of the class to secure information from the radio, television, and newspaper; why a second-grade child has been asked to read a story to his younger brother; why a family trip to a museum may be the best means by which a child gains information for a social studies unit.

How Home and School Coöperate in Classroom Projects

At school, Joe's class was interested in the different ways in which one may travel. Many books with stories and pictures of boats, trains, airplanes, and horses were on the library table. The boys and girls had brought in toy trains, automobiles, boats, wagons, and planes. They pooled their information and resources during the discussion time when they talked about trips they had taken. Joe was interested because he had been at the airport with his father. The teacher encouraged him to tell what he had seen. The result was a suggestion by a member of the group that the class visit the airport, so all might see the various kinds of planes.

Discussion followed as to what they should do before going on a trip. The answers were as many as they were varied. One child said, "We get some gas and go." Another remarked, "We must decide what we need on our trip." Still another, who had been at the airport, suggested, "Know what you want to see. There are so many planes, men, and everything." The class agreed that plans must be made. Permission should be secured from the parents in accordance with the school regulations; mothers should be invited to go on the trip; the driver of the bus should be consulted as to the day and the time. The manager of the airport should be contacted. Things to be seen and learned should be listed.

The room was a very busy one with various committees at work. One group went to see the bus driver, who suggested going on Wednesday morning. Another group went to the office to telephone to the airport. The next day, the children composed a note to their mothers which said:

Dear Mother,

Our class has planned a trip to the airport on Wednesday morning. We will leave school at nine o'clock in the school bus. Can you go with me? If I may go, will you please sign this note?

Love,
Mary

Each child read the letter, which had been duplicated, and signed his name so that his mother would understand what they were going to do. The notes, when they returned, indicated that all of the children and twelve parents were going. Then it was necessary to discuss such questions as:

1. How can we be polite on the bus and at the airport?
2. What safety rules should we remember?
3. What are the important things we want to see at the airport?

Children suggested the hangars and the runways. They talked about the people who worked with airplanes—the pilot, the stewardess, and others. Some of these terms were understood by all of the children. Others needed clarification, so the film strip, "A Trip to the Airport," was shown by the teacher. Several pictures of various models of airplanes were explained by one of the parents, an employee of a large airplane-manufacturing plant.

When the children returned from the trip, they were eager to build a model of the airport. Plans needed to be made and ideas discussed. Questions concerning location, size, and number of runways had to be answered. An account of the trip was to be written for the classbook, "Our Trips," which was to become part of the collection of such books in the school library. For the exhibition room, a class picture of the airport was planned with the various planes and buildings labeled so that the information secured might be shared with other classes.

At home each member of the family, during the dinner-table conversation, became well acquainted with the different kinds of airplanes and their importance to the country. Many of the families made a visit to the airport to clarify some of the disputed questions. It was necessary for some children to seek additional information at the library. Telephone calls were made to the airport; these were followed by letters to confirm the conversation. In this coöperative experience the children used the skills of listening, speaking, reading, and writing and had experiences with the various media of mass communication. The home experience of one boy helped to initiate the undertaking. The school then developed the project and called upon the home to coöperate at many points. The home made the school project of intimate concern to the family experience and led out in many directions appropriate for individual children.

How Parents Come to Understand the School Program

Ways of communicating and methods of learning are changing—from the hornbook to modern textbooks, from the slate to television. The acceptance of changes in educational methods and subject matter is difficult for some members both of the school staff and of the community. They have built up a resistance to change and question why things are not the same as when they attended school. Like Rip Van Winkle they suddenly awake to what is happening in education and loudly declare their allegiance to King George the Third. "Why is the alphabet not taught?" they ask. "Why is the sentence no longer analyzed? Why are the rules for the use of skills not memorized? Why is time spent preparing a radio script or writing a play instead of in learning the three R's? Why do children in the same class have different reading books?" The changes may concern methods of communication, time scheduling, use of textbooks, promotion practices, reports to parents, and many other problems which puzzle parents today.

It is exceedingly important that they understand the purposes of the school in helping the child to meet life problems effectively. It is imperative that they sense in detail how language power develops within broader activities and in social settings—that spelling, for example, is not neglected although it may not appear on the daily time schedule from two to two-fifteen.

Changed techniques in teaching beginning reading often puzzle parents who wish to assist pupils at home. The school should help them to see that much reading aloud and enjoying books together in the home is the best possible aid to learning to read at school. When children have learned to associate a good time with reading and to expect that there is a book about every new interest they develop, half the battle of learning to read is won. If a mother wishes to help her child to read, she should be urged to visit the reading class in order to see the methods in use and to offer assistance at home only under the teacher's direction.

METHODS OF HOME, SCHOOL, AND COMMUNITY COÖPERATION FOR IMPROVEMENT OF THE SCHOOL PROGRAM

The educative process is not an isolated one. It is a part of the home, the school, and the community. If the school and home program is to be an interrelated one, it is essential that it be coöperatively planned—with the layman, parent, teacher, and pupils working together. The layman knows the community and the situations in which the child's competence will ultimately be tested. The parent represents the child's immediate environment, his background, his ambitions, his needs, and interests. The teacher stresses the ideals and goals of the educator—that each pupil develop the maximum personal, social, and occupational competence of which he is capable. The child reveals his own needs and interests, the skills he is able to use, and those he is ready to learn because of his particular stage of development and because of the stimulating situations created in the school, home, or community.

Surveys by a Community Council

In many places, community councils have been formed to study the school program. They are composed of teachers and laymen who represent parent organizations and social, service, and philanthropic agencies. Their first responsibility is to become acquainted with the educational program and the community which it serves. By means of a survey, data are collected which reveal the various resources and the recreational and social facilities of the town and neighborhood, the kinds of people in it and their abilities and interests, together with the needs and problems of the community. The next step is to consider the adequacy of the educational program in meeting these needs and utilizing these resources. It is just as important for the teacher to know the community as it is for the parent or layman to know the school. The teacher actually is learning much about the child as she studies the community with its characteristic cultural patterns. She realizes also that the behavior of the child exemplifies the quality of living in the community. The parents, because of their knowledge of the community and of their children's needs, have a valuable contribution to make in the development of the school program.

Parents' Participation in School Activities

The abilities and talents of parents may be utilized in the school program by their assuming partial responsibility for dramatic clubs, radio script writing groups, broadcasting groups, or public speaking clubs. The teacher acts as advisor to such groups and in this way becomes better acquainted with the parents.

Parents come to understand the school by helping with various activities, by learning about the school program through discussion with the child or teacher, by serving as members of committees such as the one on Reporting to Parents, the Curriculum Committee, the Radio and Television Committee, and the Community Council. Thus, the parent becomes acquainted with the school program and policies. He is able to participate in developing a curriculum that will be the best one for the particular school in question and at the same time will be able to interpret the curriculum to the rest of the community.

Use of Parent-Teacher Workshops

Experience in a parent-teacher workshop is most helpful in promoting mutual understanding of school activities. Here the parents and teachers observe, participate, and assume responsibilities that pupils carry on daily in the classroom. One workshop group, conducted by a Baltimore Public School, met to discuss the objectives of language arts teaching. The types of activities which parents could observe were listed. Charts had been previously prepared and placed in the conference room so that parents might review the goals of the language arts program, the ways of living in the school environment, and the means by which the school environment could be expanded.

The parents were given a mimeographed bulletin which pointed out the purpose of the activities in each classroom. Questions were listed to guide the observers. In the first grade, they noted the use of reading material to meet the needs of each individual. Some children were reading very easy material; some were using books at the second-year level; some were writing; others were reading their favorite stories. In the second grade, the parents observed many language activities, such as making a dictionary, writing an invitation, reading library books, looking at a film strip. The third grade had prepared an exhibit of material and activities for their language arts program: books, pictures, exhibits, experiments, hobbies, and dramatization. In the fourth grade, the teacher planned ways in which the parents might help the child at home in selecting radio or television programs, using reference books and the dictionary, and choosing comic books wisely. In the fifth grade, parents were shown how individual differences are cared for by providing a wide variety of material for teaching the skills of communication. The sixth grade was in charge of the school paper and the members of the class were busy editing material, writing, and planning the format. The seventh and eighth grades explained a display of creative writing books written on a voluntary basis both in the classroom and at home. In a similar project in La Crosse, Wisconsin, the whole family had been involved in the project—a brother making the illustrations, a father binding the books, and all the family taking pride in the accomplishment. An only child, for example, wrote of her imaginary brothers and sisters. Her dedication read: "To the sandman who put me to sleep to dream up these imaginary brothers and sisters." Still another described her pets, dedicating the volume to her "Mischievous Companions." "I must have been born with a fever for pets," she wrote. "I can't get along without a furry head under my hand."

In many parts of the country the citizens' committee and the school are finding helpful ways of working together to inform the public of the community's educational plans and to secure coöperation in building the kind of program that will be the best for the children.

Means of Informing the Public

In other places, a superintendent's newsletter or bulletin is issued to the school and to the laymen. This is a public relations service which carries the school program into the home and community.

The local newspapers are usually willing to publish school news. In some places a member of the newspaper's staff known as the School Reporter visits the schools and writes feature articles. In others, the school appoints a student reporter to the staff of the local paper to forward information regarding those aspects of the program of the school which are important to the community.

Educational tours for citizens. Much information about school policies, programs, and problems may be disseminated by conducting educational tours for groups of citizens. The principal or a representative of the school may explain the program and answer questions. Subsequently, conferences of various kinds help the laymen secure information—perhaps a

planned group conference where the parents, interested laymen, and teachers discuss the language arts program on the
basis of the school observation, pupil achievement, or curriculum; an informal unscheduled conference where ideas are
shared; a class conference in which emphasis is placed on a
particular phase of the language arts program, such as the
speech of the group as recorded on a tape recorder and played
back for the parents. An individual conference may be arranged in which the parent and teacher can discuss the
growth and development of a particular child in oral and
written expression; a telephone conference may be planned
whenever face-to-face discussion is difficult to arrange. In
one instance, for example, a teacher made a telephone call or
sent a note each week to the parent telling him ways in which
his son had contributed to the school activities. This encouragement was of real value to the boy as well as to the parent.
In a short time the son was writing the note to the parent
and having it approved by the teacher. In this case, the principal had an opportunity to discuss with the parent the
progress which the boy had made in his use of language.

Reports to the home. Similarly, the understanding between
the home and school is increased by the type of written report to the home which includes the teacher's and parent's
comment regarding the child's progress. It is also fostered by
the daily work which the child takes home, indicating to the
parent the scope of the school program, by the child's folder
of written work which shows the ways in which he has improved or needs to improve, and by conferences with the
teacher when the parent visits the school to discuss his child's
growth. Parents contribute by encouraging the child in his
work, by providing enriching experiences and materials, by
expressing confidence in the teacher and school, and by planning opportunities at home for listening, reading, speaking,
and writing.

The school paper. The school paper in itself is a means of
bringing school and home together. The sixth-grade children

in a large city school publish a paper to tell both pupils and parents the school news. It also serves as a means of stimulating good writing; it furnishes activity for all age levels; it encourages the assumption of responsibility; it is a group project in which the responsibility is shared.

The desirable outcomes from this experience may be many. One is an incentive to write material clearly, interestingly, and correctly, an attitude of self-criticism as the writer evaluates and corrects his own story. It may lead to the acceptance by the pupil of any help that his classmates or teacher may give him and a feeling of responsibility to plan and carry out the plan. It may serve as a stimulus for reading, a means of developing an interest in stories and news of the entire school, and a feeling on the part of the group that they have performed a real service to the school and community.

Use of special days and weeks. In a school in New Jersey, communication was the topic for American Education Week. Teachers and pupils of all classes planned programs covering the language skills. Kindergartens demonstrated the ways in which experiences are shared; first and second grades showed examples of reading readiness and reading for pleasure; third grades composed and wrote letters; fourth grades planned a broadcast; fifth grades practiced on speech difficulties as shown by the tape recorder; sixth grades demonstrated how the library is used; seventh and eighth grades showed how reading skills are developed in the search for resource materials in science and social studies.

In a number of cities, the Business-Education and Education-Business Days have afforded an opportunity for the interchange of ideas. Teachers have been invited to visit various business and industrial organizations; and schools, in turn, have entertained groups of business men and women who enjoyed observing the work of the pupils in the classrooms.

In many communities, a tea is held to honor mothers who have children in the school for the first time. The pupils and

teachers plan the tea, act as hosts and hostesses, and entertain the guests with music and dramatizations.

Distribution of pamphlets. Distribution of pamphlets for
parents is becoming more and more common in many school
systems. For example, in Santa Barbara, California, a pamphlet called, "Yes, We Do Teach Reading," is sent to all the parents. In Baltimore, one entitled, "We Go To Kindergarten"
is given to the parent the day the child is entered for school.
"Getting Ready to Read," a booklet prepared by the Valley
Stream, Colorado, teachers and parents, was distributed in
response to a request for answers to questions concerning
reading.

THE NEED OF COÖPERATION BY HOME AND
SCHOOL IN THE WISE USE OF THE MASS
MODES OF COMMUNICATION

There is another area in which home and school feel the
need of each other in coming to grips with a common problem. That is in dealing with the place of radio, television, the
comics, and other mass modes of communication in the life
of the child.

Radio

Recreational use of radio. Parents are rightly concerned
over the number of hours children spend in listening to the
radio, and their concern is substantiated by psychiatrists who
recognize that the radio has a strong emotional effect. Blood-
curdling tales of escape from death amid the horrors of the
jungle, wild Westerns filled with pistol shooting and lawless-
ness on the part of both hero and villain, stereotyped presentations of deceit and trickery among certain peoples, and
now breath-taking leaps from planet to planet in the wonder
machines of modern science hold children of all ages spell-
bound. It is impossible to measure the effects of such programs on youngsters in general, but it is easy for parents and

teachers to observe their effects upon an individual child. Sleeplessness, nervous reactions of many kinds, the tendency to substitute wishful thinking for a straightforward approach to reality, or an insatiable appetite for books of a similar nature all tell the story of how such programs are affecting individual children. Three approaches are open to parents and teachers in this situation. One is to see that good adventure thrillers and stories in which boys and girls the age of the reader do surpassing things are available in school, home, and public libraries. Another is to encourage listening to dramatizations of well-known children's stories which appear with increasing frequency on the air; and a third is to coöperate with school and radio centers in making available for children better programs of a distinctly recreational type, which have a similar appeal.

Interpretation to parents of the function of radio in the school. Parents should be helped to see that radio is now established as a popular teaching medium on a mass basis. It may be utilized in school to enrich the curriculum by supplementing classroom instruction. Radio programs fit into the on-going curriculum in the same way as maps, globes, charts, movies, or dramatizations do. In many instances, children's literature has gained in importance as stories are told, poetry is read, choral speaking is stressed, and dramatized versions of children's classics are presented over the municipal radio stations or by means of an intercommunication system in the school.

Radio presents and interprets events as they happen. Newscasts are history in the making. Radio has also been used in cases of emergency in a community—such as the coming of floods, the spread of contagious diseases, and the sponsoring of various community drives. Listening to a program such as the presentation of a message to Congress by the President of the United States makes the child feel he is a part of history in the making. A boy or girl, hearing such a program, is much more likely to read with understanding news reports of current Congressional sessions and to visualize more concretely written accounts of similar sessions in the past.

Radio can clarify facts which have been discussed in class, at home, or in the newspaper. The forums, town meetings of the air, and commentators all present a point of view regarding topics which may have real value to the child. Hearing new ideas may arouse a desire on his part to secure additional information and to verify through books or interviews the facts found in the newspapers, magazines, discussions, or television.

When the school, the home, and the radio stations plan radio programs that suit the activities and interests of children and fit into the school curriculum, the radio is becoming another source of reference, as is the school or public library.

One of the objectives of education is to teach pupils to seek information and to evaluate the ideas presented. When a boy hears a radio program in which a theory he has accepted is questioned by authorities, he learns the importance of reaching a decision only after weighing and discussing the information secured from the newspaper or the radio.

To develop in children a desire for music, the parent and the teacher can work with the director of the radio station to have programs presented during the school day which may be utilized for teaching purposes and repeated in the evening for the family to listen to and enjoy. In many homes, phonograph records may be played in which an orchestra different from the one heard on the radio is used, and the two performances may be compared and discussed. Tape recordings are also invaluable for making programs available during school hours.

Coöperative methods of improving radio programs. Many civic and parents' associations have coöperated in an effort to improve the quality of programs offered for children. Radio and television stations are genuinely eager to produce better programs for children, most of which today must meet rigid standards before being accepted for broadcast. Parents and teachers find it profitable to study together some tests of a good program for children. The following criteria, abbreviated from an article by Dr. Reymert, are applicable to children's programs.[1]

1. The program should be interesting to the child.
2. The program should meet the standards of accepted speech.
3. The plot should eliminate horror elements.
4. The program should foster constructive social attitudes.
5. The chief characters, when they are children, should furnish models with which the various age or sex groups may identify themselves.
6. The program should contain indirect teaching techniques.

Many radio stations send the month's program to the school in advance so that it may be duplicated and distributed to the homes, thus giving the parent the opportunity to listen to the program and discuss it with the child.

The use of a school or national broadcast, therefore, may stimulate discussion, develop the ability to evaluate the program, motivate reading, lead to creative writing, encourage writing letters to various stations, provide information concerning programs, or encourage the listeners to follow the program through later series of broadcasts. This may aid in the development of habits of listening for information or enjoyment, of speaking and writing in the preparation of script, announcements, or letters, or of reading to gain additional information or pleasure.

Television

Television, because of its particular combination of visual and auditory presentation, has a stronger appeal for children than other media of communication have. Questionnaires and interviews used in various sections of the country have fully demonstrated the strong impact of television programs on the attitudes, habits, information, and ideals of boys and girls.

From this new medium of communication arises a new re-

[1] Martin L. Reymert, "Psychologists Help Radio Become a National Institution," *Printer's Ink*, XIV (November 7, 1947).

sponsibility for the parent, teacher, and director of television stations. Their working together should develop programs promoting interests in an unending variety of activities such as athletics, music, hobbies, art, and drama; programs that will stimulate an interest in science, civic affairs, cultural activities, or other material related to the enrichment of the school curriculum. Many offerings that are shared by the entire family create a stronger sense of family unity because of the common experience. Opportunity arises to discuss and relate past experiences to the present. Incentives to read more widely, to verify information, or to answer questions discussed in the program are provided.

For example, a sixth-grade boy's choice of home activities which would contribute to the work of his social studies group was to watch on television, "The Story of Williamsburg." He and his father became so interested in the historical background of the play that they planned a trip to visit the site. They sought additional information from books and from the library, by writing to the historical societies of Maryland and Virginia and by discussing the facts secured. One of the outcomes of this experience was the boy's requesting the biography of Robert E. Lee for his birthday.

Again, another child whose class was studying world relationships reported especially on "The News of the World," which was flashed on the screen as he watched a television program in his own parlor. His parents helped him find the program presenting a meeting of the United Nations and the procedures needed where different languages are spoken by the representatives of various countries. They also showed him that by turning the dial on the radio, one may hear a voice from Europe, the Orient, Africa, or the Arctic.

Television stations in several cities have an advisory council to assist in the planning of programs. It is composed of representatives of the schools, the program director of the station, various civic agencies, and parents and young people. Monthly meetings are held for the purpose of discussing and evaluating past programs and planning for the future. From this meeting a bulletin is issued to the home and school. Such a plan enables the teacher, parent, and child to select better programs and to aid in having a balanced experience with the mass media of communication.

The school has an important responsibility in the evaluation of the programs seen on television and also in the planning of those to be presented either as a public relations service, as a direct teaching technique, or as an enrichment for the curriculum.

In one Baltimore school, there is a card file of audio-visual programs. After the class discussion of each program, as to its value for the particular purpose in hand, its accuracy in terms of information the pupils have secured elsewhere, and its aesthetic appeal, a summary of the facts is written on the card, followed by a statement concerning the place of this particular program in the language arts curriculum.

Parents and teachers together should study the effects of television programs upon the child's physical, social, and emotional health through such questions as the following: Does he secure sufficient sleep? Does he go to sleep promptly? Does he enjoy watching the programs with others? Does he watch the programs alone? Does he view and discuss the programs with his parents? Does he draw constantly in his conversation and play upon melodramatic and unreal episodes seen on the screen? Does he have time left to play with children of his own age group? Does he share with others the information or fun he secures from the programs? Does he balance the viewing of television with other activities such as leisure reading and outdoor sports? [2]

Moving Pictures

The moving picture whether seen in the theater, at home, or in school is an important part of life today. The many

[2] Helps for such study appear in Chapter 15 of *The English Language Arts*, N.C.T.E. Curriculum Series, Vol. I (New York, Appleton-Century-Crofts, Inc., 1952).

studies made of the value of motion pictures indicate that they add to a child's knowledge, alter his ideas, and often affect him emotionally. Therefore, the parent and the teacher have a common concern in providing the kinds of pictures that are suited to the interests and stage of development of the child. In several communities committees of parents, teachers, and children review the current pictures and invite comments about the setting of the film, the actors, the value of the subject, the nature of the interest, and the age of persons for whom each is suitable. Reviews are written and placed in the schools and homes several weeks in advance of the showing. Reactions to the reviews are secured through the comments and discussions of those who see the pictures.

A coöperative program for reviewing motion pictures was planned in Seattle by the Junior Program, the owners of theaters, the newspaper, and the parents. As a result, the Friday edition of the daily paper carries a column, called *Playtime,* which is sponsored by the Junior Program. The films listed there meet the standards of national committees reviewing for children's entertainment. One of the important accomplishments of this publicity is that each Saturday afternoon all the moving picture houses show specially selected films for children.

The motion picture may enrich the school program by bringing to the school another source of information. A committee of pupils may have the opportunity to preview the film, to write a summary of it for the school paper, to discuss its value with the teacher and class, and, after the picture has been shown, to evaluate it in terms of its usefulness for their purpose. Many parents are willing to share with the school their films of interesting places and to act as narrators in order to clarify ideas or furnish additional information. A parent may serve as the resource person for this service and keep a file of the films which may be borrowed from members of the community or from community organizations or services.

Telephone

More than forty-four million telephones form a voice highway over the entire nation. This fact indicates that the telephone is a very important medium of communication in which the school and home have a responsibility for developing habits of courtesy, for considering the rights of others by limiting conversations and by calling at appropriate times, for providing practice in using the telephone in case of emergencies such as calling the police, the fire department, or the ambulance, or in making long distance calls. The school emphasizes these elements in its teaching, adding also matters of clear articulation and enunciation, careful identification of speaker and responder, brief and specific stating of messages, and accurate receiving and delivering of them. The latter requires careful listening, and courtesy and accuracy in relaying information. It is important for parents and teachers to coördinate what home and school are teaching and practicing in this much-used aspect of daily communication.

Newspapers and Magazines

"In spite of the rapid development of other means of communication, the newspaper remains the chief source of information regarding current affairs."[3] This fact presents a challenge to the school to teach boys and girls how to read the newspaper intelligently. Comparison of news flashes and commentaries from radio, television, and moving pictures with the headlines and editorials in the newspaper gives an opportunity to examine the information critically, to read different sources for verification of facts, and to form opinions from a variety of materials.

The newspaper has innumerable uses in a classroom and teachers have found it most valuable in many activities in-

[3] John J. DeBoer, "Using Modern Channels of Communication—Newspapers," *Elementary English*, XXVI (March, 1950), pp. 158–70.

volving reading, speaking, writing, and listening. Some of these follow:

1. Preparing a class newspaper, using the form and setup of a daily or weekly paper. This activity requires an editorial staff to write, review, and select material; reporters to secure information by interviews or observation; publishers; copy readers; a headline writer; advertisers; special feature writers
2. Learning the reading techniques required by different sections of the paper
3. Discussing similarity and difference in news presented by radio, television, motion picture, and newspaper
4. Preparing a report about the author of a comic strip and studying the strip to find out whether the author's life influences the content
5. Learning to judge relative values in comic strips
6. Studying the development of the newspaper and preparing charts to illustrate a report to the class
7. Visiting the newspaper building
8. Comparing the school newspaper with a commercially published one
9. Studying the different parts of the newspaper and considering the value of each one to the community.

If parents know that such work is going on in the school, there is much they can do to facilitate the study. Local, metropolitan, and national papers may be made available for study. Different members of the family may help by indicating which sections of the paper interest them most. Parents connected with newspaper publication may assist by telling pupils where news comes from and how the paper is published, or they may make it possible for pupils to visit the plant.

Children read indiscriminately whatever magazines are available in their homes. Parents may be persuaded to help them find appropriate sections of news and domestic magazines serving the adults in the family. There are many children's magazines which furnish valuable information and wholesome, entertaining fun and activity.[4] A joint committee of parents, teachers, and librarians such as the one appointed in Madison, Wisconsin, might well study the problem together and make recommendations to school and home.[5]

The absorption of children in the reading of comics presents a problem which home and school must attack coöperatively.[6] The popularity of comic magazines among both children and adults has been widely noted in the many studies that have been made throughout the country. A few ventures in presenting comic books of educational value have been undertaken by various organizations. Often, these illustrate problems that are of public concern or feature events of historical interest or the classics in comic-book form. From the reading of comic books, the child should be led to read other books that have many pictures and specialize in stories of adventure and suspense.

COÖPERATIVE EFFORTS IN GUIDING CHILDREN'S READING

The child's choice of comics represents his effort to get from the world of reading what he wants or needs at his particular stage of development. In addition to the adventure thrillers which parallel the children's radio and television programs, young readers seek obstreperous humor in which the incongruities of animals behaving like human beings or achieving impossible feats like being shot through cannons or

[4] See appendix for list.

[5] Magazine Committee for the Madison Public Schools, *Magazines for Elementary Grades* (Madison, Wisconsin, Curriculum Department, Madison Public Schools, 1949), or Laura K. Martin, *Magazines for School Libraries* (New York, H. W. Wilson Company, 1950).

[6] Fredric Wertham, *Seduction of the Innocent* (New York, Rinehart and Company, Inc., 1953).

———, "What Parents Don't Know about Comics," *The Ladies' Home Journal*, LXXII (November, 1953), pp. 50–53; 213–20.

catapulted into space are obvious enough to seem funny to the immature youngster. Intermediate-grade pupils add to these two varieties comics in which children like themselves commonly get the better of adults. Boy and girl heroes and the plight of adolescents become popular in the seventh and eighth grades. As parents and teachers analyze together the kinds of interests revealed in the comics or in the other reading choices of children, they may join forces to furnish in home, school, and public library better books meeting these same interests.[7]

Many parents welcome suggestions of books for pleasure reading and for reference use which should be available in the home library. Schools should make a practice of calling the attention of parents to such lists as *The Children's Bookshelf*,[8] produced by the Children's Bureau, May Hill Arbuthnot's *Children's Books Too Good to Miss*,[9] and *Adventuring with Books*[10] by the National Council of Teachers of English. Displays of both standard and new books for children may well be shown at the November meeting of the Parent-Teacher Association both because that is the month of National Book Week and because it is the time of purchasing gifts for Christmas. Speakers on the subject of the place of books in the lives of boys and girls are available in most communities. Mothers need help with what to read aloud to children. They need to be shown such collections as *Time for Poetry* or *Very Young Verses*, which should be readily accessible on the library table, because the time for a poem about a robin is when a robin hops across the lawn and the time for a poem about a steam shovel is when the monster opens its jaws on a neigh-

[7] Constance Carr, "Substitutes for the Comic Books," *Elementary English*, XXVIII (April–May, 1951), pp. 194–200; 276–85.

[8] Children's Bureau, United States Department of Health, Education, and Welfare, *The Children's Bookshelf, A Booklist for Parents*, Publication 304 (Washington, D.C., Superintendent of Documents, Government Printing Office, 1953).

[9] May Hill Arbuthnot, *Children's Books Too Good to Miss* (Cleveland, Ohio, Western Reserve University Press, 1948).

[10] National Council of Teachers of English, *Adventuring with Books* (Champaign, Illinois, The Council, 1950).

boring bank. Both teachers and parents need to be alerted to the place of poetry and reading in every experience of living.

Many homes cannot afford a wealth of books for children. Numbers of twenty-five-cent books are excellent. Many are poor. Parents need help in their selection of inexpensive editions. School and home should unite to stimulate use of the public library, for it is the public library which will serve young people after school days are over.

With the home and school working toward the same goals, the language arts program becomes a functional one, and the child gains a new sense of its importance in school and in life outside the school. The coöperative planning of the language arts curriculum for the education of children in terms of their actual needs creates a genuine partnership between school and community.

SUMMARY

The child's patterns of communication come primarily from home and neighborhood. From them, also, he brings the experiences about which he talks—some rich and educative, some barren and unproductive. From visits to the home and with the parent, the teacher learns much about the child which guides her in making school adjustments to individual needs.

At the same time, parents, visiting the school, see their child in his relations with other children and learn to understand the school program and to sense the many ways in which home and school can work together in helping the child to progress. Among these, coöperation in guiding personal reading through the use of school and public libraries and the development of the child's own bookshelf at home is particularly important.

School and home can unite to make the best possible use of the facilities of the community, to prepare children for adequate services to it, to interpret the school to its citizens, and to secure its coöperation in the best interests of boys and girls. Especially is such coöperation needed in relation to offerings in radio, motion picture, television, and the comics. Means for carrying on programs of improvement in these areas are increasing daily through the activities of home, school, and public library.

BIBLIOGRAPHY

American Association of School Administrators, *Public Relations for American Schools* (Washington, D.C., National Education Association, 1950).

APPLEGATE, Mauree, *Everybody's Business—Our Children* (Evanston, Illinois, Row, Peterson & Company, 1952).

Association for Childhood Education, *Knowing When Children Are Ready to Learn* (Washington, D.C., Association for Childhood Education International, 1947).

BENNE, Kenneth, *Human Relations in Curriculum Change* (New York, The Dryden Press, Inc., 1951).

BROENING, Angela, *Conducting Experiences in English,* English Monograph No. 8, National Council of Teachers of English (New York, Appleton-Century-Crofts, Inc., 1939).

CARR, Constance, "Substitutes for the Comic Books," *Elementary English,* XXVIII (April–May, 1951), pp. 194–200; 276–85.

———, *Substitutes for the Comic Books,* Reprint (Champaign, Illinois, National Council of Teachers of English, 1951).

Children's Bureau, United States Department of Health, Education, and Welfare, *The Children's Bookshelf, A Booklist for Parents,* Publication 304 (Washington, D.C., Superintendent of Documents, Government Printing Office, 1953).

DEBOER, John J., "Using Modern Channels of Communication—Newspapers," *Elementary English,* XXVI (March, 1950), pp. 158–70.

———, *Education and the Mass Media of Communication.* Prepared by a Committee of the National Conference on Research in English (Champaign, Illinois, National Council of Teachers of English, 1950).

Department of Elementary School Principals, *The Public and the Elementary School,* Twenty-Eighth Yearbook (Washington, D.C., National Education Association, 1949).

Florida State Department of Education, *Experiencing the Language Arts,* Bulletin No. 34 (Tallahassee, The Department of Education, 1950).

FRANK, Josette, *Comics, Radio, Movies, and Children* (New York, Public Affairs Committee, Inc., 1949).

GANS, Roma, *Reading Is Fun; Developing Children's Reading Interests,* Parent-Teachers Series (New York, Columbia University, Teachers College Bureau of Publications, 1949).

HERZBERG, Max J., *Radio and English Teaching,* English Monograph No. 14 of the National Council of Teachers of English (New York, Appleton-Century-Crofts, Inc., 1941).

JENKINS, Gladys, and others, *These Are Your Children* (Chicago, Scott, Foresman and Company, 1949).

LEONARD, Edith, and others, *The Child at Home and School* (New York, American Book Company, 1942).

LEVENSON, William B., and STASHEFF, Edward, *Teaching through Radio and Television* (New York, Rinehart & Company, Inc., 1952).

Magazine Committee for the Madison Public Schools, *Magazines for the Elementary Grades,* (Madison, Wisconsin, Curriculum Department, Madison Public Schools, 1949).

MARTIN, Laura K., *Magazines for School Libraries* (New York, H. W. Wilson Company, 1950).

Metropolitan School Study Council (New York), *Public Action for Powerful Schools* (New York, Columbia University, Teachers College Bureau of Publications, 1949).

MILLER, George A., *Language and Communication* (New York, McGraw-Hill Book Company, Inc., 1951).

National Education Association and Affiliated States Education Associations, *Skippy and the 3 R's; A 16mm Motion Picture Which Shows How a First-Grade Child Learns the Fundamentals* (Washington, D.C., National Education Association, Division of Press and Radio Relations, 1954).

OLSEN, Edward G., *School and Community Programs* (New York, Prentice-Hall, Inc., 1949).

OLSON, Willard C., *Child Development* (Boston, D. C. Heath & Company, 1949).

Radio Committee, Department of Elementary School Principals, National Education Association, *Radio and the Classroom* (Washington, D.C., The Association, 1940–1941).

REYMERT, Martin L., "Psychologists Help Radio Become a National Institution," *Printer's Ink,* XIV (November 7, 1947).

SHAYON, Robert L., *Television and Our Children* (New York, Longmans, Green and Company, 1951).

SMITH, Dora V., "Growth in Language Power as Related to Child Development," *Teaching Language in the Elementary School,* Forty-Third Yearbook of the National Society for the Study of Education, Part II (Chicago, University of Chicago Press, 1944).

STEVENSON, Elizabeth, *Home and Family Life Education in Elementary Schools* (New York, John Wiley & Sons, Inc., 1946).

STOREN, Helen, *Laymen Help Plan the Curriculum* (Washington, D.C.,

A Time—A Place—The Right Books.

Fifth Graders Flash the World News.

Parents Help Children Grow in Reading.

Child, Mother, Teacher Evaluate.

You Get the Facts When You See What's Happening.

Fifth Graders Interview the Mayor.

A Library with Everything to Offer.

Association for Supervision and Curriculum Development, National Education Association, 1946).

STRATEMEYER, Florence B., and others, *Developing a Curriculum for Modern Living*, Horace Mann-Lincoln Institute of School Experimentation (New York, Columbia University, Teachers College Bureau of Publications, 1947–48).

WEAVER, Herbert B., "Scale for Evaluating Comic Books," *Childhood Education*, XXVI (December, 1949), pp. 173–75.

WERTHAM, Fredric, *Seduction of the Innocent* (New York, Rinehart & Company, Inc., 1953).

———, "What Parents Don't Know about the Comics," *The Ladies' Home Journal*, LXXII (November, 1953), pp. 50–53; 213–20.

WHITELAW, John B., *The School and Its Community, A Guide for the Development of Dynamic School-Community Relations* (Baltimore, Johns Hopkins Press, 1951).

WITTY, Paul, and BRICKER, Harry, *Your Child and Radio, TV, Comics, and Movies* (Chicago, Science Research Associates, Inc., 1952).

CHAPTER 13

Evaluation of the Language Arts Program

EVALUATION is concerned with how well objectives are being translated into action. It aims to discover whether children are growing toward established goals through the experiences, the materials, and the procedures used.

The program presented in this volume has certain clearly defined ends in view. It stresses the importance of a rich background of experience as basic to real motives for expression and to the development of a wealth of vocabulary and ideas. It aims to develop in each child, so far as his ability will permit, those habits, attitudes, and skills necessary to effective communication through speaking, writing, reading, and listening. It recognizes the intimate connection between the growth of power in language and the personal and social development of the child. It hopes, therefore, constantly to relate the teaching of the language arts to all the activities of the school day and to the progressively developing needs and abilities of children. It urges, also, the use of language as a recognized outlet for emotional tension, as a means to creative expression, and as an instrument for social adjustment.

The school approaches the problem of evaluation from two points of view. One is to discover the adequacy of the program as a whole in experiences offered, in procedures used, and in equipment and materials furnished. The other is to study the progress of both the group and the individuals within it toward the objectives proposed, and on the basis of these findings to plan needed improvements. In both of these methods of approach, an important element will be the coöperative consideration of the problems of evaluation by teachers and administrators, by parents and other community workers, and by the children themselves.

EVALUATING THE LANGUAGE ARTS PROGRAM AS A WHOLE

Recent studies of elementary and secondary schools have begun with evaluating the program as a whole, emphasizing those major elements of setting and curriculum which make possible effective growth for children.[1]

Appropriate Criteria for Evaluation

Such questions as the following aid greatly in this kind of evaluation: How adequate are the facilities of the school for promoting the desired ends? What opportunities have children for planning, for expressing their own ideas, for carrying out their plans, and for evaluating results? How stimulating is the program to the growth of boys and girls in the areas of personal living, of social relationships, of citizenship, of habits of work? What kind of concept have the teachers of the function of a program in the language arts? To what extent is the work related to all other areas of the curriculum and to the life of the school? To the lives of the children and the community? Are teachers aware of the needs of individual pupils and how well are they adapting instruction to them? How great a wealth of material for reading is available? Does the material parallel in difficulty of vocabulary and maturity of concept the complete range of ability represented by the pupils in each classroom? By consideration of these questions

[1] Commission on Research and Service, *Evaluating the Elementary School; A Guide for Coöperative Study; a Publication of the Southern Association's Coöperative Study in Elementary Education* (Atlanta, Georgia, Commission on Research and Service, 1951).

Coöperative Study of Secondary School Standards, *Evaluative Criteria* (Washington, D.C., The Study, 1950).

the entire staff may observe, record, and evaluate the aspects of the program as they know it. Parents may add perspective to the discussion, removed as they are from the actual classroom situation and observing daily the effect of the program upon their children. The pupils also can answer these questions with a penetration often startling to adults.

Facilities of the School and the Use Made of Them

The language arts curriculum inevitably is influenced by the facilities of the school and the ways in which they are utilized. The building itself and the equipment in it, for instance, tend to determine the nature of school activities. In schools where classrooms are overcrowded, where there is no auditorium, and where the library and audio-visual services are meager, the opportunities which pupils have to speak, listen, read, and write with genuine purpose and real effectiveness are often limited. It is important, therefore, that teachers, administrators, and parents join in assessing the suitability of the school plant and equipment for the kind of program in the language arts which they wish to promote.

In spite of limited resources, however, the major objectives of the program remain the same. As a part of the evaluation, an effort should be made to determine the extent to which the teacher, her pupils and their parents, and other citizens of the community have overcome and can overcome the effects of such inadequate facilities. To illustrate, books and exhibits can be brought into the school as well as home-owned movie and slide projectors. The pupils can visit the public library and take trips into the community and to more distant places. If there is no auditorium, many smaller informal audience situations can be created. A committee of pupils may read a specially prepared story in another classroom. They may present an original play, give a planned series of brief reports, or hold a panel discussion for a neighborhood group. Individuals may campaign, room by room, for places on the school council and for other school services. Then there is the example of the class with no duplicators available which was trying to produce a school paper of the sort received by exchange from schools which had typewriters and mimeograph machines. When teacher and class agreed that sending of news bulletins to their homes was of prime importance and that the method of reporting was secondary, the boys and girls kept the daily bulletin on the board and planned ways of reporting news of the school and community orally at home or through letters to parents.

Fortunately many schools are well provided for physically. The rooms are spacious and well equipped; varied activities are possible in shop and library, in auditorium and projection room. Yet such facilities do not always afford the children rich opportunities for exchange of ideas. Under such circumstances, a program of evaluation must ask, To what extent is this school enabling children to use their daily opportunities to observe and listen, to read and report or discuss, to speak and write for significant purposes and in effective ways?

In actual practice, the extent to which good or poor school housing and equipment are made to serve the growth of children depends upon the teacher's own concept of a language arts program. She evaluates according to what she believes to be desirable outcomes. If her goals are shaped by a strong desire for a quiet classroom with pupils doing just what they are told, then she will consider her program successful so long as the children keep busy reading textbooks and writing out assignments, and talk only when called upon. On the other hand, if she thinks that in a classroom pupils should define problems, help in planning solutions, build up a background of basic understandings, develop the ability to think and to make decisions, to grow in social competence, and to build powers of observation and communication, then she will evaluate in terms of these more significant purposes. When her classroom is full of "busy noise" at times, she will think of the purpose and vitality of the pupils' activities. Since the teacher's viewpoint largely determines the nature and quality of the language arts curriculum which she provides, it is important in any program of evaluation to raise first the question of what her philosophy of teaching really is.

Relation to Other Areas of the Curriculum

Another question of importance in appraising the language arts curriculum is its relationship to the total program of the school. This relationship is twofold. On the one hand, instruction in the language arts should prepare pupils to use efficiently the skills in listening, speaking, reading, and writing requisite to effective learning in all areas. For instance, children should learn to tell stories interestingly and in good sequence, to give clear-cut and well-organized reports with all facts pertinent to the topic, and to make explanations which are precise and accurate. Guidance at the right moments in reading should enable children to use informative books with ease and skill, employing the index and the topical, marginal, and paragraph headings as aids to study.

On the other hand, activities in the social studies and science and all learning experiences of the school should provide occasions and materials for developing power in listening, storytelling, letter-writing, reporting, dramatization, discussion, giving of explanations and directions, outlining for a purpose, and various other types of speech and writing. Careful study of the extent of provision for direct teaching of language skills in the situations in which they normally develop should be a part of the program in evaluation.

Emphasis upon a Well-balanced Program

Again, evaluation seeks to discover whether the variety of offerings in the language arts contributes to the well-rounded development of boys and girls. Are all four phases of the language arts given ample recognition as important aspects of the curriculum in and for themselves? Are creative writing and imaginative reading stressed along with practical writing and informative reading? Are critical examination of what is read and improvement in the selection of books for personal reading emphasized along with accurate comprehension?

Are personal values in speech attended to as well as group discussion and business interviews? Is there a reasonable division of emphasis between the skills as such, the selection and organization of materials, and the social and personal values in language growth? Are the purposes for which children read and write and speak and listen real or artificially set up by the teacher?

Is the teacher aware of each child as a growing individual with specific assets and handicaps due to native ability, physical and emotional status, and home conditions? To what extent does flexibility in the program care for these differences and provide for growth?

Each school system, examining its own philosophy, may well prepare a series of evaluative criteria applicable to its own situation. Those presented at the end of the chapter on reading are illustrative of this kind of evaluation. Answers to these questions will come now from observation and discussion and now from actual information available on equipment and building facilities, reports of program, count and analysis of the book supply, minutes of school council meetings, and school library records. Participation in such an overview by the children themselves, by their parents, and by the community at large is of inestimable help to teachers and administrators both in assessing the strengths and weaknesses of the program and in planning and providing for next steps leading to improvement for the future.

Measurement of Skills in the Language Arts

Part of this total task of evaluation is appraisal of the effectiveness of the children's skills in listening, speaking, reading, and writing and of the appropriateness of the teaching procedures used to promote growth in them. Such evidence may be found by listening to the effectiveness with which pupils use language in group discussion, by the skill with which they find and make intelligent use of material in reference books, by the writing they do in making requests of parents, in preparing a written summary of their findings on a particular topic, or in the stories they write of their own personal experience or out of their imaginings.

Results of standardized tests enable the school to compare its achievement in detailed skills of reading and writing with national norms. The value of such measures is discussed in a later section of this chapter. It should be recognized that they are limited in the aspects of power in reading and expression which they can measure and that scores must be interpreted constantly in terms of individual growth and in relationship to the broader aspects of the language arts program. In addition, they remove the use of language from the social setting in which some of the pupil's most serious difficulties arise, and hence the results need supplementing by other informal techniques of evaluation such as anecdotal records, sociometric devices, and lists of books read by individual pupils.

The Need of Broad Criteria of Evaluation

The chief problem is to choose a suitable array of criteria for securing a well-rounded picture of results. It is perfectly possible for inappropriate or narrowly conceived kinds of appraisal to nullify good curricular practices. A school system may set up over-all objectives expressing concern for the personal and social needs of children and for the society in which they must participate and then attempt to evaluate the program solely in terms of the number of preprimers read before Christmas, the statistical results of standardized tests in reading and spelling, or the percentage of items underlined or labeled correctly in a test of language usage.

The Place of Parents and Other Members of the Community in the Program of Evaluation

Parents and other members of the community have a part in the kind of evaluation which attempts to see the program whole, to set up genuine objectives, and to establish criteria of evaluation related to the outcomes desired.

Inevitably, parents are continuously judging the school. They know whether the youngsters are happy and enthusiastic or bored and resistant. They observe daily whether their children can read and spell according to their own notions of what progress should be. They sense whether their boys and girls are growing in language power and in ability to think and act with others. Often, too, they know causes of failure which the teacher is not in a position to discover.

Without knowledge of the school's purposes and far removed from their own early experiences in learning to read and to spell, parents may expect too much and too sudden achievement. They may have little understanding of the relation of developing power in language to the total growth of the child. They may not know, for example, that usage is determined almost completely by what the child hears in home and neighborhood, that ability to express ideas comes from encouragement and practice. If parents are to realize that growth in reading, for example, progresses slowly through many and successive steps, that the child's desire to communicate is normally far ahead of his ability to spell the words he needs, that discriminating vocabulary grows out of real experiences and opportunity to talk about them, they must have some share in the establishing of such values for the school and in determining what are appropriate means of appraisal. Parents and teachers can learn much from each other—not only through parent-teacher conferences concerning individual children, but in many other broader contacts. There is no better setting for such learning than coöperative evaluation of the total program of the school.

It sometimes happens that communities, applying limited concepts of what constitutes progress in learning, cause panic among their members when children do not achieve as they think they should. The result is a repudiation of programs designed to promote broad, general development of children's powers in reading and expression and a retreat to narrowly conceived drill practices based on the kind of skills which can be measured by objective tests. For example, by constant drill on finding the main idea of a paragraph or any other single element of skill, one may produce spuriously high scores on a test of that particular element without any real change in the many functional skills involved in the reading program. Ability to pass such a test with a high level of competence is sometimes achieved at the expense of ability to stand on one's feet and express clearly and simply one's own ideas about what is read, or at the expense of a love of reading, of skill in reference use of a wide variety of books, or of growing pleasure in literature.

TECHNIQUES OF APPRAISAL

Many useful ways of measuring the growth of boys and girls are available to the teacher. Some of these are informal methods of observing and appraising the behavior of individual children in school and classroom, on the playground, and in home and community. Some are techniques developed and employed by the children themselves. Some make use of analyses of long-term activities such as lists of books read, recordings of speech, and examination of written work over a period of years. Others involve the use and careful interpretation of standardized tests.

Appraising the Growth of Individual Children

Study of the growth of individual children is the basic purpose of evaluation. It is essential to remember that while children tend to follow the same general path in their language growth and go through the same sequential steps, they develop at individual rates. Moreover, though growth is continuous, it is sometimes uneven as, for example, the slowing of vocabulary increase when the little child is learning to walk or the coming of a period of little or no progress at a time of anxiety or illness or change of homes. The wise teacher, therefore, looks at individual growth in the light of individual differences and expects each child to progress continuously from his present status toward further general and specific competence in the language arts.

In her appraisal through observation of him in a wide variety of situations she considers all the elements which affect his growth, such as native ability, special aptitudes or handicaps, emotional and physical health, and social and economic factors in home and neighborhood which influence his total adjustment. For example, if a severely retarded child has never been encouraged in early school experiences to contribute to the group's thinking, a fifth-grade teacher will be tremendously pleased if he utters a single complete and adequate sentence for an oral report. She will realize that for him this represents a sincere effort deserving of recognition.

In the same class, a bright child who talks easily may give a ten-minute report with considerable content. Yet if it is hastily presented with little regard for the effect on the class, is lacking in organization, and contains several mispronunciations, the teacher will evaluate it quite differently, for she is trying to get this child to work on good organization, clear speech, and correct pronunciation. She is helping to establish in him immediate goals in speaking that are very different from those of a silent classmate who must be encouraged to speak at all. Thus, while the teacher has certain goals in mind for the class as a whole, she realizes that each child needs to accomplish very different things if he is to grow and progress, and each must be helped to establish his own goals. She evaluates each individual's efforts accordingly. Always the child's abilities must be studied in terms of his opportunities. The quality of his speech is a product of his home and community speech habits; his vocabulary is largely that of his family and closest associates. His ability to read has been conditioned, in part, by whether his home is a reading home, by what his community has furnished him to read, and by whether those he loves and respects enjoy reading.

Informal Ways of Evaluating

Most important of all may be the teacher's day-by-day observation of children's progress as they work individually and together in the classroom. The quality of a child's reaction to a story in terms of what it does to him can be judged, if at all, by the teacher who is sensitive to his thinking and feelings. Only those immersed with the children in the real experience that gives rise to writing can gauge the value of such expression to the individual child. The teacher may study the child individually through listening to his free conversation, through observing his spontaneous interests and behavior, and through talking with him informally. From time to time she makes notes in the form of anecdotal records on significant bits of behavior. The following is an example of what one teacher wrote about a third-grade pupil:

TEACHER'S ANECDOTAL RECORD OF A THIRD-GRADE BOY
SHOWING PROGRESS IN LANGUAGE ARTS

September 15, 1952

Jack is eight years old. He lacks basic skills and also needs help in his social relations at school and at home. The other children reject him. He has an annoying habit of running his hands over everybody he attempts to talk to. When a child tries to get away from him he grabs an arm with a grip that hurts. He appears neglected. Often comes late. Complains nobody loves him. Says, "I don't even have one friend."

October 5

Today the children illustrated stories they had read or heard. Afterward they showed their drawings to the group and explained them. Jack when called on would not show his drawings. He mumbled, "I can't, I don't want to. I never did get up and do anything before everybody."

He twisted and turned, giggled and threw himself around. It took much urging to get him to hold up his drawing and say a few words.

October 17

Jack shows little interest in his reading group and never looks at books of his own accord. Talked to his mother last night. She was shocked to learn he said at school that no one loves him, but says he cries at home and makes the same complaint.

October 23

Reading Test:—Primary Battery
Grade equivalent 2.1 (first month of second year)

November 15

Jack attempted for the first time to write the spelling words. He has found a friend in Sam. They sat together today.

December 1

Jack seems to be trying to compete in the reading group with Sam, who always works to the best of his limited ability. Jack now listens carefully when the other children read. He says, "Wait a minute, I'll get it," refusing help with words.

December 12

Jack made a group of clay models, jet planes, space men, and the like. He asked, "Is it all right, Mrs. R., if I show some of the children my models? I've finished my work."

He had four or five children around his desk at a time and seriously explained what each model represented. He insisted they keep hands off the models and cautioned against loud talking or crowding.

January 8, 1953

Jack said, "Mrs. R., may I bring my space-man suit? I got it for Christmas, and a big airplane and some little space men." His pride and joy in his gifts revealed themselves in voice and face.

January 15

Jack has been reading some of the easy library books during the free choice periods. Earlier in the year he made no effort to work on the reading questions but now answers a few correctly every day.

January 23

Reading Test:—Primary Battery
Grade equivalent 2.45 (middle of fourth month of second year)

January 28

Jack said, "I know all my spelling today, Mrs. R., I worked and worked."

When I gave him his paper and he saw that he had missed six words out of ten, he frowned and said, "I'll get every one next time, you'll see." Sam, his friend, seldom misses a word.

March 17

This has been a big day for Jack. He only missed two words out of twenty in the spelling test. I asked him if he had worked at home and he said, "No, I did it all myself, every bit, right here."

March 25

Jack wrote his first original story today. It was one of the best in his group. He read it to the class with perfect ease and he was the first one to volunteer to read.

"Once there were a fairy who live in a leaf. And once there were a king who live in a castle. And sometime the fairy come out of the leaf and sing for the king and sometime the fairy would go into the leaf and go to bed."

May 15

Reading Test—Elementary Battery

Grade equivalent 3.5 (middle of Third Grade)

April 10

Sam's mother provided a birthday treat for him today. He quickly chose Jack to help him pass the cup cakes and candy. Jack remarked, "I knew he'd choose me." Selecting a girl to help was more difficult for shy Sam. Jack kept calling suggestions, but Sam didn't pay any attention to him. He pranced up and down and put on quite a clever comic skit. Finally he pointed to the favorite of the group and the others applauded. Jack looked so disgusted and said, "He learned all that from me."

April 24

Today Jack said he would like to give an original television show that he'd made up all by himself at home. He told a very good story about space men at war with earth people, with a lot of shooting, etc. Wound up his program with a snappy commercial about an imaginary product. The children were most enthusiastic. Jack repeated his performance in another third grade. He wanted to go to every primary room.

October 9

Reading Test—Elementary Battery

Grade equivalent 3.9 (ninth month of Third Grade)

December 17—fourth grade year

Jack's class had a part in the Christmas play in the auditorium stage for an all-school audience. He was the *scholar* and looked the part, dignified and poised. He listened intently for his cues, spoke his lines naturally, distinctly and with a few appropriate gestures. There was no trace of inadequacy or self-consciousness in speech or bearing.

January 13, 1954

Reading Test—Elementary Battery

Grade equivalent 4.4 (fourth month of Fourth Grade)

To be sure that her observation is systematic the teacher

may develop a check list of the standards she is seeking to achieve and use it to supplement her casual watching and listening. She may select her points from study of professional literature, from local curriculum bulletins, and from discussion with other teachers. Such check lists are best when informal, specific, and made to suit the situation in which they are being used. Her systematic study of data from records, sociograms, check lists, and the like should be summarized to enable her to draw tentative conclusions concerning the children being studied, so that she can see more clearly what they are like and how their individual needs may be met.

Can the child stay on the subject under discussion?
Does he offer facts in support of his opinions?
Can he state facts in 1, 2, 3 order?
Does he listen to information and opinions of others? Does he weigh these and make use of them in his further contribution?
Does he select words effective for making his point?

Since children's progress in the language arts is so intimately related to their contact with their own age mates, many teachers find it helpful to make up and study sociograms of the children in their classes.[2] Pupils are asked to name the children they "like best" or want to work with or sit next to. A schematic diagram is then drawn showing which children reciprocate interest in each other. This technique readily identifies the socially isolated child who is likely to be getting relatively little practice in the use of oral language. It also points out the popular children whose language may be much more effective in setting the pace and example in speech than that of teacher or parent. For in middle childhood, identification with one's peers takes precedence over adult example and admonition.

In the sociogram below, each numbered circle represents a child. Lines going from each one to others in the group indicate the persons he chose in response to the question,

[2] Horace-Mann-Lincoln Institute of School Experimentation, *How to Construct a Sociogram* (New York, The Institute, 1947).

Frieda M. Merry and Ralph V. Merry, *The First Two Decades of Life* (New York, Harper and Brothers, 1950).

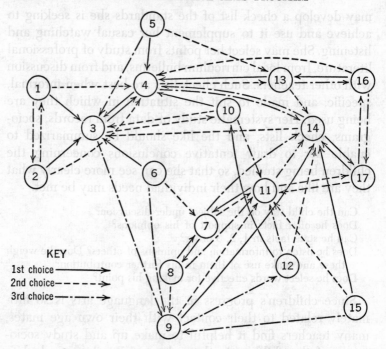

KEY
1st choice ⟶
2nd choice ----⟶
3rd choice —·—·⟶

Sociogram for Selected Children in the Third Grade

"Whom would you like to sit near or to work with?" Lines directed toward each child represent the instances in which he was chosen by another person.

Della, No. 6, is in the third month of her third-grade year. She is one of three girls in the group not chosen by anyone. She has chosen three girls, but none has reciprocated.

She is being pushed by ambitious parents beyond her power to achieve. She rates 91 I.Q. on an individual psychological test. She writes and spells at good second-grade level when the task is mechanical. However, she cannot organize and write a sentence on her own initiative. She is anxious to please and voluble with adults and children, but her language and manner are sputtery and self-conscious. She progressed last year to about second-reader level. She appears to have made no further gain in reading.

Her mother not only attempts to coach Della at home, but has a classmate help her with spelling and arithmetic. She questions classmates about Della's performance in school. They tattle. Della is unhappy, and possible friendships are sacrificed.

Della's teacher is seeking to help her in the following ways:

1. To enable her to gain some pleasure in reading through individual choice among many books
2. To encourage her to do a little writing on her own, supplying her with words as needed
3. To help her gain friends in the classroom, by abolishing the tattling and by other means
4. To persuade her parents to release the pressures and accept all Della's efforts as worthy

Self-evaluation by the Pupils

Growth in ability to evaluate one's own progress should be a significant result of all education. In their text, *The Teaching of Speech,* Weaver, Borchers, and Smith indicate the intimate relationship of such activity to all learning.[3]

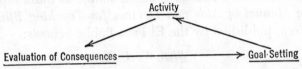

The Process of Speech Improvement

All speech takes its rise, they point out, from some activity motivating expression. Its purpose is communication and personal growth in speaking. It has direct consequences measured by its effect on the audience. Study of that effect leads to goal setting. From goal setting, the pupils go back to further activity—and so the continuous process of learning goes on.

Teachers' reports of children's activities are full of suggested standards set up by the pupils themselves in relation to speaking and writing and used by them for purposes of evaluation. One group of fourth-grade children agreed on the following goals for storytelling:

How to Get People to Listen to Your Story

1. Choose a short story.
2. Be sure you know what happens in the story.
3. Lead up to the exciting point.
4. Have a good ending.

[3] Andrew T. Weaver, Gladys L. Borchers, and Donald K. Smith, *The Teaching of Speech* (New York, Prentice-Hall, Inc., 1952), pp. 93–103.

5. When you read or tell the story, watch whether the other children seem interested.

In the sixth grade, this same group developed standards for giving a report:

Making a Good Report

1. Pick out the important facts. Don't try to tell everything.
2. Plan the order in which you are going to tell things.
3. Tell the facts in your own words.
4. Make a sketch on the board, show a picture, or display things that go with the subject.
5. Make a quick start. Stop when you have finished.
6. Find out afterward how much the listeners have learned and how they enjoyed the report.

Sometimes such standards are as simple as those reported in the *Manual of Aids and Devices for Teaching Bilingual Children*, published by the El Paso Public Schools:

What We Do

We listen quietly when stories and poems are read.
We speak so we can hear.
We make our stories interesting.[4]

The report of the elementary committee of the National Association of Teachers of Speech sets up the following standards for self-evaluation in group discussion in the upper grades. Such standards are useful chiefly as children make them for themselves.

How Good Was Our Discussion?

1. Was this a discussion or a series of reports?
2. Did the discussion develop in a logical way?
3. Was too much time spent on trivial details?
4. Did the leader listen attentively so as to keep the children on the subject?
5. Did I take an active part?
6. Did I remember the rights of others and not speak too long?
7. Did I try to enlist others to take part? [5]

[4] El Paso Public Schools, *A Manual of Aids and Devices for Teaching Bilingual Children, Grade 3* (El Paso, Texas, 1946), p. 124.
[5] *Guides to Speech Training in the Elementary School; A Report of the Elementary Committee of the National Association of Teachers of Speech* (Boston, The Expression Company, 1943), pp. 53–54.

Recent courses of study from Denver and Minneapolis are rich in suggestions for evaluating progress in such skills as ability to organize thought [6] and facility in carrying on conversation.[7]

It is important for teachers to see that the check list is used properly, and that it does not itself become the goal, obscuring the purpose of communication. If pupils are to evaluate an oral production on the spot—when, for instance, they are helping Johnny plan his announcement for the radio show—they should probably think of only the criteria that apply to that particular purpose. However, if the oral story or report has been put on a recording, they can listen to it more than once—and each time discuss it in respect to different criteria.

Pupils can profit from participating in devising appropriate check lists for speech, listening,[8] reading, and writing, and applying them to their own use of these skills. To judge their individual progress and know clearly their own current needs is to be motivated strongly for learning. Self-evaluation of a performance should be prompt and informal and should be conducted in a friendly and supporting atmosphere. When, for instance, the seventh-graders work in pairs and practice repeatedly their interview techniques, correcting their own weaknesses, they should feel that the teacher and classmates listen and advise out of a strong desire to have them succeed in the real interviews with community members. The use of check lists may easily be overdone. They probably should be discarded promptly after their immediate use and new ones should be made for new occasions.

However, self-evaluation and group evaluation are not dependent on any device. Some of the most useful informal

[6] Minneapolis Public Schools, *Communication; A Guide to the Teaching of Speaking and Writing, Grades 2–11* (Minneapolis, Minnesota, Board of Education, 1953), pp. 106–109.

[7] Denver Public Schools, *A Program in English; A Guide for Teaching the Language Arts, Kindergarten through Grade 12* (Denver, Colorado, Denver Public Schools, 1953), p. 271

[8] See pages 75, 88, 90, 101–103, 228–29, 249–56, 289, 309, 399, 401–2.

procedures in evaluation can be applied directly by the child. He can judge his own effectiveness in speaking or reading aloud by whether listeners sit still with eyes fixed on him and attention undivided. If the follow-up discussion shows that listeners comprehended and were really interested, if the questions asked are supplementary but related, if the audience seems convinced, the speaker can be reasonably sure he has expressed his ideas with some competence. If the members of the audience seem restless and discussion reveals that they do not understand, intermediate-grade pupils may profit by teacher-guided discussion of what was needed, such as a topic of more general appeal, meaningful details, better organization, a more selective choice of words, or a more pleasing delivery.

Free observation in which a child comments on something he likes in a classmate's story, substitutes a more appropriate word for one loosely used by a speaker, or commends a voice heard on a radio program, is one of the best informal procedures for appraisal. When children work together to improve a group product, genuine evaluation is going on, and they are growing not only in appropriate and effective ways of expressing themselves, but also in the ability to criticize and improve their own work.

Long-Term Evaluation of Performance in Reading, Writing, Speaking, and Listening

An important aspect of evaluation is the periodic examination of the reading records of individual pupils and of what evidence exists of their progress in writing, speaking, and listening over a series of months or years.

For example, permanent reading records for each pupil, filed and passed on to the next teacher, furnish important evidence. How much does the child read voluntarily and in relation to all areas of the curriculum? How varied is his reading in books of widely different appeal? Has he discovered that books are related to his most cherished hobbies or pastimes? Does he read cheap and ephemeral books or good wholesome material, some of it with spark and imagination? Does he have a library card? How often does he use it? Can he use the dictionary and the encyclopedia? Is he improving in his ability to take notes and to organize those notes clearly for presentation to the class? Such powers as these must be measured by informal observation of children in the classroom or by tests made by the teacher in relation to the daily uses of reading in the school program.

How much literature is the child acquainted with? Does he respond with pleasure to poetry? Has he discovered what brings satisfaction in music of line, imaginative insight into daily experience, or pictorial power of words? Does he take out poetry books from the library or, in the primary grades, does he ask for more when the teacher reads? How many poems can he repeat from memory? How often does he do so spontaneously, showing appreciation of the poem in appropriate context? [9] Has he found good books for personal reading to offset the comics and cheap motion pictures or television shows? All these are significant elements in the evaluation of a program in reading and literature.

Then, of even greater importance, what is his reading doing to him? Does his enjoyment of reading enrich his daily living? Has he gained greater understanding of himself and others through books? Through reading, has he grown more thoughtful in his approach to social problems which he can comprehend at his stage of development? Has reading influenced his attitudes toward his American heritage? Toward intercultural problems? Has he gained a sense of perspective and a sense of values which give him greater stability of character and greater steadiness of view?

Long-term records of speech and writing can be similarly evaluated. The illustration of the recording of the speech of

[9] Jean Betzner, *Exploring Literature with Children in the Elementary School, Practical Suggestions for Teaching*, No. 7 (New York, Columbia University, Teachers College Bureau of Publications, 1943), pp. 65–74.

a primary-grade child at yearly intervals which appears on page 270 shows clearly how progress can be revealed by examination of such records. Folders of pupils' writing over a period of years give opportunity for noting progress in sureness of purpose, wealth and originality of ideas, precision or suggestiveness of diction, maturity of sentence structure, and mechanical accuracy. Or a set of criteria may be adopted such as that discussed on pages 229–234: ease, clarity, suitability, and originality. Photographs of papers written by the same child over a period of eight years appear on pages 250–253. Application of any such set of standards to them will show how profitable the procedure can be.

Standardized Tests of Group and Individual Achievement

For measuring the skill aspects of reading and language, standardized tests are available which help to determine the progress of individual or class groups in comparison with national norms. Scores on such tests, based on large representative samples, help teachers and administrators keep the local situation in proper focus and assist in stabilizing the shifting standards often noted from teacher to teacher and from time to time in the same teacher.

Individual teachers and supervisors, however, will always interpret the achievement of each class in terms of the abilities and opportunities of the children concerned. Obviously, acceptable performance for a fifth-grade group of underprivileged children is different from that expected of a fifth grade in a favored suburban area.

Percentile scores available for such tests help the teacher determine the total range of performance in her class and the place of individual pupils within it. At the same time, many of the tests are helpfully diagnostic, enabling her to plan help for groups or for individuals whose specific needs are revealed in the results. Often, knowledge of these results aids the teacher greatly in her own observation of the children in the more informal types of evaluation already discussed.

Selection of test materials. Standard tests used for these purposes must be chosen for their reliability (that is, for the consistency of their results) and for their validity (the extent to which they really measure what they purport to measure), and for the size and representative character of the population on which they have been standardized. Before applying a given test in a local situation, the staff should determine whether it is fair and reasonable or valuable to compare the particular group with the population on which the test was standardized. Above all, such tests should be selected with the local curriculum in mind. It is imperative that teachers and others who are thoroughly familiar with the objectives and content of the local curriculum should assist in selecting tests for use in their schools.

Interpretation of test results. The value of any testing program lies in the intelligent and careful interpretation of results. It should be clear that a median score is by definition the point above which and below which half the pupils lie. To expect an entire fifth-grade class to be at or above the norm for the fifth grade is to show ignorance of the meaning of the term. Moreover, class scores must be interpreted in terms of the level of intelligence and the experiential background of the children concerned.

Knowledge of a child's level of intelligence is always necessary to the adequate evaluation of his performance on a standardized achievement test. Discovery of how well he has performed in terms of his potentialities is the primary aim of the testing.

When properly administered and interpreted, intelligence tests enable the teacher to discover mentally gifted children whose academic work is not reflecting their ability. She therefore examines carefully the motivation and adjustment of such children and plans ways to challenge them to better effort. In other cases the intelligence test reveals the reason for unsatisfactory academic work as due to lack of ability rather than to stubbornness or uncoöperativeness. She then accepts and praises limited performance when it represents growth for the individual child.

It should be noted, however, that intelligence tests are made up of items from what is assumed to be the normal environment of all children. Those who have had extremely deprived or limited environments, such as life in institutions or among primitive hill-folk, or whose verbal experiences have been chiefly in a different language from that of the test will not be properly measured by an instrument based on American upper-class culture. Allison Davis has pointed out that the average intelligence test may be quite unfair to the lowest socio-economic group because the experiences on which it is based are not those of this vast group of people.[10] Then, too, scores made by the same individual may fluctuate from time to time according to his health, his nervous tensions, or the effort he expends in taking the examination. For this reason the test may not always measure the child's native ability but may reveal only what he is capable of doing under present circumstances. He more often makes a low score than a high one by chance. The high scores are not likely to be accidental; low scores should be verified by other performance and interpreted in the light of the achievement of the child as he is observed by the teacher in the actual learning situation.

Special care is also necessary in interpreting evaluative measures to parents and to other members of the community, lest individual youngsters of limited ability be subject to undue pressure at home to achieve beyond what is possible for them. Acceptance of such evidence, particularly in regard to intelligence, demands an emotional adjustment of great

---

[10] Allison Davis, "Socio-Economic Influences upon Children's Learning," *Proceedings of the Midcentury White House Conference on Children and Youth* (Raleigh, N.C., Health Publications, Inc., 1951).

severity. Much evidence exists of the unhappy effect of parental pressures upon the emotional state of children and resultant severe frustrations in learning.

EVALUATION, A CONTINUOUS PROCESS

Evaluation is never an end in itself. It is always one step in a continuous sequence—activity, examination of results, goal setting, and further activity.

Relation of Evaluation to Curriculum-planning

Evaluation applies not only to individual tasks or to larger units of learning, but to the total process of curriculum-making. Goals are set for the program as a whole, experiences are chosen which are appropriate for the attaining of these ends, teaching and materials are adapted to the needs of individual boys and girls, results are evaluated, and new and more immediate goals are set in terms of results achieved. If some activities prove successful and others do not, those failing to contribute to the goals of the program are dropped and others are substituted for them. If recreatory reading has been stressed at the expense of study reading or vice versa, the emphasis will be changed. If spelling proves a problem, the selection of words and procedures in teaching will be examined. If children are successful in the presentation of reports and weak in group discussion, more provision will be made for the latter. If materials used prove too difficult for many children in the class or too remote from the normal interests of the group, more suitable ones will be provided. Thus evaluation becomes but one step in the ongoing process of curriculum making.

The Relation of Evaluation to Continuity between Elementary and High School Programs

Growth is continuous. There is no awkward break in the child's development as he moves from the elementary school to the high school, and there should be no awkward break in curricular offerings nor in the goals set for the language arts program. Hence there is a movement throughout the country toward a unified approach to the problem of planning and evaluation.[11] Vertical committees representing all levels of the school system are considering together the goals of the program in the language arts, the materials used, and the nature and extent of growth from the preschool to college. When lack of agreement on goals, on procedures, and on the nature and content of learning exists between the elementary school and the high school, frustration results for the pupils. Complaints against what the teacher failed to do lower down in the school system are often due to lack of understanding of what children are like, of how they grow, and of what can normally be expected of them. Joint criteria for evaluation coöperatively arrived at and joint consideration of results in the light of what is known about the development of children and young people can bring about increased understanding on the part of all teachers of the goals and the problems of each level of the school program. After that, consideration of needed changes in the curriculum is in order.

SUMMARY

Evaluation, then, is concerned with how well the objectives of the school are being translated into action. A clear statement of those objectives is necessarily a first step. Such evaluation has three parts: first, consideration of the adequacy of the program as a whole in experiences offered, in procedures used, and in housing, materials, and equipment furnished; second, determination of the extent of progress of both groups and individuals toward the goals set up; and third, planning improvements needed as a result of this anal-

[11] National Council of Teachers of English, Commission on the English Curriculum, *The English Language Arts*, Curriculum Series, Vol. I (New York, Appleton-Century-Crofts, Inc., 1952).

ysis. Evaluation, therefore, is always part of an on-going process—goals, activity, evaluation—then revised goals, adjusted emphasis and activity, and more evaluation, and so on throughout the school's history.

A well-balanced program of evaluation involves a study of the personal and social development of the child, his habits of work, his reading interests, his growth in language power, and his improvement in specific skills in reading, writing, speaking, and listening as revealed in the use he makes of these skills for daily purposes of social and business communication.

Many varieties of measures are needed to make such an evaluation. Sociograms are useful for determining the child's relations with other children. Anecdotal records of daily observation by the teacher reveal his willingness to participate, his habits of work, his use of the processes of selection and organization of materials, and the effect of what he says upon others.

Checklists, some made by the teacher and some by the children themselves, help to give valuable experience in preplanning and later in evaluation. Analysis of written work, of tape-recorded speech, and of records of personal reading furnishes an important basis of evaluation.

Standardized tests, when chosen with the local curriculum in mind and when interpreted with due consideration for the ability and background of both group and individuals, help keep the local situation in focus and assist in stabilizing standards.

In this process of continuous evaluation parents, community, children, and teachers all have a significant part to play.

BIBLIOGRAPHY

American Council on Education, Commission on Teacher Education, *Helping Teachers Understand Children* (Washington, D.C., The Council, 1945).

American Educational Research Association, "Methods of Research and

Appraisal," *Review of Educational Research,* XXI (December, 1951), pp. 327–62.

Association for Supervision and Curriculum Development, Alice Miel and Kimball Wiles, Co-Chairmen, *Toward Better Teaching; a Report of Current Practices* (Washington, D.C., National Education Association, 1949), pp. 226–55.

BETZNER, Jean, *Exploring Literature with Children in the Elementary School,* Practical Suggestions for Teaching, No. 7 (New York, Columbia University, Teachers College Bureau of Publications, 1943), pp. 65–74.

BUROS, Oscar K., *Fourth Mental Measurements Yearbook* (Highland Park, New Jersey, The Gryphon Press, 1953).

Commission on Research and Service, *Evaluating the Elementary School; A Guide for Coöperative Study; a Publication of the Southern Association's Coöperative Study in Elementary Education* (Atlanta, Georgia, Commission on Research and Service, 1951).

COOK, Walter W., "Evaluation in the Language-Arts Program," National Society for the Study of Education, *The Forty-Third Yearbook, Part II, Teaching Language in the Elementary School* (Chicago, University of Chicago Press, 1944), pp. 194–214.

Coöperative Study of Secondary School Standards, *Evaluative Criteria* (Washington, D.C., The Study, 1950).

DAVIS, Allison, "Socio-Economic Influences upon Children's Learning," *Proceedings of the Midcentury White House Conference on Children and Youth* (Raleigh, N.C., Health Publications, Inc., 1951).

DAWSON, Mildred, *Teaching Language in the Grades* (Yonkers-on-Hudson, New York, World Book Company, 1951), pp. 301–15.

Denver Public Schools, *A Program in English; A Guide for Teaching the Language Arts, Kindergarten through Grade Twelve* (Denver, Colorado, Board of Education, 1953).

El Paso Public Schools, *A Manual of Aids and Devices for Teaching Bilingual Children, Grade 3* (El Paso, Texas, 1946), p. 124.

Florida State Department of Education, *Experiencing the Language Arts,* Bulletin No. 34 (Tallahassee, Florida, The Department, 1948).

GREENE, Harry A., JORGENSEN, Albert N., and GERBERICH, Joseph R., *Measurement and Evaluation in the Elementary School* (New York, Longmans, Green & Company, 1952).

HILDRETH, Gertrude, *Child Growth Through Education* (New York, The Ronald Press, 1948), pp. 418–25.

Horace-Mann-Lincoln Institute of School Experimentation, *How to Construct a Sociogram* (New York, The Institute, 1947).

KEARNEY, Nolan C., *Elementary School Objectives.* A Report Prepared for the Mid-century Committee on Outcomes in Elementary Education (New York, Russell Sage Foundation, 1953), pp. 101–13.

LEE, J. Murray and Dorris May, *The Child and His Curriculum* (New York, Appleton-Century-Crofts, Inc., 1950), pp. 650–86.

MERRY, Frieda M. and Ralph V., *The First Two Decades of Life* (New York, Harper and Brothers, 1950).

Minneapolis Public Schools, *Communication; A Guide to the Teaching of Speaking and Writing, Grades 2–11* (Minneapolis, Minnesota, Board of Education, 1953).

National Association of Teachers of Speech, *Guide to Speech Training in the Elementary School; A Report of the Elementary Committee of the National Association of Teachers of Speech* (Boston, The Expression Company, 1943).

National Council of Teachers of English, Commission on the English Curriculum, *The English Language Arts*, N.C.T.E. Curriculum Series, Vol. I (New York, Appleton-Century-Crofts, Inc., 1952), pp. 417–40.

National Society for the Study of Education, *Reading in the Elementary School*, Forty-Eighth Yearbook, Part II (Chicago, University of Chicago Press, 1949), pp. 284–97.

SHANE, Harold G., and McSWAIN, Eldridge T. "Evaluation of the Educational Program," *Review of Educational Research*, XXIII (April, 1953), pp. 171–80.

STRICKLAND, Ruth G., *The Language Arts in the Elementary School* (Boston, D. C. Heath & Company, 1951), pp. 348–51; 275–78.

TIDYMAN, Willard F., and BUTTERFIELD, Marguerite, *Teaching the Language Arts* (New York, McGraw-Hill Book Company, Inc., 1951), pp. 77–78; 160–62; 228–29; 354–55; 364–65; 373; 422–25.

WEAVER, Andrew T., BORCHERS, Gladys L., and SMITH, Donald K., *The Teaching of Speech* (New York, Prentice-Hall, Inc., 1952).

Appendix

HELPS FOR TEACHERS

American Council on Education, *Reading Ladders for Human Relations*, Staff of the Intergroup Education Project in Coöperating Schools, (Washington D.C., The Council, 1949).

The American Library Association, *Basic Book Collection for Elementary Grades*, Miriam Braley Snow, Chairman (Chicago, The Association, 50 E. Huron Street, 1951).

———, *Booklist (The): A Guide to Current Books* (Twice monthly except monthly in August) (Chicago, The Association).

———, *Inexpensive Books for Boys and Girls*, Catherine E. Adamson, Chairman (Chicago, The Association, 1952).

Arbuthnot, May Hill, *Children and Books* (Chicago, Scott, Foresman and Company, 1947).

———, *Children's Books Too Good to Miss* (Cleveland, Western Reserve University Press, 1948).

Association for Childhood Education International, *Adventuring in Literature with Children* (Washington D.C., The Association, 1200 Fifteenth Street, N.W. 5, 1953).

Becker, May Lamberton, *First Adventures in Reading* (Philadelphia, J. B. Lippincott Company, 1947).

Child Study Association of America, *Books of the Year for Children* (Annually) (New York, The Association, 132 East 74th Street).

———, *Today's World in Books for Boys and Girls* (Revised) (New York, The Association, 1952).

Children's Bureau and U.S. Office of Education, *The Children's Bookshelf*, (Washington D.C., Superintendent of Documents, 1953).

Children's Catalog, Ruth Giles and Dorothy E. Cook, compilers (New York, H. W. Wilson Company, 1951, with Supplements 1952–1953).

Duff, Annis, *The Bequest of Wings* (New York, Viking Press, Inc., 1944).

Eaton, Anne T., *Reading with Children* (New York, Viking Press, Inc., 1940).

———, *Treasure for the Taking* (New York, Viking Press, Inc., 1946).

Elementary English, Monthly publication of the Elementary School Section of the National Council of Teachers of English (Champaign, Illinois, 704 South Sixth).

The Horn Book Magazine (585 Boylston Street, Boston, Massachusetts).

Meigs, Cornelia L., and others, *A Critical History of Children's Literature* (New York, The Macmillan Company, 1953).

National Council of Teachers of English, *Adventuring with Books* (Champaign, Illinois, The Council, 704 South Sixth Street, 1950).

———, *We Build Together* (Revised), Charlemae Rollins, Chairman (Champaign, Illinois, The Council, 1948).

Rue, Eloise, and La Plante, Effie, *Subject Headings for Children's Materials* (Chicago, American Library Association, 1952).

Rue, Eloise, *Subject Index to Books for Intermediate Grades* (Chicago, American Library Association, 1950).

———, *Subject Index to Books for Primary Grades* (Chicago, American Library Association, 1943, First Supplement, 1946).

Smith, Lillian, *The Unreluctant Years* (Chicago, The American Library Association, 1953).

LIST OF CHILDREN'S BOOKS MENTIONED

Abeita, Louise	*I am a Pueblo Indian Girl*	New York	Morrow	1939
Ackley, Edith F.	*Dolls to Make for Fun or Profit*	Philadelphia	Lippincott	1938
Ackley, Edith F.	*Marionettes, Easy to Make! Fun to Use!*	Philadelphia	Lippincott	1929
Adams, Helen S.	*The Wonderful Year*	New York	Messner	1946
Adams, Veotta M.	*Captain Joe and the Eskimo*	Eau Claire, Wisconsin	Hale	1952
Alcott, Louisa M.	*Little Women*	Boston	Little	1946
Andersen, Hans C.	*It's Perfectly True and Other Stories* (tr. Paul Leyssac)	New York	Harcourt	1938
Anderson, Clarence W.	*Big Red*	New York	Macmillan	1943
Arbuthnot, May H.	*Time for Poetry*	Chicago	Scott	1952
Armer, Laura G.	*Waterless Mountain*	New York	Longmans	1931
Asbjornsen, Peter, and Moe, Jorgen	*East o' the Sun and West o' the Moon*	New York	Macmillan	1928
Becker, Charlotte	*Necessary Nellie*	New York	Coward	1945
Bannon, Laura M.	*Manuela's Birthday in Old Mexico*	Chicago	Whitman	1939
Barrie, Sir James	*Peter Pan*	New York	Scribner	1950
Beaton, Mabel F. and Leslie	*Marionettes*	New York	Crowell	1948
Baker, Charlotte	*Judy's Farm Visit*	Eau Claire, Wisconsin	Hale	1943
Beim, Jerrold	*Andy and the School Bus*	New York	Morrow	1947
_____	*The Smallest Boy in The Class*	New York	Morrow	1949
Beim, Lorraine L. and Jerrold	*Two Is a Team*	New York	Harcourt	1945
Bemelmans, Ludwig	*Hansi*	New York	Viking	1934
_____	*Madeline*	New York	Simon & Schuster	1939
Bendick, Jeanne	*All Around You: First Look at the World*	New York	McGraw	1951
Bendick, Jeanne Robert	*Television Works Like This*	New York	McGraw	1949
Benet, Rosemary C. and Stephen V.	*Book of Americans*	New York	Rinehart	1933
Bennett, Richard	*Shawnee and the Gander*	New York	Doubleday	1937
Beskow, Elsa	*Pelle's New Suit*	Eau Claire, Wisconsin	Harper	1929
Best, Allena	*One String Fiddle*	New York	Hale	1939
Bishop, Claire H.	*The Five Chinese Brothers*	New York	Coward	1938
Bone, Stephen, and Adshead, Mary	*The Little Boy and His House*	Philadelphia	Winston	1950
Boulton, Rudyerd	*Traveling with the Birds*	New York	Donahue	1933
Bowman, James C.	*Pecos Bill*	Chicago	Whitman	1937
Branley, Franklyn M.	*Lodestar, Rocket Ship to Mars*	New York	Crowell	1951
Brewton, John E. and Sara W.	*An Index to Children's Poetry*	New York	Wilson, H.W.	1942
Brier, Howard	*Phantom Backfield*	New York	Random House	1948
Brink, Carol R.	*Caddie Woodlawn*	New York	Macmillan	1935
Britton, Katharine	*What Makes It Tick?*	Boston	Houghton	1948
Bro, Marguerite H.	*Sue-Mei's Golden Year*	New York	Doubleday	1950
Brock, Emma L.	*One Little Indian Boy*	New York	Knopf	1932
_____	*The Three Ring Circus*	New York	Knopf	1950
Bronson, Wilfred S.	*The Grasshopper Book*	New York	Harcourt	1943

Brooke, L. Leslie	*Johnny Crow's Garden*	New York	Warne	1904
	The Three Little Pigs	New York	Warne	1906
Brown, Francis J., and Roucek, Joseph S.	*One America*	New York	Prentice-Hall	1952
Brown, Margaret W.	*Red Light, Green Light*	New York	Doubleday	1944
———	*The Runaway Bunny*	New York	Harper	1942
———	"Willie's Walk to Grandmama's" in *Willie's Adventures*	Chicago	W. R. Scott	1954
Bryant, Bernice	*Everybody Likes Butch*	Chicago	Children's Press	1947
Buff, Mary M. and Conrad	*Peter's Pinto; a Story of Utah*	New York	Viking	1949
Burton, Virginia	*Katy and the Big Snow*	Boston	Houghton	1943
	The Little House	Boston	Houghton	1942
Carr, Mary J.	*Children of the Covered Wagon; A Story of the Old Oregon Trail*	New York	Crowell	1943
Carroll, Lewis (pseud.)	*Alice's Adventures in Wonderland*	New York	Macmillan	1923
Carryl, Charles E.	*Davy and the Goblin*	Boston	Houghton	1928
Carson, Rachel L.	*The Sea Around Us*	New York	Oxford	1951
Cavanah, Frances	*Our Country's Story*	New York	Rand	1945
Cavanna, Betty	*A Girl Can Dream*	Philadelphia	Westminster	1948
Clark, Ann N.	*In My Mother's House*	Eau Claire, Wisconsin	Hale	1941
———	*The Secret of the Andes*	New York	Viking	1952
Clark, Eugenie	*Lady with a Spear*	New York	Harper	1953
Cleary, Beverly	*Henry Huggins*	New York	Morrow	1950
Clemens, Samuel L. (Mark Twain)	*Tom Sawyer*	New York	Harper	1917
Coggins, Jack, and Pratt, Fletcher	*Rockets, Jets, Guided Missiles and Space Ships*	New York	Random House	1951
Collodi, Carlo	*Adventures of Pinochio*	New York	Macmillan	1951
Conger, Marion	*Rosie the Rhino*	Nashville, Tennessee	Abingdon-Cokesbury	1948
Cormack, Maribelle	*First Book of Stones*	New York	Franklin-Watts	1950
Coy, Harold	*The First Book of Presidents*	New York	Watts	1952
Craig, Gerald S.	*Science All About Us*	Boston	Ginn	1946
Crawford, Phyllis	*Hello the Boat!*	New York	Holt	1938
Credle, Ellis	*Down, Down the Mountain*	New York	Nelson	1934
Crockett, Lucy H.	*Pong Choolie, You Rascal*	New York	Holt	1951
Curle, Richard H.	*Stamp Collecting*	New York	Knopf	1947
Dalgliesh, Alice	*The Little Wooden Farmer*	New York	Macmillan	
Dana, Richard H.	*Two Years Before the Mast*	Boston	Houghton	1911
Daugherty, James	*Daniel Boone*	New York	Viking	1939
	The Landing of the Pilgrims	New York	Random House	1950
———	*Of Courage Undaunted*	New York	Viking	1951
Davis, Julia	*No Other White Man*	New York	Dutton	1937
Davis, Lavinia	*Roger and the Fox*	New York	Doubleday	1947
Davis, Norman	*Picken's Great Adventure*	New York	Oxford	1949
De Angeli, Marguerite	*Bright April*	New York	Doubleday	1946
———	*Ted and Nina Have a Happy Rainy Day*	New York	Doubleday	1936
———	*The Door in the Wall*	New York	Doubleday	1949

———	*Yonie Wondernose*	New York	Doubleday	1944
De Leeuw, Adele L.	*With a High Heart*	New York	Macmillan	1945
Dennis, Wesley	*Flip and the Cows*	New York	Viking	1942
———	*Flip and the Morning*	New York	Viking	1951
Duvoisin, Roger	*A is for the Ark*	New York	Lathrop	1952
———	*Mother Goose*	New York	Heritage	1943
Eastman Kodak Co.	*How to Make Good Pictures*	Rochester	Eastman Kodak Company	yearly
Edmonds, Walter D.	*The Matchlock Gun*	New York	Dodd, Mead	1941
Elting, Mary	*First Book of Baseball*	New York	Franklin-Watts	1950
———	*The First Book of Indians*	New York	Franklin-Watts	1950
Epstein, Samuel, and Williams, Beryl	*Real Book about Pirates*	New York	Garden City	1952
Estes, Eleanor	*The Moffats*	New York	Harcourt	1941
———	*Ginger Pye*	New York	Harcourt	1951
———	*The Hundred Dresses*	New York	Harcourt	1944
Ets, Marie H.	*Oley, the Sea Monster*	New York	Viking	1947
Faulkner, Georgine, and Becker, John L.	*Melindy's Medal*	New York	Messner	1945
Fenner, Phyllis R.	*Pirates, Pirates, Pirates*	New York	Franklin-Watts	1951
Fish, Helen D.	*When the Root Children Wake Up*	Philadelphia	Lippincott	1941
Flack, Marjorie	*Ask Mr. Bear*	New York	Macmillan	1932
———	*The New Pet*	New York	Doubleday	1943
———	*Tim Tadpole and the Great Bullfrog*	New York	Doubleday	1934
Gag, Wanda	*Millions of Cats*	New York	Coward	1928
———	*Nothing at All*	New York	Coward	1941
Gall Alice, and Crew, Fleming H.	*All the Year Round*	New York	Oxford	1944
Gannett, Ruth S.	*My Father's Dragon*	New York	Random House	1948
Gates, Doris	*Blue Willow*	New York	Viking	1940
Geisel, Theodore (Dr. Seuss)	*And to Think that I Saw It on Mulberry Street*	New York	Vanguard	1937
———	*If I Ran the Zoo*	New York	Random	1950
———	*The Five Hundred Hats of Bartholomew Cubbins*	New York	Vanguard	1938
Geismer, Barbara P., and Suter, Antoinette B.	*Very Young Verses*	Boston	Houghton	1945
George, John J. and Jean C.	*Meph, the Pet Skunk*	New York	Dutton	1952
Gibson, Katharine	*Goldsmith of Florence*	New York	Macmillan	1929
Grahame, Kenneth	*Wind in the Willows*	New York	Scribner	1933
Gray, Elizabeth J.	*Adam of the Road*	New York	Viking	1942
———	*Fair Adventure*	New York	Viking	1940
———	*Jane Hope*	New York	Viking	1933
Greener, Leslie	*Moon Ahead*	New York	Viking	1951
Grimm, Jakob L. K. and Wilhelm K.	*Household Stories*	New York	Macmillan	1882
Hader, Berta H. and Hader, Elmer	*Cock-a-Doodle-Doo, the the Story of a Little Red Rooster*	New York	Macmillan	1939
———	*The Big Snow*	New York	Macmillan	1949
———	*Spunky*	New York	Macmillan	1933
Hall, Ruth M. and Albert N.	*Home Handicraft for Girls*	Philadelphia	Lippincott	1941
Harkins, Philip	*Southpaw from San Francisco*	New York	Morrow	1948
Haywood, Carolyn	*B Is for Betsy*	New York	Harcourt	1939
———	*Eddie and the Fire Engine*	New York	Morrow	1949
———	*Here's A Penny*	New York	Harcourt	1944

Heinlein, Robert A.	*Farmer in the Sky*	New York	Scribner	1950
Hemingway, Ernest	*The Old Man and the Sea*	New York	Scribner	1952
Henry, Marguerite	*King of the Wind*	Chicago	Rand	1948
	Misty of Chincoteague	Chicago	Rand	1947
Hoffman, Eleanor	*Mischief in Fez*	New York	Holiday	1943
Hogben, Lancelot T.	*The First Great Inventions*	New York	Chanticleer	1950
Holberg, Ruth L. and Richard A.	*Mitty on Mr. Syrup's Farm*	New York	Doubleday	1936
Holling, Holling C.	*Paddle-to-the-Sea*	Boston	Houghton	1941
	Book of Indians	New York	Platt and Munk	1935
Hubbard, Alice M., and Babbitt, Adeline	*The Golden Flute*	New York	Day	1932
Hubbard, Freeman H.	*The Train that Never Came Back and Other Railroad Stories*	New York	McGraw	1952
Huber, Miriam B., Salisbury, Mrs. Frank S., and Gates, Arthur I.	*The Ranch Book*	New York	Macmillan	1943
	Rusty Wants a Dog	New York	Macmillan	1943
	Smoky, the Crow	New York	Macmillan	1943
Hull, Eleanor	*The Boy's Cuchulain*	New York	Crowell	1910
Humperdinck, Engelbert	*Hansel and Grettel*	Bridgeport, Conn.	Columbia Records, Inc.	
Hunt, Walter Bernard	*Bent Hunt's Whittling Book*	Milwaukee	Bruce Pub.	1944
Huntington, Harriet E.	*Let's Go Outdoors*	New York	Doubleday	1939
Hutchinson, Veronica	*The Circus Comes to Town*	Eau Claire, Wisconsin	Hale	n.d.
Ipcar, Dahlov J.	*One Horse Farm*	New York	Doubleday	1950
Jackson, Caary P.	*Shorty Makes First Team*	Chicago	Wilcox	1950
Jacobs, Joseph	*Celtic Fairy Tales*	New York	Putnam	1893
James, Will	*Smoky, the Cowhorse*	New York	Scribner	1926
Johnston, Charles, and Spencer, Carita	*Ireland's Story* (new ed.)	Boston	Houghton	1923
Jordan, Emil L.	*Nature Atlas of America*	Sandusky	Hammond	1952
Juta, Jan	*Look Out for the Ostriches! Tales of South Africa*	New York	Knopf	1949
Kane, Henry B.	*Wild World Tales; the Tale of the Moth, the Mouse and the Crow*	New York	Knopf	1949
Kelly, Eric P.	*In Clean Hay*	New York	Macmillan	1953
	The Christmas Nightingale; Three Christmas Stories from Poland	New York	Macmillan	1932
Keto, Emma	*Ting Ling and Mee-Too*	New York	Grosset	1937
Kipling, Rudyard	*The Jungle Book*	New York	Doubleday	1932
	Just So Stories (illus. by Nicolas, pseud.)	New York	Garden City	1952
Kjelgaard, James	*Big Red*	New York	Holiday	1945
Lampman, Evelyn S.	*The Bounces of Cynthiann'*	New York	Doubleday	1950
Lang, Andrew	*The Arabian Nights*	New York	Longmans	1946
	The Blue Fairy Book	New York	Longmans	1948
Lanier, Sidney (Ed.)	*The Boy's King Arthur*	New York	Scribner	1917

Lattimore, Eleanor F.	*Little Pear*	New York	Harcourt	1931
Laverty, Maura	*The Gold of Glenaree*	New York	Longmans	1945
Lawson, Robert	*Rabbit Hill*	New York	Viking	1944
	Robbut	New York	Viking	1942
Leaf, Munro	*The Story of Ferdinand*	New York	Viking	1936
Lenski, Lois	*Cowboy Small*	New York	Oxford	1949
————	*Let's Play House*	New York	Oxford	1944
————	*The Little Airplane*	New York	Oxford	1938
————	*The Little Family*	New York	Doubleday	1932
————	*The Little Fire Engine*	New York	Oxord	1946
————	*The Little Train*	New York	Oxford	1940
Lent, Henry J.	*Straight Down!*	New York	Macmillan	1944
————	*Straight Up!*	New York	Macmillan	1944
Lipkind, William, and Mordinoff, Nicholas	*Finders Keepers*	New York	Harcourt	1951
Lofting, Hugh	*Story of Dr. Dolittle*	Philadelphia	Lippincott	1920
MacLeod, Mary	*Book of King Arthur and His Noble Knights*	Philadelphia	Lippincott	1949
MacManus, Seumas	*The Donegal Wonder Book*	Philadelphia	Lippincott	1926
Maginley, C. J.	*The Toymaker's Book*	New York	Harcourt	1948
Malory, Sir Thomas	*Boy's King Arthur* (Ed., Sidney Lanier)	New York	Scribner	1917
McCloskey, Robert	*Blueberries for Sal*	New York	Viking	1948
————	*Lentil*	New York	Viking	1940
————	*Homer Price*	New York	Viking	1943
————	*Make Way for Ducklings*	New York	Viking	1941
McCormick, Dell J.	*Paul Bunyan Swings His Axe*	New York	Caxton	1936
McGinley, Phyllis	*All Around the Town*	Philadelphia	Lippincott	1948
Medearis, Mary	*Big Doc's Girl*	Philadelphia	Lippincott	1950
Meyer, Jerome S.	*Picture Book of Astronomy*	New York	Lothrop	1945
Milhous, Katherine	*Patrick and the Golden Slippers*	New York	Scribner	1951
Mills, Winifred, and Dunn, Louise M.	*Marionettes, Masks, and Shadows*	New York	Doubleday	1927
Milne, A. A.	*The House at Pooh Corner*	New York	Dutton	1928
	Winnie the Pooh	New York	Dutton	1950
Mitchell, Lucy S.	*A Year in the City*	New York	Simon & Schuster	1948
Mother Goose	*The Real Mother Goose*	Chicago	Rand	1916
Munchausen, Baron	*Tales from the Travels of Baron Munchausen*	New York	Heath	1900
Newberry, Clare T.				
Norton, Mary	*Smudge*	New York	Harper	1948
Nutting, Wallace	*The Borrowers*	New York	Harcourt	1953
	Ireland Beautiful	Framingham	Old America Co.	1925
O'Brien, John S.	*Silver Chief, Dog of the North*	Philadelphia	Winston	1933
Parrish, Anne	*Floating Island*	New York	Harper	1930
Petersham, Maud (Fuller) and Miska	*Miki*	New York	Doubleday	1929
Pistorius, Anna	*What Animal Is It?*	Chicago	Wilcox	1947
Posell, Elsa Z.	*This Is An Orchestra*	Boston	Houghton	1950
Potter, Beatrix	*The Tale of Peter Rabbit*	New York	Warne	1903
————	*The Tale of Benjamin Bunny*	New York	Warne	1904
Pyle, Howard	*The Merry Adventures of Robin Hood*	New York	Scribner	1946

Rankin, Louise S.	*Daughter of the Mountains*	New York	Viking	1948
Rawlings, Marjorie K.	*The Yearling*	New York	Scribner	1938
Renick, Marion	*Nicky's Football Team*	New York	Scribner	1951
Rey, Hans A.	*Cicely G and the Nine Monkeys*	Boston	Houghton	1942
———	*Curious George*	Boston	Houghton	1941
Rey, Margaret and Hans A.	*Spotty*	New York	Harper	1945
Robertson, Lilian	*Picnic Woods*	New York	Harcourt	1941
Rollefston, T. W.	*The High Deeds of Finn*	New York	Crowell	1923
Rourke, Constance M.	*Davy Crockett*	New York	Harcourt	1934
Ruskin, John	*The King of the Golden River*	New York	Macmillan	1926
Sackett, Rose	*The Cousin from Clare*	New York	Macmillan	1937
Sawyer, Ruth	*Journey Cake, Ho!*	New York	Viking	1953
Salten, Felix	*Bambi*	New York	Noble	n.d.
Scholz, Jackson V.	*Gridiron Challenge*	New York	Morrow	1947
Scott, William R.	*This Is the Milk that Jack Drank*	New York	W. R. Scott	1944
Seredy, Kate	*The Good Master*	New York	Viking	1935
Sewell, Helen	*Birthdays for Robin*	New York	Macmillan	1947
Shippen, Katherine B.	*Mr. Bell Invents the Telephone* (Landmark)	New York	Random House	1952
Snedeker, Caroline D.	*Theras and His Town*	New York	Doubleday	1924
Sperry, Armstrong	*Call It Courage*	New York	Macmillan	1940
———	*The Voyages of Christopher Columbus*	New York	Random House	1950
Steiner, Charlotte	*Kiki Dances*	New York	Doubleday	1949
Stephens, James	*Irish Fairy Tales*	New York	Macmillan	1920
Stevenson, Augusta	*Booker T. Washington, Ambitious Boy*	Indianapolis	Bobbs	1950
———	*Buffalo Bill, Boy of the Plains*	Indianapolis	Bobbs	1948
Stevenson, Robert L.	*Treasure Island*	New York	Scribner	1924
Stolz, Mary S.	*Organdy Cup Cakes*	New York	Harper	1951
Stong, Phil D.	*Honk, the Moose*	New York	Dodd, Mead	1935
Swift, Hildegarde	*North Star Shining*	New York	Morrow	1947
Tensen, Ruth M.	*Come to the Zoo*	Chicago	Reilly & Lee	1948
Thorne-Thomsen, Gudrun	*East o' the Sun and West o' the Moon*	Evanston	Row	1946
Tippett, James	*The Singing Farmer*	New York	World Book	1927
Tooze, Ruth	*Monkey See, Monkey Do*	New York	Grosset	?
Tresselt, Alvin R., and Duvoisin, Roger	*Follow the Wind*	New York	Lothrop	1950
Tresselt, Alvin	*White Snow, Bright Snow*	New York	Lothrop	1947
Tunis, John	*All American*	New York	Harcourt	1942
———	*The Kid from Tompkinsville*	New York	Harcourt	1943
Turnbull, Agnes S.	*Elijah the Fishbite*	New York	Macmillan	1940
Van Loon, Hendrick W.	*The Story of Mankind*	New York	Liveright	1951
Van Stockum, Hilda	*The Cottage at Bantry Bay*	New York	Viking	1938
Wadsworth, Wallace	*Paul Bunyan and His Blue Ox*	New York	Doubleday	1925
Warner, Gertrude	*Children of the Harvest*	New York	Friendship Press	1940
Webber, Irma E.	*Travelers All*	New York	W. R. Scott	1944
———	*Up Above and Down Below*	New York	W. R. Scott	1943
Whipple, Gertrude	*Airplanes at Work*	New York	Macmillan	1944

White, Elwyn B.	*Charlotte's Web*	New York	Harper	1952
Wilder, Laura I.	*Little House in the Big Woods*	New York	Harper	1953
———	*Little House on the Prairie*	New York	Harper	1953
Williamson, Margaret	*The First Book of Bugs*	New York	Watts	1949
Wright, Ethel	*Saturday Walk*	New York	W. R. Scott	1941

CHILDREN'S MAGAZINES

American Girl (*The*)	Girl Scouts of America 155 E. 44th St., New York, N.Y.
American Junior Red Cross News	American National Red Cross 400 S. Front St., Washington, D.C.
Boy's Life (Boy Scouts)	Boy Scouts of America 2 Park Ave., New York 16, N.Y.
Collins Magazine	Wm. Collins & Sons, Ltd. 14 St. James Pl., London, England
Child Life	Ernest D. Frowley, Publisher 136 Federal St., Boston, Mass.
Children's Activities	Child Training Association 1018 S. Wabash Ave., Chicago, Ill.
Current Events	American Education Publications 400 S. Front St., Columbus, Ohio
Children's Digest	The Children's Digest, Inc. 52 Vanderbilt Ave., New York 17, N.Y.
Children's Playmate	3025 E. 75th St. Cleveland, Ohio
Humpty, Dumpty	Parents Institute 52 Vanderbilt Ave., New York 17, N.Y.
Jack and Jill	Curtis Publishing Co. Independence Square, Philadelphia, Pa.
Junior Natural History Magazine (*The*)	American Museum of Natural History Central Park W. at 79th St., New York, N.Y.
Junior Scholastic	Scholastic Corporation 351 Fourth Ave., New York, N.Y.
My Weekly Reader	American Education Publications, 400 S. Front St., Columbus 15, Ohio
National Geographic	National Geographic Society 146 16th St. N.W., Washington, D.C.
Nature Magazine	American Nature Association 1214 16th St., N.W., Washington, D.C.
Newstime	Scholastic Corporation 351 Fourth St., New York, N.Y.
Mechanix Illustrated	Fawcett Publications 67 W. 44th St., New York 36, N.Y.
Open Road for Boys	729 Boylston St. Boston, Mass.
Popular Mechanics	200 E. Ontario St. Chicago 11, Ill.
Popular Science	353 Fourth Ave. New York 10, N.Y.
Science News Letter	Science Service 1719 N. St. N.W., Washington, D.C.
Seventeen	Triangle Publications, Inc. 488 Madison Ave., New York, N.Y.
Story Parade	630 Fifth Ave New York 10, N.Y.
Young Citizen	Civic Education Service 1733 K St. N.W., Washington 6, D.C.

Index

Adolescence, development during early, 37-40. *See also* Upper-grade children

Adventuring with Books, National Council of Teachers of English, 381

Airport visit project, 362-364

Allen, Marion, book week project, 307*n*

American Library Association, 145

Anderson, Irving H., on reading, 151

Announcements, listening to, 93

Appalachian community school, 341-344

Arbuthnot, May Hill, book list, 381

Arizona State College, workshop visits, 293

Arts, used in book-making project, 273-274

Assemblies, listening to, 93-94

Attention span, 30

Audio-visual aids, 188, 338

Aviation Readers (Series), Henry J. Lent and others, 188

Bailey, Etta Rose, 297*n*

Baker, Harold V., group discussion studies, 20

Baltimore schools, pamphlet issued by, 371; parents' workshop, 367

Basic Life Spelling Vocabulary, A, J. A. Fitzgerald, 66

Boney, Dewitt, on reading, 157

Book-making project, language arts development through, 271-282

Books, 144-150, 167-168; adventure, 60, 147, 173, 174, 178, 308, 311; biographies, 174, 178, 179; classroom "library," 330-331; fairy tales, 55, 56, 59, 60, 173, 183, 219, 305, 347; humor, 56, 57, 60; informational, 34, 35, 148, 149, 163, 167, 174, 178, 219, 305, 310, 311; kindergarten, 264-265, 267; lists of, 308, 381; primary, 278-280; sports story, 174, 310; teen-age, 310; upper grades project on, 307-312. *See also* Literature *and* Reading

Books for Reluctant Readers, Dunn, Jackman, and others, 308

Books for You, National Council of Teachers of English, 308

Book Week, 145, 381; project emphasizing, 307-312

Boy Scouts, encouragement of reading, 145

Business-Education Days, 370

Caldecott medal, 145

Camp Fire Girls, encouragement of reading, 145

Capitalizing, 226, 240

Chart reading, 157-158

Child development and growth in language, creative writing and dramatics in, 6-7; curriculum and, 18-41; evidences of, in achievement, 175-180; relation of home to, 150-153; through listening, 71-105; through reading, 55-66; through speech, 106-143; through writing, 206-208, 215-216, 225-241

Childhood Education, book review section, 145

Children-of-the-world project, 298-301

Children's Bookshelf, The, Children's Bureau, 381

Children's Books Too Good to Miss, Arbuthnot, 381

Children's Bureau, book list, 381

Choric speaking, 92, 122-123; oral reading and, 182-183; speech improvement through, 131

Classroom, home and school coöperation in projects, 362-364; influence on language development, 329-335; school organization and the, 335-337. *See also* Education, Elementary school education, *and* Schools

Comics, 146, 381

Communication, basic nature of skills, 3-13; moral aspects, 15-16; home patterns of, 358-359; wise use of the mass modes, 371-380

Community councils, surveys of school programs, 365-366

Community life, education and, 339-342, 393-394; language needs and technological development, 3-4

Comprehension, natural unit of, 79

Context clues, reading, 160

Conversation, 89, 116-117

Core Vocabulary Series, Huber, Salisbury, and Gates, 188

Creative writing, early adolescent, 39-40; book-making project and, 274-282; intermediate grade, 234-236; kindergarten, 211-213; personal development and, 6-7; primary grade opportunities, 218-219; upper-grade, 242-245

Critical thinking, as a goal, 347-348

Curriculum making in the language arts, continuity in, 409-410; coöperation in, 342-344; evaluation of, 390-391; home habits in reading and use of mass modes of communication, related to, 371-380; influence of community on, 339-342; relation of, to child development, 18-41

Cursive writing, 220

Davis, Allison, on intelligence tests, 408

Dearborn, Walter F., on reading, 151

De Mars, Muriel, 72*n*

Departmentalization, upper-grade, 335-337

Dictation, 211, 214, 215, 271

Diction, 239

Dictionary, use of, 51, 171, 176, 237-238, 327

Discussion, kindergarten, 268-269; listening to, 89-90; speech experience in, 117-119

Drama, as a literary type, 179

Dramatic play, kindergarten, 263; speech experience through, 121-122

Dramatization, child development through, 6-7; oral reading and, 182-183; "play broadcasting," 95; speech experience through, 121-122, 131

Drill, wrong use of, 394

Education, community and, 339-342; continuity of program, 409-410; curriculum-building and child development, 25-40; early childhood, 261-282; function of language in school program, 4, 319-329; impact of forces outside the school, 337-339; in-service training, 343; learning readiness, 23-24; reading basic to, *see* Reading; record-keeping, 54-55; sequential nature of learning, 324-329; ten major goals of a program, 345-355. *See also* Elementary school education

Educational tours, citizens, 368-369

Education-Business Days, 370

Edwards, Alice D., 271*n*

Elementary English, book review section, 145

Elementary school education, basic skills in teaching, 7-12; continuity aspects, 42-54; intermediate grades, *see* Intermediate grade children; language arts curriculum, 25-40; language needs and responsibilities, 13-16; learning "readiness," 29; listening and child development, 71-105; primary grades, *see* Primary children; reading, *see* Reading; school organization, 335-337; speaking and child development, 106-143; spelling, 63-66; upper grades, *see* Upper grade children; writing, *see* Writing. *See also* Education *and* Schools

Encyclopedias, 170-171, 176

English Journal, The, 145, 310

Environment, community influence on schools, 339-342; home influence on schools, *see* Family; individual pupil differences and, 328; influence of school on language growth, 329-339, 344-345. *See also* Community life

Evaluation, appraising growth of individual children, 394-396; continuous nature of, 409-410; criteria for, 387-388, 392; goals of, 349; kindergarten, 270; language arts program, 386-411; long-term, 404-406; parent and community in, 393-394; pupils', 401-404; standardized tests for, 406-409; teacher's day-by-day, 396-401; upper grade, 311

Evans, Clara, on reading, 182

Experience charts, reading, 157-158

Family, evaluating the language arts program, 393-394; guidance in use of mass communication facilities, 371-380; relieving tensions through language arts program, 192-194; reading readiness and, 151-153; role in language development, 9-11, 359-365; school participation, 360, 364-368; writing activities in, 206-208. *See also* Environment

Fifth-grade listening study, 71-75

Films. *See* Motion pictures

First Book Series, 188

Fitzgerald, James A., 66

Fourteen Questions on Elementary School Organization, 335-336

Gateways to Readable Books, Strang and others, 308

George P. Phenix School (Hampton, Va.) project, 312-315

Girl Scouts, encouragement of reading, 145

Gorman's School, 339-341, 344

Grammatical usage, 238-239, 314

Graphic materials, 188

Group, citizenship training role, 14; goals of participation in, 352; growth in reading and, 162-165; learning to work in, 309-312; reading aloud to, 181-183; speech experience in, 116-125

Handbook of English for Boys and Girls, Kibbe, Brant, and Pooley, 241

Handwriting, 238; growth in skill, 249-256; guides and self-help materials, 335; primary school, 219-225; intermediate grades, 238; upper grades, 248

Hearing, 77, 82, 133, 139. *See also* Listening

Helping Children to Read, Hildreth and Wright, 198

Herald Tribune, New York, book review, 145

Hildreth, Gertrude, 151, 198

Hogan, Ursula, listening experiment, 101-102

Home. *See* Environment *and* Family

Horn Book, The, 145, 310

Human relations, language arts related to furthering, 12-13

Humor, children's love of, 56, 59-61

Index to Children's Poetry, John E. and Sara W. Brewton, 57n

Individual differences, evaluation of, 394-396; family and, 328; guidance of, in reading, 165-166; in writing, 242-246; materials adapted to, 167-169; promoting growth in terms of, 185-201

Intelligence quotient (IQ), 195

Intelligence tests, 407-408

Intermediate-grade children, 32-37, 44-46, 48, 50-53, 71, 283-301; books for, 167-168; listening habits, 71-75, 88; maturity in reading, 169-175; pageant project, 297-301; programs in listening, 101-102; reading interests, 58-60, 173-178; reference library project, 283-297; writing experience, 227-241. *See also* Elementary school education

Interrelationships among the language arts, 324-329
Interviews, intermediate-grade children, 286-287
Irish study of contribution, 302-307

Jersild, Arthur T., 172
Junior high schools, 307, 336-337
Junior Program, Seattle, 377
Junior Scholastic, 290

Kiefer, Mildred S., 283*n*
Killarney songs and legends, 304-305
Kindergarten, language arts opportunities in, 263-270; musical activities in, 268; reading program, 154-155; writing in the, 209-213; year's program detailed, 262-270. *See also* Preprimary children

La Crosse, Wis., parent-teacher workshop, 368
Lafayette School (Norfolk, Va.) book-making project, 271-282
Landmark Books, The (Series), 188, 351, 353
Language, arousing interest in, 61; classroom influence on, 329-335; goals of, 346-352; four aspects of, 71; impact of innovations on, 337-338; importance to children related to modern living, 3-17; personality development and, 20-22; power of words, 218-219, 247; role of home and school in developing, 359-365; social effects of, 19-20. *See also* Language arts
Language arts, child development and, 18-41; continuity in growth, 42-67; curriculum building and, 25-40, 390-391; early childhood experiences, 261-282; functions in the school program, 319-329; instruction related to goals, 4, 345-355; intermediate-grade experiences, 294-295, 301; interrelationships among, 324; sequential relationships, 324-329; subject matter and values inherent in, 322-324; textbooks, 332-335; upper-grade

experiences, 303, 307, 311-312, 314-315. *See also* Language *and* Language arts program
Language arts program, 344; curriculum relationships, 25-40, 390-391; environment and, 340-341, 344-345; evaluation of, 386-411; facilities of the school, 388-390; impact of forces outside the school, 337-339; intermediate grades, 283-301; kindergarten, 261-270; listening methods, 101-104; measurement of skills in, 391-392; pageant project, 297-301; primary grades, 271-282; reference library project, 283-297; techniques of appraisal, 394-409; total program of the school and, 390-391; upper grades, 302-315. *See also* Elementary school education
Leisure Reading, book list, 308
Letter-writing, 210, 267-268, 327
Libraries, children's reading, 145; skills in the use of, 175. *See also* Books *and* Reading
Library Journal, The, 145
Listening, 71-105, 320-321; book-making project and, 276-277; classification of kinds, 80; educational significance, 75-77; essentials of effective, 81-86; evaluation of progress, 404-406; methods of teaching, 97-103; nature of, 77-81; oral language situations, 88-97, 182; problems interfering with, 85-86; reading compared with, 78-80; sequence of development, 86-88
Literacy, 13-14
Literature, development of skill in reading, 179; growth in appreciation, 55-66; personal development and, 5-6; special demands of, 173. *See also* Reading
Longfellow School (Madison, Wis.) fifth-grade project, 72*n*

Madison, Wis., 72*n*; magazine committee, 380
Magazines, 52, 145-146, 290, 378-380

Maib, Frances, report on reading, 168
Manuscript writing, 219-220
Mass communication media, 371-380
Maturity, and readiness for reading, 151; in reading growth, 349-350
Maury School (Richmond, Va.), United Nations project, 297-301
Moral perception goal, 347
Motion pictures, 97, 269, 275, 311, 338; guidance in attending, 376-377
Music, 123-124, 268

National Conference on Research in English, 241
National Council of Teachers of English, 345-346, 381
Neilson, Theodora N., 312n
Newbery medal, 145
New Jersey, school communication project, 370
Newspapers, 378-380
Number concepts, kindergarten, 268

Ohio State University, kindergarten program, 262-270
Olson, Willard C., quoted, 23
Oral reading. See Reading
Originality, in writing, 234

Pageant project, 297-301
Pamphlets, for parents, 371
Paragraph structure, 246-247
Parents. See Family
Parent-teacher workshops, 367
Parker, Randall G., 312n
Pennsylvania Dutch school, 339-341
Personal development goal, 346
Personal interest goals, 349-350
Personality, language relationship to, 20-22
Personal sense of values goal, 347
Phoenix (Ariz.) school library project, 283-297
Phonic analysis, 161, 163
Place of Subjects in the Curriculum, The, bulletin, 329
Planning, 15; intermediate-grade children, 285-286; listening skills needed in, 91; speech experience in, 117-119; teacher-pupil, 292-293
Poetry, 50, 174, 167, 179; human relationship teaching through, 62; introducing children to, 57-63; listening to, 92-93; narrative, 178; writing of, 235. See also Creative writing
Pooley, Robert, 239, 241n
Practical project, language values of, 312-315
Preprimary children, 25-26, 154-155; kindergarten program, 262-270; listening experiences, 82-83, 99-100; reading experiences, 154-156; writing experiences, 206-213
Preprimers, 159
Primary children, 26-32, 43-44, 47, 49-50; book-making project, 271; introduction to literature, 55-58; listening conditions, 83-85, 87-88; reading experiences, 155-165; spelling, 225-226; writing experiences, 213-227. See also Elementary school education
Primers, 159
Problem-solving, 266-267
Program-listening, 93-94
Promotion, 157
Public relations service, school's, 368-371
Punctuation, 211, 214, 226, 240-241

Radio, 76-77; guidance in use of, 371-374; listening to, 94-95; methods of improving programs, 373-374
Rainwater, Cleo, on classroom equipment, 331
Ramsay (Minn.) Junior High School project, 307-312
Rankin, Paul T., 76
Readiness, learning, 23-24; listening, 78; reading, see Reading-readiness
Reading, 154-169, 202, 321; aloud, 120-121, 161-162, 180-184, 218; causes of retardation in, 189-201; challenge of modern world, 144-147; children's interests, 173-178; clinics for, 201; development of

Reading (*continued*)

skills in use, 169-173; early adolescent, 39; early childhood, 28-29; easy books for older children, 188-189; evaluation in, 177, 404-406; group, 162-165, 197-198; guidance by home and school, 146-147, 380-382; individual help in, 165-166, 168-169, 198-201; interest-building, 191-192; intermediate-grade children's, 33-37; interviewing and, 194-195; kindergarten, 264-265, 267; life attitudes directed through, 218-219, 347; listening compared with, 77-80; oral, 180-184, 195-197; period of rapid growth in, 166-169; personal development and, 5-6, 173; primary level, 31-32; rates of growth in, 185-186; readiness for, *see* Reading-readiness; selective, 170, 176; teaching techniques in, 364-365; upper-grade achievement, 175-180; vision and, 190-191; wide range of material necessary, 186-189. *See also* Books

Reading-readiness, 127; ability grouping, 165; child development and, 150-153; first learning experiences, 156-162; kindergarten program, 154-155; prereading program, 155; stimulation of interest, 161-162

Real Book Series, 188

Recordings, 95-96, 338

Reference books, 52, 148, 170-171, 176-177

Reference library project, 283-297

Reporting, speech experience in, 117-119

Reports, listening to, 90

Retardation, reading, 189-201; speech problems and, 136-137

Reymert, Martin L., on radio, 374

Schools, coöperation of home and community in program, 365-371; facilities and objectives, 384-390; guidance in use of mass communication facilities, 371-380; public information in, 368-371; sharing with home in language development, 359-365. *See also* Classroom, Education *and* Elementary school education

Sentence, the, 211, 214, 216, 239-240, 247-248

Sequence in the language arts program continuity in growth, 42-54; evaluation and, 404-410; in listening, 86-88; in literary appreciation, 55-66; in reading, 169-175, 324-329; in skills, 325-327; in speech, 126-127; in writing, 249-257; school's influence on, 329-339

Skills, sequence in learning, 325-327

Slow learners' project, 312-315

Sociogram, evaluation, 399-400

Sounds, learning sequence, 126-127; variety of, 100-101

Speech, 78, 91-92, 106-143; activities emphasizing, 113-125; all-pervasive nature of, 106-107; beginning stages, 108-109; book-making project and, 276-277; child growth and development of, 109-113; defects and their improvement, 133-141; evaluation of progress, 404-406; face-to-face situations, 114-116; factors that affect proficiency, 125-126, 137-141; goals in, 129-130; learning sequence, 126-127; normal activities and improvement in, 130-131; "public speaking" situations, 123-125; sharing experience, 116-117; small group situations, 116-123; standards and patterns, 111-113, 131-132; teacher's example, 128-130; three types of, 113-114

Spelling, 63-66, 225-226, 313; intermediate grade, 237-238, 287-288; textbook in, 334-335; upper-grade, 248-249

Standardized tests, 392, 406-409

Storytelling, 91-92, 120-121

Stuttering, 133

Sutcliffe, Ann, 283n

Swales, Cecile, 263n

Syllabication, 237

"Teachable moment," 23-24, 29, 34. *See also* Readiness

Teacher, *passim;* as example and guide, 128-130, 332; coöperative curriculum building, 342-344; home visits, 361-362; listening experiences and habits of, 98-99; literary appreciation, 63; methods for teaching reading, 154-169; primary importance of, 345; responsibility to keep abreast of current attractions, 337; speech-centered activities, 114

Teaching English Usage, Pooley, 239

Telephoning, 89, 378

Television, 52, 76-77, 96-97, 375; guidance in use of, 374-376

Textbooks, language arts, 332-335

Time for Poetry, anthology, 218, 265, 381

Times, New York, book review, 145

Transcriptions, 95-96

United Nations pageant project, 298-301

Unzicker, Cecelia, original studies by, 189

Upper-grade children, department organization and, 335-337; developmental aspects, 37-40; maturing powers and interests in reading, 60-63, 175-180; projects involving language arts, 302-315; reading rate of, 185-186; writing experience, 241-249. *See also* Elementary school education

Valley Stream, Col., pamphlet on reading, 371

Very Young Verses, anthology, 218, 265, 381

Vision, reading and, 190-191

Vocabulary, 31, 53, 138-139, 171-172, 211, 216, 328

Vocational role goals, 351-352

Whittier School (Phoenix, Ariz.) project, 283-297

Willard School (Cleveland, O.) project, 302-307

Wilt, Miriam, listening study, 76

Words, disciplined use of, 247; power of, 218-219, 247; recognition of, 158-159, 161, 163-166, 171; structural analysis, 163-164

Work-habit goals, 350-351

Writing, 78, 206-258, 321-322; acceptable usage, 248; basic goals in, 229-234; book-making project, 277-282; children's need of, 207-208, 213, 227-228, 241, 245-246; clarity in, 230-232; creative, *see* Creative writing; development illustrated, 249-257; evaluation of progress, 404-406; grammatical usage, 238-239; handwriting, *see* Handwriting; mastering of skills, 237-241; maturity and childhood needs, 206-208; middle grades, 227-241; organization in, 246-248; positive approach, 218; preschool experiences, 209-213; primary grades, 213-227; progression of steps for, 228-229; punctuation, 226, 240-241; real motives for, 246; spelling, 225-226, 237-238; suitability in, 232-234; techniques based on growth rate, 215-216; therapeutic values, 236, 281-282; upper grades, 241-249; wide range of achievement, 242-245